EXAMINED LIFE

EXAMINED LIFE

Excursions with Contemporary Thinkers

Edited by Astra Taylor

THE NEW PRESS

NEW YORK
LONDON

Requests for permission to reproduce selections from this book should be mailed to:
Permissions Department, The New Press, 38 Greene Street, New York, NY 10013.

Published in the United States by The New Press, New York, 2009
Distributed by Perseus Distribution

LIBRARY OF CONGRESS CATALOGING-IN-PUBLICATION DATA

Examined life : excursions with contemporary thinkers / edited by Astra Taylor.
    p.   cm.
   ISBN 978-1-59558-447-2- (pb)
   1. Philosophy, Modern—21st century.   2. Philosophers, Modern—Interviews.
I. Taylor, Astra.
   B805.E82   2009
   190.9'04—dc22   2009004831

The New Press was established in 1990 as a not-for-profit alternative to the large,
commercial publishing houses currently dominating the book publishing industry.
The New Press operates in the public interest rather than for private gain, and is
committed to publishing, in innovative ways, works of educational, cultural, and
community value that are often deemed insufficiently profitable.

www.thenewpress.com

Production photographs taken from the film *Examined Life* © 2008 Sphinx
Productions and the National Film Board of Canada. All rights reserved.

Composition by dix!
This book was set in Minion

Printed in the United States of America

10   9   8   7   6   5   4   3   2   1

CONTENTS

PREFACE

Are the philosophers dead? How do you keep the audience from falling asleep while watching academics walk and talk for nearly ninety minutes?

These are the questions that frequently greet me after I describe *Examined Life*, the companion film to this volume. The first question reflects a common view of philosophy as a rather antiquated activity and assumes that my documentary is historic in nature—an exploration of a quaint and heady pursuit for which no one has the time or patience any longer. The second always causes me to marvel that a field devoted to exploring the power and limits of human knowledge, to pondering basic, intractable questions at the heart of our collective condition, strikes otherwise curious, knowledgeable, and vibrant people as wearying.

There are various reasons for philosophy's rather musty reputation. Our current culture's anti-intellectualism plays a strong role, standing in stark contrast to a country like France, where philosophers possess comparatively significant cultural and political influence, helped in part by a decades-long tradition of televising philosophical discussions. The turn away from liberal education, with its emphasis on the humanities, critical thinking, and the arts, in favor of more market-friendly disciplines certainly hurts philosophy's cause. Without a doubt, the professionalization of the field and the narrowing of its language has contributed to this situation as well— can the public really be blamed for finding current academic debates a bit arcane, if not wholly incomprehensible? As a consequence, where people may have once turned to philosophy for consolation, they now look to self-help; when they seek insight into human nature or the world we inhabit, they look to science. At the same time, communication technologies have immersed us in the ecstasies and agonies of ubiquitous and relentless—if often fleeting—"connectivity," eroding both patience and stamina for the unique sort of contemplation and dialogue philosophy invites.

Examined Life attempts to address this disconnect by using cinema and the simple art of conversation to relate philosophy to everyday experience. The title refers to Socrates' famous maxim "The unexamined life is not worth living." The figure of Socrates, as transmitted by Plato, has come to symbolize the birth of Western philosophy: the posing of ceaseless questions about truth and appearances, the origins of creation, the meaning of the good, and the fickle nature of common wisdom. His maxim also announced a timeless contradiction addressed by several of the philosophers in this book. The examined life is indeed hard; it has driven many a mind to crippling doubt or even madness and has invited, in the case of Socrates and countless others from diverse cultures, the wrath of panicked communities. But a life of questioning is also a dearly vital one, studded with passions and rewards and a courage all its own.

Examined Life draws in another sense on the example of Socrates, who, in the words of Cicero, called philosophy "down from the heavens." He did so by wandering the Athenian agora, engaging everyone he encountered in passionate discussion, allowing no assumption or assertion by vexed interlocutors to escape his playful scrutiny. Over the intervening centuries the peripatetic impulse remained strong, manifesting in Rousseau's *Reveries of a Solitary Walker,* Kierkegaard's melancholic rambles, Immanual Kant's famously punctual strolls, and Walter Benjamin's enigmatic urban flaneur. As Nietzsche wrote in *Twilight of the Idols,* "A sedentary life is the real sin against the Holy Spirit. Only those thoughts reached by walking have any value." Slowly but surely, though, philosophical thinking moved indoors, into college classrooms and onto book-shelves. *Examined Life* takes philosophy outside again, playing off its long and salient relationship to walking by inviting eight thinkers to share their ideas in the streets and on camera.

The philosopher's walk is straightforward enough, but it also possesses numerous registers of significance. Given its historical precedents, it resonates with philosophy's past. Cinematically, the walking motif provided an opportunity for movement, gesture, and variation of scene, saving me from conducting stagnant sit-down interviews. Symbolically, the walks take philosophy out of the ivory tower and into "the real world." Politically and culturally, these conversations unfold against a backdrop of diminishing public space in a society that worships speed and efficiency while placing little value on the peaceful reflection—with its unpredictable revelations and chance encounters—walking encourages. Yet as soon as I devised the pedestrian approach I knew I wanted to diverge from it. Thus, for me, the three excursions that ultimately utilize other modes of transportation—a car, a rowboat, and a wheelchair—expand the original concept and bring it up to date, a process pushed to further limits by Judith Butler's penetrating conversation with my sister, Sunaura Taylor, which challenges our most elemental, everyday understanding of what it means to take a walk.

Upon conceiving *Examined Life*, I began to focus on thinkers primarily concerned with social and ethical issues, a decision that reflects both my personal interests and my belief that serious reflection is a crucial ingredient of any effort to improve our collective condition. As a result, there are many branches of philosophy not touched on in this book, including linguistic philosophy, logic, philosophy of science, phenomenology, and philosophy of mind, among others. This is not a comprehensive introduction to philosophy; instead, I tried to attain some sense of thematic unity while featuring a diversity of thinkers and perspectives—from varied geographies, cultures, and intellectual traditions—not often found together. I settled on a rough balance between individuals associated with the analytic, pragmatic, and utilitarian traditions and those identified with what has come to be called "theory," incorporating continental philosophy, psychoanalysis, queer studies, post-Marxism, and deconstruction.

The people I invited to participate in this project are ones who have left a mark on my thinking over the years. I wagered that if their work managed to produce a lasting effect on me, the same might be true for an audience and a readership. I was twelve years old when I read Peter Singer's *Animal Liberation*, which gave me a new ethical framework for understanding vegetarianism. As a teenager wrestling with what it meant to be a "feminist" and a "woman" (or a "man," for that matter), I pored over Judith Butler's *Gender Trouble*. Years later, Martha Nussbaum's work on the position of people with disabilities in our society would help frame my thinking on the topic and understand better Sunaura's experiences. Slavoj Žižek (with whom I collaborated on my documentary *Žižek!*) and Michael Hardt consistently provoke me to reevaluate my political assumptions, much as the divergent methods of Cornel West and Kwame Anthony Appiah have impacted my understanding of race and identity, as well as the relationship between the local and the global. A graduate seminar led by Avital Ronell (co-taught by the late Jacques Derrida) coincided with my initial foray into documentary filmmaking, inspiring my first inkling of desire to make philosophy more accessible to a nonspecialized audience. Film and philosophy have always struck me as uniquely simpatico. Different theories present opportunities to look at the world anew, shedding light on difficult issues from various angles; film has a similar ability to shift perception, to transform the way we see and appreciate what's around us.

Yet philosophy can be very technical in its argumentation, relying on analytic categories that may seem, at first blush, cosmically and even comically complex. But, as Isaiah Berlin, echoing Bertrand Russell, once said, "The central visions of the great philosophers are essentially simple." I agree with Berlin, and my aim was to present the basic impetus or insight of the philosophers profiled in a way that was free of jargon and that resonated with common experiences and concerns. Indeed, perhaps the greatest thrill brought by doing philosophy is the moment when a concept that initially appeared impenetrable all of a sudden becomes clear, perfectly illuminating some problem, situation, or sensation that had previously eluded comprehension. I experienced many exhilarating moments in the conversations recorded here and hope similar epiphanies might be sparked in the reader.

Much of the credit for these moments of course goes to the thinkers featured in this book. They are, I quickly learned, possessed of exceptional intelligence, intensity, charisma, and even irreverence. But they also are all deeply committed to communicating their ideas to the broader world, often in defiance of our culture's antiintellectual bent. Crafting accessible presentations of their own complex ideas, they have written for major newspapers, collaborated with artists from various disciplines, given public lectures, appeared on radio and television, and been guests on cable news shows. They have championed, in other words, the democratic nature of learning and knowledge.

As the chapters in this book reveal, each conversation centered loosely on a specific concept, something intrinsic to the philosopher's work that I felt would play well against the topics to be tackled by other participants. At the same time, the project was designed such that all the philosophers are, in key respects, talking about two overarching themes—the search for meaning and our responsibilities to others in a world rife with inequity, persecution, and suffering.

In these pages I have also tried to retain a sense of the environment as a central character providing more than just passive scenery. While conducting these interviews I looked forward to interruptions from passersby, to small details igniting my subjects' imaginations, to the geography of a place determining what way we were or were not able to move. While some of the topics we settled on immediately lent themselves to a specific location, as in Peter Singer's discussion of consumer ethics (he cleverly suggested we shoot along Fifth Avenue, one of Manhattan's upscale shopping districts) and ecology for Slavoj Žižek (I immediately knew I wanted to film in a garbage dump), other settings were less obviously illustrative (as in the case of Michael Hardt rowing around a lake in Central Park or Cornel West's car ride across Manhattan), each environment possessed its own significance and elicited reactions and insights we could not have planned or anticipated. In the wake of this project I am far more aware of our dynamic relationship to the space we occupy, to how it frames and influences us, guides our physical movements, affects our states of mind, intrudes on our thought processes, and shapes our sense of what is possible.

I shot anywhere between ninety minutes and four hours of material for each philosopher's walk, eventually whittling down these marathon conversations to approximately ten minutes. In that process many moments—by turns incisive, provocative, and humorous—had to be abandoned. Knowing these scenes would be disseminated through another medium made the editing process less painful. Cinema has many charms, but the format also has its limitations, chiefly compression. Here the interviews are presented in their entirety, providing greater nuance and the possibility of sustained engagement, allowing the reader to set her or his own contemplative pace. Though I strove to maintain the informality and freewheeling nature of the exchanges, the dialogues in this book have been revised and restructured in order to abide by the stricter cadences of written prose.

No doubt the conversations in this volume raise more questions than they answer. But, as Cornel West says at the end of the film, our romantic desire for wholeness, for absolute truth, can be problematic. The salient message may be that the multiplicity of perspectives presented here does not lead to a quagmire of moral relativism, as some may fear, but instead to an expansive ethic of intellectual inquiry, compassion, and political commitment. This project doesn't wrap everything up or pretend to provide a definitive answer to the difficult issues addressed in it—after all, if our answers were incontrovertible, we wouldn't need philosophy. Rather, for those readers already committed to philosophical discourse, *Examined Life* may evoke the sense of curiosity, wonder, and moral indignation that initially attracted them to this discipline, while providing a reminder that ideas are always rooted in people, place, and time. For readers new to this field, I hope *Examined Life* ignites an endlessly inquisitive momentum. If this effort inspires some people to pause and ponder how they came to hold the beliefs they do, to question the ethical assumptions and preconceptions they take for granted, to reconsider their responsibilities to others, or to see a problem in a new way, I'll be content. But I'll be most pleased if, after watching the movie or reading this book, they get swept up in enthusiasm for the everyday practice of philosophy and find it to be an irresistible, if demanding, pleasure.

CORNEL WEST

Truth

As dusk fell over Manhattan, I stopped to pick up Cornel West from his midtown hotel. He agreed to let me conduct an interview while driving him to the New School, where he was scheduled to give a lecture with the philosopher Simon Critchley. Although Examined Life *was conceived as primarily pedestrian, the car ride seemed an appropriate way to bring the peripatetic concept up to date. How else would a modern-day flaneur travel? The cameraman sat in the front passenger seat; West and the sound man, who also operated the second camera, took the back. I did my best to guide the conversation while navigating rush-hour traffic.*

CORNEL WEST: So here we are in the middle of the Big Apple.

ASTRA TAYLOR: Since we haven't settled on a theme in advance, let me throw some possibilities at you: truth, faith, love—

WEST: Truth is fine, truth is fine. Absolutely.

TAYLOR: OK, let's go for truth. A big topic. [*The engine starts and we begin our drive downtown.*]

WEST: I think in many ways it is the ultimate question: What is truth? How do we understand truth and what are the ways in which we wrestle with truth? And I believe that Theodor Adorno was right when he said that the condition of truth is to allow suffering to speak. He said that the condition of truth is to allow suffering to speak—that gives it an existential emphasis, you see, so that we're really talking about truth as a way of life, as opposed to a set of propositions that correspond to a set of things in the world.

TAYLOR: When we settled on this topic, my mind immediately went to Plato.

WEST: Well, in many ways I wish people would think of Plato, rather then Bertrand Russell. Bertrand Russell, one of the grand exemplary analytic philosophers, tried to convince us that truth really was about propositions that correspond to objects in the world, whereas Plato always understood truth as tied into a way of life, as a certain mode of existence. And so what he's trying to get us to enact is *paideia**, which I think at the end is really at the center of any serious philosophic project. How do you engage in that formation of attention? For Plato, that's to move from becoming to being, but I would just characterize it as moving from the superficial to the substantial, moving from the frivolous to the serious, and then cultivating a self to wrestle with reality and history and mortality and, most importantly, promoting a maturation of the soul. And for Plato, that had to do, of course, with a turning of the soul, so that you become a

---

* Broadly defined as training or teaching, but not in the sense of learning a trade. Greek *paideia,* according to Xenophon, was "the process of educating man into his true form, the real and genuine human nature."

certain kind of person. So I'm actually with the classics in general in terms of understanding truth in an existential mode. Therefore, philosophy becomes more a way of life as opposed to simply a mode of discourse.

TAYLOR: Let's talk about that transformative aspect of philosophy. The title for this project is "Examined Life." So what we're trying to do is bring the Socratic imperative to the big screen.

WEST: Absolutely. How do we examine ourselves in a Socratic manner? "The unexamined life is not worth living," Plato says in line 38a of *The Apology*. How do you examine yourself? What happens when you interrogate yourself? What happens when you begin calling into question your tacit assumptions and unarticulated presuppositions and begin then to become a different kind of person? You know, Plato says philosophy's a meditation on and a preparation for death. By death what he means is not an event, but a death in life because there's no rebirth, there's no change, there's no transformation without death, and therefore the question becomes: How do you learn how to die? Of course Montaigne talks about that in his famous essay "To Philosophize Is to Learn How to Die." You can't talk about truth without talking about learning how to die because it's precisely by learning how to die, examining yourself and transforming your old self into a better self, that you actually live more intensely and critically and abundantly. So that the connection between learning how to die and changing, being transformed, turning your world upside down, inverting your world the way in which that famous play by Ludwig Tieck* highlights so that you actually are in a different kind of zone, you have a new self. That's why love is so inseparable from any talk about truth and death, because we know that love is fundamentally a death of an old self that was isolated and the emergence of

* *The World Turned Upside Down.*

a new self now entangled with another self, the self that you fall in love with.

TAYLOR: Let's talk more about love. It seems to me that might be something that folks may not see as a properly philosophical concept.

WEST: I think love is central to any philosophical discourse. Plato understood that you have to talk about eros in talking about truth. That's why philosophy is in fact a quest for wisdom based in *sophia*; that quest for wisdom has everything to do with a love of wisdom. I mean, my criticism of Plato is that he's too in love with the abstract forms as opposed to loving concrete human beings. [*West pauses to look out the window. The street overflows with people queuing for an event.*] Oh, we're having an opening. Isn't that nice. A line on both sides—this is New York. Red carpet and everything!

Eros is at the center of it all. Remember, Socrates defined eros in an autobiographical way. It's lack on the one hand and it's ingenuity on the other. Plato's definition of eros emerges out of his wrestling with love in *Symposium*, which is his great text on love, you see. So that eros is crucial. There's simply no philosophizing without a love of wisdom, absolutely.

TAYLOR: I like this idea of the transformative power of philosophy. When I say the tagline for this project is "philosophy is in the streets," does that resonate with you?

WEST: I think philosophy is all about lived experience, which is to say life in the streets, life in a variety of different contexts. I don't want to make it just urban; you can have life in the streets in the country. But it's fundamentally about how you come to terms with living your life and trying to do it in a wise manner, and, for me, that means decently and compassionately and courageously and so forth. See, I put it this way: that—for me—philosophy is fundamentally about our finite situation. We can define that in terms of we're beings towards death, we're featherless two-legged linguistically conscious creatures born between urine and feces whose bodies will one day be the culinary delight of terrestrial worms. That's us; we're beings towards death. At the same time, we have desire while we are organisms in space and time and so it's desire in the face of death. And then, of course, you've got dogmatism, various attempts to hold on to certainty, various forms of idolatry. And you've got dialogue in the face of dogmatism. And then of course structurally and institutionally you have domination and you have democracy. You have attempts of people trying to render accountable elites, kings, queens, suzerains, corporate elites, politicians, trying to make these elites accountable to everyday people, to ordinary people. So if you've got on the one hand death, dogmatism, domination, and on the other you've got desire in the face of death, dialogue in the face of dogmatism, democracy in the face of domination, then philosophy itself becomes a critical disposition of wrestling with desire in the face of death, wrestling with dialogue in the face of dogmatism, and wrestling with democracy, trying to keep alive a very fragile democratic experiment in the face of structures of domination, patriarchy, white supremacy, imperial power, state power, all those concentrated forms of power that are not accountable to people who are affected by it.

TAYLOR: So is philosophy about speaking truth to power?

WEST: Absolutely, very true. But you also speak truth to the powerless—see, the powerful have no monopoly on greed, hatred, fear, or ignorance. [*We stop at a red light. A large crowd of people is gathered around a group of performers on the steps of the New York Public Library.*] Look at these folks dancing right there. Oh yes, we got a little hip-hop here. That's the break-dance dimension of hip-hop. Isn't that nice? I was at a session last night; we had four hours of dialogue with all the great hip-hoppers in the country.

TAYLOR: I just saw your CD.

WEST: My *Never Forget: A Journey of Revelation* with Prince, André 3000 of OutKast, the late great Gerald Levert, M-1 of Dead Prez, and KRS-1. Towering, prophetic, and progressive hip-hop artists. KRS-1 is a philosopher, you know—dropped out of school at thirteen, grew up on the streets until he was nineteen, and was in on the first wave of hip-hop.

TAYLOR: So let me ask: What is your definition of a philosopher? Do you have to go to school to be a philosopher?

WEST: Oh, God no. God no. Thank God you don't have to go to school. No, a philosopher's a lover of wisdom. It takes tremendous discipline, takes tremendous courage, to think for yourself, to examine yourself. The Socratic imperative of examining yourself requires courage. William Butler Yeats used to say it takes more courage to examine the dark corners of your own soul than it does for a soldier to fight on the battlefield. Courage to think critically. Courage is the enabling virtue for any philosopher—for any human being, I think, in the end. Courage to think, courage to love, courage to hope. That's what I like about brother Simon Critchley's work and the debate we'll have tonight.

TAYLOR: This is an old idea, right? Going back at least to the death of Socrates. That philosophy both requires and instills courage. Is music a similarly courageous endeavor?

WEST: You see, the thing to keep in mind for me is line 607b in book ten of Plato's *Republic*, on the traditional quarrel of philosophy and poetry. And of course there what Plato's trying to do is to displace Homeric *paideia* with Platonic *paideia*. Homer, representing the poets, has his own way of getting us to live our lives wisely, and Plato thinks he has a better way. And of course the death of Socrates was at the center of Plato's whole project: how do you keep alive the memory of Socrates, the legacy of Socrates, in the face of what he considers to be an inferior form of *paideia*, which is Homer? And in this first section of book ten in Plato's *Republic*, Plato talks about his traditional quarrel between philosophy and poetry. Now for me, I believe philosophy must go to school with the poets; it's not either/or, it's not over or against.

TAYLOR: Are you getting at different kinds of knowledge?

WEST: Different kinds of knowledge and the degree to which the poetic is shot through the philosophic and the philosophic shot through the poetic. Now, I think what separates me from most philosophers probably is that, see, I'm a bluesman in the life of the mind, I'm a jazzman in the world of ideas. Therefore, for me music is central, so when you're talking about poetry, for the most part Plato's talking primarily about words, where I talk about notes, I talk about tone, I talk about timbre, I talk about rhythms. See, for me music is fundamental; philosophy must go to school not only with the poets, philosophy needs to go to school with the musicians. Keep in mind Plato bans the flute in *The Republic* but not the lyre. Why? Because the flute appeals to all of the various dimensions of who we are given his tripartite conception of the soul—the rational, and the spirited, and the appetitive. The flute appeals to all three of those, whereas he thinks the lyre, with one string only, appeals to one and therefore it's permissible. Now, of course the irony of Plato was that on his deathbed, what did he do? Well, he requested the Thracian girl play music on the flute. Isn't that interesting? And you remember she forgets the melody; he has to hum it right before he dies.

TAYLOR: So he knew it.

WEST: So he knew it! The same way he had Aristophanes under his pillow. So that Plato unfortunately juxtaposes philosophy over and against poetry in his project even though his writing is so poetic—of course his practice defies his own ideology. Because Plato was very much a poetic philosopher and a philosophic poet. But for me it's not just about being a poetic philosopher or a philosophic poet; it's also about being musical. Now, what's very interesting is that Plato refers to the musical life once and it's in his dialogue *Laches*—and in *Laches*, what is he talking about? He's raising a question: What is courage? And for him a musical life is the most courageous life. Now, what does he mean by that? He's not referring to somebody that plays an instrument, but he's really referring to somebody who's trying to weave together a certain kind of melody and harmony, though he knows there's no melody and harmony without dissonance, without minor keys. But I'm a bluesman, which means that I put an emphasis on the minor keys.

TAYLOR: I just want to ask you a basic question. What do you mean when you refer to your work as "prophetic"?

WEST: Well, for me the prophetic has to do with mustering the courage to love, to empathize, to exercise compassion, and to be committed to justice. Now of course, as a Christian I come out of premodern narratives, I come out of Hebrew scripture. Micah 6:8: "Do justly, and to love mercy, and to walk humbly with thy God." *Hesed*—*hesed* is the Hebrew word for steadfast love. Now, of course you know in a capitalist society and a market-driven culture, love tends to be viewed as a wayward sentimental feeling—it's sentiment. Whereas for the Hebrew scripture and Christians and for many secular folks influenced by the legacies of Jerusalem, love is fundamentally a steadfast commitment to the well-being of the other, with that other being especially the most vulnerable. Leviticus 19:18: "Love thy neighbor as thyself." The twenty-fifth chapter of Matthew: keep track of "the least of these," the widows, the elderly, the disabled, those who have been victimized by white supremacy or homophobia or patriarchy or imperial subjugation and so forth, those Frantz Fanon called "the wretched of the earth." So that the prophetic fundamentally means this attempt to courageously live and speak on behalf of the dejected, on behalf of those whose humanity has been rendered invisible, those whose humanity is hidden and concealed. So that the notion of being a philosophical prophet or poetic prophet or what have you is integral to my own conception to what it means to be a lover of wisdom. Therefore, again, we're back to philosophy in the generic sense. And because, you see, the condition of truth is to allow suffering to speak, it means then that if you have a prophetic sensibility, you are committed to loving others and if you love others, you hate injustice. That's why Jesus goes into the temple and runs after marketeers when he first enters Jerusalem, right? That this unbelievable righteous indignation—I know my dear brother Simon Critchley calls it anger. I don't think it's anger, though. I think anger's different; anger's not the same as righteous indignation. Anger can be a bitterness that devours your soul while righteous indignation is morally driven, it's ethically driven. Now Simon agrees with that cause—he, as you know, wants strong ethics.

TAYLOR: Earlier today I was filming with Michael Hardt and our theme was revolution. We got a bit tangled up in the question of violence.

WEST: Well, I'm not a pacifist at all; I think there is a notion of "just war" that can be persuasively argued. I think in the face of Nazis, in the face of apartheid, that I would have joined those armies. But that's the last, last resort. I think nonviolence and the mediation of conflict by means of respecting civility must be promoted. But being the kind of beings we are—you know, wrestling with greed, and wrestling with fears and security, anxieties, wrestling with hatred that's shot through all of us—wars are here to stay. And the question is how do you very selectively choose, so when you send your soldiers out to fight Hitler, it's still a tragicomic affair, but you're going to have to kill the mother-huckers because they want to dominate the world, put Jewish brothers and sisters in concentration camps, and subordinate the women, and eliminate people of color.

TAYLOR: Let's talk about this idea of the market more. You mentioned its effect on love and its preference for sentimentalism. But what about thinking? What is philosophy's place in a market-driven society? What's the market's effect on philosophical or intellectual discourse?

WEST: On the one hand, you know, you've got professionalized philosophy, which is in professional/managerial spaces, namely universities, that conduct philosophy as a technical expertise rather then a way of life, rather then a mode of existence. And of course it's tied to the market in the sense that these multiversities, these highly specialized and professionalized multiversities and universities, are parasitic on corporate capital for the most part and there's often very cozy and intimate relations between the corporate elites who rule and the universities who are financially and disproportionately dependent on the wealth and monies of the corporate elite. So for the most part you tend not to look to the history of universities as being places for serious radical political action, radical political ideas, radical political paradigms, and so on. There are exceptions but for the most part I've never had high expectations of the academy. I mean, American history, my God, if we had waited for universities to fight wars against male supremacy and white supremacy and the wealth and inequality generated by corporate greed, then we'd have very few victories. See, much of the courage has come from the demos—from ordinary people, from below—and the academicians are then affected by the social movements and respond thereto.

TAYLOR: And they can do valuable work in that capacity.

WEST: Absolutely—well, not only that, but I mean there's a certain pleasure of the life of the mind that cannot be denied. There's a certain pleasure about being around people who enact a playfulness when it comes to the world of ideas.

TAYLOR: Let's hear more about this. Convince the audience.

WEST: Oh yes, I mean, intellectual hedonism has its place. I'm a Christian, but I'm not a puritan. I believe in pleasure and orgiastic pleasure has its place, intellectual pleasure has its place, social pleasure has its place, televisual pleasure has its place. I like certain TV shows. My God, when it comes to music, Beethoven's great string quartet, Opus 131—unbelievable aesthetic pleasure. The same goes for Curtis Mayfield, the Beatles, or what have you, on different levels. So that intellectual pleasure's very important—it's just that we have to be honest that it presupposes certain kinds of structures and institutions, like universities, and they have histories. So its pleasure, no matter how desirable, is never innocent: it's always presupposing and assuming a certain kind of social order, one usually shot through structures of domination.

TAYLOR: Last night I was talking to Simon Critchley and he made the case that to be a philosopher, to be an intellectual, is already to be half-dead. You're like a corpse. How pleasurable can that be?

WEST: No, I wouldn't agree with that, though. The conversation with the dead is one of the great pleasures of life. My God, somebody who is sitting there reading Chekhov, Beckett, reading Toni Morrison— you are not in any way dead, in many ways you are intensely alive. I mean, when my dear brother Simon reads Wallace Stevens in his wonderful book *Things Merely Are*, he's very much alive. It's impossible to be dead and dull reading Wallace Stevens's intricate and subtle plays of mind. So it's true that you might be socially isolated because you're in the library at home and so on, but you're intensely alive. In fact you're much more alive than these folk walking the streets of New York in crowds, with no intellectual interrogation and questioning going at all. But if you read John Ruskin, or you read Mark Twain, or, my God, Herman Melville, you almost have to throw the book against the wall because you're almost so intensely alive that you need a break! It's time to take a break, get a little dullness in your life, take *Moby-Dick* and throw it against the wall the way Goethe threw von Kleist's work against the wall. It was just too much. It reminded Goethe of the darkness that he was escaping after he overcame those suicidal impulses with *Sorrows of Young Werther* in the 1770s that made him move towards neoclassicism in Weimar. There are certain things that make us almost too alive: it's almost like being too intensely in love—you can't do anything. It's hard to get back to chronos, it's hard to get back to everyday life, you know what I mean? The *kairotic** dimension of being in love with another person—everything is so meaningful you want to sustain it. You just can't do it, you know? You've got to go to the bathroom, get a drink of water!

TAYLOR: Let's veer back to the idea of truth, or rather, the idea of truth as connected to lived experience.

WEST: We started with the existential conception of truth: Truth is a way of life and mode of existence. And there, as in Plato's *Seventh Letter*, you usually have truth inexplicably tied to mystery because we fallen finite human beings are unable to ever gain any monopoly on Truth (capital T). We might have access to truths (small t), but

---

* From *kairos*, meaning a propitious moment for decision or action. Whereas chronos conveys the linear or quantitative aspect of time, *kairos* stresses the qualitative element.

they're fallible claims about truth, they could be wrong, we have to be open to revision, and so on. So there is a certain kind of mystery that goes hand in hand with truth. This is why so many of the existential thinkers, be they religious like Meister Eikhart or Paul Tillich or be they secular like Camus and Sartre, they're accenting our finitude and our inability to fully grasp the ultimate nature of reality, the truth about things. And therefore you talk about truth being tied to the *way* to truth, because once you give up on the notion of fully grasping the way the world is, you're going to talk about: What are the ways in which I can sustain my quest for truth? How do you sustain a journey, a path, towards truth, the way to truth? So the truth talk goes hand in hand with the talk about the way to truth. And scientists could talk about this in terms of inducing evidence and drawing reliable conclusions and so forth and so on. Religious folk could talk about this in terms of surrendering one's arrogance and pride in the face of divine revelation and what have you, but they're all ways of acknowledging our finitude and our fallibility.

TAYLOR: You're talking about philosophy as an exploration of limits?

WEST: Yes, our finitude. I mean, "limit" strikes me as a little bit too bureaucratic a term, even though Karl Jaspers has this wonderful notion of limit situations in life—he's another great European existential philosopher, of the twentieth century. But I want to talk about it much more in terms of finitude because I'm much more of a historicist. See, I want to talk about organisms in time and space. And we linguistic organisms in time and space, our finitude's always wrapped up with culture, history, society, structures of domination, ways of resisting structures of domination. "Limits" tends to emaciate that kind of language, you know what I mean? I want all of the rich historical colorations to be manifest in talking about our finitude. Being born of a woman in stank and stench—what I call funk—being introduced to the funk of life in the womb, and the love push that gets you out. Here Vico is so much better then Heidegger. Vico talks about it in terms of being a corpse. See, Heidegger doesn't talk about corpses, he talks about death—it's still too abstract. Read the poetry of John Donne; he'll tell you about corpses that decompose and so forth. Well, see, that's history, that's the raw funky stanky stuff of life. That's what bluesmen do, you see, that's what jazzmen do. So that, yes, "limits" has a certain way of signifying the fact that we're not masters of the universe. But when you actually talk philosophically in terms of being a lover of wisdom, the question becomes, "OK, you're born of this particular woman, will she love you or not?" If she doesn't, that's going to fundamentally affect your life; if she does, it's going to fundamentally affect your life. Now what are her beliefs? What kind of culture does she come from? What kind of orientations will she transmit and bequeath to you? What about your community? What about your religious/nonreligious institutions that will shape you? So that, once you're really bitten by the Socratic bug, you're going to be questioning some things. Something's got to be in place.

I mean, brother Simon again, I hate to keep going back to my dear brother, but he's on my mind. I mean, it's clear that he's got Romantic problems, right? So disappointment is always at the center, failure is always at the center. Well, where does Romanticism come from? Why begin with Romanticism? You see, I don't begin with Romanticism, Chekhov didn't, but Simon does. And there's nothing wrong with that because, you know, for many people German idealism is the ultimate horizon of thinking. That's my dear brother Žižek—and I've had wonderful debates with him at Harvard and Princeton—but for Žižek, and in a sort of sense it's true for my dear brother Simon, German idealism is the ultimate horizon of human thought and therefore you begin with Romanticism. Can you totalize? Can you make things whole? Can you create harmony? If you can't: disappointment. So disappointment is relevant to what you're rejecting, you see? Chekhov was never Romantic. Therefore, when he talked about fragments and ruins and relics, it wasn't in relation to a whole, because he was never socialized into a Romantic sensibility, you see. I'm a Chekhovian Christian to the core, to the core.

TAYLOR: It seems to me we could relate Romanticism back to our conversation about capitalism. There's a rather one-dimensional pressure to be happy, for example, and feelings of doubt, melancholy, or alienation are to be suppressed in our society. This could be related to the Romantic desire for wholeness that you're talking about.

WEST: One of the aims at the market—Marx is absolutely right in that wonderful language of the *Manifesto*—you want to melt everything down, you want to flatten out the rituals, you want to flatten out all of those moments that equip us to deal with death in various forms, and you want a life on the surface that is driven by cash nexus, driven by profit making, driven by pleasure taking. It's a very superficial, immature way of living, but it becomes a way of sustaining a whole economy in the end, a way of life, a market way of life that Marx projected though he never could have conceived of how we live now in the twenty-first century. Where market affects every nook and cranny from bedroom to classroom, and therefore it's a sheer act of resistance to try to hold back, to some degree, the market sensibility. It's a very, very difficult thing to do. I mean, Adorno spends much of the last thirty years of his life looking for some form of resistance against the ubiquitous presence of the market and its pernicious consequences.

TAYLOR: He couldn't find it then, and the situation is much more intense today. The market has penetrated much further into our lives.

WEST: Well, he found it in some Schoenberg gestures of atonality. Of course, Beckett for him becomes the exemplary artist too because Beckett does resist—even at the level of form he does resist. You know that wonderful line in Beckett where he says, "Heidegger and Sartre talk about being. That's too abstract for me. I call it the mess"? It's what I call the funk as a bluesman in the life of the mind, right? And the mess for Beckett is so overwhelming that it overflows into your form. That's why he breaks with Joyce, his mentor. Joyce is a maximalist; he's still trying to find a form he can impose upon the chaos of history. "History is the nightmare from which I'm trying to awake," Stephen says in *Ulysses*. And Beckett says, "Joyce, no, I'm a minimalist, I'm not a maximalist. The mess is so overwhelming, right, that I know the mess is going to be in my incomplete form, that it is a form of failure." Now, at the end of Joyce's life, Joyce knew he failed anyway, but he didn't intend to. Whereas Beckett says from the very beginning, "I enact an art and aesthetics of failure."

TAYLOR: So which position resonates with you, maximalist or minimalist? Or is there something else?

WEST: Again, you see, the language of failure and disappointment, disenchantment, disillusionment, is a little bit Romantic for me. You see, Chekhov never called his art failure; Beckett did. It is failure of a certain sort but I'm not sure that would be the first word I would use. See, part of the problem is that when you have a Romantic project, you're so obsessed with time as loss and time as a taker, whereas as a Chekhovian Christian, I want to stress time as a gift as well as time as a giver. So that, yes, it's failure, but how good a failure? It's done some wonderful things. And Beckett can say, "Try again, fail again, fail better" in *Worstward Ho*—that wonderful line, it's about page 89 in the French. Fail better—well, OK, but why call it failure? I mean, why not have a sense of gratitude that you're able to do as much as you did? That you're able to love as much and think as much and play as much? Why think you need the whole thing? Where's the expectation that you need the whole thing coming from? It's a Romantic project, you see what I mean?

And this is even disturbing about America. The paradisial city and all the other mess and lies and so on. I say no, no, America's a very fragile, democratic experiment predicated on the disposition of the lands of indigenous people and the enslavement of African people and the subjugation of workers and women and the marginalization of gays and lesbians. It has great potential, but this notion that somehow we had it all or ever will have it all—that's got to go, you've got to push it to the side. And once you push all that to the side, then it tends to evacuate the language of disappointment and the language of failure. And you say, OK, how much have we done? How have we been able to do it? Can we do more? In some situations you can't do more. It's like trying to break-dance at seventy-five, you can't do it anymore! You were a master at sixteen; it's over! Does that make you a failure? Hell no! You're seventy-five years old—some things you can't do. You accept it for what it is. That's the wisdom that Sophocles is looking for in his plays. It's a situated judgment where you accept it for what it is. You don't need to be disappointed you can't break-dance at seventy-five the way you did at fifteen. The way you can't make love at eighty the way you did at twenty—so what? Time is real!

TAYLOR: You're not trapped in this Romantic view that's always longing for some totality or some ideal past—

WEST: Longing for more or some wholeness or harmony or overcoming alienation, all of the Romantic tropes that have thoroughly saturated the discourse of modern thinkers—I resist that.

TAYLOR: I'm concerned about you being late for your lecture. But I want to talk to you more about this.

WEST: We got good time. You take whatever time you want to take.

TAYLOR: Are you sure? I want to make sure you have time to prepare.

WEST: It's not so much a matter of me preparing. I'm ever ready.

TAYLOR: So, we have to love the world in all its flaws.

WEST: Remember what Beethoven said on his deathbed. He said, "I learned to look at the world in all of its darkness and evil and still love it." And that's not Romantic Beethoven. This is the Beethoven of the string quartets, the 131, the greatest string quartet ever written—of course, Beethoven is a grand master. But the string quartets, you go back to those movements, there's no Romantic wholeness to be shattered as in early Beethoven. He's given up on that, you see. This is where Chekhov begins, this is where the blues starts, this is where jazz starts. You think Charles Parker's upset because he can't sustain a harmony? He doesn't care about the harmony: he's trying to completely ride on dissonance, ride on the blue notes. Of course he's got harmony in terms of his interventions here and there, but why start with this obsession with wholeness? And if you can't have it, you're disappointed and want to have a drink, melancholia, blah blah blah. No, you see, the blues, my kind of blues, begins with catastrophe, begins with the angel of history in Benjamin's *Theses on the Philosophy of History*. It begins with the pillage, the wreckage, of one pile on another. That's the starting point. The blues is personal catastrophe lyrically expressed. And for black people in America and in the modern world, given these vicious legacies of white supremacy, it is: How do you generate an elegance of earned self-togetherness so that you have a stick-to-it-iveness in the face of the catastrophic and the calamitous and the horrendous and the scandalous, the monstrous? You see it in Kafka with Gregor. The first line of the story *The Metamorphosis* is what? He's in a catastrophic situation, that he wakes up one morning transformed into a huge insect, vermin, however you want to talk about it, *unheimlichkeit*, the uncanniness of that. Dealing with the catastrophic. Kafka, Benjamin, Adorno, Said—these are people that understand this. But I understand it as a bluesman, so it has much more connection to my own situation as a black man. You don't have to be a black man for that—I mean, Tennessee Williams understood, he's a white literary bluesman. You know his first collection of plays was called *American Blues*? White brother born in Mississippi—Columbus, Mississippi.

TAYLOR: No doubt the conditions of our life influence our sensibilities.

WEST: Absolutely. I mean, you could begin with a mother that doesn't love you. I mean, look at the finest playwright in song ever produced in the American theater, Stephen Sondheim, whose mother never loved him. In fact, when she was in the hospital about to get heart surgery, they asked her to write one last thing before she died. She wrote one sentence. It was a note to Stephen: "I have no regrets in life other than the fact that I gave birth to you"—that's it. That's it. And you look at Sondheim's *Passion*, you look at *Follies*, look at *Company*. Of course, Eugene O'Neill had the same problem. *A Long Day's Journey into Night* is about the same problem, a mother who wished she had never given birth to Eugene.

That catastrophic beginning! I mean, in some ways it's almost primordial in a historical sense. It's much deeper than the kind of blues that I live because I have a mother who loves me deeply and a father who's dead but once loved me too. I don't experience the catastrophic at that level. So, as a black male, I can deal with white supremacy and so forth, and imperial subjugation, what have you. But not at that deep primordial existential, quasi-ontological level of having a mother who wishes she never gave birth to you. That's Sondheim, that's O'Neill, that's deep stuff, I tell you. I don't want anybody to go there, but I thank God for Stephen Sondheim, I thank God for Eugene O'Neill.

TAYLOR: So this non-Romantic view of the world—

WEST: It's not even non-Romantic. You don't even want to use Romantic as a point of reference!

TAYLOR: So what do you call it?

WEST: Just "blues sensibility."

TAYLOR: Blues sensibility.

WEST: There you go! There you go!

TAYLOR: It seems liberational.

WEST: Absolutely, I think it is. But I don't want to fetishize it either. I think that it has some emancipatory consequences but also has some debilitating ones.

TAYLOR: What are those?

WEST: Well, I think there's a way in which a blues sensibility could easily downplay, for example, the essential role of mathematics. I mean, the tradition of Pythagoras is still an important one. Somebody like Ralph Waldo Ellison, author of *Invisible Man*—named after Ralph Waldo Emerson, one of the founding fathers of American intellectual culture—for him the blues was always tied to a humanistic project. And there's nothing wrong with that, but it could be limiting and could downplay the crucial role of science, and mathematics, and physics, and biology, and chemistry, and so on. I've got fellow Christians who are afraid of Darwin, afraid of evolutionary biology, afraid of the sciences because somehow that's going to pull the rug from under them. I say no. I think nothing human ought to be alien to us, including numbers. Numbers are at the essence of reality. That's Pythagoras. He turns out to be more right than almost anybody else when you look at modern physics these days, right?

TAYLOR: It's true. One thing I was going to say earlier is that your concept of philosophy seems to be allowed to investigate everything.

WEST: It's tied to that level of wisdom in that broad sense, you're absolutely right. You're absolutely right. It's not relativistic in the sense that it does believe there are better views of the world, better interpretations of the world, because I put a premium on justice. Nazis are wrong, you know, Bush is wrong, Cheney's wrong, and I think we can generate some arguments to show that, you see what I mean? Living and dying for oppressed people I think is noble. I think it's a great calling. I don't think it's normative to be a radical, I don't think martyrdom ever ought to be normative in any project. But a certain kind of martyrdom is noble, it has a magnanimity to it. So I do believe in making judgments, you know what I mean? I don't in any way have anything to do with this kind of sophomoric relativism where anything goes.

TAYLOR: So maybe this can lead us back to the quest for truth, something that guides our judgments.

WEST: Back to existential truth. Because in the end, you see, a skeptic can't live his or her skepticism. See, if you're really a skeptic all the way down, the death of a fly on the wall has the same status as the death of your mother. Now, if somebody's able to reach that conclusion, I think they become so detached from my conception of what it is to be human that I don't find it interesting. I have nothing against flies or insects, but I just don't give them the same status as you all in this car. So if you see some insect that gets crushed, I'm not going to say a prayer (I'm not going to celebrate either), but if you all get crushed, I'm rushing you to the hospital, we got a fight on our hands. We got to make sure you all bounce back. You see what I mean? And that means I'm ascribing a certain value to you all that I'm not to that fly, which means I can't be a thoroughgoing skeptic or an anything-goes relativist.

TAYLOR: I keep wanting to return to the idea of faith and your source of that within what you call the blues sensibility. We've talked about this market-driven society and the desire for a more just world. But here we are driving through New York, the center of it all, and the buildings are so material, so big, so immovable, so gray. It's hard to imagine things changing.

WEST: It's true. There's a wonderful line in the New Testament, Luke 18:8, that says, "When the Son of Man returns to earth, will he find any faith?" It's a powerful formulation. And he's not just talking about religious faith because there is a fiduciary dimension of being human, of the fiducial constitution of human existence in which we all need some degree of trustworthiness in order to go on in some way. Now, of course there's Beckett, "I can't go on, I do go on, I can't go on, I go on" and so forth, but there's some fiduciary dimension there. It may have a little to do with God, may have little to do with church, mosque, synagogue, what have you. But why get up in the morning? Why not kill yourself? Why not get hit by the car because you don't care, because you've become so thoroughly indifferent, coldhearted, that you've lost trust in everything? You see what I mean? So at that very deep level of the fiduciary dimension of the human condition, a faith in that sense—very, very small f, very small f—we're not talking about falling in love, which is a thicker faith but has nothing to do with God, nothing to do with religion, right? And then, by the time you get to God talk, things have really thickened out. You've a very thick conception of faith. But at this very threadbare notion of faith, why go on? Why have any fidelity to a friend? Why have any loyalty to a mother? These are fiduciary dimensions of faith, you see. And for some of us it has to do with piety—you know the wonderful treatment of piety in Plato's *Euthyphro*? What is piety? Piety is the indebtedness to those things that help us make our move from womb to tomb.

From a mother's womb to tomb, from womb to tomb. It's indebtedness. Santayana makes much of this: "natural piety." John Dewey writes about natural piety. We are all pietistic in some sense because we're indebted to those who came before. Why? Because we have a language. The very afterlife of the language we speak has to do with our giving life now. And we didn't create our language, we're indebted to the very strong structure of the language that we deploy, that we're taught, and so on. And from language, you can go all the way up, you know, to culture and society and love, through religious God talk.

TAYLOR: So it's an act of faith to even get up in the morning.

WEST: It's a tremendous act of faith. I mean, again, I think Beckett is quite relevant here. It's almost a Kierkegaardian leap of faith in Beckett's universe. But the irony is, of course, in killing oneself the expectations were too high. Why did you expect more? It's a Romantic act, you see what I mean?

TAYLOR: My final question is for the faithful who manage to get out of bed. One theme that keeps coming up is the phrase "a meaningful life." Do you think it is philosophy's duty to speak on this: How to live a meaningful life, what is the meaning of life? Are these even appropriate questions for a philosopher?

WEST: I think it is. I think the problem with meaning is very important. Nihilism is a serious challenge, meaninglessness is a serious challenge. Even making sense of meaninglessness in itself is a kind of discipline and achievement. The problem is, of course, you never really reach it. It's not a static, stationary *telos* or object or end or aim. It's a process that one never reaches; it's Sisyphean. You're going up the hill, looking for better meanings or grander, more ennobling, enabling meanings, but you never reach it. In that sense, you die without being able to have the whole in the language of a Romantic discourse. [*West looks out the window and sees we're approaching his destination.*] You can just let me off here on the corner.

[*West gets out of the car, heading off across Union Square into the night.*]

AVITAL RONELL

Meaning

I had the good fortune to take a course co-taught by Avital Ronell and Jacques Derrida in the fall of 2000, so Ronell was always on my radar for Examined Life. *Not long after I got the green light for the movie, I ran into her in the middle of a snowstorm in the East Village. I asked her on the spot if she would consider participating in the project. While meeting at a café some months later, we resolved to film without planning or predetermining the discussion to come. The walk took place in Tompkins Square Park, one of the rare public spaces in lower Manhattan that retains some of its distinctively quirky, gritty character.*

AVITAL RONELL: So I was trying to figure out what you were getting me into here and how we are implicated or co-implicated in this walk, what steps we should take toward a work that sounds very intriguing. But also, given my high levels of hermeneutic suspicion, I had to wonder what you had up your sleeve. I tried to understand what I was being inscribed in by you, and with you, which is to say this walk is not just an off-ramp in terms of my own projects but has a very real place and, more generally, belongs to a history of thought in and besides the kind of work that I have been trying to do—not only in terms of what it might mean to "walk the walk" or "talk the talk" or to do both at the same time. I was going to interview you and ask you what you thought you were doing. Perhaps you want to say something and I could be responsive to that?

ASTRA TAYLOR: It occurs to me that there are in fact two answers to the question of why I've undertaken this project. There's a public answer and a more private answer. Publicly, when I've pitched this film to people, I've struck a very confident pose and said I want to bring philosophy to the streets and show an audience that philosophy is relevant and important. That's how I've framed the film in those contexts. But I think, on a more personal level, I'm challenging philosophy to see if that's actually true. I haven't articulated my private yearning for and doubts about philosophy's relevance when I describe the film to others.

RONELL: OK, well, those are fighting words, and now I feel I have the upbeat and I can start to work with you in a rather authentic, if worrisome, way because I share your yearning and longing to get philosophy to show up, to present itself as something extremely relevant, poignant, irreversible, necessary, and desirable. And yet, certainly, in our culture, the culture we share—I'm sure we share many cultures and subcultures—but in the dominant culture, ever since Socrates was pummeled to death by the state and told to shut the fuck up, essentially, philosophy has been terrorized by powerful structures and shoved into a kind of place of irrelevance. I would like to see us transvaluate that into a kind of sacred irrelevance, because what counts as relevant is often scored from business interests, is asked, very violently, to yield results and to reduce or simplify things by articulating them in a purportedly clear and intelligible way.

From the place that I am speaking to you now, anyone who has asked for clarity or transparency or relevance has kind of been on the enemy side of things. When a politician says, "Let me say something very clearly," it has that right-wing scary machete edge to it. Or "Read my lips." The clearer and simpler the things around us appear to be and the louder the spokespeople advocate for "clarity," the more insidious, dangerous, and outright pernicious this demand turns out to be. So there is a problem; we now find ourselves in a kind of snag or impossibility because I cannot, unless I were to translate this into a sort of dissimulation or something dishonest, I can't speak for relevance or for the kind of fulfillment of longing that we both nonetheless share.

TAYLOR: That's exactly why I used the word yearning, because I thought you could speak to the longing or desire for absolute meaning or for wholeness that always eludes us. I suppose I can't help but relate things to the challenge of making this film. I imagine that some people in the audience will respond to this project with frustration because it won't provide any answers—it will just raise more questions.

RONELL: I can understand your concern. We should remember and summon all sorts of hermeneutic helpers right now. First of all, the reception end of this film is of importance. The audience has to be brilliant, open, vulnerable, prepared to co-produce genius. If something's to happen here, that something and that happening can't be grasped ahead of time, or we can't be certain to be able to program it ahead of time. We don't know when, in a speculative sense, the film is going to come out, when people are going to receive it, or even where—where in their orifices, on their bodies. Because Lacan has said, for example, that every word of an intense analytical session—which this may be, for all we know—enters the body and becomes body. We don't know where this film is going to land, whom it's going to shake up, wake up, freak out, or bore. But even boredom as an off-shoot of melancholy interests me as a response to these dazzling utterances that we are producing. [*Laughs.*]

Don't forget that Heidegger ditched philosophy for "thinking" because he thought philosophy as such was still too institutional, academic, too bound up in knowledge and scientific results, too cognitively inflected. So he asked the question, What is called thinking? And he had a lot to say about walks, about going on paths that lead nowhere. One of his important texts is called *Holzwege*, which means "a path that leads nowhere." In Greek the word for path is *methodos*. So we're on the path, we're following a method that isn't determined or entirely programmed.

[*Ronell points to a trash can our film crew is about to crash into.*] Except there's garbage, which is part of what we are trying to include in our work and our thought, which is to say, we are attentive still to what remains, what gets tossed away and off. We want to include the trash in many ways, thinking of this refuse according to all sorts of disposal systems.

TAYLOR: Maybe we can begin with the central relationship of speech to writing. And then, I was wondering if you have any thoughts about film as a form of writing, as something that evokes a person's presence, but of course that person isn't there. This seems like a subject that may be appropriate given your background both as someone associated with deconstruction and one who has written a lot about technology.

RONELL: Thank you. I've been concerned about film and video, in particular in terms of television and different levels of feed, whether live or dead. I have many subpersonalities, a number of intellectual profiles, and one of them involves trying to work on questions concerning technology and media. So certainly I've been thinking about transferences and translations into different media and what film inscribes and enacts, and what kind of exteriority it promises in relation to an outside, so I'd have to think about that surprise question.

In regard to film I would say, very provisionally, that what interests me is the medium as something that sustains an "interruption in presence" as it produces the illusion of immediacy and presence. What speaks to me is how film is on the haunted side of things and the way it participates in a kind of mourning disorder, a failure to mourn, to let go, and is at the same time only ever in mourning over its objects.

TAYLOR: I am curious how you feel about the prospect of being represented in that way or to be something that's haunting?

RONELL: You mean our project now? Oh, it's very distressing; it's a disturbance. If I can allow for an autobiographical trace, I think one reason that I took to writing in the way I did was in order to avoid all those empirical scandals that go into getting up in the morning and trying to put oneself together. Each time I teach a class, I am cursing and upset and practically crying because I have to suddenly present my so-called self in front of an audience. Writing (so I tell my so-called self) promised me that I could hide under her skirt, in a way. And thus coming out to talk and work with you is really a personal homage to you, because I tend to avoid this sort of thing, the extreme exposure to which you are subjecting me.

TAYLOR: It's funny, I'm feeling suddenly relaxed. I've been in a state of panic since we started walking. I think it's good for me to feel what it's like to be in front of the camera and what a terrifying experience it is to be recorded while having to think on your feet.

RONELL: Or to think with one's feet. As Nietzsche has said, one must learn to read him by taking one's boots off.

TAYLOR: Let's go back to writing and speech and the central status of that relationship in the kind of work you do and in philosophy more generally.

RONELL: Well, writing is what continues to be massively repressed and rejected, as my mentor and friend Derrida pointed out in his sustained reflections on the predicament of writing. Writing has always been associated with the excremental, the secondary. There's the discussion that Plato has about drugs and writing and how worrisome the introduction of writing is; he sees the invention of writing as a peril. The same way we talk about video games or anything that is related to violence and mimetic impulses, like kids miming or imitating what they see on television, writing was seen to be extremely dangerous when first presented to the king. The king said, If I allow writing into my kingdom, then people will forget everything. Writing, a kind of secondary supplementary device, effaces as it inscribes. It promotes forgetting.

I am reminded of something that happens in *Hamlet*, something altogether scandalous. After their first interview, which is traumatic and shocking, the ghost of Hamlet's father says, "Remember me," which could in English—glorious luscious English—also mean "bring me back my phallus": re-member me. Hamlet, the son who has just heard the atrocities revealed by his ghost father, is supposed to, according to the codifications and conventions of drama and tragedy, whip out his sword and say, "I will avenge you, Dad!" Instead Hamlet agrees to remember his father but whips out a little writing pad and writes it down, which is a scandal. This kind of shift to writing that Hamlet enacts suggests that he has to put a Post-it on his refrigerator to remember the revealed crime. It's a note to self: "Your father was murdered by your uncle" or something like that. In this moment there's the irony of Hamlet forgetting his father, maybe killing his father—maybe this is another parricidal moment—because he whips out the writing pad or his little technoberry.

TAYLOR: I'd like you to continue to articulate this division between speech and writing and the historical privileging of speech over writing. Again, it relates to something I've been thinking about in regard to this project, which is film's relationship to the written word and the fact that filmic language often condenses or simplifies things compared to writing.

RONELL: If I were your analyst I would wonder what makes you say that, because it sounds like it comes from a place of self-humiliation or despair. So if this were an analytic session, I would ask you to say more about the place from which the denigration of filmic writing is coming from because I would differ in this regard: I see film grammar or its particular syntax as something that explores the limits of what can be said and what can be shown. But you may want to say more about why you want to subsume it under other types of writing.

TAYLOR: I'm specifically thinking about the challenge of making a film about philosophy, which obviously has a spoken element but is typically written. Book form allows you to explore something so in depth: three hundred, four hundred, five hundred pages exploring a single concept. Whereas in a feature-length film you have eighty minutes in the form of speech that has been recorded, and in the case of this film, each person has ten minutes.

RONELL: Yes, that is an outrage. I would understand that the others would have ten minutes but to bring me down to ten minutes is inadmissible, there's no doubt about it. [*Laughs.*]

But let me say that it's a matter of a different temporality, a different approach or way of attacking similar problems or issues of, for example, phenomenological import. The film does ask: What can I show? What can I tell? How can I try to make a narrative or destroy a narrative and deconstitute it?

[*We begin to pass through the corner of the park where the punks hang out. They don't respond very warmly to the presence of our camera.*] And here you are, opening up to the public's face our linguistic pollutants. This is also a response to the work we are doing, which is to say that there is some fascination—people are turning their gaze toward this project right here. Very kind, very curious, very intellectually alert, as you can see. Very high on what we are doing. [*Some people on the park benches make obscene gestures at the camera; others hide their faces, though a few don't seem to notice us at all.*]

But let me get back to what we were discussing. First of all, for my part, I tried to destroy the sovereignty of the book many years ago, though books have certain claims and pretensions and I'm of course addicted to them, cathected onto them irreversibly. But the hierarchies that begin with the difference you evoked between speech and writing are very dangerous and quite pernicious. Speech is considered to be on the side of presence and fullness and immediacy; by contrast, writing is what always lags behind, needs to be denied. Rousseau always railed against writing. Others railed against writing and always made it part of a logic of substitution: I'd rather be with you than write to you. Then there's Goethe, who wrote on his mistress's back, meaning that he already confused those differences and separations. So speech was the living Logos. Writing was always considered to be on the side of death and *techné* and so on and so forth. It was always the degraded one in any binary standoff. [*In the distance a few kids in the background yell "Fuck you" at us.*] I think we have a great audience! [*Laughs.*]

[*A teenage punk jumps up and starts skipping alongside us, holding up a bottle of beer for the camera.*] When I used to teach at Berkeley, the administrative assistant said she always knew when my seminar was up because these were my students. So you see we're being squeezed from all sides, including this debilitated side of those who are completely wasted and couldn't care less. Though I assure you that when they get high and stoned they can have serious and deep reflections about the meaning of being!

TAYLOR: Well, you have written about addiction in your book *Crack Wars*, so maybe we can take this opportunity to say something about that.

RONELL: I was interested in different types of memory, which is something that we've already started to talk about. In Hegel there's the difference between *Erinnerung*, which is the internalizing memory when you have something at heart or in your heart and you don't need to write it down the way Hamlet did. That, in contrast, would be on the side of what he calls *Gedächtnis*, which refers to the more mechanical and technologically driven prompters. When you have to prompt yourself or remind yourself or write a memo to yourself, that means, as you're remembering, you're forgetting or you will have already always forgotten. But then there are other types of memories that have to do with getting high or intoxicated, and the image in film of some guy sitting in front of some glass of alcohol and remembering with melancholic music in the background. This has to do with a resurrectionist memory, and you wonder what they are preserving in alcohol, these guys.

TAYLOR: Memory and forgetting were the themes of the class I took with you and Jacques Derrida at NYU in 2000. We were focusing on Derrida's book *Memoires for Paul de Man*. Certainly film and video play a big role in forging collective memories and the whole archival process, in how we remember certain things and forget others. And here we are, creating a visual and auditory record of this moment.

RONELL: But that means that even at the moment of filming—this is what I meant by mourning or the structure of mourning—we are already part of an archival index of the dead. So the moment of this address, as present and vibrant as it might seem here in the park, is already part of a death march.

TAYLOR: Let's talk about the drive to archive, to capture moments like this one.

RONELL: Derrida wrote that beautiful work *Archive Fever*. Judy Butler has considered archival aspects of some of the scandalous photographs that came out when it turned out American soldiers were torturing detainees. So there's quite a lot to be said about the national archival impulse. The question might be: To what extent are we addicted to archiving ourselves or to what has been called by Derrida "anarchivisation," preserving everything without a necessary order or intention?

TAYLOR: I've noticed over the last few days that so much of what we capture with our camera is people taking photographs. Everywhere we go there are people taking photographs and immediately looking at them.

RONELL: Yes, it's absolute mediation. It's also a kind of concession to a traumatic theory of existence, which is to say you're not truly present to your experience. It first has to be captured or deadened and then presented to you from the Other, which could be a photograph or a film. It often has to be circuited in that way.

TAYLOR: John [*the director of photography*] said recently that if he doesn't take a photograph of something he's experiencing, then it doesn't happen.

RONELL: That's right. That shows the lag or the deferral, because what you see in the photograph gets reconstituted as what may have happened. Experience as such no longer carries authority—it lacks the substance of a grounding or unshakable occurrence.

TAYLOR: That's part of the process of how we give meaning to an experience.

RONELL: If we insist still on giving meaning, and there's definitely a craving for that.

TAYLOR: Let's talk about that craving, because meaning, the idea that life should have a meaning, the quest for the meaning of life, are recurring themes, especially in books that attempt to pitch philosophy to the general public.

RONELL: They tell you that your life should have a meaning?

TAYLOR: Sure, these common questions associated with philosophy: What's the meaning of life? What makes a meaningful life? These questions that speak to the longing for meaning, which even you confessed to feeling.

RONELL: I used to and still do in my adolescent surges feel a longing for meaning that gets translated in different ways. I do believe that some things are purposeful—I'm thinking here of Kantian "purposefulness without purpose," part of his definition of art—it doesn't get subsumed under a concept, cannot be forced to yield meaning or serve a purpose. Nonetheless, for Kant, art proceeds as if it did have a purpose and goes along with this energizing fiction.

I'm very suspicious historically and intellectually of the promise of meaning. Meaning has often had very fascistoid nonprogressivist edges, if not a problematic core. Very often the emergency supplies of meaning brought to a given incident, structure, or theme in one's life are cover-ups, are ways of addressing the wound of nonmeaning. I think it's very hard to keep things in the tensional structure of the openness, whether it's ecstatic or not, of nonmeaning. This is very difficult, which is why there is then the quick grab for transcendental signifiers—for God, for nation, and for other master signifiers. The widespread craving for meaning has tended to be very misused and abused by certain types of, let's say, power guzzlers or by more innocent, if needy, people toward dubious ends.

And I understand it. I understand the compulsion to secure meaning. I'm not saying we need to eradicate it; that effort would be an error because it would bring surplus meaning back on the rebound like the return of the repressed. But the clamor for meaning is something that should be recognized as a symptom and often as a sickness, a sign of weakness. Though it's something that we are in constant negotiation with—everyone wants something like meaning to back up finite, often impoverished existence.

[*We turn a corner, passing by the dog run. A dozen or so large dogs chase each other in circles while their owners watch over them.*] For instance, when you see these dogs play, why reduce the frolic to meaning rather than just allowing for the arbitrary eruption of something that can't be grasped or explicated as such, but it's just there in this absolute contingency of being? Now they are sniffing each other. So, OK, that I can reduce to meaning! But when you slip meaning onto things, very often it reduces and darkens the entire horizon and can function as a first step in a kind of rallying cry that is to be held in suspicion.

TAYLOR: Your comments made me think about current events and the desire to slap a meaning on September 11th, to distill that event into a rallying cry for retaliation that has led to the wars in Iraq and Afghanistan.

RONELL: I agree. Again, I want to just say that life in its grand complexity very often eludes meaning and is in excess of it. Things happen that you can't account for. When you wrap things up—and who wouldn't want to wrap things up?—and you think, "Well, I've got so I can close the book on it and that's it," that's cheating, that's not enabling the intense excess and surprise of what is happening.

TAYLOR: How does that relate to your work, which often takes a single concept, like stupidity, and explodes it, exploring it from many different angles?

RONELL: Precisely to the extent that these things are inexhaustible. They call us, they summon us, and they force us to pay attention. If something had a meaning that could be tagged and decided on once and for all, we wouldn't be called ethically to go over it again and again and to review things, to question them, to open cold cases and rethink our common certitudes. All of this requires intellectual labor, the boost of our ethical, first-responder kind of instincts. All of this requires us to be on it and all over it—without, however, presuming that we have been able to master something.

TAYLOR: My thought is that this ties into philosophy more broadly. This is why philosophy is never finished, right? It speaks to questions that we can never pin down and close the book on. It's a sort of endless process of questioning, of reopening books even when certain thinkers thought they had closed them for good. Do you see yourself as part of an ongoing conversation with thinkers throughout history? Where do you see this conversation heading?

RONELL: Yes, I am involved in conversation, what Blanchot calls an "infinite conversation." I'm devoted to those who are at the edge of philosophical thought, which is to say those who are really thinking and struggling with the limits of what's possible but also at the same time I am very, very respectful of the great thinkers such as Kant, Nietzsche, Heidegger, Derrida, and others—Freud. I'm very open to, and captivated by, psychoanalysis, though that's often a rendezvous that's very troubled, full of static and friction. It's not always an easy coupling.

I don't know what the future of philosophy can be, especially in North America. Here, what we think—well, let me say, if there's a "we" I wouldn't be part of that community, I don't think I would be welcomed or included necessarily. In Europe I'm considered an American philosopher; in America I don't know what I'm considered. I don't want to know! But for the most part, no one gives a shit what we think or say in this country.

I think it might interest people to consider what kind of a wildlife preserve this is—who are these people dedicated to thinking about things, to writing about things, to knowing that they are firing blank shots? Immanuel Kant, the great philosopher, said that it's the theorist's *duty* to try to open a little private war theater against the state precisely because no one cares—you're just firing blanks anyway. So it's your duty to be very loud, to say what you think, to express your sense of scandal and disappointment, and to do it with a lot of integrity even if you are convinced that no one is listening. That would be the kind of responsibility that I try to enact, which is to say, keep on saying it, keep on walking. If no one is watching, no one's listening, so what? Someone has to have done this, even if it stays off the public record. And that would be the nature of responsibility—that you respond to things even if there isn't an audience, even if it's non-profit to the max or inevitably self-marginalizing.

TAYLOR: It reminds me of when you spoke about being called, ethically, to go over things again and again. On the one hand, you're being called to this kind of work, but it's not necessarily the audience that's summoning you. The simple question, I guess, is whom do you feel you're writing for?

RONELL: Well, I'm very surprised that I'm writing for anyone who's more or less alive. I am accustomed to writing for the dead. I used to be called into service by something I read or a book that was neglected or by a discarded problem or cluster, something that was abandoned. I write for the community of those who have no community. I have never declared any identitarian politics that might stabilize me somewhere or give me an acceptable password. I think the Derridians, for inexplicable reasons, don't necessarily love me, yet in some sectors I'm considered a Derridian. I've never made myself welcome or flashed an ID that would permit me to feel comfortable or at-home somewhere. I think I practice a politics of non-belonging, without being isolationist or narcissistically autarkic at all. So the audience isn't there prior to it all. I don't have anyone in mind. I do invite and welcome. I imagine that someone will take my call. Maybe, or maybe not. That's the risk—you should do it even if no one is going to take your call. You can do it, or you *must* do it. Your destiny is to remain ignorant of your destination.

One must wonder why one feels so duty bound. One aspect of the kind of work we do—I don't know if this also assails you in any way—is that it's exhausting and entails a real degree of carceral isolation. Coming out here, trying to bring philosophy to the streets, is a joy even though it's very anxiety provoking. I remember I had an idea that I wanted to spend my holidays in Port Authority standing on a little box and teaching philosophy. When I taught at Berkeley, I thought every holiday I would teach and give a little certificate to the people or something like that. Those were very idealistic and performance-oriented moments.

TAYLOR: What appealed to you about that idea?

RONELL: What appealed to me were several things. One was the dislocation of the space of writing and speaking and teaching. What happens when pedagogy moves out of institutionally sanctioned spaces? Well, you could be a nutcase. The difference between me and someone screaming in a park, or at what was called Sproul Plaza a long time ago at Berkeley, was that I'm on the architecturally defined inside of the mapping of where speech is sheltered. But I could also be ranting.

TAYLOR: So who gets to rant with legitimacy and who doesn't? All of the philosophers in this film have PhDs. As someone who was unschooled for most of my childhood, I tend to be a bit skeptical about formal education. Is there a certificate you can get and suddenly become a philosopher?

RONELL: It's not sudden, but it can be from one day to the next. Obviously I was a baby philosopher. When I was two I was bossing people around and I had ethical intrusions on my poor parents. I already had that Socratic finger in the air.

Look, a PhD, as silly as it sometimes is—I'm all for the impossible discipline that it implies and presumably awards. The scholar sits and sits and studies with tremendous discipline that isn't often going to be socially acknowledged or properly accommodated on the brutal job market, such as it is. The relation to the granting institution (granting a seat, library access, teaching, a PhD) is often ambivalent and dispiriting. Very often, as you know, schools are mausoleums, there to ensure that nothing creative or inventive happens. Very often they're the sanitation department of knowledge, and things get transmitted that are supposed to get transmitted, and there's a real cleanup apparatus responsible for what is taught and learned in schools. So much gets discarded that would lend vitality and brilliance to our lives.

When I was a graduate student it was to a significant degree sheer torture. I was very, very unhappy, miserable, when I was at Princeton. In some respects it couldn't have been more unwelcoming, white, right-wing, self-congratulatory. And yet there's a part of me that's also inscribed by an Asian sense of discipline and love of learning, and there's the masochistic streak that was deepened, even exalted, by the Princeton experience. I'm not saying the masochistic streak is Asian—that's my contribution, my singularity. I forced myself, or superego forced me, to work very, very hard to no ostensible end. There was just the pure work that goes into nothing graspable. You feel you're all alone within your library carrel. You're in the kind of world where nothing responds to you; at most, you hear an internal voice or archival broadcast system or podcast going on in your ever-tightening head, but there's certainly no guarantee of any reliable sort that anything or anyone is listening.

RONELL: I want to go back and pick up on the theme of meaning and ask you about ethics. I feel that some people might be troubled and wonder, how do you function ethically or behave ethically if there is no ultimate meaning?

RONELL: Thank you, because I'm sure that this needs to be clarified and that we need to really open a conversation about this so I don't seem like a complete outcast in a bizarre realm of thought, or I don't give you a mistaken sense of unbounded irresponsibility. Quite to the contrary, I hope. Precisely where there's the pretense or claim for ultimate meaning and transparency—precisely where transcendental guarantors are stamping everything as meaningful, when no one needs to do the anxious guesswork of how to behave or what to do— that's when you are *not* called upon to be strenuously responsible, because the grammar of being, or the axiom of taking care of the Other, is spelled out for you. According to several registers of traditional ethics, things are pre-scripted, they're prescribed. You know everything that you are supposed to do; it's all more or less mapped out for you. What becomes difficult and terrifying, and what requires infinite translation of a situation or of the distress of the world, is when you don't have those sure markers. You don't have the guarantee of ultimate meaning or the final reward or the last judgment and must enter into unsolvable calculations, searing doubts. Anyone who's sure of themselves, of their morals and intentions, is not truly ethical, is not struggling heroically with the mandate of genuine responsibility. It is impossible ever to be fully responsible because you are never done being responsible or never responsible enough— you've never given or offered or done enough for those suffering, for the poor, the hungry. That's a law shared by Dostoyevsky, Levinas, and Derrida: one never meets one's responsible quota, which is set at an infinite bar (hence the invention of the figure of Christ, our infinite creditor).

You know, Plato invented hell (thank you, Plato!) because he thought the citizens weren't up to the level of philosophical rigor. Why don't we invent hell, he offered, and give them a sense of this infantile punishment resort, or last resort, and let's add heaven— although he didn't occupy himself with heaven too much. It was hell that was supposed to strike fear in the citizens of the polis. And we still have that kind of habit of reverting to very simplistic and fantastical models that are supposed to keep people doing the right thing, keep their blinders on and fear factors in gear. But when those are lifted and you remember that it was a myth, a fiction, meant to scare people into behaving themselves and there's no clear prescribed remedial directive that you are supposed to follow, and there's no parental guidance on any level of being, then you are on your own. That's more work than having this kind of prefab superego-transmission system telling you, "That's bad. That's good."

There are things that are very difficult to decipher, that require the really difficult labor associated with hermeneutic anxiety. You have to figure out why this is happening, why didn't that happen, what is my relation to the bottomless neediness of the world and the constant summonses that one must respond to? So precisely where there isn't a guaranteed direction or the yield of palpable meaning, you have to do a lot of work and you have to be megaethical. Clearly, it's much easier to live life as though we knew "this you should do and this you shouldn't do" because someone said so and commands your every move.

TAYLOR: So what's the work of philosophy in all this? Does it play a part in encouraging us to question these rules or maxims that are handed down from on high? Plato's invention of hell suggests otherwise.

RONELL: Philosophy is also guilty of producing rules and regs and specs and all of the above (or below). Philosophy is like a parallel universe or a rival team that also comes up with all of this prescribed bullshit; it's very will to power. I mean, philosophy wants to be powered up, fueled by its immense capacity for positing and performativity. So I wouldn't always trust philosophy, either. But at least, to a certain degree in any case, philosophy does not act on its nonknowledge, does not throw the book at the innocent bystander.

You know, the FBI, by the way, does not have a theory or any knowledge of drugs or addiction. They have "schedules." The difference between hard and soft drugs has not been theorized. You could not ask someone who is in law enforcement to actually reflect on the fundamental structure that permits a social body to condemn an addict. That's where philosophical thinking, I think, should come in and open dossiers, ask impossible questions, live with impossibility. The things that are possible don't interest us. Well, they interest some people and some philosophers. But if it's possible, no one needs us to intervene.

I would say that your question is really crucial. I hope that if there's something else that I did a fast drive-by with, you will ask me to speak a little more clearly than I've been able to do spontaneously.

TAYLOR: So if not meaning, then what are you working toward? Could we say that you're concerned with working toward meaning without believing you'll ever get there?

RONELL: You're right, the work toward meaning is unavoidable and can't be reverted. There's a relation to meaning that probably can't be repudiated or denied. What I have been working with has been the necessity, in my view, of attacking all of these presuppositions and precomprehensions with which we think. I start by interrogating the basics. Like, what is understanding? What is comprehension? What is happening or what is prevented from happening if you think you've understood something? It may be that you are mistaken. It may mean that you haven't heard it at all because you "preunderstood." This is what hermeneutics says. There's something called the hermeneutic circle: you have already understood what you are about to learn. So it's very hard to break that habit or that circle and to ask, what does it mean to understand?

This is why I also wrote a book called *Stupidity*. This is an ethically hard nut to crack, I think. I was trying to consider the debilitated subject, the one who is in a stupor; I was bringing the focus on those who fail to understand. Of course, I try to show how sacred that can be in some cases—the sacred being who knows nothing of this world, who has no apparent interiority or demand, who simply and stupidly is. Nonetheless, ethically what do you do with this sort of figure? We had some characters behind us—I don't know if you are going to retain them in the editing room—who were totally stoned out of their minds and nonpresent. I'm sure they're not stupid, but I'm also sure they're in a stupor or near stupor. Now, what about ethics and people whose consciousness is nearly extinct? That is something I raise that I haven't seen in other works concerned with ethics. I also take the politics of dumbing down quite seriously.

TAYLOR: Since the beginning of philosophy, recognizing what you don't know, being acutely aware of your own ignorance and basing a claim for wisdom on that awareness, is a tradition of sorts. Do you see yourself as part of that?

RONELL: Well, I would say if there's a tradition that I'm purportedly part of, it's the tradition of misfits. Also what Nietzsche calls (very lovingly, I might say) the buffoon, which is to say someone who disrupts, invades, breaks up smooth totalities. Think of the court jester, someone who gets to say things, very recondite things, to the king in Shakespeare, for example, and gets away with that kind of truth telling. Also, politically I always thought it to be my duty to be a pain in the ass, to make trouble, to create skirmishes that those gendered as guys usually can't do without getting into mangling fights. I would go up to ROTC people and really kind of harass them with wit and linguistic daring, because I felt that I could do that as a woman and they wouldn't necessarily beat the crap out of me. In many of my actions I feel the gender of female that I provisionally carry in public allows me to do and get away with certain subversive maneuvers. So there is a lineage and there is a German, and also ironic, kind of trajectory consisting of those who have broken into and raided the main lines and main streets of philosophical thought. I would maybe try to situate myself there along with the great poet (if I may) Heinrich Heine. That lineage, which I honor—I don't know if one can claim membership—is the one that is always troublemaking but also more interested in producing interference and static and parasitical utterances, things that aren't a part of what we think is sanctioned as "thought," things that aren't necessarily viewed as legitimate or worthy of serious contemplation. That's where I've parked and squatted and made noises in my work. I could argue that this is where thought needs to be ever since that gadfly Socrates started rumbling in the streets. There is the matter of locating the verve of the pre-Socratics as well, but I'll leave that for another walk.

TAYLOR: Since you brought up gender and there are so few women philosophers, why don't you say a few words about that?

RONELL: Well, one even continues to hear in this day, in the twenty-first century, people say—and I've heard it many times—that women can't philosophize. And maybe that's true if philosophy, which is part of a stronghold, a phallogocentric fortress—

TAYLOR: Maybe we should have you define "phallogocentric."

RONELL: This word that I'm citing comes from Derrida. He shows to what extent we have inherited, and are marked by, such thinking and habits and cultural institutions that are constituted by the fantasy of the phallus, that are determined by logos, which is to say reason, and their calculated centrism—this is where we're centered. Of course this is the nano–sound bite that I offer, sparing you my forty-hour lecture on this term and its relation to carnologocentrism, which brings meat into the blend.

Returning to the phallus and its mighty heritage, however: Philosophy, metaphysics in particular, is dependent on the exclusion or withdrawal of woman. In Hegel, woman is named the enemy of the community and at another point she is designated as the irony of the community. So one could take it from a kind of Valerie Solanas perspective, if that's what it is: The violence against women in philosophy is so serious and so radical and so unrelenting that it would be foolish to just counter with "No, there are woman philosophers." Yeah, maybe, but unwelcome, disfigured, and without address. Of course there are great agitators such as Lyotard and others who say we need to change addresses. Who or what is being addressed by philosophical thought has to change, it has to be more radical, has to even range toward the posthuman, maybe include plants and animals, other species, other companionable and uncompanionably marked species! All of that has to be interrogated and shaken up, that's for sure.

So I would be on both sides of that question, because it might be deluded of me to think that there are women in philosophy, even though anatomically, according to some construct, we have seen and we do see women philosophers, truly outstanding ones like Sarah Kofman, Judith Butler. But checking off names places me squarely in a trap, so I'll cut my losses here and halt the roll call.

On one level, one can try to answer by conceding the attendance of women in the philosophical colloquy. Are they miming another's enemy discourse? Are they hiding behind defenses? Are they in drag? Are they unconscious? Are they hyperconscious? Are they the unhappy consciousness or the voice of conscience? What are they doing there? What kinds of economies of sacrifice account for their presence or faux presence? To what extent have they struggled with what is essentially psychoticizing, viewed as they have been as the unwelcome intrusion, a parasite, or a joke? Institutionally, you have to deal with the man, the still-musculating victory of patriarchy, with which Freud says we have yet to contend. As a woman you constantly have to back off, back up, ass up—I don't know what to say, but there are days when it's only psychoticizing, and there's no covering this fact over. Yet then one gears up to enter the better neighborhoods of symptomal response, one gets dressed up for the uptown scale of hysteria. There's a whole book of hysterical outbursts provoked by institutional and philosophical pressures. Hysteria sometimes becomes a woman, as far as breakdown dialects are concerned. It works in some extraordinary ways and, as Hélène Cixous has shown, produces a revolutionary stir, seriously stirs up trouble—becoming the feminine mask put to good strategic use.

So yes, one could say, "Yeah, statistically there's a couple more women doing philosophy," but that doesn't mean women are welcome in the house of philosophy and it doesn't mean that men don't sometimes *become women* as they philosophize. Deleuze said that in writing there's an inevitable process of "becoming woman." Of anyone who writes, it can be shown that there's a feminization, there's something that happens that you undergo—a regendering, a new zoning ordinance of what you are, and you go through things that can't be accounted for by rational means. You simply baffle logocentrism's common claims.

TAYLOR: Women are always characterized as unreasonable, as hysterical. This is a timeless trope.

RONELL: Absolutely. There's a whole vocabulary of the type of utterances that women emit, such as moaning and bitching and groaning and complaining. So women are on the sidelines, in the suburbs of great discursive formations. That's something I try to claim rather than saying, "No, I have nothing to do with these depopulated utterances or these minoritized traces." I want to stay with them and listen to them. You know, I try to negotiate with the very thing that's marginalized, which is not that unusual. It's like incorporating, even though it's controversial on all sides of the barrier, the N word into your speech. Or saying, "We're queer, we're here" and accepting and hijacking the very word—here's the trash can again, watch out—that is meant to insult and hurt and devastate. You take it on, you appropriate and use it like a ballistic shield or wield it as a weapon.

TAYLOR: So is that part of your ethical project? Do you have an ethical project? I want to get back to ethics.

RONELL: Well, the thing is that ever since Bataille—he's a great, crazy French writer who wrote on eros and all sorts of desirably disgusting things. He was a great thinker who transgressed so many limits, let's say—let's leave it at that provisionally, because transgression is one of his big words.

[*A cop car with siren blaring cruises through the park.*] Oh, here's the police, better watch out.

I bring up Bataille because he proved highly suspicious of the word "project." He said project is always in a certain way a work of death; in other ways it's also closural, it's self-inclosing, and it's servile to an agenda. That's why I don't know if I have an ethical project or a different relation to ethics, like an ethical requirement of myself or my work.

At the same time, this is something that Derrida has taught: If you feel that you've acquitted yourself honorably, then you're not so ethical. If you walk away with a good conscience, then you're kind of worthless. Like, if you think, "Oh, I gave this homeless person five bucks, I'm great," then you're basically irresponsible. The responsible one—and this I also see in Levinas, who of course quotes Dostoyevsky—responsible beings are those who feel they've never acquitted themselves, they've never been responsible enough, they've never taken care enough of the Other. And they don't even have an ethical project, because that would be too grandiose a statement.

There's something on the side of Levinas, who's a spectacular thinker and an often disrespected thinker—a lot of people still attack him, including a lot of people who you are going to interview for this film—but, anyway, he developed, among other things, a thought of the most passive passivity, bowing before the Other. The Other is so in excess of anything you can understand or grasp or reduce that this in itself creates ethical relatedness, a relation without relation. You can't presume to know or grasp the Other. The minute you think you know the Other you're ready to kill them. You think, "Oh, they're doing this or that, they're the Axis of Evil, let's drop some bombs." But if you confront the possibility that you don't know, you don't understand this alterity—that it's so Other that you can't violate it with your sense of understanding—then you have to let it live in a sense. Of course I simplify and falsify here. I wish we could go into seminar now.

TAYLOR: I like what you're saying, but it strikes me, just in a simple way, that it could be a difficult perspective to maintain, never acquitting yourself, never feeling you understand completely. It could be a bit overwhelming.

RONELL: That's very, very true. It's something that embraces or acknowledges failure without the nihilistic bounce of "Yay, failure, I crashed and burned!" Again, it's something that can't be very proud of itself. It's infinite, it's unending hesitation, trauma, persecution, as Levinas says. In Heidegger's *Being and Time* one of the fundamental categories or qualities of being is *sorge* or concern, care—it's been translated as both—or anxiety. So Heidegger says that anxiety as a mode of being is what makes us want to understand. If we're not anxious, if we're OK with things, then we're not trying to explore or figure anything out. Anxiety is the mood par excellence of ethicity, I think. Now I'm not prescribing anxiety disorder for anyone. However, could you imagine an infusion of anxiety for Mr. Bush, who doesn't give a shit when he sends everyone to war or the electric chair; he expresses no anxiety to speak of. And they're very proud of this, they don't lose a wink of sleep, they express no anxiety as part of a codification of a murderous disposition. That's the nonethical stance. Not that Heidegger was a big ethical example. Nonetheless, he called the crucial shots concerning our age of criminal blunder and he made it very important for us to think alongside him.

But it's a real stress, you are right. We don't want to literalize the modality of anxiety that ontology in Heidegger, for example, marks. At the same time, there is the trace of the literal with which to contend. On the one hand, Heidegger wants to avoid psychologizing. On the other hand, there is an anthropological tendency in the voyage that *Dasein* undertakes. At any rate I, for my existential part, am very anxious. I am distressingly freaked out, I cringe and cry, and I am very upset about what's going on in this world. And it lands in my stomach, I know exactly where it's transiting. When things are shameful and pathetic in our sorry-ass country, I, like others, am carrying it in my body. I have a permanent headache or a stomachache, or I want to throw up.

You know, Nietzsche was the great philosopher of throwing up. For him that was a reversal of dialectics, the opposite of assimilating thought and putting up with philosophical laboriousness. So many metaphors of thinking relate to figures of digestion and assimilation. So the need to throw everything up for Nietzsche was a healthy thing to do, to get rid of historical poisoning. Nietzsche loved cows because they ruminate, they have four stomachs, or folds that count as stomachs. They have a very good digestive tract and take their time. They are unresentful. Nietzsche discovered the trope of *ressentiment* and saw how resentfulness or suppressed rage seriously upset so many collective systems and stomachs.

Anyway, this is a question: What are the symptoms, and where are they located, of any citizen of our day who is halfway conscious? It would be a needed inquiry to find out where you have been affected by the Bush administration. Let us one day look at the body politic according to different scanners. You know, where do you take it? You know we've been taking it up the ass. Where are your symptoms? Where do your hives come out, according to what algorithm of despair? I've had shingles. I don't know if you know what that is—

TAYLOR: Yes, I had them too! Funny, I got them in exactly the circumstances you describe, when I was producing a documentary about Arab and Muslim people who were illegally detained after 9/11 in New York, going into those devastated communities where I felt totally impotent to help and overcome by what was happening. At the height of the project I had a horrible case of shingles. So I definitely agree there's a kind of moral certitude that's very dangerous in this world—the certitude that can lock an innocent person away in solitary confinement for years on end without trial is only one type. Can you speak more about resisting this sort of certainty and the ethical vigilance, the comfort with ambiguity, you have been outlining, and also say more about why this is such a difficult position for us to maintain?

RONELL: Living in a tensional structure, holding the tensions that won't resolve, is difficult. In the beginning you asked about frustration and the audience; perhaps we can link these questions. I'm interested in the hermeneutics of frustration. By all means, frustration is difficult and unpleasant. Yet isn't this what is required if we are to be vigilant: to acknowledge that we haven't understood and that we understand that we haven't understood, that we enter the pressure zone of the frustrating impasse? Freud said that people are very narcissistically comforted by a closing statement or any closural gesture, by thinking we have understood, by wrapping things up. But to leave them open and radically inappropriable, admitting that we haven't really understood, is much less satisfying, more frustrating—and more necessary, I think. A lot of people have been fed and fueled by promises of immediate gratification, in thought and food, and junk thought and junk food. So there's a politics that we probably have to put in practice that consists in refusing that gratification without succumbing to pessimism or asceticism. And I know that's crazy-making, but I think that's where we have to pull the brakes.

[*A little girl, around six or seven, carrying a soccer ball walks up to Ronell. The whole crew pauses when she approaches.*]

GIRL: Are you a boy or a girl?

RONELL: What do you think?

GIRL: A boy. [*Laughs.*] Are you making a movie? I like movies.

PRODUCTION ASSISTANT: What's your favorite movie?

GIRL: There's a girl and her mom and she has a fight with her mom and then the mom went into one room and the girl went into another and they read the thing and there was lightning and when they wake up they were in—

PRODUCTION ASSISTANT: Switched bodies? *Freaky Friday*?

GIRL: Yeah! I forgot what it was called.

RONELL: Do you want to ask me again if I'm a girl or a boy, but this time for the camera?

GIRL: No! [*Feigns fear and runs away to her older sister.*]

RONELL: It's funny. She had a real narrative compulsion and pretended not to.

CAMERAMAN: Why do you think she stopped?

RONELL: It was a very Bataillean moment, the horror and fascination together. So she was fascinated and came into the frame and then was horrified by her desire. And there was a sexual thing to it, too, a libidinized attachment to the possibility of showing up in the film.

TAYLOR: I overheard them saying they were pointing out homosexuals.

RONELL: Is that what it was? So it was part of a homophobic sweep. She has good gaydar, I have to say, for that age especially. Though the homos and the phobes are getting younger by the day!

TAYLOR: Let's change paths for a bit. Could you trace your intellectual trajectory for us?

RONELL: I have two, let's say, internalized histories of myself in regard to this question. I used to be a Kantian and, within limits, I expected intelligibility from the world. Then I converted and switched to Bataille, where things are not easily reducible to sense. At one point Bataille says, "Stop making sense!" Making sense is a production consisting in a willful and will to power kind of takeover of the world. I don't expect things to make sense anymore. That doesn't mean that I don't have my witness consciousness on, as they say in yoga. It doesn't mean that I am inattentive. On the contrary, I am more attentive, since I don't recognize what's happening. It's not prepackaged sense. It's not what we are calling meaning in its totalizing form.

TAYLOR: Would you like to say something about Derrida, on what his thinking bequeathed to you? It's apparent that he had a profound effect on your work.

RONELL: That's very poignant. I was very close to Derrida. Toward the end we taught at NYU every fall. He bequeathed so much to me.

I was thinking also about our conversation prior to this filming. You suggested filming in a library and that I could speak about my favorite books. I noticed you did that with Žižek in your first film. He names his three favorite movies. By the way, I was very jealous because you bought him those DVDs! Do you remember that scene, the gift you bought? So I was thinking if we were in a library and you were to ask me to point at three or four weighty books—well, I thought how impossible that would be for me. I can say that for many of the books that have been very important for me, the influence often has been very negative.

TAYLOR: How do you mean?

RONELL: You know, Kafka says that a book should hit you like an ax in a frozen sea. So maybe if you were to ask me, what works have dented you, thrown you overboard, proven to be very disturbing, or devastated you? Maybe I could have had a sense of that kind of traumatic influence. Because very often the things I return to in my work are the things that have harmed me.

Whereas Derrida, I am sure to the extent that I have incorporated him and felt very, very adherent to him and grateful to this masterful thinker, who is generous and kind and brilliant and modest in many ways—though he also had his narcissist counterpoints—but to the extent that he's given me so much, I wouldn't be able to say what it was. Certainly his thought on the gift, on forgiveness, on sexual difference, destination, and Kantian respect. . . . It's truly endless, I wouldn't know where to begin to express my gratitude. Because, you know, when I was little, you don't know how whitewashed the university was. Derrida also led in all the freaks, people who were not welcome—he forced an opening. No wonder that he wrote on hospitality, on radical, unconditional hospitality, and what that would be and require. He was also politically very involved in bringing dignity to the homeless and the undocumented ("the paperless") in France. So I wouldn't know where to start or to end, but as Slavoj said about me in your film, I am a Derridean. So you know what I could offer is a thought on what it means to do that to a name—"Derridean"—and what's the difference between Derridean and Derrida and in what ambivalent ways Derrida has been honored.

TAYLOR: Derrida has been a huge target from not just the conservative media but also the mainstream media, even the liberal media over the years. For a while it seemed like bashing Derrida, bashing the postmodernists, was a way to prove one's bona fides.

RONELL: That's a strategy that has become quite noticeable, though maybe it's no longer as pertinent as it once was. There was a lot of hostility from various sides. Also the tendency to homosexualize and feminize his work became prominent in some sectors, to some extent because he was a beautiful writer. Ever since Kant, writing philosophically requires a nonbeautiful attitude. In fact, fairly recently Chantal Mouffe said she used to write beautifully before she became a philosopher. And that's not just an accidental utterance. If you write beautifully, you are not counted among the hard-bodied philosophers.

TAYLOR: Yes, many believe a real philosopher must write without passion—very dryly, very analytically—even though there are so many philosophers who are fantastically enjoyable to read: Plato, Montaigne, Schopenhauer, Nietzsche, Deleuze and Guattari. But copying the prose style of these guys may not get you very far today.

RONELL: No, that would not bode well in the more strict and severe philosophical precincts, because if you have claims and make claims to be close to the truth, you shouldn't, according to Kant, be accessorizing and stylizing or having a relation to poetical utterances that overshadow stark language usage. Of course the poets are always served eviction notices. So there's already a strict monitoring of style, which is why Nietzsche took on Kant—Nietzsche, who wrote beautifully and had many styles.

Some think if you are telling the truth, and you have truth on your side, you shouldn't be choosy about which color and which style would look best. You just write with your boots on, you're cloddy, you are awkward, but you have truth. You have to practice a type of stylistic asceticism. Still, if you are negotiating with the limits of metaphysics, something often happens that puts you at the mercy of language in a very serious and poignant way. You feel it, you deal with it, you really maneuver only under its command. And you let language circuit through you and force your hand in certain ways. So you have a very acute relation to language that you might not if you were "making sense" or on a mission from truth, which doesn't tolerate fussiness or delight in language beyond a certain point.

TAYLOR: It's true that historically, continuing through to this day, many philosophers want to distance themselves from art. They rather prefer to think they're doing science.

RONELL: Right, the thing is, the more creative and art-prone the philosophical utterance, the less legitimacy it can supposedly hold. So if those out there in the audience want to seriously be considered philosophers, they should not write beautifully, they should not be inspired or have their sails billowing with inspiration from favorable winds of linguistic invention. No, that would not be a good idea. Not a good career move.

The question concerning the relation of art and poetry to philosophy is important, and it opens a new dossier—your question is by no means just some contingency. In Heidegger, art is capable of fundamental disclosure. It discloses being in a way that philosophy may or may not be able to attain. He speaks of the twin peaks of poetry and philosophy. So there's so much to be said for that relationship and also about the Kantian envy of the good writer. Kant was very shrewd because in the preface to his *Critique* he says, I am a shitty writer, I didn't have time to write, but that's because I am pinched by time, and I have to get down to the truth. So I don't have time for fancy-footing writing. This is my translation from the German original. Ever since Kant made this avowal of his inability to write pretty prose, something happened to philosophical writing; it became almost an imperative that it not be appealing to the senses, that it lose the beauty. However, Kant pulls a fast one on us, because at first he says, Look, I can't help it, I can't write beautifully. But at the time he abruptly switches the whole power game and says that in order to be a serious thinker, you shouldn't endeavor to write beautifully. In the end he makes it a matter of his will and philosophical necessity. Jean-Luc Nancy has developed this logic further and I have run with it in *Stupidity*, where I write about the popularity of the ridiculous philosopher.

And again, as I said, the reproaches tend to be made on the level of sexual difference. Kant trades in his ballet slippers and walks a more manly stride (see, I'm still treading on our topic and path, that of walking): it's really too femme to go out there in ballerina slippers when performing philosophically. The ballet slippers put the emphasis on writing beautifully. Henceforth, that's not philosophy, not hard, not serious (a beloved word of philosophers).

TAYLOR: So what do you think about taking philosophy to the streets?

RONELL: Well, I think that's the call to take. I remember when I started something called Radio Free Theory at Berkeley. In the end it didn't get the support it needed to truly get off the ground and into the airwaves. Nancy, the French philosopher, said to me at the time that he wished that he had tried to take philosophy through other possibilities and channels and medial transmitters. And that has always been a wish of mine: rather than bypass the questions or dispositions relating to technology and the effects of what Heidegger calls the technological revealing, to dwell in it, to work with it, to see how we're rewritten by film, by TV, by the technological incursion and its many facets. So the question is to imagine what this involves, what kind of openings, some of which are also pernicious and undermining, to be sure, while others are welcome or to be welcomed.

That's why I really admire the effort that you are making because you start, I assume, from the premise of the seeming incompatibility of philosophical thought—its elaboration—and your work. Is the co-belonging of film and thought a matter of incompatibility or is it, on the contrary, as Heidegger said when he was on TV, inextricably related? He mysteriously and enigmatically said that television was disclosive of his thought. Television somehow revealed to him the essence of his thinking.

What that might mean is not clear to me, but it does signal that there was a kind of welcoming extended to acts of filming and showing even in the most recalcitrant neighborhoods of philosophy. Also, Lacan was on TV and explained the structures of transference and racism, the relation to the *jouissance* of the other that TV plays out. I myself have worked on television, and wrote for *Artforum* at the time a piece called "Trauma TV" that investigates the secret channels, the often-invisible channels, that television harbors. So what is film doing? What kind of possibilities for thought and as thought are being inscribed in acts of filming? What kind of syntaxes are being created or decreated? All this is something that we still need to be attentive to, especially when political decisions and enactments continue to be dependent on TV's particular types of representation.

Filming and television appear to be radically incompatible with thinking and writing—a statement you would have to be very suspicious of, not the least because it sounds conservative and old-fashioned, foreclosive, and fast on the trigger. I suppose we could locate some sort of cohabitation, and calling from one zone to the other that is very crucial for us to work with today. Work, "work to failure," "work to destruction," "work out," as they say in the gym, "work through," drawing from the psychoanalytic idiom—there's a lot of work to be done here, a conversation among these different modalities of thought and registers of medial articulation. I think we are doing similar things, the same thing. Writing is not nontechnological, obviously. You know it's already on the side of death and technology. So we are on the same side in so many ways.

At the same time, even though we share quite a bit in terms of aim, intention, structure, planning, you're on a faster track in some regards than I could ever allow myself to be. I have a Germanic habit of having abundant footnotes wherever I go or write, of being concerned about each turn of phrase and its calamitous itineraries. Still, this is not supported widely for the writing disposition. Even publishing houses don't want to hear about these footnotes and anxious gasps of writing anymore. One is reduced to minimal sound bites everywhere, without backup or archive. This is something that Heidegger predicted. He said the way we abbreviate things is already an effect of technology. When we say "NYU" or any abbreviation such as FBI, POV, LAX, etc., the reduction of language to little signals or text messages is something that is an effect of technology and changes our rapport to Being. He bemoaned this eventuality, he lamented the linguistic abduction. Let's say that the diminishment of language squeezes and harms us in ways we haven't begun to understand.

TAYLOR: As I said, that's my concern. This is the fundamental source of my anxiety—wanting to honor my subjects, to not be too reductive, to resist the temptation of sound bites. And I do ultimately agree with you and am working under the assumption that filmic language has other levels of significance—the visual, the aural, the gestural— and that people will also read the environment, the park, and the life here and our response to it in ways that give them different levels of insight.

RONELL: I think that's a struggle for everyone who's involved in something like representing the unrepresentable or in diffusing something that is trying to negotiate with the limits of possibility. Yes, there will necessarily be those struggles, and I guess that anyone who entered into a contract with you also has to submit masochistically and happily, without the shadow of dissent, to the director's cut.

PETER SINGER

Ethics

I met Peter Singer near Central Park, at the giant cube that marks the location of the Apple Store. It struck us as a fitting monument given that we arranged to discuss ethics and consumerism while walking down Fifth Avenue, one of New York City's glitzy shopping districts, to Times Square, now a site of corporate seduction ablaze with giant television advertisements and three-dimensional billboards. It was a perfect summer day, and the streets were crowded with shoppers and tourists as we made our way downtown.

ASTRA TAYLOR: I want the ideas to bounce off the environment, so feel free to reference things you pass by or to pause and talk about things that have caught your eye.

PETER SINGER: So we are here on Fifth Avenue in New York, which is obviously the shopping strip par excellence for all the top brands, for all the top designers—Gucci, Hugo Boss, Escada, whoever that is.

They're here, they are selling stuff at incredible prices, thousands of dollars for a dress or a handbag or whatever it might be. And at the same time, of course, we are living in a world in which there are about a billion people who are struggling to survive on less than one U.S. dollar per day.* With some more aid from the developed world, untold deaths could be prevented.

So obviously that raises an ethical issue. I mean, there are people who have the money to buy from these stores and who don't seem to see any moral problem about doing that. But what I want to ask is: Shouldn't they see some sort of moral problem about that? Isn't there a question about what we should be spending our money on?

And that's why the existence of stores like these raises a lot of serious ethical issues that I hope people will think about a little bit. All of us, even if we are not the type to shop at Gucci or Louis Vuitton, have some spare cash. All of us in the developed countries, in the affluent world, spend money on luxuries and frivolities that are really not things that we need. So the question is one that affects you as much as it affects someone who shops in these types of stores. What should I be spending my money on and what does that say about me, about my priorities, and about what I might take to be important?

[*Singer notices some exorbitantly pricey shoes in a nearby window. It seems like a good place to pause for a moment.*]

So we are outside Bergdorf Goodman, where they have got a display of Dolce & Gabbana shoes. It's kind of amusing to me because about thirty years ago I wrote an article called "Famine, Affluence and Morality" in which I ask you to imagine you are walking by a shallow pond, and as you walk past it, you notice there is a small child who has fallen into the pond and is in danger of drowning. You look

* This figure held until 2008, when the World Bank set the poverty line at $1.25 per day. There are currently 1.4 billion people living under this line. It should be noted that the figure has been adjusted by the World Bank to reflect an amount of goods and services—whether earned or homegrown—comparable to what can be purchased in the United States for $1.25.

around to see where the parents are, and there is no one in sight. And you realize, unless you wade into this pond and you pull the child out, the child is likely to drown. There is no danger to you because you know the pond is just a shallow one, but you are wearing a nice pair of shoes and they are probably going to get ruined if you wade into that shallow pond.

So of course when I ask people this, they say, well, of course forget about the shoes, you just have to save the child, that's clear. And then I stop and I say, OK, well, I agree with you about that, but for the price of a pair of shoes, if you were to give that money to Oxfam or UNICEF or one of those organizations, they could probably save the life of a child, maybe more than one child in a poor country where they can't get basic medical care to treat very basic diseases like diarrhea or whatever it might be.

So just looking at the shoes here at Dolce & Gabbana, they are probably going to be worth quite a bit more than just your basic kind of shoes, and it made me think, if you are wearing these kinds of shoes and you still want to wade into the pond, that's probably a large number of children's lives they could save.

And that's one of the reasons it's interesting to be here on Fifth Avenue talking about ethics, because ethics is about the basic choices that we all make in our lives. And one of those choices is how we spend our money, and as you walk past stores like Bergdorf Goodman and Gucci and Louis Vuitton, they are all around, they are calling to you—spend your money here, buy these pricey designer items.

It is obscene that people are spending thousands of dollars on a handbag or a pair of shoes when there are a billion people in the world who are living on less than a dollar a day. As UNICEF tell us, there are 27,000 children who die every day from avoidable, poverty-related diseases and malnutrition. And clearly there is something we could be doing about that, there is something we could be doing to help them.

TAYLOR: Good start. You've given us a concrete example, so maybe our discussion can get more abstract. What does it mean to think ethically? How can we have ethical standards without some ultimate authority in the universe?

SINGER: I look at all the people around who are strolling here—of course, most of them are tourists who are not going to buy a lot. But nevertheless, this is the center of one of the world's richest countries and one of the most expensive places in it, and it does raise that ethical question: What should we be doing with our lives, what should we be spending our money on, have we got the right set of priorities? And that of course is what ethics is all about. Ethics is asking us to reflect on what is important to us, on what the ultimate questions are and trying to get standards that help us make decisions. That's what I have been thinking about for most of my life.

A lot of people think that you can only have ethical standards if you are religious, or you thought there was a god who handed down some commandments or inspired some scriptures that tell you what to do. I don't believe in any of that. I think ethics has to come from ourselves. But that doesn't mean that it's totally subjective, that doesn't mean you can think whatever you like about what's right and wrong, because we are reasoning beings, we are thinking beings. And because of that, we can reflect on our situation.

For me, ethics begins with the idea that we have certain needs, certain basic wants and desires. And when we think about our place in the world, we realize that there are lots of other people—or, more precisely, lots of other sentient beings—who have interests, and they care about their interests in similar ways to the way we care about our interests. And the point about ethics is that, rather than just thinking about our own interests, we have got to put ourselves in the position of others. We have got to think, what would it be like for them? That is something that is in scriptures, though not only in scriptures—the idea of asking myself how would I like it, if I'm going to do something to someone else, how would I like it if they were going to do that to me? That seems to be an almost universal moral principle that you find in all of the major ethical traditions. Not only in Christianity, not only in Judaism or Islam, but also in the Hindu traditions and the Confucian traditions. It's a thought that occurs to people independently at some stage when they want to justify their conduct, when they want to justify how they are going to act in terms that other people can accept. And that's where ethics gets going.

TAYLOR: Can you talk more about taking others' interests into account? How do we do it? I wonder if you could speak about the relationship between reason and empathy.

SINGER: These are ethical issues because if you go right back to the start of the Western philosophical tradition, you find Socrates saying, Well, we are talking about how we ought to live. That's the most serious thing we can talk about. And for Socrates, of course, this was a matter of reasoning, of trying to understand. So ethical choices are not just something where you say, "This is what I feel" and "This is how you feel," as if it were all entirely subjective.

Of course emotion plays a role in ethics, in particular our sympathy to others, our capacity to empathize with those children who are dying or the families that are watching their children die in developing countries. We have to be able to empathize with them or we don't get to first base in terms of what we are doing. But then we actually want to involve our reason, we want to think about what is the best thing to do in these circumstances. What is right? What is wrong? And that means putting yourself in the position of others, taking on their interests and asking yourself, What would I choose if I were to be in their position, rather than my position?

Suppose that I was living both the life of a family with a child who was dying of diarrhea because they couldn't get even the most basic health care and my own life. Would I rather have a situation where I have the handbag and my child dies? Or would I rather have a situation where the child lives, but I don't get the handbag? Well, of course that choice is very easy.

And that's the basic idea in ethics: to put yourself in the position of others. And that means that you are taking into account their interests, that you are including everyone—and in fact, I would say, every sentient being, because animals have to count too. As long as they are capable of feeling, of experiencing something, we shouldn't exclude them. So we take the interests of everyone into account, and then we try to decide what would be the best thing to do from that more universal perspective.

TAYLOR: I think an essential point for us here is that you're not just making the case for not shopping or refraining from spending money. You want people to use their money to do good. Not only that, you believe they have an ethical responsibility to do so.

SINGER: Right. I should make that clear. One of the most obvious things that emerges when you put yourself in the position of others is the priority of reducing or preventing suffering. Because ethics is not only about what I actually do and the impact of that; it's also about what I omit to do, what I decide not to do. And that's why, given that we all have a limited amount of money, questions about what you spend your money on are also questions about what you *don't* spend your money on and what you don't use your money to achieve. And a lot of people forget that. They just say, "Oh well, I'm not harming anyone if I go and spend a thousand dollars on a new suit," but, in fact, given the opportunities that they have to help and given the way the world is, quite often you actually are failing to benefit someone. And we have moral obligations to help, just as we have moral obligations not to harm.

TAYLOR: Could you expound on what you mean when you say "the way the world is"? How can your seemingly straightforward observation about shoes have such extreme consequences for how people should live their lives and spend their money? How is it that our ethical obligations extend around the globe?

SINGER: It's to do with the way the world is today. Some simple ideas can have very radical impacts. If you didn't have much that was spare, much that was surplus, and if you lived in a community, let's say in the Middle Ages, where you couldn't travel to other places, it was hard to think about what you could do beyond the community that you live in. But now we live in a global world where we have these enormous contrasts between affluence and poverty. And that means we have different opportunities and obligations.

Consider quite simple ideas, like the idea that if you can prevent something really bad from happening at very small cost to yourself, then you ought to do it. That sounds pretty commonsensical. Most people would agree with that—until they stop and think that in the world in which we live, at a very small cost to myself, I can actually save the lives of children who are starving in different parts of the world. So that makes the obligation much more demanding. And people get a bit surprised and they ask, "How can that be?"

I think the reason it can be is that we live in a strange world, in a world in which, in one sense, there is an ongoing emergency, an ongoing crisis: those 27,000 children dying every day from preventable diseases. And yet, we are insulated from that, we don't necessarily see it. We live in a world where there's affluence surrounding us, and so we don't always understand that our obligations extend far beyond what is in front of us.

TAYLOR: Some philosophers, including your colleague Anthony Appiah, whom I have also interviewed, argue we should each do our "fair share," whatever that may be, to address global poverty—no more, no less. What do you have to say to critics who say you place an unreasonable demand on people by making the case, as you have, that we should donate money to the point where, if we were to donate any more, we would be sacrificing something nearly as important as the lives we could save?

SINGER: In brief, if others are not doing their fair share, and we can easily save lives by doing more than our fair share, we should do it. To refuse to do more than your fair share in these circumstances is to get your priorities wrong. Imagine, for instance, that there is not just one child drowning in that shallow pond, but ten. And coincidentally, there are ten adults near the pond, each able to rescue a child. You are one of them. So you wade into the pond, rescue a child, and assume everyone else will do the same. But once you have safely deposited your child on the grass, you are shocked to see that five of the other adults have not rescued a child at all. So there are still five children in danger of drowning in the pond. Should you and the other four adults who rescued a child say, "Well, we've done our fair share of rescuing," and just walk away? No. Even though it may be unfair that you have to go twice into the cold water when others haven't done anything, it would still be wrong to leave a child to drown when you could easily rescue her.*

TAYLOR: You're well known as a utilitarian thinker, a philosophy developed by Jeremy Bentham, John Stuart Mill, and others in which the morality of an action is determined by its outcome, the good should be maximized and the bad minimized. Thus you seek solutions for problems that have the best consequences for all affected and that minimize suffering. And best consequences, for you, means the ones that satisfy the most preferences. Does a person have to be a utilitarian to adopt your ethical views? That seems like something we should address.

*For a fuller discussion of this dilemma, please see Singer's book, *The Life You Can Save: Acting Now to End World Poverty* (New York: Random House, 2009).

SINGER: Now, a lot of people ask, does this position I'm putting forward depend upon any particular ethical view or on some form of consequentialism or utilitarianism? Certainly the consequences are really important. We should constantly be considering the consequences of what we do. But I don't think that you have to be a utilitarian to take this view that there is something wrong with spending money on luxuries when other people are starving. You could, for example, defend a view of natural rights. The Catholic philosopher and theologian Thomas Aquinas in the Middle Ages said that we have a natural right to property to meet our needs, but if we have met all our needs, if we have what he called superabundance above and beyond our needs, and there is someone else who can't meet their needs, then we don't have a right to our property that trumps that person's right. So we have an obligation to use our wealth to help those who are in real need. And in fact, Aquinas said if they were to take our property, if they were to take our bread to feed their family, that's not theft because if we have more bread than we need and they can't feed their family, our natural right to property has disappeared. So you can get these radical conclusions from quite different sorts of perspectives, quite different kinds of ethical perspectives, and they become radical because of that state that we're in.

TAYLOR: Since you brought up natural rights, let me ask how or if utilitarianism is compatible with a theory of rights more generally. Specifically, in regard to animal rights, the topic that made your reputation with the publication of *Animal Liberation* in 1975, what fundamental rights would you have granted to animals and on what basis? Perhaps you could talk about the Great Ape Project and the recent progress that has been made on that front. I am also wondering about the idea, discussed by some theorists, that animals have a fundamental right not to be property.

SINGER: I'm a utilitarian. I do not ground my ethical theories on the basis of rights. I find the concept of rights useful in political and legal contexts. So to say that great apes have rights to life, liberty, and protection from torture—as the Great Ape Project does—is a political demand and a useful shorthand for saying that they are the kinds of beings who would benefit from being treated in certain ways, and the law should recognize that. In a historic vote earlier this year, a commission of the Spanish parliament agreed that the government should support these rights for great apes.

For the same reason, I agree that animals should not be property. They are sentient beings, and to give them the status of property ignores that crucial distinction between them and, say, cars.

TAYLOR: Let's go back for a moment to your comment about utilitarianism and natural rights. If we can come up with different arguments defending the same ethical position, what's the basis for this whole discussion? Where do ethics begin?

SINGER: People often ask where ethics comes from, and if you are asking how does it originate, we have to look to an evolutionary understanding of human beings. Ethics is not a human invention. It builds on things that our primate ancestors, perhaps other social mammals, already had. That is, they were able to interact with each other and they developed feelings like concern for their children, obviously, concern for their kin, which becomes our obligation as parents to look after our children. Also the idea of reciprocity, which is central to ethics and you can find it in lots of nonhuman social animals—that if someone does a good turn to you, you do something back for them, and if they do something nasty to you, you are going to do something nasty to them. I think those basic ideas of justice actually come out of our evolutionary heritage.

But as we develop language, as we develop the capacity of reason, we take this to a new level. It becomes much more sophisticated, and we have the need to justify what we are doing to others, in linguistic terms. And we extend our capacities to think about the consequences of what we are doing, to imagine what it does to others. And also, of course, to develop certain rules for general conduct so that society can guide its members in how they should behave. In every society there are some basic rules about not killing other members of your society, about not cheating, and so on. But as we develop and as we think about our situation, we can become critical of these rules, so that the rules are not the last word. The rules are there; they are socially useful for functioning in society. But we can be critical of them, we can evaluate if they are really working. Are they doing the job that we want them to be doing? And then we can make choices about whether to obey those rules in all circumstances. So sometimes when it's clear that a rule gets in the way of something that is good or important, we should change it.

TAYLOR: Can you give us an example?

SINGER: The rule against killing innocent people is generally obviously a good rule, but if someone is terminally ill, suffering from cancer, they know that they only have weeks or months to live and they don't want to go through those last weeks or months with a quality of life that they think is not worth having, then we ought to be able to change that rule and say that if they ask for assistance in dying, somebody ought to be able to help them to die.

TAYLOR: Thinking about the fact that social rules sometimes need to change, you mention briefly in one of your essays that we're quite fortunate to be able to protest and challenge commonsense morality in our society, though sadly few seem to bother to take advantage of this freedom. I think it's a point worth repeating.

SINGER: Ethics is an ongoing process of thought about how we ought to act, about the choices that we make. And we are very fortunate now, in this era, because we are not bound by traditional custom. In many societies, if you challenge a custom you become a heretic, you're cast out, you are burned at the stake. Things like that can still happen in some parts of the world. But at least in developed, democratic, open societies we can challenge the rules, we can think about them, and if we don't like what's happening, we can protest, and we're not going to get stood up against the wall and shot for doing that. So we have a lot of opportunities to not only act ethically but to look at our own ethical judgments on the basis of discussion, on the basis of thinking about ultimate principles and deciding what we ought to do.

TAYLOR: Speaking about our comparatively open society, you have written about Marx and Hegel. And you are obviously well aware that the drive for profit is a huge part of what fuels the factory-farming industry, as you make clear in *The Ethics of What We Eat*, for example. Yet you generally emphasize individual choice and the power we all wield either as consumers or as people who can donate money to charitable organizations. Why isn't a more traditionally Marxist perspective compelling to you?

SINGER: I haven't written a lot about Marx and Hegel. I've written two very short introductory books, one on each of them. Although both of them have had ideas that have contributed to our self-understanding, I've never been a Marxist. Marx was wrong when he predicted that capitalism would produce an ever-larger army of impoverished workers, and he was wrong when he said revolution was inevitable, and he was wrong when he said that under communism, the state would "wither away." Capitalism is a highly productive system, and although there are some aspects of it that I don't like, we don't have a workable economic system that produces better results. Capitalism isn't any more responsible for animal suffering and environmental degradation than communism—check out what happened to animals and the environment in the Soviet Union. Whatever system we have, much will depend on the extent to which people want to prevent animal suffering and environmental degradation. If consumers and voters want to prevent it, they can do so under capitalism as well as, or better than, under alternative systems.

TAYLOR: Let's step back for a bit. What drew you to the subject of practical ethics? Can you give us some personal background?

SINGER: I started thinking about these issues back in the 1970s, when, for one thing, there was the crisis in Bangladesh, where there were millions of people who were in danger of starving because of the repression of the Bangladeshis by the Pakistani army. And that made me think about our obligations to help people who were in danger of starvation.

Also around the same time I happened to meet an ethical vegetarian who got me asking myself, am I justified in continuing to eat meat? What is it that gives us the right or that justifies us in treating animals the way they get treated before they end up in our lunch or dinner? And I read about factory farming and intensive farms and the way they confine animals, which was something that was getting going at that time. And I thought that you can't justify this. We humans have simply taken it for granted that we have the right to use animals whichever way we want to. And that isn't defensible. The boundary between species is not something that is so morally significant that it entitles us to take another sentient being who can suffer or feel pain and do as we wish with that sentient being just because we happen to like the taste of its flesh.

So these two issues got me thinking about applied ethics, which at this time, the beginning of the 1970s, wasn't really a field. It wasn't something philosophers thought was proper philosophy. But it was a good time to start thinking about these issues because of the student movement, the radical movement of the '60s and early '70s, which had increased interest in these issues and raised the question, can we make our academic studies more relevant to the important questions of the day? Questions like the Vietnam War, for example, civil disobedience, the protest against that war. So I was interested in trying to bring these issues into philosophy, and there were a few other people at the time too who were developing the idea of applied ethics, which is really not new, it had been done by great philosophers of the past. But from the 1920s to the 1970s it was not something that was thought to be part of philosophy.

I think that it's important to engage philosophy in the world, and of course to do that, you have to bring in a certain amount of factual background to understand how things actually are. So, in order to raise questions on what we should be spending our money on, you need to know something about what aid can do in the world, about the prices of those items over there, what could be done if the money was given to organizations like Oxfam; you need to know about whether such organizations work, how they can be made effective. That becomes part of applied ethics. In the case of the treatment of animals—[*We're stopped by an inquisitive man working as a security guard for a Bank of America branch.*]

MAN: My question for you is how are you going to get your idea close to that 5 percent or 1 percent of Americans who holds the greatest wealth to distribute it?

SINGER: Well, firstly, it's more than that, because most of us have got a little bit, so maybe we can't give away like [Bill] Gates or [Warren] Buffett, but we can still do something. Secondly, you know, some of those people are receptive. Obviously Gates and Buffett are the best examples, but since I had that article in the *New York Times*, "The Singer Solution to World Poverty," which essentially argued that money spent on luxuries, not necessities, should be donated to overseas aid agencies, I've had a lot of people write to me who are giving away quite significant amounts of their wealth. So I am hopeful that it's spreading. How did you recognize me?

MAN: I just like to know things. It's been a pleasure. Thank you for your response. I'll do my share also.

SINGER: Nice to meet you. Great. Cheers.

TAYLOR: Wow, that was a very strange encounter. But he kind of seemed convinced. Now, if you can, please go back to the issue of animal rights. In fact, why don't you make the case to my camera assistant here, who likes to make fun of me for being vegetarian? Convince him, too! [*Laughs.*]

SINGER: When I was a graduate student at Oxford, I just happened to have lunch with another graduate student, a Canadian called Richard Keshen, who didn't eat the meal that was on offer because it had meat in it. So I started talking to him about why he wasn't eating meat, and that conversation challenged me to say, how is it that we can justify the way we treat animals in order to turn them into food? Of course this is against the background of knowing that we don't really need to eat meat; there are plenty of people who are vegetarian or vegans who live long and healthy lives, perhaps on average healthier than people who do eat a lot of meat. So eating meat is not a necessity; it's a luxury of some sort. Some people say they enjoy the taste of it. So how much weight should we give our enjoyment of that taste, our desire for a particular kind of dish, for chicken or ham or pork or whatever it might be, as compared to a vegetarian dish? How much suffering does that justify us inflicting on animals? And, of course, killing them in the end in order to have that particular kind of taste. And when you think about it, we do inflict a lot of suffering on animals, particularly as we have developed intensive farms where we crowd animals indoors, take them off the land. They never get to go

outside. In some cases they are so crowded that they can't even move
or turn around in their stalls, or, if they're the hens that lay our eggs,
they can't even stretch their wings. They live there for pretty much
their entire lives, for a year or more. So can we defend this treatment
just to get our eggs or meat a little more cheaply than we would if the
animals were allowed to go outside? It doesn't seem to me we can. Of
course, that question leads you to go back and to say, Well, what is it
about animals that justifies us, or makes us think that we're justified,
in treating them in this way? Not just in using them for food but also
for research, in circuses for entertainment, or trapping them and
killing them for their fur, or whatever else it might be. And when I
started thinking about that, I began to realize that this is just another
prejudice, this is just another example of that kind of prejudice that
we are so familiar with, from looking at racial discrimination or discrimination on the basis of sex.

So when you think about the position of animals, it's really another prejudice like those that we're familiar with, like the prejudice
that people had against people of another race that enabled them, in
the eighteenth century, to go and capture them and enslave them and
use them as tools for whatever they wanted to do with them. That's the
same kind of relationship, really, that we have with animals: we just see
them as a different group, an inferior group, and we develop an ideology that enables us to use them. Think about it: the boundary line of
species is not something that in itself is of great moral significance. It's
a biological difference, but it's not morally significant for that reason.
If we say, well, just because they are not a member of the species *Homo
sapiens*, that gives us a right to use them in whatever way we want to,
are we going to defend the racist that says, well, because they are not
Europeans and don't have white skin or because they come from
Africa, we can use them in whatever way we want to? I think the two
are similar phenomena. They're not identical, but there is a certain
parallel between them. Some people will say it's because we are more
rational than animals are, or we can use language, or we have a higher

level of self-awareness, and of course those things are typically true; there are differences between humans and nonhuman animals, but there are circumstances in which these differences do not hold. Not all humans are rational: human infants are not rational, humans with severe intellectual disabilities may be less rational, less self-aware, even less able to communicate than a chimpanzee or an orangutan. But we don't therefore think that these less rational humans have no rights. We don't think that we can use them as we wish, that we can experiment on them in ways that are painful or lethal because we want to find something out. Yet these are things that we do to animals, including chimpanzees. So it seems that it is the boundary of species that's making the moral difference—it's not really these other characteristics like rationality or self-awareness that are determining how we treat a being.

TAYLOR: Can we go back to your student days, since we were interrupted? You brought up the fact that Socrates, through Plato, was concerned with the question of how ought we to live. So why did that sort of interrogation go out of style for a while there?

SINGER: When I started studying philosophy, when I was an undergraduate in the mid-1960s, philosophy was mostly about analyzing the meaning of words. It was the period of linguistic analysis, so ethics was just about saying: What do the words "good" or "bad" mean? There was no substantive content about what we should be doing, and in fact some philosophers, leading philosophers, like A.J. Ayer and C.D. Broad, actually said philosophy doesn't tell you what you ought to do. It has nothing to do with that.

But, as I was saying, the '60s saw the movement against the Vietnam War, the black liberation movement, the student movement—and as those things started happening, people started demanding more relevance in their studies. Some people started to think, well, the big issues of the day are at least in part ethical issues, and philosophy should have something to say about those. So I got interested in that area of philosophy, which developed into applied ethics. I wrote my thesis at Oxford on the question of whether there is an obligation to obey the law in a democracy, which, of course, was an issue that was very relevant during the Vietnam War when there were a lot of protests, acts of civil disobedience, and even violence as a protest against the war. So that was one issue of applied ethics that was clearly a philosophical issue—the question of the obligation to obey the law is a traditional question in political philosophy. But I then got interested in some other questions that hadn't been discussed so much. One was the question of our obligation to help the poor. Again, that became very relevant in the early 1970s because of the crisis in what's now Bangladesh. When Pakistani troops were engaged in the repression of the population of East Pakistan, millions of refugees fled across the border into India, and they were in danger of starving. India at that time did not have resources to feed them. So that was an occasion for one of my first articles in applied ethics, about the obligations of the rich to help. And finally, as I already mentioned, the other issue that I started working on was the question about the treatment of animals, which is also very much a practical question that shows how philosophy connects with everyday life because we are involved in the issue of how to treat animals every day; most people eat meat twice or three times a day. So this question is just there. It keeps coming up.

Questions about the ethical status of animals, the ethical standing of animals, are questions we should be thinking about because if we've got this wrong then we are doing something wrong every day when we buy the products of industrialized farming and thereby are giving our resources, our money, to people who are doing this to animals, effectively encouraging them to keep going, to keep putting more chickens in sheds with twenty thousand other chickens, to keep cramming more hens into cages to produce the cheapest possible eggs, or to put pigs in stalls where they can't even turn around. These are examples of ways in which ethics can be applied. It's important that philosophy should think about these issues, that it shouldn't just be a matter of analyzing the meaning of words or writing articles for academic journals that only other philosophers will read. These are important issues that we should all be thinking about, and philosophy has a role to play in helping us to think about those issues, raising the level of discussion, clarifying our ideas and concepts and putting the arguments out there for everyone to think about.

TAYLOR: Can you give another example of a contemporary ethical issue, perhaps something from bioethics since that's an area you are deeply involved in?

SINGER: Bioethics studies the ethical issues that arise from medicine and the biological sciences. Obviously there are a lot of people who practice in this area—doctors, scientists, and so on—and they're intelligent and thoughtful people, but there is a noticeable difference between somebody who was just trained in medicine or science and somebody who brings an understanding of philosophical arguments to those issues. Doctors, for example, when discussing euthanasia, will often quote this verse: "Thou shalt not kill; but need'st not strive, Officiously to keep alive." And they use that to justify the idea that it's OK for them to allow patients to die, but they should never actively hasten a death. Now, in fact, if you look at that verse, it is not some piece of ancient wisdom. It was written as part of a satirical poem. When you analyze it, it is dubious to claim that there is a big moral distinction between, on the one hand, allowing someone to die by turning off a respirator or pulling out a feeding tube, and, on the other hand, actively killing a patient by giving a lethal injection. It's something that's difficult to justify since the patients are both equally dead, their deaths are the result of your decision, and their deaths were equally certain once the respirator was turned off or the injection given. That's something that be-comes clearer when you start to bring a different perspective, a more critical, reflective, philosophical perspective, to the way in which doctors have been dealing with these issues in hospitals for several decades.

TAYLOR: This seems like a good moment to segue into the topic of disability, an area in which you have caused some controversy and a theme in some of the other interviews I'm conducting for this project. In *Practical Ethics*, you write that disabled people's "lives are less worth living than the lives of people who are not disabled" and have made the case for selective infanticide. But what makes a life worth living? Community, companionship, planning for the future, problem solving, creativity, purpose, romance—all of these are as open to disabled people as able-bodied people.

As a utilitarian you want to reduce suffering. But disabled activists and disability theorists argue that it is not being born into an impaired body that causes severe suffering (even if a physical condition includes living with pain), but instead it is the cultural aversion to disability that causes the most suffering—that is, living in a world that discriminates against and stereotypes disabled people while offering limited access to public life, housing, education, meaningful work, and so on. Disabled people are the largest minority in the world and all of us begin and (if we live long enough) end our lives in a state of dependency, so it seems to me that by changing cultural perceptions of what being disabled means and opening up social opportunity, we would eliminate far more suffering than we can by supporting assisted suicide, certain infanticides, and disability-related abortions for those relatively rare cases.

SINGER: First, I do recognize that there are prejudices against people with disabilities, and that is just as bad as prejudices against people because of their skin color or ethnic origin. We should do what we can to fight that, and we have made some progress in recent years. I strongly support legislation making it illegal to discriminate against people with disabilities in employment, for example, where the disability does not affect a person's ability to do the job.

Second, I agree that we should make it as easy as possible for people with disabilities to live the richest, most fulfilling life they can. That includes making buildings and public transport wheelchair accessible and ensuring that schools can meet the needs of children with disabilities. Again, we've done a lot of that. There is some extra expense involved in that, obviously, and there have to be limits somewhere, but in general it is something we should do.

But when all that is said, it just isn't credible that the only problem with having a disability is the cultural prejudice against people with disabilities and the consequent failure of society to adequately accommodate the needs of people with disabilities. You say that we will all end our lives in a state of dependency. Yes, and how many of us are indifferent whether that state comes earlier or later? Look around you: millions of people in middle age go to the gym to keep fit, they eat food high in antioxidants because they believe—without much evidence—that this will keep them healthy and independent longer, and the first drug company that really does find something to prevent Alzheimer's disease will make billions of dollars. While I am sure I could still find life worth living if I were in a wheelchair, I enjoy physical activities like hiking and surfing, and I think my life will be diminished when I can no longer do such things.

On this issue—that it is, other things being equal, better not to have a disability than to have one—it is your view, not mine, that is contradicted by almost everything we do. Why do we discourage pregnant women from smoking, drinking alcohol, and taking drugs? Do you think we were wrong to ban thalidomide? Pregnant women found it quite a useful aid to sleeping. If the disabilities that their children had as a result did not make the lives of those children worse, why shouldn't we continue to use it?

Next, everything you say in your question is based on physical disability. I've never really understood why people like Harriet

Johnson* think that just because they are in a wheelchair, they have a better sense of what it is like to be severely intellectually disabled than people who are not in wheelchairs. The one has nothing to do with the other. Not all disabled people are capable of all the things you mention above that make life worth living—planning for the future, problem solving, creativity, purpose.

Finally, you ignore the interests of parents. If they want to raise a child with serious disabilities, of course they should be able to do so, and society should assist them, as I've said, in giving that child the best possible life. But conversely, if they don't want to do that, I don't think they should be coerced into doing it. Nearly nine out of ten pregnant women who are told that they are carrying a child with Down syndrome opt to terminate the pregnancy. Is that just cultural prejudice? Is it unreasonable to prefer to have a child who will develop into someone with whom you will, eventually, be on equal terms intellectually, and who may even have children of his or her own?

TAYLOR: I still think judging people's quality of life is risky business. Also, given the goals of challenging speciesism and granting equal consideration to all beings, I wonder if it would be more effective to accept people's concern for extremely physically and mentally impaired individuals and try to convince them to extend that concern to nonhuman animals.

In any case, the positions we're discussing challenge very fundamental assumptions, like the belief in the sanctity of human life, for example, which is a view many hold dear. Can you talk more about philosophy's role in challenging things we take for granted, even if that causes us some initial discomfort?

* The late Harriet McBryde Johnson was a physically disabled lawyer who wrote about her debate with Singer for the *New York Times*: "Unspeakable Conversations," *New York Times Magazine*, February 16, 2003. See also Singer's obituary for Johnson: "Happy Nevertheless," *New York Times*, December 28, 2008.

SINGER: When you do applied ethics, you often find that thinking things through leads you to challenge commonsense morality, the ideas that most people have. This is consistent with a very ancient philosophical tradition. It's exactly what happened with Socrates when he started asking people, "What is justice?" They thought they knew what justice was and they started thinking about it and they realized that they didn't understand it. And Socrates ended up being forced to drink the hemlock because he was accused of corrupting the morals of the youth. Now, fortunately, that doesn't happen to philosophers today, but it could well be said that, from a conservative point of view, applied ethics does corrupt morals—"corrupt" is the wrong word, but it certainly challenges morals and might lead us to think differently about some things that we have held very dear for a long time, like that idea that it's always wrong to kill an innocent human being. Think about some cases of people dying from painful diseases who request assistance in dying. Or take the idea that we can use animals as we wish, which again is another commonsense moral idea that we might want to challenge.

Commonsense morality has developed in various ways. In part, it is the outcome of our evolved ways of thinking, partly it is made up of local customs, sometimes it's a heritage of religious teaching. Here in the West we've had two thousand years of Christian teaching and that has had an enduring effect on our morals. Even if many people now reject the specific ideas of Christianity—they don't accept the idea of the scriptures as a sacred text, for example—nevertheless, some of those ideas are still around and are having an influence on the way we think. So we should be able to challenge those ideas, we should be able to say, well, some people may of course be religious and want to follow a religious ethic, but that doesn't mean that everybody else should. And so some of the ideas about the doctrine of the sanctity of the human life, for example, or the idea that humans are made in the image of God and animals are not, those things which may have an influence over our moral judgments and our moral attitudes, maybe these are ideas that applied ethics is going to lead us to reconsider.

TAYLOR: Can we talk a bit about psychology? Because it seems to me some critics may say that your philosophy doesn't take into account human beings as they are. A lot of people argue that we're hardwired to be selfish, for example. If that's true, your ideas go against human nature.

SINGER: Sometimes the ideas that we might come up with, through applied ethics, might be ones that people find actually difficult not just to accept but to act on—they might be quite demanding. In various ways human psychology is a factor that has to be taken into account. Obviously we need to try and suggest what's best for human beings as they are; it's no good having a morality that's only for human beings as we might wish them to be. But at the same time, perhaps morality does play a role in changing how human beings are. It's not as if we are permanently fixed; there's at least some flexibility. You can think about changing institutions, changing structures, so that people become a little more generous than they are, so that they think less selfishly. That's important and can be part of what ethics does. So the psychological questions and the ethical questions are always intermingled, but we shouldn't just assume that psychology is fixed and unchanging, no matter what kind of ethical arguments we put forward.

[*At this moment we arrive in Times Square. Billboards and television screens cover every surface, reaching skyward.*]

TAYLOR: Here we are, in the belly of the beast. It's seems we should return to the topic of consumerism.

SINGER: Times Square is the epitome of selling things. Everything around here says, "Buy this, buy that," and of course that's what people often unreflectively do. It's a recreational activity. But we need to stop sometimes and reflect on how we really want to live our lives—that's the ultimate question. We shouldn't just accept this message that the way to live is to buy more, to consume more, to pursue pleasure in all of the ways that are offered to us.

The ultimate ethical question is: How are you going to live your life? And the answer that Western culture often seems to give is: Consume a lot, buy a lot, and seek your own pleasure. And I wonder if that is the most fulfilling way to live your life. The ancient Greeks had this idea that they called the paradox of hedonism, that is, if you try to get pleasure for yourself by directly aiming at it, by setting out and saying, "I'm going to do what will bring me pleasure," you often find that it evaporates, that it retreats in front of you. You don't find it satisfying or really enjoyable in the end. But if instead you do something else that you think is worthwhile, perhaps something that is ethically important, then you find that you get a satisfaction in doing it, and then that's not only the more enjoyable thing to do, but of course also the more meaningful and fulfilling thing to do. Your life actually becomes more enjoyable, more rewarding, and as you pass through it you think, yes, this is really what I want to spend my life doing, this is something that is worthwhile. Rather than just having that empty feeling and saying, well, I pursue pleasure and I enjoy myself, now that's over, that's it.

TAYLOR: So does life have a meaning? I can't think of a more dramatic final question than that.

SINGER: Over the thousands of years of the history and development of philosophy, a lot of philosophers have asked: Does life have a meaning, and if so, what is it? Sometimes when people ask that question, they are asking if there is some sort of external meaning to it, whether there is a god who has given life some meaning or something of that sort. I don't believe that, but I do believe that we can give our own life some kind of meaning. A lot of philosophers have also discussed this, they have asked: How are we to live? What makes our life most meaningful, most fulfilling?

And that's a question we can give an answer to, and the answer is: We make our life most meaningful when we connect ourselves with some really important causes or issues and we contribute to them. So we feel that because we live, something has gotten a little better than it would otherwise; we have contributed in however small a way to making the world a better place. And it's hard to find anything more meaningful than doing that, than reducing the amount of unnecessary pain and suffering that there has been in this world and making the world a little bit better for all of the beings that are sharing it with us.

KWAME ANTHONY APPIAH

Cosmopolitanism

I considered various locations for my interview with Kwame Anthony Appiah, including a brief fantasy about traveling with him to Ashanti, Ghana, where he grew up. Constrained by the film's budget, we eventually decided to meet at the Toronto Pearson International Airport as Appiah disembarked from an early morning flight. He was in town to give a lecture on cosmopolitanism, a theme which also provided the focus of our interview. It was relatively quiet in the terminal and we strolled without supervision. It's worth noting that the cultural diversity of the space was expanded more by the airport employees, who seemed to come from all parts of the world, than by the many travelers we passed.

ASTRA TAYLOR: We've decided to focus our conversation on the topic of cosmopolitanism, which is a main theme of at least two of your books, *Cosmopolitanism: Ethics in a World of Strangers* and *The Ethics of Identity*. Perhaps you could begin by giving some insight into why you began working on this topic and what's at stake more broadly?

KWAME ANTHONY APPIAH: I started thinking about the difference between the context in which we evolved as a species and the present, this age of globalization, and one way to think about that is to notice that if you live a modern life, if you're traveling through an airport, you're going to be passing lots and lots of people. And within a few minutes you'll have passed more people than most of our remote ancestors would ever have seen in their entire lives. And that's just a tiny proportion of the people you're going to meet because if you go to another airport, you'll meet other people in other places.

As a species that was designed for living in bands of a hundred-odd people for much of its evolutionary history, we have to figure out how we're going to live in a planet with 6, 7, 8 billion people. Billions not divided into lots of little bands of a hundred, but constantly interacting—and interacting in units of hundreds of millions. The United States, for example, has a population of 300 million right now. So as an American, you exist in this kind of virtual relationship with 300 million people. If you're lucky enough to be Chinese, your virtual relationships are soon with 1.5 billion people or something like that.

So I think that's a way of dramatizing the challenge that we face. We're good at small, face-to-face stuff; that's what we were made for. We know how to be responsible for children and parents and cousins and friends, but we now have to be responsible for fellow citizens, both of our country and fellow citizens of the world. The question is, can we figure that out?

TAYLOR: Why don't we linger on the word "globalization" since it's a rather contested concept? It would probably be good to clarify your definition.

APPIAH: "Globalization" is a word used to describe many processes. One of these is the process that took us from being humans who lived in these bands of a hundred people, mostly in Africa, to being a global species. So that somewhere between 80 and 120,000 years ago (they keep changing the numbers on us) a band of people, who are the ancestors of all modern humans outside Africa, left Africa for the Arabian Peninsula and within ten thousand years there were people in Australia. So in one sense, globalization is just what humans do. We've moved pretty swiftly in terms of biological time to cover the whole planet.

But then this word "globalization" is also used to talk about economic processes, some important ones that began in the nineteenth century and some of which began in the fifteenth century.

Nowadays, however, it's used above all to talk about the fact that we live in a world that is connected by information. So I have ancestors in Africa and I have ancestors in Europe. A hundred years ago, if something happened among my African ancestors, it would have taken a very long time for any of my European ancestors to hear about it. Now I'm e-mailing my nephews in Namibia, in Nigeria, in London, and within milliseconds I can find out what's happened, if somebody in the family is sick or has had an accident, for example. We live in many countries but all know about it instantaneously.

So there's nothing wrong with calling any of these things globalization so long as you don't mix them up. But I think all of those processes of increasing economic interconnectedness, increasing informational interconnectedness, increasing biological interconnectedness—because now flu viruses, which often evolve in China, almost inevitably end up in the United States and the rest of the world—count as globalization, which is a sort of underlying fact of reality at this point. What we need is a term for how we respond to this fact. And my term for how I think we should respond to globalization is cosmopolitanism. It's an old word, one invented in the fourth or fifth century B.C., but I think it nonetheless very timely. Cosmopolitanism comes from the Greek phrase *kosmou polites*, which means citizen of the cosmos, of the world. And we need a notion of global citizenship.

TAYLOR: I think we need to make clear that you're not talking about being a global citizen in the context of there being a single global government, a monolithic power presiding over every human being.

APPIAH: Yes, you're right. One response to someone who says we should be global fellow citizens is to say, "Well, that means you want a global government," in other words, to have all power collected somewhere centrally and everybody to be under one lot of controllers. And the great cosmopolitans that I look back to would have been horrified at the thought of putting anybody in charge of the whole planet.

Diogenes, the first person we know who said he was a citizen of the world, was very, very antigovernment. He was much admired by Alexander the Great, who generally had a high opinion of philosophers and was a student of Aristotle. Alexander the Great actually met Diogenes once, who was a pretty weird fellow. Diogenes was in a hole in the ground for some reason and Alexander stood above him on a sunny day, looked down, and said, "What can I do for you, O philosopher?" And Diogenes said, "Get outta my light!" So I don't think Diogenes was a great fan of Alexander, even though Alexander was a great fan of Diogenes. In fact, Alexander famously said, "If I hadn't been Alexander, I'd have liked to be Diogenes." So it must have been a bad day for Alexander when he found out what Diogenes thought of him.

I think that anecdote reflects Diogenes' general feeling that we have to take moral responsibility for one another the way fellow members of a city-state, a polis, did, but not by imposing some global megastate or monarch on top of us.

TAYLOR: Could you say more about Diogenes? He is perhaps the most colorful character philosophy has ever produced.

APPIAH: Diogenes was the founder of a movement called Cynicism, a word that did not mean then what it means now. Sometimes when I'm talking to students I say that by "cynicism" I do not mean the official ideology of American high schools. [*Laughs.*] I mean the view of Diogenes. The reason he was called a Cynic is because *kunikos* in Greek means "doglike" and he did various things in public that human beings are not supposed to do and that dogs do. Diogenes was making a point about not being bound by convention and local mores. So Diogenes' cosmopolitanism—[*We're momentarily interrupted by a sudden blast of the loudspeaker: "Do not leave your bags unattended! Do not take items from strangers!"*]—his brand of cosmopolitanism, the idea of global citizenship without global government, went into Stoicism, which is a sort of successor movement to Cynicism. Stoicism became the elite ideology of the Roman Empire at the time Christianity was getting started, and as a result, I think, it got into Christianity. And of course through Christianity, it gets into Islam and it's also in Rabbinic Judaism, which begins in the Eastern Empire at about the same time, after the destruction of the Temple.* So all of the sort of major religions of the Western world—Judaism, Christianity, Islam—have roots, among other things, in these Stoic traditions of global citizenship.

When you think of the great Stoics like Marcus Aurelius, the Roman emperor, he said, "We are fellow citizens of the cosmos." And yet even though he was an emperor, he didn't think it followed from that that he should take over the whole world. So he was talking about a sort of spiritual affinity, taking responsibility for each other because you feel a kind of spiritual affinity. Marcus Aurelius says that the bond between humans is not just of the blood but of the spirit.

* The destruction of the Second Temple in Jerusalem by the Romans in 70 A.D.

And if that sounds a little bit Christian to you, that's because it is, as these ideas were created around the same time. So when St. Paul says, "In me there is no Jew, nor Greek,"* that's also an echo of this kind of global community that is implicit in the Stoic ideal that became part of Christianity as Christianity becomes the official ideology of the Roman Empire.

TAYLOR: As a thinker you go to great lengths to carve out a space between the extremes of universalism and cultural relativism, and we should get into that distinction as well. But perhaps you should first outline the main tenets of cosmopolitanism as you interpret it?

APPIAH: That's pretty easy. As I say, you have to begin with the metaphor of global citizenship. That means, first, we're responsible collectively for each other as citizens are, but second—and this is what differentiates cosmopolitans from other kinds of people who are universalists, who say everybody matters—cosmopolitans think that it's OK for people to be different. They care about everybody, but not in a way that means they want everyone to be the same or like them.

There's a certain kind of philosophical universalism, which is often associated with evangelizing religions, where, yeah, we love everybody but we want them to become like us in order to love them properly. There's a great German proverb, which says, "Und willst du nicht mein Bruder sein, So schlag' ich Dir den Schädel ein"—"If you don't want to be my brother, I'll bash your skull in." And that's the opposite of cosmopolitanism. It's the universalist who says, "Yeah, I want you to be my brother, but on my terms," whereas the cosmopolitan says, "I want to be your brother figuratively, your fellow citizen, but I don't make it a condition of that that we come to be the same."

---

* "There is neither Jew nor Greek, there is neither slave nor free man, there is neither male nor female; for you are all one in Christ Jesus" (*Galatians* 3:28).

TAYLOR: But there's a related sort of universalism as well, right? The universalist injunction not to privilege any cultural tradition or group. It promotes the ideal of viewing everyone equally, of total impartiality, even nonattachment to individuals. Could you talk about that?

APPIAH: Well, if you think that everybody matters but everybody is entitled to be different, then you can allow for rootedness.

But, as you say, there is a kind of universalism, which some people call cosmopolitanism too, that I find absurdly demanding because it says your local attachments, your rooted connections to your family, your community, your country are all morally arbitrary. It says you should really recognize that your primary obligation is to humans as such, and that it's wrong to favor anybody, to be partial to anybody. There is a long tradition of this sort of thought in philosophy. William Godwin, in the famous nineteenth-century version of it, discusses whether if you see a great humanitarian in a house that's burning down, but his servant is your father, whether you should save your father or the great humanitarian. Godwin says obviously you should save the great humanitarian because that is better for humanity.

That kind of denial of the moral appropriateness of partiality— attachment to family, friends, lovers, and so on—just makes this view seem preposterous. People thought Godwin's view was preposterous, and even Godwin thought Godwin's view was preposterous. He said, "Of course I understand that you wouldn't trust somebody who didn't automatically feel that they in fact had to save their father." So the form of cosmopolitanism I defend is one that recognizes that people are, and are entitled to be, partial. That they're entitled to think that if there is a choice between saving your wife and a stranger, you shouldn't be weighing up the moral merits of your wife versus the stranger—you should be saving your wife! Or your child or your parent or your friends. That's fine.

But even if we have more sense of responsibility for people who are closer to us, which is fine, that isn't grounds for not recognizing that we have wider responsibilities as well, and we have to balance them. One way to say this is, we have fundamental responsibilities to everybody, which are so fundamental that we must meet them whenever we can.

TAYLOR: I want to get to that later, the idea that we have fundamental responsibilities to everybody that must be met whenever we can. But for now, let's tackle cultural relativism, which is, obviously, the counterpart to universalism.

APPIAH: Yes, of course. One kind of person who is open to strangers, open to the world, accepting in a way that abandons all judgment—that perspective produces a kind of cultural relativism in which you say, "Whatever they want to do, that's fine, and I'm interested in it, I'm curious about it; I have a cosmopolitan curiosity about it. I'm willing to talk to them about it but there's no place for me, standing outside, to make any judgments, any moral judgments, any ethical judgments about what they're up to." That is one position that I wanted to distinguish myself from. I think it's very important that, in the global conversation of human beings, which cosmopolitans recommend, one of the things we're doing is exchanging ideas about what's right and wrong and that it's perfectly appropriate to do so. But on the other hand, I don't think this has to lead to a kind of moral universalism that doesn't allow for the fact there are legitimate ways of living differently. There isn't only one good or best way for humans to live, and therefore you have to have a deep appreciation for the way a form of life works before you can distinguish what's good and bad in it.

I think that often what motivates cultural relativism is a perfectly legitimate observation, which is that high-minded sort of liberal moralists of human rights, for example, will enter into another society and make judgments all over the place immediately without having done the work to figure out what's going on and to understand why people are doing what they're doing, what the meaning is of what they're doing, what the effects of it really are in the minds and the lives of the people who are there. But if you are engaged with a place and you do appreciate and understand those things, it seems to me perfectly proper in the course of the conversation to say, "Well, I understand what you're doing, but here's something that strikes me as morally objectionable," and "This is a conversation, so you can tell me why you don't think it's morally objectionable, and you can also tell me if I'm doing things that you find morally objectionable."

I think we should think about moral questions as a global conversation, one in which if we come to the right answers, we'll come to the same answers. But among the same answers may be "It's OK to do something differently in one place from the way we do it in another."

Now, we all accept this in the realm of the aesthetic. We all think you'd have to be crazy to think that there was one best kind of music and that therefore all other music should be criticized for not being, for example, nineteenth-century, classical, Romantic music. It would be absurd to listen to Chinese opera and say the trouble with Chinese opera is that it doesn't sound like Verdi. Everyone understands that Chinese opera can be terrific and Verdi can be terrific, too.

TAYLOR: I think a concrete example would probably be helpful here. Perhaps we could take an illustration from your book, where you talk about different ways of organizing families.

APPIAH: So I've been very abstract about this. Let's be concrete. Let's be concrete in the way that I'm able to be concrete because I have, as it were, two very different family histories.

My mother came from England and my father came from Ghana. It happens that in Ashanti, where I grew up, kinship—that is, the family—is organized in a very different way from the way that it's organized in England. In particular, your family membership depends exclusively, basically, on who your mother is. So we're what anthropologists call matrilineal. That means that the most important adult male in a child's life isn't his mother's husband—that is, his father—it is his mother's brother, his maternal uncle. There's a word for that: *wofa*.

So I have these eight people in the world, two young women and six young men who are my nephews and nieces. I'm their *wofa*, and by our tradition, since my sisters don't have any other brothers, I'm the guy who is responsible for their education. If anything bad happens to them, I'm supposed to look after them and so on. Now of course in England, if you have a father, that's his job. Your mother's brother might or might not be helpful, but it would never occur to you to think that he had the primary responsibility. When we were growing up, my father supervised the education of his sister's children, and their school reports didn't go to their dad, they came to him. I mean, their dad was interested in them, he loved his children, but he didn't see himself as having the primary responsibility.

So these are two ways of doing it. These are two ways of organizing intergenerational responsibility for the raising of children. Both work perfectly well. And that means that if you're working in the Ashanti context and you are a *wofa*, you are a maternal uncle, you have obligations which are contingent upon the fact that your society is organized in that way. And similarly, if you're an English father, you have obligations contingent upon the fact that it's organized in the way that it is in England, as a patrilineal system.

There's a certain kind of universalist who believes one of these has to be correct. Here's what I believe: If you could show that it was very, very difficult to bring up children well in the matrilineal system or very, very difficult to bring them up well in the patrilineal system, that would be an argument for shifting from one to the other. But as far as I'm aware there's no serious evidence for either of those propositions and so these are two ways of doing it, and as long as they do the thing they're supposed to do—which is to make sure that there's somebody who's responsible for raising and, apart from the mother, primarily responsible for the children, someone who can contribute in the way that a male relative can—provided they do that job, it seems to me absurd to suggest that one has to be better than the other or that one should be universalized for any reason.

TAYLOR: So you were raised by a mother from a patrilineal society and a father from a matrilineal society—no doubt that's pretty unusual. How did your family get started?

APPIAH: My mother's family is from the west of England, the border of Oxford and Gloucester. Her parents were, I think, more open to the world than the average people in their little village when she was growing up, so my grandparents knew, for example, people from other continents when a lot of English people didn't.

Nehru was a friend of my English grandfather and Indira Gandhi played with my mother in her home in England when she was a girl. They were more open to the world than most people, so I suppose it wasn't too surprising that one of the things my mother did after the Second World War (she spent part of it in Moscow when my grandfather was the British ambassador) was travel quite a lot. But another thing she did after the war was become the secretary to a man called Colin Turnbull who was running an organization called Racial Unity, which dealt with problems of racism experienced by students from the colonies, from Africa and Asia, in Britain. So through her work for Racial Unity with Turnbull, she met the president of the West African student union in London, who was my dad, who was a Ghanaian. He was studying law and also agitating for independence. He used to go and stand on Hyde Park Corner on a Sunday and lecture the British on how come, if they had been fighting for democracy against the Nazis, they hadn't introduced democracy into the colonies.

So they met, and they would neither of them tell us exactly how they met or exactly what it was that drew them to each other, though my father always said that my mother had a splendidly un-English behind, that she actually had a more African behind and he found that attractive, so I don't know! Anyway, they met. They fell in love. My mother went to her mother (her father was very ill at the time) and said, "I think I might want to marry this African." And my grandmother said, "Well, if you're going to marry somebody from the Gold Coast," as it then was, "you should probably go to the Gold Coast to see what it's like before you commit yourself to living there."

And so my mother traveled to the Gold Coast and met my father's family. People thought it was very strange, because her father was a British cabinet minister and nobody could understand why the daughter of a British cabinet minister who had recently died was traveling with all of these anticolonial agitators who were my father's friends. People like Kwame Nkrumah, who was going to be the first prime minister and president of Ghana. But she said she arrived and she sort of felt within about twenty seconds that she was in the right place. She loved it immediately. So she went back home and said to her mother, "As far as the place goes, it's going to be fine."

So that's how, as it were, we got started. I was born while they were still in London but my sisters were all born in Ghana, where we returned when I was one. Kumasi, my father's hometown, was a place full of people from many places. It was a city that had been the capital of an empire, the Ashanti Empire, and it had residents from other parts of Africa, people from the Middle East, Lebanese and Syrians, Indians, Indian traders, and so on. It was a mixed-up kind of a place and it was happy to be so; people were welcome there.

And so, as it happened, as a result of all this mixing and so on, I had a Lebanese uncle and so that means that, as a child, I got to experience the pleasures of feasting during Ramadan, because people fast during the day and then they have to eat! Then at the end of Ramadan, at Eid al-Fitr, the great festival, the food, at least the way

Lebanese people do it, is pretty terrific. So I had half-Lebanese cousins and a Lebanese uncle. My older sister married a Norwegian, my middle sister married a Nigerian, my younger sister married a Portuguese and then has, in succession, married quite a large number of other people, often from other places. Some from Ghana, one half-Malian, and so on. She's added considerably to the collection of my in-laws and ex-in-laws in terms of countries! And on my mother's side, I think partly, as I say, because my English grandparents were quite un-parochial, one of my English cousins lives in Thailand and is married to a Thai, one married a Kenyan. I even have some cousins who made the mistake of marrying Americans. [*Laughs.*] We have French cousins—some of them are Jewish and some of them are Christian—so it's a sort of rather interesting mix of people in the family and that's very enjoyable. It makes it possible for me to learn about all kinds of things just by visiting relatives.

So that's the background and there's obviously a sort of privilege to come from a family that allows you so many family connections to many places, but it's increasingly common.

TAYLOR: In your book you write eloquently about the challenge of understanding different cultural traditions, even seemingly innocent ones. You would say this work of making sense is essential if we're going to avoid destructive cultural conflict, right?

APPIAH: Yes, certainly. In fact, one thing that people talk about all the time these days are conflicts of values across cultures, and often people think that they're kind of inevitably irreconcilable and that they are the root of all the difficulties in the world.

The first way I think you need to work to disentangle all the problems of that way of thinking is to recognize the huge diversity of values by which people are guided. Some of them are very local and particular and hard to make much sense of until you've been in a place for a while. For example, taboos—people have very specific ideas about what you can and cannot eat and so on in different places and you just have to learn them. At first they do not necessarily make much sense to you, but there they are. You can understand food is the type of thing that people have taboos about, so on that level you recognize them. Think about manners. If you're trying to figure out how things work in another place, one of the things you have to figure out is what it is to have good manners. And you can come to recognize what counts as polite in a place. You can recognize that what is at issue is a kind of politeness, even though the things that are preoccupying people strike you as unfamiliar or perhaps even crazy.

So, for example, where I grew up you never give anybody anything with your left hand. It's very rude to give somebody something with your left hand, and if you come from a place where that's not one of the rules, you'll find yourself offending people all the time until you figure that out. Now, Ashanti is a pretty cosmopolitan place, so they know this is a rule that other people don't have; they're not going to begin by assuming that you're trying to be offensive. They'll just assume that you're an ignorant person, not properly brought up perhaps, but still, they'll forgive you. [*Laughs.*] Again, you can see that what you're arguing about is politeness even if you have different notions of what's polite.

So that's a kind of intermediate case between the ones that you may have a hard time really making sense of, the serious taboos. You can understand that some people might think you shouldn't eat cats and other people might think you shouldn't eat dogs and other people might think you shouldn't eat horses, but the idea that you shouldn't eat red peppers on a Wednesday, for example, which is one old taboo that belongs to certain groups of people in Ashanti who worship certain shrines, that might just seem, you know, you might have to take that as given because you can't make sense of it. How on earth could that be a sensible thing not to do? How could anybody think that was a value worth living by, worth being guided by? Nevertheless, some do, and you just have to accept it. With the politeness thing, you are closer to it because all cultures have notions of politeness. Or when it comes to values, things like gratuitous cruelty, for example, that's a pretty universal taboo. There are a few cultures recorded in the ethnographic record where it looks like they think it's not obviously bad, but in general, in most places you'll find when you get to them that they share some of these powerful general values. To the extent that they didn't in the past, I think people are coming increasingly to do so, which is why notions of human rights have gone powerfully global.

Now clearly the fact that there are all these different kinds of values and the fact that we can recognize so many of them are a reflection of the fact that we're all human beings, that we share what you might call a moral nature. We're different. The cosmopolitan thinks we're entitled to be different and that it's predictable that people will be different and that it's permissible that they should be different in certain ways. But the cosmopolitan also assumes that because we have this shared moral nature, anywhere you go, however remote it seems to you to begin with, you will eventually be able to do what anthropologists have always found a human being can do with another bunch of human beings, which is gradually figure out what they're doing, what they care about, what's going on—especially if they want you to. If they want to help you, you can learn, and the reason you can learn is because you have a shared humanity. Wittgenstein famously said that if a lion could speak, we wouldn't understand him. And the point is that animals other than us have different natures and so we don't have this shared background of sameness, of fundamental commonality, to start with. But with humans, with other humans, no matter how different our ways of life may appear, we always do.

TAYLOR: It strikes me that this may be part of why so much wisdom from faraway times and radically different cultures still strikes us immediately as timely and insightful. Diogenes, whom we owe this conversation to, was born over 2,400 years ago, yet his provocative statements still resonate. This is perhaps, as you say, not only a testament to his unique intelligence but also a consequence of our fundamental commonality. What I'm trying to get at is values. Are values timeless, cross-cultural universals rooted in our shared humanity? Or do you think they're something less grandiose?

APPIAH: A lot of values, including moral values, are fundamentally practical. They shape what we do, and they shape what we do very often without our having much rational basis for them. So people often agree about what ought to be done without having a very elaborate or good story about why. Often, because we're a rationalizing species, if you force people, they'll tell you some story about why they ought to do it, but it's a story they've made up afterwards. Beforehand they just saw they had to save the child. If you ask them why they had to save the child, well, they'll say something. But in the end it's the practical conviction, as it were, that is at the heart of their response and the rest of it is a kind of gloss.

Philosophers try to give a rational account of how we should behave. That's something that every human being does, give ex post rationalizations of things that they feel very strongly ought to be so, and philosophers are particularly good at it. Nevertheless, it turns out to be remarkably hard to come up with exceptionless generalizations that actually match the texture of our moral views. One of the attractions of a view like utilitarianism is that it answers every question in a simple way. It tells you what you need to find out in order to decide what to do in terms of one recipe. The trouble is it very often tells us to do things that most people have strong inclinations to think we shouldn't do.

I think that, for practical purposes, what matters is our practical convictions and our practical agreements. Much of the time we don't need a theory about why the baby should be saved. All we need to do is jump in the river and get the baby out.

When we are faced, as we sometimes are within societies and across them, with disagreements about what to do, of course we may then try to use the structure of reasons, the structure of rationalizations, to get at the possibility of some kind of agreement. And that can work. But very often what you discover in the course of such conversations—which is really what they are, they're exchanges of reasons—what you discover first of all is that the kinds of disagreement we have about what we should do are often not grounded in differences in value at all. The most characteristic reason why people do things that we think are bad for children, for example, isn't that they think it's good to do bad things to children, it's because they think that what they're doing is good. So they don't realize that if you take water that looks clear but actually has bacteria in it, the children will suffer. So they go on giving the infectious water to the children, not because they want the children to suffer, but because they don't have any reason to believe that it could possibly be the water that's making them sick. So you have to persuade them. You have to tell them a story about what's going on in the water that they come to believe. Then it turns out they'll boil the water, they'll do exactly what you would do. It's not a disagreement about values, it's not a disagreement about the value of the life of the child; it's just a misunderstanding about what's going on.

Much of the time, when we actually explore disagreements about what to do, we're going to discover all kinds of background facts that explain the disagreement. Often it won't be because there's some deep and irresolvable conflict of values. Nevertheless, sometimes there may well be. That's one of the things that we're going to have to live with if we share the world with strangers who have legitimate differences. They're also going to have differences that we don't think are legitimate, and when we come across those we have a practical problem, which is, what to do? The answer depends on the particular facts of the situation. How bad it is, whether there's anything we can do that will stop them, whether there's anything we can do that will stop them that's consistent with respect for them. If what they're doing is sufficiently bad, we may have to intervene in a way that's not consistent with respect for them because we have to protect, say, a third party from harm from them and so on. So it's a complicated question: What do you do in practice once you recognize that there is a serious disagreement? But my point is that most of the disagreements in the world aren't like that. We haven't even had the conversation that's necessary to figure out where they come from, and that's in part because, as I say, most of our value commitments are not theoretical, they're practical, and most of what we say in justifying them is a kind of rationalization.

TAYLOR: So instead of constantly rationalizing our actions after the fact, do you think we humans would be better off if we were more rational to begin with?

APPIAH: Would we be a better species if we were guided by a sort of pure rational morality? I've no idea because it seems to me that that species wouldn't be ours, a species guided that way. It's very important that intuition and feeling are central to the shape of moral response in humans, and becoming more like Spock, becoming more purely rational, would be, as *Star Trek* suggests, just becoming something other than human.

TAYLOR: But obviously you'd like people to be a bit more reasonable, right? That seems to be something a good number of philosophers encourage.

APPIAH: Of course, to say that one either doesn't hope or expect people to become totally guided by a kind of rational morality isn't to say that one's against reason. As you say, it would be hard to be a philosopher and be totally against reason and reasoning. And so where we can reason about things together and where we can come to rational consensus, there's nothing wrong with it. Great. I'm just pointing out that we can live together without rational consensus and that very often the reason we can is that, while we have different theoretical accounts on the matter, we agree about what needs to be done. We agree that, you know, pollution is bad, mortality is bad. These are all relatively uncontroversial across the species, and to the extent that there are things that we can do about them, it's pretty uncontroversial that we should do them.

I want to combine respect for reason with an acknowledgment that it isn't the only thing that matters in practical life. In fact, the texture of our humanity is so tied up with its not being the only thing that matters in practical life.

TAYLOR: I think more could be said about values. To rephrase my previous question, what are values, exactly? Are they, as Hilary Putnam might put it, "in the head"? That is, are values simply personal preferences, like preferring the color pink over blue, or are they out there somewhere?

APPIAH: I think a lot of modern people are kind of taken by what certain philosophers call a positivist picture, which you've hinted at. It says that when we talk about values we're really just talking about what we like. We're just expressing our desires, our passions, our emotions, and, as a result, values are kind of "in the heads" of different people and, since people are different, values are different. That leads pretty quickly to a sort of relativism according to which there are no extrapersonal standards of judgment, and therefore no conversation can be had about these things as there's no standard of judgment that we both feel bound by or responsible to. Then I just say what I desire and you say what you desire, and that's sort of the end of discussion.

So one of the reasons why this view is wrong, I think, is because moral language is precisely the language that aims to guide shared practices of life. We use moral language because we live together, we share problems, we share communities, and we use it to try to come to agreement about things to do. So moral language is out there in the world, it's a public practice, it's a public thing. It's not the expression of some private inner set of feelings. It's a public practice whose point is to regulate things in a public way. So morality requires conversation. That's one of the reasons why even the great apes can't really have morality. It is because morality is about shaping a collective life through symbolic exchanges, through conversation, through coming to having a shared vocabulary for talking about things, a vocabulary in which cruelty is articulated and understood. We understand what it is to be cruel, and the badness of cruelty is something we come to recognize collectively and therefore we can use the word "cruel" as a powerful reason why you shouldn't do something.

Of course, each of us, in entering into this public practice of forging shared moral values, brings his or her own feelings. A person who has merely an abstract understanding of the wrongness of cruelty but doesn't have an instinctive revulsion towards it is someone who's morally in a bad place. Our sentiments should certainly align with the correct moral view—I'm not denying that. I'm just saying that it doesn't follow from that that moral views are just expressions of private sentiments.

TAYLOR: I think an even more powerful example is science. Few of us—except maybe conservative politicians and corporate elite who want to confuse the public about climate change—accept the concept of scientific relativism, right?

APPIAH: Yes, I can speak about that. It does seem everybody's terribly tempted by moral relativism, but hardly anybody is tempted by relativism about physics or chemistry or biology. Again, I have this privilege of having grown up in a couple of places, and in one of the places people did and do believe in witchcraft. When bad things happen, you go to people who practice good witchcraft to try and deal with them. When my father died and things were going wrong, at least in the view of some members of my family, they went to a Muslim *malaam malaam* and slaughtered a white sheep in order to, as it were, put the spiritual stuff back in balance. Now, I think many people in the West are inclined to think that this is an unreasonable belief and they ought to give it up as quickly as possible. My own view is that killing sheep is not a good way to prevent bad things from happening to you. I agree with that. But I do not agree that the people who hold the belief about slaughtering sheep are especially unreasonable.

One way to think about this is to ask how people respond in, say, New York City when there are certain kinds of problems in their lives. When, for example, they feel a bit under the weather, they feel a little bit sick, what do they say? They say things about viruses. But what do they know about viruses? Most people don't have the faintest idea about the underlying biology. They talk about viruses because that's just what the medical people in our society talk about: "Oh, you've got a virus." Even most scientists in our society couldn't tell you what the evidence is. Most people in our society apply the science that they apply in the same sort of way that people apply witchcraft belief. That is, they just take them as given from the society around them, they apply them, and it sort of seems to work. Somebody says you have a virus, you'll be better in a few days. You're better in a few days. Somebody says you're suffering from witchcraft. You slaughter a sheep and they say you'll be better—and you are better in a few days, right? The evidence looks pretty much the same.

Now, I'm not a relativist about the truth here. Whether there are viruses or not I take to be a completely objective question. I am saying that we're not entitled to be as pleased with ourselves as we are in the West about the correctness of our views because we are no more rational, no more reasonable, than people anywhere else. Most of what we believe, we believe for the boring reason that somebody told us. That's why most people believe what they believe in the world. One of the values, actually, of cosmopolitan conversation is that people who've been told one lot of things meet people who've been told a different lot of things and then they can start to entertain the possibility that, you know, maybe what you were told wasn't right. And you can make progress.

Witchcraft beliefs are giving way in many places to other ways of responding to misfortune. Traditional medical practices in some places are being replaced. Other practices in other places are being shown scientifically to be actually quite helpful and so they're not being replaced, they're being added to the armory of scientific medicine.

[*At this point we decide to move to another terminal in the airport. But first, we pause in one of the main halls to film a few cutaways of Appiah walking by all of the ticket counters. We make two attempts and then pause briefly near an escalator where a group waiting for their connecting flight stands and stares at us.*]

OBSERVER: What are you people doing, walking back and forth like that? And who's he? [*gesturing toward Appiah*] He looks like a prince! [*The group laughs boisterously. They tell us they are already drunk even though it's barely noon.*]

TAYLOR: He's a philosopher, actually. Who are you?

OBSERVER: We're from Newfoundland. We're going to Cuba. To the beach!

[*For the next few minutes they continue to explode into laughter every time we walk by in an attempt to get the perfect shot. It takes some effort to ignore their running commentary and accompanying laugh track.*]

TAYLOR: I really do like conversation as a metaphor for global citizenship because it entails both speaking and listening. That is, you first have to articulate your own assumptions and beliefs in order to explain them to other people—which is something we do surprisingly rarely—and then we have to consider why other people think and do the things they do. And of course that process will lead to plenty of opportunities for "contamination," another wonderful word you highlight.

APPIAH: Yes, one of the ideas that I have found useful in thinking about what's going on in the complicated cultural exchanges happening across the planet now, as we become increasingly informationally globalized, is an idea that, again, is a very old one: contamination. And I like using a word like contamination, which sounds bad, to talk about something that I think is actually good as a way of shocking people into recognition of something.

Much of what is most interesting about what humans do comes not from purity but from contamination. The Roman poet Terence has used this word because he was writing Latin dramas but he was drawing on Greek originals to construct them. Sometimes he would make a play that was based on two Greek originals and sort of bring them together. So he would, as it were, contaminate. Some people criticized him by calling it contamination and he said, Yeah, that's exactly what it is and, furthermore, I think that's a compliment.

When somebody brought back pasta from China to Italy, it was the origin of a great human invention. The way pasta noodles are used in Italy is very different from the way they use them in China and that's part of what's great about it. They took something from one place, mixed it up with ideas from a second place, and of course with products from other parts of the world because Italian cuisine evolved in the context of a trading civilization, and there you have it. Now, that happens all the time. Think of the way in which Athens in the fifth century was a great intellectual center. It was because it was open to people like Diogenes who came from Sinope, which is a town off the Black Sea in the north of Turkey. The people who created Greek philosophy as we think of it came from all around the region. They came from parts of Italy, from the islands, Cyprus, and so on. And of course their philosophy was deeply shaped in the end by interactions with Persian culture and with the sort of cultural discoveries that came as a result of Alexander going as far as India or into Egypt. So great civilizations and great cultural moments are usually the result not of purity but of the contamination and combination of ideas to produce new things.

As you say, conversation is a metaphor for global citizenship; it's a metaphor that has to be interpreted and applied. I think of it as, first of all, involving actual literal conversation, that is, people talking to each other who are from very different backgrounds, whether we're in the same society or across social boundaries, but also consisting of an engagement with the cultural lives of other places through anthropology, through literature, through movies, through the arts, through following the news on the Internet and on television. All of these are ways of taking up the cosmopolitan insight that we will be enriched by ideas and knowledge from other places just as other places can be enriched by knowledge and ideas from us.

TAYLOR: I want to return to a provocative thing you said earlier—provocative because it sounded like common sense, but I suspect it's a bit trickier than that when you get down to it. You said, "We have fundamental responsibilities to everybody, which are so fundamental that we must meet them whenever we can." What does this really mean in practice?

APPIAH: If cosmopolitanism means that we have responsibilities to everybody, then it's reasonable to ask what they are. Now I think it's predictably a rather hard question, but I do think that I can say some things about constraints on a sensible answer. And I think one of the things we can say is that human beings have fundamental needs and interests in order to have a dignified existence, the sort of human existence that's really worth having. Surely one thing that we ought to hope for is that we should accept collectively the responsibility of making sure that everybody has those necessary things. Now those things will vary from place to place but still we'll be able to identify people who fall below that standard and recognize that we have a collective responsibility to them.

I believe that the best way to achieve real progress in this area as an individual, at least in a rich country, is to focus on making sure that your country behaves as a responsible county in the community of nations, in a way that reflects its resources and capacities and that acknowledges the difficulties of doing something but nevertheless takes seriously the fact that, if there are people falling below this line, something must be done about it. Rich people will find it easier to do more, so we should probably do more. But I think that the best way to do that is by reshaping trade and aid policies, by reshaping politics of the planet, and by trying to guarantee these minimum standards for everybody.

Of course that's not the only obligation you have because trying to get your country to do something doesn't mean that it'll do it, and if it isn't doing anything, you haven't discharged your responsibility, which is—and here's my formulation—to do your fair share of the collective obligation. So there are two problems. What does the collective obligation amount to? I say it amounts to guaranteeing that everyone has a shot at a decent human life. That I think is something that's obviously difficult to interpret in practice but I think it's something we can get widespread agreement on, I hope, in theory.

The really hard question is: What is the fair share? Does my fair share depend on how rich I am, for example? And more importantly, and I think more difficultly, can my fair share go up because other people aren't doing their fair share? Someone like my friend Peter Singer might say, Look, what matters is that these needs are met. It's not enough to say that you're doing your fair share because your fair share will meet those needs only if everybody does their fair share. And we know that other people aren't doing their fair share, so you and I may have to do more. The trouble is the logic of that position leads to the idea that I should go on doing what's necessary to help make sure everybody has the shot at a decent existence down to the point of making my existence the bare minimum existence—that I should abandon my own projects, my own life, my own family, my own community, my own friends if necessary, if other people aren't doing their fair share. Now that's one of the kinds of demands that I think if a philosophical theory makes, people are just going to ignore it. If somebody says you have to abandon your life, you have to abandon all the things you care about because there are people suffering out there and because other people aren't doing their fair share to remedy it, I think you're entitled to—well, whether you're entitled to it or not, most of us will just walk away. We'll just say, "Well, if that's what you're asking of us, we're not gonna do anything!"

So the form of cosmopolitanism that I'm endorsing takes seriously not just the fact of human partiality—the fact that we take more care of our kin than we do of strangers, and of our fellow citizens than we do of citizens of other places—but our right to do so. Provided you're doing your fair share to guarantee the basic shot for everybody, it's OK to do more for the people you care more about. That is one of the ways this form of cosmopolitanism, in acknowledging that important fact about how people are and how they are entitled to be, makes demands on them that are more reasonable than the demands that would be made by someone who says, "No, you're not entitled to have any preferences, you must treat everybody the same." Once you grant that there is a legitimate place for partiality, for treating your family better than other people in your community and people in your community better than people in other communities, then you can go on to say, "But nevertheless, there is this huge, unmet human need. There are a billion people living on a dollar a day and two billion people living on less than two dollars a day. That just cannot be enough to sustain a decent human life and so we have an obligation, a collective obligation, an obligation we can mostly meet through politics to do something about it."

TAYLOR: But it's very easy, as an individual, to look at everyone else and imagine you're doing enough simply because others are doing so little. Surely that's not an acceptable standard. Is it really possible to do enough to help others?

APPIAH: My view is it's a hard question. But whatever the answer is, it can't be that those of us who care about these things have to abandon our lives in order to face this challenge. Rather, as I say, I think we should mostly focus on using our political clout in democratic societies to get our governments to do what they should be doing, which is making sure that we do, collectively, our fair share. And they can do that most easily by deciding what needs to be done and then raising the taxes to do it.

The fact is, we have to figure out how to live in a world in which our responsibilities are, not to just a hundred people with whom we can interact with and see, but to six or seven billion people whom we cannot see and whom we can affect only in indirect ways. That is, I think, the great challenge. And cosmopolitanism for me is meant to be an answer to that challenge. It is meant to say you cannot retreat to the hundred. You can't be partial to some tiny group and live out your moral life there; it's simply not morally permissible. But you cannot abandon your local group either, because that would take you too far away from your humanity. So what we have to do is to learn how to do both.

MARTHA NUSSBAUM

Justice

Immediately after I invited her to participate in Examined Life, *Martha Nussbaum suggested we conduct the interview while strolling along Chicago's lakeshore, a path she visits almost daily. It was a late fall morning with clear skies, and we walked briskly and purposefully, though we had no particular destination, spurred on by the chill in the air and Nussbaum's rousing elocution. Only later did I recognize what a fitting location a public park was for our discussion. As parents played with their children, elderly people took in the scenery, and locals passed by with their dogs, Nussbaum presented an impassioned critique of the traditional social contract theory, envisioning a society based on mutual care instead of mutual advantage.*

ASTRA TAYLOR: I've invited you here to talk about justice, an inquiry that takes us back to the beginning of philosophy, to Plato, who famously asked: What is justice? Perhaps you could begin by letting us know what motivates you to wrestle with this sort of topic.

MARTHA NUSSBAUM: For the first part of my career, I worked on ethical issues, not issues of justice. I moved into that area when I found myself presenting a paper at an international institute for development studies connected to the United Nations. There, learning a lot more about inequalities of opportunity around the world, I saw how urgent the issue of global justice was and how little philosophers and economists had done to confront it well. So I decided to focus at least part of my work, from then on, on that question.

TAYLOR: You make a good point in the beginning of your book *Frontiers of Justice* when you articulate why theories of justice need to be abstract, a point that relates more generally to this project, which is all about encouraging abstract thinking while also trying to make philosophical issues concrete and palpable. So let me ask you: Why do we need to generate theories, to think in abstraction, specifically when it comes to justice?

NUSSBAUM: Theories of justice need to be abstract because if we remain immersed in the prejudices of our immediate time and place, we may create theoretical structures that are unfair to people in other places. So we need to rise above the details of our immediate situation and create theories that have the power to cover many different times and places.

But when we do that, there's also a risk, and that is that we will be too abstract. We'll forget some very important things that the real world contains. So we always have to keep testing our abstract theories against the real world and asking ourselves, have we forgotten something very, very important? So for example, for a long time theories of justice simply forgot about the family. They created theories that were fine for the big political space outside the home, but because they weren't thinking much about women's lives, they didn't see that there were justice and injustice inside the family as well. And of course, that was true all along, and the theories were therefore too abstract, or abstract in the wrong way, because they did not zero in on the tremendous injustice and inequality of opportunity that goes on in the family. So that's an example of how a theory can be abstract in the wrong way. When we notice that we have to correct, we have to go back to the real world, look at the problems it contains, and then come back to the theoretical plane with a new theoretical structure.

TAYLOR: That makes sense. So is this the work of philosophy?

NUSSBAUM: I think a lot of it is the work of philosophy. But philosophy, of course, has to be responsive to people who are actually struggling for justice. So in this case, the feminist movement was a very important catalyst for philosophy to do better work. Philosophy also has to know something about economics and has to know about history. So philosophers may be the ones that do the abstracting, but they have to be in conversation with people in these other disciplines.

TAYLOR: Do you think we're making progress on this front? Are our theories, specifically about justice, improving over time?

NUSSBAUM: Well, you know, I think the funny thing is that things were better longer ago in some way, because Aristotle had the ingredients of an idea that I think is very powerful. And that is that it's the job of a good political arrangement to provide each and every person with what they need to become capable of living rich and flourishing human lives. Now, of course, he didn't include all the people: he left out all noncitizens, which meant all women and slaves and some agricultural and manual laborers. It took the Stoics, who came later, to introduce the idea of human equality. When you include everyone, you have to change all the structures, as I said. But he at least had that idea of supporting human capabilities that's the foundation of my own approach.

Now then, in the seventeenth and eighteenth centuries, a very powerful new approach came on the scene and that was the social contract approach: Hobbes, Locke, Rousseau, Kant. The social contract approach was inspired by the background culture of feudalism, where all opportunities were distributed unequally to people according to their class, their inherited wealth, and their status. And so what these theorists said is, try to imagine human beings stripped of all those inherited advantages, placed in what they call the "state of nature," where they had only their natural bodies and their physical advantages, and try to imagine what kind of arrangement they would actually make. Because then we'll see that the artificial advantages of power and wealth are gone, and only the body is there, which is pretty much the same for all people, and so they will choose a certain kind of more equitable political arrangement.

Now that was a wonderful idea, and I think it really illuminated the structure of justice for a very long time. But, of course, they made certain assumptions that aren't always true. They assumed that the parties to this contract really are roughly equal in mental and physical power. Now that was fine when you're thinking about adult men with no disabilities, but as some of them already began to notice, it doesn't do so well when you think about women, because women's oppression has always been partly occasioned by their physical weakness compared to men. And so if you leave out that physical asymmetry, you may be leaving out a problem that a theory of justice will need to fix. But it certainly does not do well when we think about justice for people with serious physical and mental disabilities. And in fact some of the theorists who noticed that said this is a problem, but we'll just have to solve it later. We'll get the theory first, then we'll work on this problem at some other point. Well, my thought is that this is not a small problem. There are a lot of people with serious mental and physical disabilities, but not only that: it's all of us when we're little children and as we age. And the populations of the world are aging, so the whole lifespan of a person in the old days with a physical or mental disability may have been shorter than the span that some of us will spend when we are aging with serious disabilities of our own.

So this is a vast problem. How do you think about justice when you're dealing with bodies that are very, very unequal in their ability and their power? And perhaps even harder: How do you think about it when you're dealing with mental powers that are very, very unequal in their potential? And I think this is a really serious political problem. We have only just begun to understand how to educate children with disabilities, how to think about their political representation, how to design cities that are open to them. I mean, the bridge we walked across to get to this path, a person in a wheelchair can go over that bridge, but, you know, fifty years ago that would not have been the case. There would have been steps and that person could not get to see this beautiful lakeshore. So we've just begun to think about these things, and we have to have theories that help us think better.

TAYLOR: So the traditional social contract approach looks at people with disabilities in terms of what they contribute or what they offer in terms of mutual advantage?

NUSSBAUM: Yes, the contract approach, when thinking about mental and physical disabilities, wants us to ask, "How much do these people contribute to our gross national product and how much do we pay to educate and sustain them?" Well, usually those figures don't balance out. To educate a child with Down syndrome and to care for all of the physical needs of that child will actually be very expensive. And that child will not repay, in economic terms, that input. But that's why thinking about the contribution in such a way is much too narrow. Children with Down syndrome contribute immensely to our larger culture as members of families, as friends—and even as members of a political community, because adults with Down syndrome are voters—they're able to participate in political life. And they also contribute simply by showing their lives and showing the dignity of a life that can overcome great disability. Children who are mainstreamed along with a child with Down syndrome really understand something about the diversity of humanity and its capacities for overcoming difficulty that will stand them in good stead as they get older and encounter similar disabilities themselves and others. So once again, thinking about these people who have lifelong disabilities helps us—each and every one of us—think about our own bodies as we age and become physically and cognitively impaired ourselves. Once again, we don't want to say about people who are aging, "Oh, well, let's see how much they contribute to the economy." We want to say there are different kinds of contribution—life experience, understanding, just being there as who they are and being objects of love in families—that enrich all of our lives.

TAYLOR: In a moment, I want to ask you about the other populations that are, you argue, left out by the traditional social contract model, namely, people in other countries and animals. But first, I want to make clear just how relevant to our lives this topic actually is. It may seem like we're discussing some obscure philosophical proposition when, in fact, the social contract is really part of everyday ideology. Can you talk about that?

NUSSBAUM: I'd be happy to. The social contract tradition is, of course, an academic, philosophical tradition, but it also has had tremendous influence on popular culture and our general public life because every day we hear things like, "Oh, those people don't pay their own way" or, when advocates propose supporting some new group of people, "Well, they'll be a drag on our economy." So the idea that the good member of a society is a producer who contributes advantage to everyone—that is a very live idea. It lies behind the decline of welfare programs in this country. I think it lies behind many Americans' skepticism about Europe, about European social democracy. You hear terms like the "nanny state" as though there is something wrong with the idea of maternal care as a conception of what society actually does. We also see it in another way, in images of who the "real man" is. The "real man" is sort of like these people in the state of nature. He doesn't deeply need anyone. He isn't bound to anyone by ties of love and compassion. He is the loner who can go his own way, and then out of advantage he'll choose to have certain kinds of social arrangements.

TAYLOR: I think your observations reveal the power of ideas and the influence of philosophical thinking on daily life. It's also good to remember that philosophers are not always mavericks challenging the prevailing assumptions of their time; being human, all philosophers have blind spots and many have provided eloquent rationalizations and defenses of the status quo, as the earlier example of Aristotle shows. In any case, as I mentioned, you argue that there are two other populations left behind by the social contract approach. Could you talk about them now?

NUSSBAUM: The traditional social contract theory assumes a rough equality in both physical and mental powers among the people who make the social contract, imagining, basically, roughly equal, adult, male bodies capable of functioning pretty well and possessing rationality, language, and so on. Now this leaves out, very obviously, people with severe physical and mental disabilities and the part of "normal" human lives that involves dependency, when we are very young or aging and need care. But in a more subtle way it leaves out people in different countries. For example, one of the most severe deprivations of poverty in developing countries is nutritional and physical disadvantage. The people of the world are just not equal in physical and mental power because even before they're born, maternal malnutrition has affected their physical capacities, and there's such a large proportion of the children of the world who do not have access to adequate nutrition. So we really have large numbers of people in the world who are unequal in physical power because of their nation, because of the poor situation into which they've been born. Thinking about global justice includes having to think about that.

And then we finally have nonhuman animals, and I'm very interested in having a theory of justice that includes them. I think that nonhuman animals are entitled to have decent and flourishing lives. Now, of course, some nonhuman animals are very powerful, but let's face it, we dominate them. And the whole point of the state of nature was to say that no one can really dominate—that's why you have to make a fairly egalitarian bargain. But, with nonhuman animals, we dominate them. We have totally won that battle, as it were, and we've created a world in which they exist in fairly restricted places, and whenever we want to we can restrict that sphere still further. Even a creature as powerful as an elephant is not equal to us in power, and that's a fact. So we can't presuppose this rough equality of power if we're going to have the right kind of theory that includes nonhuman animals.

And I think these three areas are the frontiers of justice. I call them that because I think they are now the places where we're breaking new ground in the theory of justice. I think we've done pretty well with a lot of the older problems, problems of class, of status, and even with equality of gender. We at least have theoretical structures that handle those problems pretty well now. We know what it would be to correct those problems. But with these three issues the theory is under a new kind of pressure and we can no longer rely on the old theoretical structures. So I think we need to think again. And when we do, we may find that this will reshape all of our thinking about justice.

TAYLOR: It seems obvious that people have motivations other than mutual advantage when they enter into relationships. Why does the social contract model ignore this?

NUSSBAUM: Theorists of the social contract made a simplifying assumption that people only cooperate for the sake of mutual advantage, and they didn't necessarily deny that people have, in real life, other motives for cooperation. But they thought it would be simpler if you could use the minimal assumption, that it's only advantage people are looking for, and see whether you can get an adequate theoretical structure out of that.

Now, actually, I think that just didn't work. You really need to record and include in your theory the fact that people cooperate for love of one another, out of compassion, out of respect for human dignity in one another, but also just simply out of love of humanity. All those things are real, but they're also theoretically important because they show us why we would want to create a society that fully included people with mental and physical disabilities. Now, mutual advantage cannot answer that question because many, many people with mental and physical disabilities do not repay, by their economic input, the expense that we take in caring for them—medically caring for them and then educating them adequately. Those who say, "Oh, those people don't pay their own way"—well, that kind of thinking is what has made it very difficult to solve this problem politically. That's why we need to build into our theoretical structure itself the fact that just love of a person is an adequate reason to include that person in one's political structure and as a full equal.

So the social contract theory is not meant to be a total account of human nature; it's meant to be a very simple one. And so they try to rely on very thin assumptions, and the assumption is that people cooperate for the sake of mutual advantage. Unfortunately, however, this gives us a theory that's much too thin to include all that we want a theory to include. We need to include beneficent and compassionate motivations, and we need to include the relationships in which we stand to one another. If we think of these people as isolated, anatomic beings in the state of nature, we don't get a rich enough sense of what they're trying to build, which of course includes relationships very, very prominently.

TAYLOR: Let's move beyond the contractual model and get into the capabilities approach, which you've been developing for many years.

NUSSBAUM: The capabilities approach, as I've developed it as a theory of justice, begins with the idea of the dignity of a human being. Now, we'll get to animals later, but as a first point we begin with an idea that all human beings have an inherent dignity and what they require is life circumstances that are worthy of that dignity, which I believe is equal in everyone. So what does that mean? Here I draw on Aristotle and I also draw on the young Marx, who talked about a life that is truly human (as opposed to subhuman, as it were) a life in which we can use all our basic human equipment in a way that's not just minimal but flourishing.

In my view, it's the job of a decent society to provide all the people in that society with the underpinnings of that decent human life. And the way I think of it is that all citizens should have ten central capabilities, which means they should all be ready to be able to go out and choose that thing (for example, health care, employment opportunities, political participation). If they don't use the opportunity, that's up to them. But the areas of life that seem to me particularly important when we think about the capabilities are: of course, life (it's the most basic one); bodily health; bodily integrity; the development of the senses, imagination, and thought; the development of practical reasoning; the development of affiliations, both more informal in the family and friendship but also in the political community; the development of the ability to play and have recreational opportunities; the ability to have relationships with other creatures and the world of nature; developing emotional capabilities—because I think a lot of theories leave out the fact that we don't want to have lives that are filled with fear, for example, so emotional health is another one on my list; and then, finally, control over one's material culture, some degree of control over property, and control of some sorts over one's workplace. It turns out that equal access to property rights is a very important ingredient of women's equality, and access to decent working conditions that give workers some control over their own labor is of urgent importance for all.

Now all of that is elaborated a lot further in the theory, and my idea is that each country would elaborate it even more specifically in accordance with its own history and its own constitution-making process. So the idea, which I work out in a fairly abstract way, is that each nation would then put something like that into its constitution, articulating a sense of where the threshold for each capability lies. So each culture has to say, health has to come up to this level, the provision of health opportunities for our citizens has to meet this standard. The protection for bodily integrity has to come up to this level or it's not a minimally just society. So that's the basic idea, and then of course I get into a lot more detail about each element on the list, and with animals we have to shift gears entirely.

TAYLOR: So to be very clear—and to return to the original question—according to your theory, some basic level of social justice is achieved when a society's citizens are not denied these basic capabilities. Right?

NUSSBAUM: Yes, that's the minimum if we've set the threshold level correctly. Societies can then go on to ask how to handle inequalities that rise above the threshold level. That I do not discuss because getting everyone above the threshold is already such an ambitious goal.

TAYLOR: Let's go a bit more in depth with the capabilities approach, which emphasizes what people are able to do and to be. What is new about taking such a perspective and why is it necessary?

NUSSBAUM: It is not so new in philosophy. As I said, Aristotle had many of the ingredients of the idea. In international development economics, however, the approach came to prominence, in the work of my collaborator Amartya Sen, as an alternative to theories that measured the quality of life in a nation by looking only at GNP per capita. That simple approach did not even look at distribution, so it could give high marks to nations with huge inequalities. By focusing on the social contract approach in *Frontiers of Justice*, I am, by choice, focusing on a subtle and admirable opponent, having already had my say about the cruder and less admirable views that currently dominate the development debate in my earlier book *Women and Human Development*.

TAYLOR: It occurs to me that the enduring appeal of the social contract approach may be partially attributed to the myth of man in the state of nature. This very simple origin story is a powerful thing and an important reason why this theory is so pervasive and persuasive to many. Can you think of a new founding myth that would convey the essence of the capabilities approach in an equally direct, cogent way?

NUSSBAUM: Well, you know, my theory is antimythical in the sense that it insists on looking at real people in their historical and political conditions. Only in that way can we see the obstacles that stand between them and their really being able to go out and choose the capabilities on my list. So I open the book *Women and Human Development* with two real-life stories, both of poor working women in India, and I look at how the governments of the two states in which they live (Gujarat for one, Kerala for the other) have enabled them to attain those capabilities or have not done so. I keep returning to real-world examples all through the book.

TAYLOR: You mentioned Aristotle and the young Marx. What did each of these thinkers bestow to you and how did you incorporate their lessons into the capabilities approach?

NUSSBAUM: Aristotle was the topic of much of my earlier scholarship since I began my career as an expert in ancient Greek philosophy, so he is important to me for many things, but in this connection he supplies the idea that the purpose of government is to put people in a position of capability to lead a flourishing human life. Part of this idea is the crucial insight that the important things in life are plural and not singular, so we don't want one single measure of the quality of a human life; we want to look at each area separately and make sure all the areas are going well. Marx supplied the idea that what we are after when we do this is a life that is truly human, worthy of human dignity, and that there's a way of merely living that is not worthy of our humanity.

TAYLOR: By inviting thinkers to take a walk with me, to talk about their ideas out in the open like this, I'm trying to illustrate philosophy's connection to urgent real-world dilemmas, problems at the heart of human existence, on both the personal and political level. That's why I chose the tagline "philosophy is in the streets" for the film. So one reason I was keen for you to be part of this endeavor is your commitment to addressing issues like global poverty, to combining theory and practice. Could you talk about your experiences in India, which I understand had an immense influence on your intellectual trajectory? I'd also like to hear about the capabilities approach's impact in the realm of international development, as I want to make sure people realize that the ideas you've outlined are actually being put to use around the world and that your aim is social transformation.

NUSSBAUM: I focused on India because I wanted to show how my theories apply to a single nation that I could get to know well. I don't like it when people use scattered examples from different countries without understanding the history or internal politics of any. For *Women and Human Development*, I spent a lot of time studying women's groups in different parts of the country. But since I love the country, this has led to a lifelong engagement with it, and I recently wrote a book entirely about India's struggle with religious violence, *The Clash Within: Democracy, Religious Violence, and India's Future*. As for social transformation, that takes a partnership between theory and practice, so we've formed an international association, the

Human Development and Capability Association, which brings people together across the theory-practice divide to think about new scholarship in this area but also issues of implementation.

TAYLOR: Let's take a moment here and shoot some cutaways. I want to focus the camera on your hand movements.

NUSSBAUM: It would be easier if I kept talking, as I tend to talk with my hands. I like moving around when I talk. I never like to talk sitting still. If I come into a lecture room and I'm at table, it's just dead. I like to stand.

TAYLOR: It's true that moving around, getting your blood flowing, walking like this, helps one think better.

NUSSBAUM: Well, it's also like theater. It is theater, lecturing. I used to be an actress at one point. I had a brief stint as a professional actress and I learned something from that.

TAYLOR: I had no idea. It's interesting you say you incorporate a theatrical element into your lecturing, as some seem to think philosophy should be undemonstrative, unadorned. But here I'm trying to dramatize philosophic debate, to make it resonate, by putting what is usually an academic discussion into a different context. You've written very inventive philosophic dialogues, for example, so it seems you've experimented with making philosophy more accessible and absorbing as well. Is there anything you want to say about that effort?

NUSSBAUM: Well, I love writing, and I did turn the first chapter of *Upheavals of Thought* into a dialogue in which my mother, my father, and I were characters discussing grief. It was performed by some wonderful actors in Sweden. I also wrote another one about patriotism and cosmopolitanism, with the philosopher Marcus Aurelius as a lead character, which was performed at a fund-raiser for one of Chicago's theater companies. I'd like to do more of that sort of writing, but even in my "regular" writing I try to be clear and to use examples in a dramatic way.

TAYLOR: I want to go back to a topic touched on earlier, nonhuman animals, as I'm very intrigued by your treatment of animal rights as an issue of justice and not just as an ethical or moral issue. Typically people, animal-rights activists and philosophers alike, focus on animal suffering instead of animal abilities and their potential to flourish. Why do you think that is?

NUSSBAUM: You know, a lot of people think that the problems of cruelty to animals are ethical problems, and that these are the sort of ethical problems that don't raise issues of justice. And it's tricky to talk to people about this because justice is a very elusive notion. But what I think is that whenever you have a creature that is an agent—one that's got a point of view on the world and is actively striving to achieve a certain kind of life for itself—then you already have the question of justice on the table because then things may block that effort to live a decent life. Sometimes it will just be an accident, but sometimes blameworthy action is the cause of a creature being blocked, and that's where we typically bring in the notion of justice. Creatures are entitled to be able to pursue a certain kind of rich and flourishing life, so I just think there's no reason to draw the line at the human race. Again, the very idea of agency and striving is enough to put the question of justice on the table. I'm unclear whether the creatures that Aristotle called the "stationary animals" like sponges and mollusks really are subjects of justice—that would be the gray area. And plants for me are not. They're of interest to us for many, many reasons; we have ethical duties to plants and the nonhuman environment but not duties of justice. But most animals—the ones who are moving around, desiring things, moving toward what they desire, trying to live—those are the ones where we do have duties of justice.

And of course, that means modifying my capabilities approach to justice in many ways, but I think the same basic list is actually still a pretty good one because animals don't just want freedom from pain; they do want healthy lives, lives with bodily integrity, the ability to move around in an environment that's pleasing to their senses. Animals want affiliation. There's a lot of good new research about the social bonds of animal communities, and even animals as simple as mice and rats have complicated social perceptions. So all of these things can be modified, and we can think of dignity in a new way. Dignity is not just a human affair. Nonhuman animals also have their dignity, and I think it's a useful notion when we think of what's wrong with the factory-farming industry, for example—namely, a creature that should have its dignity respected is being humiliated.

TAYLOR: There have long been appeals in philosophy to the intrinsic dignity of human beings, and many have denied animals this dignity. So I'm very pleased that you extend this attribute to animals. But I wonder what, precisely, you mean by dignity? And also, why make dignity central to your argument about justice?

NUSSBAUM: The notion of dignity is slippery, and I believe it has to be defined as part of a family of interrelated notions, including respect, capability, and justice. John Rawls was correct when he said that it has no obvious content all on its own. But basically, it is the worthiness of a living being, that which inspires our respect and awe.

TAYLOR: You mentioned the social contract approach not being an account of human nature earlier. But doesn't every theory of justice make implicit assumptions about human nature? If that's the case, then what is the view of human nature at the center of the capabilities approach? And should theories take into account and focus on human nature as it is, or is human nature something more malleable, something that theories should perhaps aim to transform?

NUSSBAUM: No, it's not true to say that all political theories are built on theories of human nature. No good one is, in my view. The reason for that is that all modern nations contain many different religious and secular views of life, each with their own views of human nature, and I agree with John Rawls that this means that our political principles must avoid taking divisive positions on such issues. So my capabilities theory is a normative theory of political obligation, not a theory of human nature.

TAYLOR: I don't want to forget to ask you about emotions. You've done a lot of important work on this front, for example, your book *Upheavals of Thought: The Intelligence of Emotions*, which you just mentioned. Why have emotions often been pushed to the sidelines by philosophical thinkers?

NUSSBAUM: Well, I think that it's an old story in philosophy, that there was a very, very long period where male philosophers were embarrassed by the emotions. It was a particularly English phenomenon, I think. But if you go back to the Greeks and the Romans, they talked about emotion all the time, and they had very powerful theories of emotion. But then there was a gap, and I think it was around 1916 when a few people in Anglo-American philosophy very courageously started writing articles on the emotions. But it was actually a result of feminism that this topic became part of the agenda for philosophy in a big way. Interestingly, it was men who had to begin it because I think that if women had done it first, they would have been laughed at—and they were. But there were people like Bernard Williams, for example, who began talking about the role of emotions in philosophy in a way that then gave permission for other people to go much further and talk about it more.

TAYLOR: In your work, you also broach the topic of negative emotions, like shame and disgust, which you argue are a defense against our inherent vulnerability as human beings. Could you talk about vulnerability, which seems to be a theme that deeply compels you? Why is vulnerability a central aspect of your work and how does vulnerability relate to the problem of justice?

NUSSBAUM: Well, yes, that could be said to be the question that links all my work together. Vulnerability has a positive aspect: unless we are willing to be vulnerable to one another, we will not be capable of love, and the denial of vulnerability is one of the sources of aggression and violence. On the other hand, some types of vulnerability are just bad and should be eliminated—a child should not go hungry, women should not be raped, etc. So figuring out which sorts of vulnerability are good and which sorts a decent politics should remove is where my work on emotions connects up with my work on political justice.

TAYLOR: Very succinctly, if we could distill this conversation about justice to its essence, what would your message be?

NUSSBAUM: I guess at the heart of this discussion is the question: Why do people get together to form a society in the first place? And, really, it's not because they're afraid and they want to strike a new deal for mutual advantage; it's much more out of love—it's out of the love of humanity and the love of human dignity that they want to join with others in creating a world that's as good as it can be.

MICHAEL HARDT

Revolution

When I first envisioned Examined Life *as a series of walks, I always imagined that there would be some exceptions. As long as the film maintained its nomadic, roving character, the specific means of motion didn't seem all that significant to me. Given Michael Hardt's connection to Venice, Italy—home of his longtime collaborator, Antonio Negri, and a location we briefly considered—I had already daydreamed about filming in a gondola. When we arrived at one of Hardt's favorite spots, Central Park's Bethesda Terrace, the nearby boathouse immediately caught my eye. Hardt, the cameraman, and I clambered into one rowboat, while the camera assistant and soundman, his giant boom microphone swinging overhead, got into another. As I held the two boats together and Hardt provided the rowing power for the whole team, we made quite a spectacle. Tourists snapped photos of us from the shore as we discussed revolution.*

MICHAEL HARDT: For my generation, in the mid-eighties, when I was in my twenties and just starting to do politics in a serious way, it seemed like the only outlet for revolutionary desire was to go to Central America. So a lot of people went to Nicaragua. My friends and I were mostly interested in El Salvador. But the thing I realized, at a certain point, was that all we could do was observe their revolutions. The defining moment for me came in a meeting with a group of students at the University of El Salvador. A friend there said, "Look, we are really grateful to these North American comrades who've come to help us, but what would really be best for us is if you all would go home and make revolution in the U.S. That would really be better than coming to help us here."

And it was true. I don't think any of these North Americans were particularly helpful in Nicaragua and El Salvador, etc. But I said, "Reagan is in the White House; I don't know what it would take to make revolution in the U.S." And he said, "Don't you have mountains in the U.S?" And I said, "Yes, we have mountains." And he said, "It's easy. You go to the mountains, you start an armed cell, and you make a revolution." And I was like, "Oh shit"—it did not correspond to my reality.

So there were two things that were helpful for me. One was that I think there was a feeling among my generation that we couldn't make revolution in the U.S. The U.S. wasn't a site of revolutionary activity. We thought revolution could only be made in the subordinated countries that suffer most from the global capitalist system. The El Salvadorans didn't share that feeling. They thought that it *was* important to make revolution in the U.S. So that was helpful to know. And the other thing that was helpful was that the models we had for how to make revolutions did not correspond to our lives. Like those notions of constructing the armed cell in the mountains and sabotaging things—it didn't make any sense at all. So, on the one hand, I realized they were right: it's not that we are excluded from revolution. But what was also clear is that we really had no idea how to do it. Not just that we didn't know practically—we didn't know which rifles to take up to the mountains, for example—but rather, the whole idea of what it involved was lacking. And really required a conceptual rethinking.

ASTRA TAYLOR: Fredric Jameson and Slavoj Žižek have both noted that it's easier to imagine an immense catastrophe, an asteroid hitting the earth or a virus wiping out humankind, than it is to imagine a modest change in the capitalist order. Why is it so hard to talk about revolution today? And on more specifically, can you speak about the Left's relationship to the notion of revolution, which I would say is pretty ambivalent?

HARDT: We're living in a period when, in order to ensure its legitimacy, the Left has had to abandon the notion of revolution. So what's left after the possibility of a radical transformation of society has been written off? What's left, for the Left, are practices of resistance, practices of critique and of civil disobedience. In other words, it's a strictly negative vocation.

I'm not saying that these are not important practices—they certainly are. They can temper how bad things are and they can in some ways undermine or subvert things. But what's lacking is that positive propositional element. In fact, there's even a feeling—or at least this is the sense I have—that there's a great dignity in criticizing things and that you're kind of stupid if you actually propose something. First of all, if you propose something on the Left today, you know what happens: you get critiqued by everybody because they are great at critiquing things. So I think that part of my, I guess it would be, diagnosis of why the Left has consigned itself to this critical role is precisely because it's cut off the possibility of revolution. I'm not saying that hasn't been for some good reasons. But it seems to me that totally abandoning the notion of revolution limits the Left to a strictly defensive and critical posture.

Without being able to think revolution, the Left ends up with only half a politics, it ends up only with its ability to critique, to resist, to disobey power—but not able to construct an alternative. That's why it seems to me that without a revolutionary imaginary, without being able to imagine an alternative to the current situation, and without figuring out how we can construct mechanisms to get us there, the Left is lost in a kind of long-term holding pattern.

TAYLOR: A quick question: Are you talking about the old opposition between reform and revolution?

HARDT: There is a conventional opposition posed between reform and revolution, and I don't think that's what we're talking about. What I'm interested in here is the division between practices of resistance and the possibilities of revolution. As I said earlier, certainly practices of resistance are necessary and important: think about resistance to the war in Iraq, resistance to corporate globalization around the WTO, the World Bank, and the IMF. These all seem to me important practices of resistance. But on their own, as such, they are not able to propose an alternative society. What they can do, of course, is make marginally better the society we have now—but ultimately they're critical, negative practices. And it's for that reason one has to think about the possibility of revolution and develop practices that would constitute revolution by transforming human nature so that people are able to rule themselves without masters.

TAYLOR: The word "revolution" is thrown around quite often by the Right, who boast about the Republican revolution that took place over the last four decades. Again, the Left doesn't speak like that. Any more thoughts on why this is the case?

HARDT: I think part of the reason it's so hard to talk about revolution, it's so hard for people to hear the word, is not so much just a practical question. It's a conceptual question. It's a question of what revolution means and what revolution could mean. There's one definition of revolution I find really useful: that every modern revolution has to be aimed at freedom. This is what Hannah Arendt proposes. That seems to me a first useful criterion or starting point. But actually, I think it's even better to think of revolution as being aimed at democracy, which is, let's say, continuous with or inclusive of freedom, but at the same time different from it.

But even then, when we say revolution is aimed at democracy, we're in a way stuck conceptually, I think, by many of the modern ways revolution is thought. It seems to me that there are two dominant or received (or almost clichéd) ways of thinking revolution and its relationship to democracy today and that they cancel each other out.

We're in a sense stuck between what we might call realist versus idealist notions of revolution. On the one hand, there's the realist notion of revolution—and this is in fact how most of the twentieth-century revolutions turned out—that merely involves the substitution of one ruling elite for another ruling elite. This new elite may be a much better one, one that makes great improvements for society and so forth, but nonetheless doesn't lead to any deep democratic change.

Opposed to that is another notion of revolution, the idealist notion, which I think is equally discredited from exactly the opposite point of view. It's the notion of revolution that thinks of revolution as just the removal of all those forms of authority—state power, the power of capital—that stop people from expressing their natural abilities to rule themselves. And this is in fact based on a notion of human nature that says not only are people fundamentally good, but they're also capable of ruling themselves, capable of cooperating. So the first one, the realist view, is discredited because, in fact, it's not democratic and doesn't lead to democracy. The second one is discredited, and properly so, by the realist perspective, which says, Look, people today aren't capable of cooperating, they aren't capable of ruling themselves, they aren't capable of democracy.

TAYLOR: So there's the romantic view and the cynical view, in a sense.

HARDT: Yeah, exactly. So in some ways this disqualification of revolution conceptually boils down to a question of human nature. On one side, it's based on the notion that human nature's good and that therefore we can have revolution by taking away the ruling structures, letting people express their natural beliefs. On the other side, it's based on the notion that human nature is essentially—I don't know if "evil" is the right word—but, in some sense, incapable, and so we need a ruling elite, some sort of vanguard or leadership to direct things.

In some ways, it all being about human nature actually is quite revealing. The question of whether human nature is good or evil has long been part of political philosophy. In fact, I'm sure everyone had some stupid evening in college smoking way too much and talking, where you end up with a discussion where you disagree with your friend because she thinks human nature's evil, you think human nature's good, and you can't get further. I mean, I think that kind of stupidity has affected a lot of the history of political philosophy and I think the relevant fact for politics—[*We hit a rock in the middle of the pond, which briefly interrupts the flow of thought.*] We're running aground. Shipwrecked! [*Laughs.*]

The relevant fact for politics is really that human nature's changeable, that humans can become different. Human nature isn't good or evil. Human nature is constituted—it's constituted by how we act. Human nature is in fact part of a history of habits and practices that are the result of past struggles, of past hierarchies, of past victories and defeats. And so this is, I think, actually the key to rethinking revolution: recognizing that revolution is not just about a transformation for democracy—revolution really requires a transformation of human nature so that people are capable of democracy. It's a process that not only destroys habits of servitude and develops capacities for self-rule but also inspires people's political imagination and expands their desires, which can press far beyond the present political situation.

At least for me, this is really Lenin's fundamental insight. When writing about revolution—I'm talking 1916, just on the eve of the October Revolution—he says, the people of Russia today aren't capable of democracy. They have masters at work; they need a master in politics.

But he adds to this. Lenin poses the project of revolution as a project to transform human nature so that people will be capable of democracy, and that's how he thinks of the process of communist transition. He doesn't expect the revolution to happen overnight. Conceptually, this seems to be a great advance on Lenin's part, and it is something that I think is extremely important. But at the same time, the Bolshevik experience and Lenin's solution to the problem is another moment in discrediting revolution.

I say discrediting revolution because Lenin's solution to the problem—the problem of how you transform human nature so that people will be capable of democracy—is a properly dialectical one. He thinks (and this is in fact in a large part what the Soviets enact) that there has to be a negation of democracy, call it "dictatorship of the proletariat," some sort of hegemonic state that would operate the transition, that would transform human nature, and then we would eventually arrive at the time when people are capable of democracy, when the state's no longer necessary, etc.

There are two obvious problems with this: The first one is—and I think it would be obvious to anyone—that whenever people start talking to you about transitions, they're always trying to trick you. These transitions never end. But the more general problem, the more important problem, is that you can't arrive at democratic capabilities, you can't transform human nature to be capable of democracy, by its opposite. It's precisely the dialectical nature that bothers me, that seems, to me, mistaken—dialectical, here, in a very simple precise sense, meaning that you negate democracy through dictatorship, in order to then negate that negation to finally arrive at democracy. Now, I think that this kind of dialectical formulation in this instance makes no sense. In other words, how do people learn democracy? How does human nature change to become capable of democracy? Not by its opposite. It can only be done in a sort of positive development; you can only learn democracy by doing it. And so that seems to me the only way to be able to rehabilitate the conception of revolution today.

[*At this moment we float under a beautiful stone bridge. The microphone, perched at the end of a six-foot pole, disturbs a flock of nesting pigeons. They take off dramatically as Hardt finishes his thought.*]

TAYLOR: Aren't you also proposing a period of transition as well, though?

HARDT: But this poses a different notion of transition. Going back to Lenin, transition is traditionally that period where we're not yet ready for democracy, where we have to suffer through a kind of purgatory in order to arrive at the paradise when people are capable of democracy and our utopia can be realized. What I'm posing is a different notion of transition, one that refuses that dialectic between purgatory and paradise. The revolutionary process would focus on the transformation of human nature for a truly democratic society but wouldn't postpone that end towards the future. It would be enacting that end in its very process. So imagine a situation like the Paris Commune, or even the ward system proposed by Thomas Jefferson. In those contexts people are transformed by practicing autonomy and participating in government. This is not the end of the revolutionary transition but instead its primary means.

To put it another way, what I've been calling Lenin's notion of transition is often cast in terms of a division between means and ends. What I'm saying is that the separation between means and ends is what dooms the process of transition. At least in this case, the means can't be separated from the ends. There can't be that deferral of utopia towards some future moment because the means themselves have to be democratic. So this also involves a notion of transition, maybe a notion of permanent transition, but it's a transition that isn't purgatory deferring our ends; rather, it's instigating utopia everyday.

Now, I'm not saying it's easy—in fact, such a conceptual solution only poses further practical problems. What are democratic means that can transform human nature to make people capable of democracy? How can people be trained to be capable of cooperating with each other and ruling themselves collectively? These seem to me enormously difficult practical questions. But at least conceptually, things seem clearer to me.

TAYLOR: I want to pause on two words: democracy and politics. Let's take democracy first. To some, we already live in a democracy, so they may wonder why the hell we're going on like this. Others would contrast direct or participatory democracy with the current, rather impoverished democratic arrangement. Could we clarify our terms for a moment?

HARDT: Sure. Democracy is one of those concepts that seems to have been almost completely corrupted today. In some cases, it's used simply to mean periodic elections with a limited choice of rulers. In other cases, when one thinks especially of international affairs, it often means following the will of the United States—exactly the opposite of democracy!

But then, the concept of democracy itself is not that difficult. Democracy means and democracy has meant throughout the modern era—at least for the last four or five hundred years—the rule of all by all. It means everybody involved in collective self-rule. Of course, there need to be mechanisms for instituting this, and that's what's difficult. But conceptually it's not difficult.

I think that democracy is one of those concepts that have to be struggled over. Part of the political process is struggling over such concepts. In fact, I find myself often confronted by the fact that terms that are important to me—democracy is certainly one of them, communism would be another—have a popular understanding, not just in the press but even among colleagues on the Left, that's the complete opposite of what I think they mean. Like communism, which in common usage means state control—the opposite of what I think it means. Or democracy, as we've just seen. So you're faced with a choice, which is either you invent a new concept and say, OK, let's let democracy mean what Bush says it means, or freedom mean what Bush says it means, and so let's invent some other term for it, or you struggle over the concept.

In fact, one of the things I like so much about reading U.S. political history is that the so-called Founding Fathers didn't call just anything democracy; they knew what they were proposing wasn't democracy. They were guarding against democracy and were clear about that. People like Madison, who has many great attributes, recognized the representative nature of the government as a block against democracy. They thought it was important to keep a gap to ensure the people don't rule because they're not prepared to rule. We need an elite to rule and what the constitution does is create that elite. At least they're honest about it. What's so irritating today is the dishonesty that goes around with the concept of democracy. It's a kind of knowing dishonesty because, like I say, you don't have to be some great scholar to figure out what democracy means.

TAYLOR: OK, how about politics?

HARDT: Politics, in many respects, is conventionally conceived as what I would call the administration of people, like constructing structures that will administer and thereby control how people act in society, how society is organized. But there is a second conception of politics that in ways is posed against this, that focuses on the subjects and their freedom. In other words, politics in this second conception is conceived as the form in which we express ourselves. Politics in this sense is speaking in the presence of others, so that we think of the subjects already as foundational—who we are—and that we can then construct our society. I'm thinking here of a third conception, which is slightly different in that who we are isn't something fixed and primary. Who we are is something that is changing. Then, in this sense, politics is not the administration of society, and it is not the free expression of subjects in a public space; it is, rather, a project to transform human nature, to enter the process of this constant transformation of who we are. Politics is about the production of subjectivity.

Now, once you say "transform human nature and produce subjectivity," there's something vertiginous about that. I think this vertigo is something that we have to confront. What humans are and what we're capable of is something that changes. And it seems to me that how we enter into and direct that transformation is the primary object of politics.

There is a common criticism of postmodernist relativism that might spring to people's minds here that says, "Oh, so you think that we can just wake up tomorrow and be completely different." I'm not saying that at all, which is why I think it's useful to think about this in terms of habits. There are certain habits of thought, certain habits of practice, which have a consistency and even an inertia. We can't be transformed overnight. It's a much more glacial process. But nonetheless, I think that this is what politics should aim at and, in fact, what already happens through politics.

TAYLOR: Let's go back to Lenin's insight, that people are used to having masters at work; they need masters in politics.

HARDT: I think that's true. It's a matter of habit, and that's why people require training in democracy. I'm not saying people don't have those capacities in their nature. What's in their nature doesn't make any sense or difference to me. What's true and important is that democracy is what people are trained to do—people aren't trained to rule themselves, and people aren't trained to cooperate collectively with each other.

So it seems to me the most pressing question about democracy and revolution is: What are the mechanisms for such training? "Training" is obviously a difficult term here because training implies there's some trainer who's going to set you on a regimen and teach you how to do it, but by the terms we've talked about, it would have to be a kind of self-training. Or imagine it like the kind of training that you do to run a marathon. It's not that it even has to be something mysterious, it's only that one can't expect to do it immediately. You just can't go out and run a marathon one day; you've got to train for it. It takes a while. You're training, changing the body. And I think we have to think the same way politically on a larger scale.

So when Lenin's talking about what people are capable of, he's not talking in absolute terms like "Russian peasants are stupid" or something like that. It's that they have certain habits and those habits were learned. So the question is, what are the social mechanisms or social structures that might allow people to learn how to act democratically? What are the economic structures?

TAYLOR: It's time for the inevitable questions. What *are* the social structures that can lead to a more democratic society? How do we begin this revolutionary process?

HARDT: When someone says, "OK, Mike, you want revolution, so how do we do it?", it's not only that I'm not smart enough (I'm certainly not smart enough), it's also that it's much more useful to look at the examples that already exist.

For instance, think about the Bolivarian Revolution in Venezuela today. Given this notion of revolution I'm proposing, how would we evaluate it? Because there are many ways in which, especially from the perspective of the U.S. media or the opposition media in Venezuela, there is a distinctly authoritarian or centralized element at work there. You know, the idea that Chávez and the government and now the party are transforming Venezuelan society but not doing it through democratic means. One facet of what's going on in Venezuela does have to do with the state and Chávez himself, but there's another facet that's going on as well, which is that the Bolivarian Revolution consists of new structures of community-controlled and autonomous neighborhood, citywide, and rural networks of self-rule. So it's a mixed situation.

What I'm trying to propose are the terms we would use to evaluate and even maybe to guide such a revolutionary process. Of course, it's also not quite as divided as I was just saying because a lot of what's done through the state authority of the Chávez government provides the necessary foundations for people to act democratically. In other words, without the so-called *misiones* that provide health care, education, and other certain basic needs, none of this discussion about self-rule, democracy, and cooperative networks makes sense. So what interests me about Chávez is not him as a central authority, the charismatic leader, but rather the way that his government fosters or makes possible the practicing of democracy. In all the Leftist governments in Latin America today—Bolivia and Ecuador might be even better examples than Venezuela—the dynamic at stake here is the relationship between government and social movements, the extent to which a leftist government can open space for, and empower, the social movements that brought them to power.

TAYLOR: I want to dig deeper into this concept of training. You said it didn't have to be very mysterious. So is it in fact small everyday activities? Or does it require something more substantial, like the backing of a larger social movement?

HARDT: When I say training in democracy, you may think that some-times it doesn't involve very much. Maybe it can be very humble: people participating in local government decisions, participating in decisions about not only their local government but their conditions of work, joining the school PTA, etc. And that's true and that's im-portant, but one has to realize also that there's a certain amount of participation that can be allowed within the current system, and then there are obstacles.

For this reason I like very much this notion of exodus, taken from the biblical process of exodus, which is that, you know, at a certain point the pharaoh won't just let you leave. It's not like you can just abandon the kinds of hierarchy and forms of authority we have today—they don't let you go peacefully. There's a certain point in which you've got to fight in order to free yourself from slavery. And so exodus is not just a kind of line of flight, it's an often armed and vi-olent form of freeing oneself from these mechanisms.

So what do I mean exactly by that? Taking the example of work, there're some ways in which capitalist work relations are extremely unfree and hierarchical. There are limits. Someone will say, "I have a great job because I can make my own hours, I can work from home," and that's true but to a limit. There's a limit because the fact is you have a boss, even if sometimes you're made your own boss, which can be even worse. Capital requires a boss. It also requires that someone else profit off what you do, which is another internal element of authority within the structure itself. I'm not saying capitalism is slavery, al-though it has certain elements of it and there are specific populations for whom that's a better analogy. What I'm saying is simply that there are limitations to the possibilities of freedom within it and there are limitations to the development of democratic relations within it. And it's those limits, then, that a process of revolution has to confront.

TAYLOR: Confronting the limits of democratic possibility—let's talk about that. I'm thinking about Žižek's work here, which in many

ways yours contradicts. He would agree, though, that there's a necessarily violent element to revolution, even though it's hard for some of
us to accept.

HARDT: Whenever you talk about revolution someone will say to
you, "Oh, does revolution have to be violent?" It's an annoying question. But it's true; revolution does have to be violent precisely because the pharaoh won't let you go. If the pharaoh would let you go,
revolution wouldn't have to be violent. If capital would let us go, no
problem. But the thing is, at a certain point there is a moment of conflict, and it's in this way that I would say revolutionary struggles, the
violence of them, is always a defensive violence. It's in the same way
that Israelites Aaron and Moses are conducting a defensive battle;
they're organizing a defensive battle against the pharaoh's armies.
And so that's why I think revolution as exodus, in this way, has a violent element.

TAYLOR: Let's talk more about work before we move on. I saw you
give a talk a few years ago in which you focused on immaterial production and affective labor, and that's something you write a lot
about. It seems to me it could be relevant to our discussion.

HARDT: I agree. It seems one major site we have to talk about is work,
because work dominates most of our lives and is the site of the greatest unfreedom we experience. But at the same time, I think that work
can also be on the side of learning new capacities.

So when we talk about where a training in democracy may take
place or what tools are already available for such a training in democracy, it seems to be useful to consider these questions in terms of our
work life. Already in the factory—even though I think that the era of
the dominance of factory production is obviously ending—you can
recognize the great capacities of workers. I mean, there are of course
great restrictions, but there also is great learning, great compassion,

the great pride of worker's movements, etc. Union agitation has always been about the knowledge of the workers. They know how to make everything; they are the ones who make society. So it seems to me that what we would have to do today is think about how work has changed and ask what the dominant forms of work and the dominant capacities that people learn from work are.

It's in this regard that Toni [Negri], my co-author, and I always turn to look at the transformations of labor. The classical term for this is "the composition of the working class." So what we mean by this is—well, here's our hypothesis. Our hypothesis is that just as there was a dominance of industrial production over the economy for the last 150 years, say from the time of Marx, today there is emerging a new dominance of what we call "immaterial production," or better called "biopolitical production." And this dominance may not be in quantitative terms. When Marx was writing, it's not like most of the people were in the factories. In fact, most of the people were in the fields. Most people today are probably still in the fields. So it's not a quantitative thing, it's a qualitative thing. The point is the qualities of industry were imposed over other forms of production and over society itself. We argue that today industry no longer has that role, but rather immaterial production—meaning the production of things that have largely immaterial components, like the production of ideas, the production of images, the production of communication, the production of affects—have become, together, the dominant form of production, dominant in the sense that the quality of this production is progressively becoming the norm.

So think about the qualities of these kinds of productions when people work to produce affects, for example. One of the standard examples is flight attendants. Of course they produce material things, they do material things, tasks like passing out pillows, going through safety procedures. But a lot of the work they do is affective. They produce affects in the sense of being there, being nice to people, calming people down. I think the same is true of some health care workers.

You can see it with fast-food workers—"service with a smile." These are all producers of affects, the production of relationships. Now, this involves some horrible kinds of exploitation and imposes some horrible limits on our abilities to cooperate and rule ourselves collectively. Yet still, in some ways, it's arming people with the capacity to create social relationships.

OK, you can easily mock my perspective and say, "Oh, someone working in a call center in Delhi, they are doing affective labor, they are the new revolutionaries" or something. But the point is the capacities of affective labor and immaterial production involve the direct production of social relations, and that is an enormously powerful ability. When you think about an old industrial union, the pride of the worker in a factory—the auto-factory worker who knows how to make every part of the automobile, the engineers only know a little bit, and the owner knows nothing—it's a great pride in those productive capacities. If we try to translate that to the current situation, what happens? Now what about these people who are involved in affective production and immaterial production, in the production of culture, in the production of images, etc.? What they are becoming expert in is producing social relations. Now, to come back to close the long circle: That, I think, is the terrain on which the training in democracy can happen—the training and the collective ability to produce social relationships.

Again, of course the way it happens now isn't democratic. Marx's notion of alienation never made much sense to me when I was thinking of it in classic terms, but here it does: something intimate is made external to you, into something you have to sell for a wage. When you think of this affective labor in flight attendants, to go back to that example, something we imagine as so important and intimate—the ability to be friendly, to love, to be kind, etc.—is being commanded of them. They have to service people who don't deserve it while under the command of the boss. I think it's the fact of things not being democratic that makes some of these jobs so horrible.

TAYLOR: But how does this imply revolution or even an anticapitalist stance?

HARDT: Thinking about work in this way, particularly the capacities that one learns and the capacities that are frustrated and thwarted at work, does imply the notion of revolution I am talking about—revolution as the transformation of human nature to make us capable of democracy. And it is an anticapitalist project, but in a very specific way. Because it's not just a refusal of all capitalist society and capitalist production has created: I won't go see their movies, I won't participate in their world, I'm going to remove myself. No, it's not that. It is rather a subversion from within. So what do I mean? As I said, there are certain elements within capitalist social relations and work relations that require circuits of cooperation. It's transforming the capacities and abilities we already have, in a way liberating those elements within capitalist labor, within capitalist production, within capitalist society, from the command that capital that always operates on them.

Already starting in the factory, with the birth of industrial production, there is a requirement of a certain kind of cooperation among workers in the plant, among workers around the machines, which is what many of the communist revolutions in the past have been based on. The Bolshevik ideal is in part based around that—that the cooperation of the factory, the structure of organization of workers in the factory, will provide the model for the revolutionary vanguard. But with the new, increasingly dominant forms of production that are outside the factory, cooperation is required more and more. Today what we have to think about is a much more generalized, more horizontal network of the kind of cooperation and communication that is implied and required by capitalist production, the kind of cooperation and communication that are both required but also thwarted by capital. I think this can serve us as the basis for instituting the training in democracy that we are just talking about, perhaps providing a springboard or a standpoint for imagining an anticapitalist or postcapitalist alternative.

TAYLOR: So where do intellectuals, folks who are involved in the immaterial production of ideas, fit into all of this? Are you all supposed to provide the road map to this new revolutionary world?

HARDT: I don't really have an answer, but an anecdote comes to mind. Once, when I was giving a lecture in Columbia, at the national university there, I was talking about these topics: my co-authored books *Empire* and *Multitude*, the concept of revolution, etc. And for the first question, someone got up and said, "You are the great North American theorist. Please tell us what to do." And, you know me, I was uncomfortable, I was stuttering, and I said, "Don't ask me what to do. Look at the examples around the world." For the second question, someone got up and said, "Who do you think you are—the North American theorist coming here telling us what to do?" And I felt like, shit, I really walked into that one. But I mean, it's true. I certainly agree with the second questioner.

First of all, philosophers shouldn't pretend that their theories will somehow solve things and be put into active practice. Secondly, people shouldn't ask them such questions. In general, my usual response for these things is, don't ask what is to be done. Don't even try to answer that question. Instead, ask what are people already doing and then look at the kind of theorizing that's going on collectively in the movements.

I grew up intellectually and politically with a prejudice against theorists and philosophers, against the old-fashioned French model of the master of thought, you know, who always has disciples and then even has political movements that follow him—always *him*. I'm much more on the side of thinking that actual innovations in thought actually happen collectively, not as a result of lone philosophers. Sometimes philosophers manage to condense and represent what people are doing. So when people ask me, journalists ask me, about antiglobalization movements, for example—"How does it feel to have all these people doing and following what you said?" I say, "Nobody's following me. I'm following them."

Look at those turtles over there. [*We float by a rock covered in turtles sunning themselves. We're all struck by how picturesque and bucolic the scene is.*] I think we need to say something about the location.

TAYLOR: About the fact we're in a boat. Yes, I suppose it may seem a bit strange, given our topic of conversation.

HARDT: Yeah. I mean, there's something that feels immediately quite inappropriate about talking about revolution in what would be a sort of almost aristocratic—I mean not even bourgeois, but aristocratic— location. You know, rowing on a beautiful pond in a park with the rich of New York all around. It seems like almost an absurdity.

TAYLOR: Well, where would we pick that would be the revolutionary spot? Over the last few months we discussed and decided against some seemingly more appropriate locations, like along the wall that marks the border between Mexico and the United States, or around abandoned factories in North Carolina.

HARDT: The problem is, any revolutionary spot would be cliché already.

TAYLOR: Exactly. And that's why I finally decided we should just film here, as it was convenient for both of us and Central Park is a place you said you enjoyed visiting when you used to live in New York. But you're right, the division between what we're talking about and the environment is a little incongruous. But maybe you can say something about that?

HARDT: It is difficult to think of a location that would represent revolution. . . . In fact, in some ways, it seems like we're in the worst location, in the sense that we're in the middle of all of the wealth and power that prevents the type of revolution we're discussing.

So here the cliché would be that you either choose as a visual site a scene of poverty or a scene of labor and production because then you would show the ones who would benefit from it and even the subjects, the actors, that would conduct it. But it strikes me in another way that it might be appropriate to work against such a conception of revolution as a loss and as deprivation. In other words, I think another reason the notion of revolution has been discredited is its association with misery, as if revolution would involve giving up all of the pleasures that everyone enjoys. I think I would much rather frame notions of revolution within the context of wanting everything for everyone so that it does have to do with pleasure and the realizations of desires. It's not that revolution would mean everyone in the world suffers equally. On the contrary, I think that revolution would have to be a transformation through which we can all find pleasure in the world and in each other. So I suppose being here is at least useful for countering the notion of revolution as poverty and helps us to think about the pleasures in the world and the greater pleasures that we could have in a different world.

So maybe, in a perverse way, it's an appropriate location for doing this. It's such an idyllic and seemingly anti- or even counterrevolutionary location, one associated with old wealth and the stability of power, the leisure activities of the rich. Maybe, in a strange way, it will help us work through some of these issues like who can think revolution, who wants revolution, where we can think revolution, and who would benefit. Maybe this seemingly strange location can help us cast away what seem to me destructive limitations on how we think about this.

TAYLOR: It seems like we're always trying to posit an agent of revolutionary change out there: Third World peasants, workers, the poor, people of color, even students. One thing this does is let us off the hook. It's always another social group's responsibility to create social change, not ours.

HARDT: You're right. I think that there's a relatively widespread contemporary notion that revolution can only be made by the poorest and the most excluded in the world. In some ways, I think this is a perfectly justified compensation for previous notions that claimed either that only white male factory workers could make revolution, or, more generally, that only Europeans or only the world elite can actually shape history and advance society, etc. But I think now we have a kind of symmetrical difficulty in thinking revolution: only the most excluded, only the most poor, can make revolution.

It's in this regard that I, perhaps naively, have this kind of equal-opportunity theory of revolution. It's in all of our interests, it's all of our responsibility, to think about how to transform the world and make it more democratic.

Again, it makes little sense to me to say, "Revolution can't be made in the United States" or "Revolution can't be made in Europe" because everyone's too comfortable, because they have too much to lose. They too have an enormous amount to gain. When we say a better world is possible, we don't just mean a better world for those who are worst off today. We mean a better world for all of us.

SLAVOJ ŽIŽEK

Ecology

What better place to film a conversation about ecology than a garbage dump? The choice was particularly self-evident as I had spent some time the previous summer documenting the lives of "pickers" who lived and worked at a massive toxic landfill in Tijuana, Mexico; I wanted a similarly apocalyptic atmosphere for this scene. Slavoj Žižek was in London the dates we chose to shoot, so some intrepid local friends helped me find a trash depot willing to put up with a six-person crew plus a subject (we were all decked out in mandatory safety gear— orange vests and green hard hats). A pit stop for detritus before it moves on to a final resting place in the countryside, the place was bustling with activity. A dozen relatively tidy recycling stations provided the depot's public face. Inside we found mounds of used building materials, forlorn household appliances, and assorted junk, as well as enormous moun- tains of fetid refuse. As an army of trucks and tractors moved the piles around with no discernable logic, some strange spray filtered down on us, a futile attempt to mitigate the stench. Meanwhile, it was a beautiful

day: blue skies, birds singing. The contrast couldn't have been more
appropriate.

ASTRA TAYLOR: OK, we should get started. [*Ironically*] Act natural!

SLAVOJ ŽIŽEK: Don't tell this to me, because I am naturally unnatural.

TAYLOR: That's why I said it—to harass you.

ŽIŽEK: Yeah, yeah. Like, "Be spontaneous." This is how you ruin people, the same as in sex. If a man has trouble with impotency, the worst
thing a woman can tell you is "Just relax, be spontaneous." That ruins
you completely. Because then that is the absolute order: "Do it, you
have no excuse."

TAYLOR: So, act unnatural, then! Does that help? [*Laughs.*] I was surprised when you wrote to me suggesting we focus on the theme of
trash and the environment. Why this topic?

ŽIŽEK: We are on? OK. I think ecology, the way we approach ecological problematics is maybe the crucial field of ideology today, and I
use ideology in the traditional sense of an illusory, wrong way of
thinking and perceiving reality. Why? Ideology is not simply dream-
ing about false ideas and so on; ideology addresses very real problems, but it mystifies them, often almost imperceptibly.

    This is why for me, to use my big example, tolerance is one of
the main ideological notions today. Of course the problem is real,
there is intolerance: racism, sexism, people are raped, killed. But
what is the problem? Of course there is racism, but why do we
today automatically translate or perceive racism in the terms of intolerance and tolerance? The notion of tolerance, I claim, is ideology
today. Why? Because it names real problems—sexual, racial, religious intolerance—but it mystifies them precisely by perceiving

them as problems of tolerance. For Martin Luther King, racism was not a problem of tolerance. He does not ask the whites to tolerate the blacks. That would be ridiculous. For him racism was a problem of equality, economic justice, legal rights, and so on. Today we perceive racism as a problem of tolerance, which means we perceive it as a problem of cultural differences, cultural intolerance, which is really a mystification. The whole field of economy, public space, and so on disappears.

I claim that in our postpolitical era, where economy is a matter for experts, the only struggles that remain are cultural struggles. All conflicts have to be translated into cultural conflicts. Thus racism is not an effect of exploitation, but is an effect of our intolerance of other cultures, and so on. So you see how the fight for tolerance—of course it's a good cause, I am not for intolerance—involves a mystification in how we describe it.

The same thing goes for ecology. Of course ecology is the question today, where the fate of humanity literally will be decided. We may all disappear. But the way ecology is formulated, the way problems are perceived, always—as a rule, I claim—involves mystification. Mystification starts at the very base, with the notion of nature as some kind of harmonious balance, which is then disturbed and derailed through human hubris, through excessive human desire to exploit nature, to dominate nature, and so on, and so on.

TAYLOR: Let's spend a bit more time on ideology and how it colors real problems. Can you give another example of how ecology has become ideologically invested?

ŽIŽEK: So ecology is the problem today, but the reason we are not able to approach this problem properly is because ecology is the site for ideological investment. First, one of the elementary ideological mechanisms is what I call the temptation of meaning. When something horrible happens, our spontaneous tendency is to search for meaning, it must have a meaning. Like AIDS: it was a trauma, and conservatives came and said it is a punishment for our sinful ways of life, and so on and so on. Even if we interpret a catastrophe as a punishment, it makes it easier in a way. It is not some terrifying blind force; it has a meaning. It is better when you are in the middle of a catastrophe to feel that God punished you than to feel that it just happened. If God punished you, it's still a universe of meaning. I think that is when ecology as ideology enters. The field of ecology is massively invested.

It's common to read ecology as a punishment for human hubris, excessive development. Like we wanted to dominate nature, we wanted to become masters of the universe, we forgot that we are just modest humans on the earth, and nature, God, whoever, a higher agency, is punishing us. That is why I claim that ecology will slowly turn into the new opium of the masses—the way, you know, Marx defined religion. In what sense? Namely, what we expect from religion is this kind of an unquestionable authority: it's God's word, so it just is; you don't debate it. The function of religion is to appear as an agency of ultimate authority. If you can justify a measure, a prohibition, an injunction as part of a divine commandment, there is no debate. I think today, more and more, ecology is starting to function as the ultimate agency of control.

This brings us to another paradox: the conservative function of ecology. Today, I claim, ecology is taking over more and more the role of a conservative ideology. Whenever there is a new scientific breakthrough, cryogenic development, whatever, it is as if the voice that warns us not to trespass or violate a certain invisible limit—like "Don't do that, it would be too much"—that voice is today more and more the voice of ecology. Like don't mess with DNA, don't mess with nature, don't do it. This basic, conservative, archideological mistrust of change, this is, today, ecology.

Ecologists, on one hand, try to convince us that if humanity is to survive, we have to change. But at the same time whenever there is a new breakthrough in the sciences, in technologies and so on, ecologists begin to worry. The ecologists' idea is "Let's not disturb the existing balance, whatever we might do; there are unknown risks and we might lose the balance." It's really the implicit premise of ecology that the existing world is the best possible world, in the sense that it is a balanced world undisturbed by human hubris. So why do I find this problematic? Because I think that this notion of nature, nature as a harmonious, organic, balanced, reproducing, almost living organism, which is then disturbed, perturbed, derailed through human hubris, technological exploitation, and so on, is, I think, a secular version of the religious story with a fall. The answer should be not that there is no fall, that we are part of nature, but on the contrary that *there is no nature*.

A lesson we should all learn from good Darwinists like Stephen Jay Gould is that nature is not a balanced totality, which then we humans disturb. Nature is a series of unimaginable catastrophes. We profit from them. What is our main source of energy today? Oil. Are we aware what oil is? Oil reserves under the earth are material remains of unimaginable catastrophes. We all know that oil is composed of remains of animal life, plants, and so on. Can you imagine what kind of unthinkable catastrophes had to occur on earth? So that's good to remember, that nature is crazy in itself. Nature is not this harmonious natural rhythm; nature is fundamentally imbalanced. So that is the first myth to dispel. So there is no nature as a norm of self-balance, of self-reproduction, to which we should return.

[*A large truck drives up and dumps a huge load of garbage. A tractor comes up from behind and begins to shovel the trash on top of an enormous heap, compacting the pile, and then adding more to it. We pause due to the noise.*]

Look at that—that suitcase. Now it's covered. The blue one. It looks quite nice. They must find good stuff here. I wonder, what do they do with it?

TAYLOR: They take it home and sell it. I am worried that with all the tractors moving everything around that the background will keep changing and none of our shots will match. The garbage keeps changing places.

ŽIŽEK: Ah, but you see, that would have been true Hollywood style— and what does it matter? It's a great film you are making—that you would hire like two hundred people to exactly reconstruct the same piles of garbage comparing it with photos.

TAYLOR: Next time that's what I'll do.

ŽIŽEK: Yes, next time. That would be true cinema-making. But you should follow Sam Goldwyn, the greatest—you know that this is one of his most famous Goldwynisms. In one of these recession poor-boys/hooligans-turning-good-Christians movies, he reproached a director, saying that the set looked too dirty. The director told him it was supposed to be a slum, and Goldwyn said the studio spent so much money on the slum it should look clean!

TAYLOR: Well, I only paid a few hundred dollars to film here. Maybe that's why it's so dirty—and loud. OK, they've stopped for a minute. Let's go back to ideology and ecology. I think you were going to explain another ecological myth.

[*We begin walking again, now up a ramp toward the main section of the depot.*]

ŽIŽEK: That brings us to the second popular ecological myth: the idea that we Western people, in our artificial technological environment, are alienated from our immediate natural environments, that we should not forget that we humans are part of the environment, the living earth. We should not forget that we are not abstract individual theorists, engineers who just exploit nature, but we are part of nature and nature is our unfathomable, impenetrable background. I think that, precisely, is the greatest danger. Why? Let me make a simple mental experiment. Think about a certain obvious paradox. We all know what danger we all are in: global warming, the threat of other ecological catastrophes, so on and so on. Why don't we do anything about it? It is a nice example of what in psychoanalysis we call disavowal. The logic is that of "I know very well, but, nonetheless, I do not believe it. I act as if I don't know."

[*At this moment the crew turns into the depot's central space, where everything that cannot be recycled ends up. The air is almost unbearably rank and we hear rats scurrying in the piles.*]

For example, precisely in the case of ecology, I know very well there will be global warming, that everything will explode, will be destroyed. But after reading treatises on this, what do I do? I step out and I see not the things I see behind me now [*gesturing at the steaming mountain of refuse behind him*], that's a nice sight for me, but I see nice sights, birds singing. Even if I know rationally that it is all in danger, I do not believe that it can be destroyed. That is the horror of visiting sites of catastrophes like Chernobyl. In a way we are not evolutionarily equipped, not wired, to be able to imagine something like that. It is, in a way, unimaginable.

So I think what we should do to confront properly the threat of ecological catastrophe is not this New Age stuff of breaking through from this technologically manipulative mood to find our roots in nature, but, on the contrary, to cut off even more our roots in nature. I claim that it is our roots in our natural environment that prevent us from taking seriously things that we already know: that all this normal life we see around us can disappear. We can imagine it, but we do not really believe it—I mean we don't effectively act upon it.

So again my paradoxical formula is: ecology is the greatest threat, but to confront it properly, we need to get rid of the very notion of nature, meaning nature in its ideological investment, nature as some kind of a normative model of balance and harmonious development. We should become more artificial.

TAYLOR: To be fair, many ecologists have long advocated "appropriate technologies," leading innovation in areas like wind and solar energy. However, it strikes me that the deep ecologists you are talking about, the antitechnologists, wouldn't even know global warming was a threat if it wasn't for science.

ŽIŽEK: Yes, let's not forget that even those who fight scientific exploitation of nature have to rely on science. For example, the ozone hole: no matter how much you look up, you see no hole there. The ozone hole is a metaphor for a precise scientific notion. Maybe science is, up to a point, the cause, the origin, of trouble, but let's not forget that science and technology are also our only true solutions and the proof of the reality of these problems.

TAYLOR: I want to go back to something you said a few moments ago. What do you mean we should become more artificial? How?

ŽIŽEK: When we are standing where I am standing now, with a lot of trash behind me, this is where we should start feeling at home. I think in our daily attitude—not only with trash like this but with more literal trash like excrement—in our daily perception, the reality is that this disappears from our world. When you go to the toilet, shit disappears. You flush it, and while, of course, rationally you know that it is there in canalization, at a certain level of your most elementary experience it disappears from your world. The same happens with trash. But the problem is that trash doesn't disappear. Coming to terms with trash is our problem today. The special irony is that one of the leading ideologies today is that we are moving from material to immaterial production, that today the main productive work is intellectual work, programming, servicing people, and so on and so on. But at the same time, ecological problems and problems with disposing trash mean that there is more material production going than ever.

TAYLOR: Well, what should we do with it all? How would becoming artificial help?

ŽIŽEK: There is more and more of this trash, and I think maybe even the greatest challenge is to discover trash as an aesthetic object. What do I mean by this? I am not trying to have any of these pseudo-avant-garde, masochistic ideas of "shit is art" or whatever, but something much more elementary. Whenever we are engaged with the world we use objects. It is, for me, always a mysterious moment when you see an object that originally was a functional object, part of our system of needs, as no longer of any use and changed into trash. At that point you should accept it. Which is why, for me, the most metaphysical experience that I can imagine in my dreams is to visit the Mojave Desert in the United States where there is the big cemetery of planes. So you have a couple of hundred planes doing nothing over there—and there is something so shocking in all those objects that have become, all of a sudden, trash, useless. I think that a true ecologist should not admire pure nature, trees and so on, which are there before we use them and that can still be part of our technological exploitative universe. The true spiritual change is to develop, if you want, a kind of emotional attachment to, or to find meaning in, useless objects.

Here we should follow Romantics, I claim. I am against Romanticism as such, but something great in Romanticism is that Romantics discovered ruins, remainders, useless objects as potentially aesthetic objects. In Romanticism they were building houses so that they already looked like ruins. I think there is something deep about this. To come to terms with life around you would mean, precisely, to step out of this eternal active engagement and to accept objects in their uselessness. And this doesn't mean escaping technology. It means something else, using technology in different ways.

What do I mean by this? The conservative critics of modernity claim we should not get too involved with technology. Instead we should rediscover simple pleasures of walking in the forest, sitting at a table, just drinking water, whatever, that is still part of a technological universe for me. The really subversive thing is something that was going on some ten years ago and is still going on: using technology to produce objects that are functional but ridiculous on account of their very excessive functionality. It is a whole movement in Japan to build objects that meet two conditions. First, they must be feasible and really function but be so ridiculous as to be commercially unviable. For example, glasses with windshield wipers so you can walk in the rain, or an inverted umbrella so that you walk in the rain and the water is collected so you can drink fresh water, or butter in lipstick tubes so that you can apply butter just like that—this ridiculous use of technology, which still is technological but kind of suspends the seriousness.

TAYLOR: What about more serious technological issues like genetic engineering, for example, that blur the distinctions between natural and the artificial? How does this relate to the aesthetic turn you're advocating?

ŽIŽEK: Something concerning our ecological sensibilities is happening today with our most elementary experience of life. Once, with DNA analysis, one can isolate the basic genetic structure of life, then something in a way terrifying happens. There is no longer a distinction between real life and artificial life. There are now already projects to develop artificial life, which is life where you don't just change the biogenetic structure of an organism but you create it, as if it were, from a zero level. But what is the problem? The problem is that once you can do it artificially, then natural life itself is perceived in the same way, just as a different formula of life. So in a way, nature is no longer nature. Nature loses its organic impenetrability. You know, it's the same as with your sense of freedom. If you can regulate your moods with pills or if you can enhance your intelligence with pills, you cannot say, "OK, now I am artificially manipulating my intelligence, but otherwise I am natural and spontaneous." If you can change your mood with certain pills, chemicals, and so on, this means that even when you don't use pills, your moods already depend on chemicals in your body. You know this psychological spontaneity is lost, and the same happens with life. That's, I think, extremely difficult for us to accept, that once life becomes something that you can manipulate, re-create technologically, it's not only that we have on one hand natural organisms and then on the other artificial organisms, but that nature itself is perceived as just another artificial program. You can analyze it, re-create it, and so on.

Nature loses its natural character and that's difficult to accept, but I think it's crucial to accept it. In other words, according to my formula, the new type of humanity that we need is not the one rediscovering the spirituality of nature, rediscovering this mysterious, deep, unfathomable impenetrability of nature, but, on the contrary, nature should disappear as nature, as the mysterious dark background. We should develop, I think, a much more terrifying new abstract materialism, a kind of mathematical universe where there is nothing, there are just formulas, technical forms and so on, and the difficult thing is to find poetry, spirituality, in this dimension.

Gilbert Keith Chesterton, my favorite English Catholic theologist, had a wonderful idea once when he observed that in old love poetry we refer to the sunset or the moon and we say, "I will kiss you at sunset." Now that we know that the sun doesn't really go down, it's just that the earth moves around the sun, the true poetry would have to be something that does not return from astronomy to our naive perception of sunset but that discovers the poetic dimension of this scientific truth. For example, imagine a lover telling his beloved not "I meet you at sunset" but "I meet you at one quarter of the turn of the earth." The point is to rediscover a poetry in all this, in abstract technology, in mathematics, in trash and so on.

Since we are here in London, this is why one of my favorite

British writers is Ruth Rendell, the detective writer. I think this is her big achievement, rediscovering things almost like this. That is to say, she rediscovered those famous decaying poor London suburbs, the back of the house—the front of the house may even still look nice—but in the back you find those half-abandoned gardens with old bathtubs and decaying old fridges, desks and so on. To rediscover a poetic dimension to this sort of scene is, I think, the proper reaction to ecology. To rediscover the aesthetic dimension of life, not in the sense of let's get rid of the trash, let's re-create the beautiful universe, but let's re-create, if not beauty, then an aesthetic dimension in things like this, in trash itself.

That's the true love of the world. Because what is love? Love is not idealization. Every true lover knows that if you really love a woman or a man, you don't idealize him or her. Love means that you accept a person with all the failures, stupidities, ugly points, and, nonetheless, the person is absolute for you, everything that makes life worth living. You see perfection in imperfection itself, and that's how we should learn to love the world. The true ecologist loves all this. He's not afraid to look at this with friendliness. A true ecologist, I think, is horrified at perfect gardens, clean surroundings, and so on. That's what he fears, that's the nightmare for him.

The true ecologist must also accept that nature is the ultimate human myth, that we humans, when we perceive ourselves as beyond nature, exploiting nature and so on, we also, through this opposition, create a certain image of nature. And that idealized image of nature is the ultimate obstacle to ecology. So, again, this is why my formula is ecology without nature. The first duty is to drop this heavily ideologically mythological, invested notion of nature.

TAYLOR: Let's go back to ideology at a really basic level. It seems to me someone could wonder how ecological issues could be ideological. Isn't it just a straightforward matter of scientific fact? We're releasing carbon dioxide into the atmosphere and the climate is changing—

end of argument. Though I guess it would be hard to believe that given certain political realities. But you get what I'm saying.

žižek: Yes, it may appear that ecology has nothing to do with ideology. It's not about politics or passion, how just a society should be and so on. It's simply about a cruel reality, that we are polluting the environment, that it may kill us all. But the problem is it is always this way with ideology. Ideology is always about real problems, but it is kind of a screen that distorts reality, making us perceive the real problem in a slightly twisted, perverted way.

So the catch of ideology is that it transforms or mystifies the problems themselves. For example, let's take the most violent, brutal ideology of them all: Hitler, Nazism. It was not only that Hitler proposed wrong solutions—kill the Jews and so on. The catch was that in order for his solution to have been feasible in the eyes of the Nazis, he already had to rephrase or reformulate the problem. The real problems—economic crisis, poverty, political crisis and so on—were supplanted by the figure of the Jew. Only with this background does the solution work. Again, Hitler did not just propose an ideological solution—kill the Jews—for the real social problems in Germany in the '20s; he already proposed his own mystifying interpretation of the crisis itself, interpreting the problem as a Jewish plot.

I think that it is crucial that we perceive ecology as ideology in this sense. In other words, ideology is not the solution. Rather, you should always step back and look at what problems it is trying to solve, how it mystifies the problem itself. This brings us back to ecology because, it's a horrible thing to admit, but the Nazi regime was the first political regime, probably in the entirety of human history, to practice a fully conscious, even scientifically supported ecological policy. Not only at the level of the environment, protecting forests and so on, but also at the level of individual lives, promoting health, eating whole-grain bread. It is interesting to learn that the first legal measure, symbolically, the very first legal measure when Hitler became chancellor, was to prohibit animal torture. Ironically, it was, of course, a stab at the Jews—the idea was to outlaw Jewish rituals for killing sheep. But you see, the fact that the first ecologically fully conscious regime in Europe was Nazi Germany, if nothing else, proves that ecology is not always as innocent as it appears, that it is always contaminated by ideology.

[*We come to the part of the depot that's open to the public, where people sort their refuse into massive recycling bins: plastic, metal, paper, cardboard, wood, yard clippings, old fridges, broken furniture.*]

TAYLOR: I want to ask you about recycling here, particularly the emphasis on recycling as opposed to production in most mainstream environmental conversations. This seems to me ideological in precisely the way you're talking about because it takes a real problem—overproduction, the fact that capitalist economies thrive on the production of things we don't need, on excessive packaging, on planned obsolescence—and individualizes it. Suddenly it's the consumer's job to reduce, reuse, recycle and not the manufacturer's job to produce more responsibly or the government's job to regulate affairs.

ŽIŽEK: I think that already such a neutral notion as recycling involves one of the fundamental ideological myths today, that of clearing the plate, of erasing one's guilt. I think that our obsession in ecology with recycling is part of the same phenomenon as debt in collective ideology, of restitution, repaying the old debts, collective crimes. In the United States there is talk that the whites should collectively repay the blacks for slavery. They are talking about enormous sums, a couple of hundreds of billions of dollars. Everybody knows that the origin of society, of every form of social life, is some primordial crime. But the ultimate postmodern political correctness utopia for me is that somehow through legal restitution, repaying your constituting debt, you can erase your dark origin.

The ultimate conclusion would have been—in one of my books I have developed this in a mocking way—the end of the class struggle. The capitalist would collectively repay the workers their claim. Again, in ecology, the idea of recycling is the same myth, that we humans are spoiling nature, but by recycling we can ideally reapproach the zero level. The circle of nature is reconstituted. I think this is ideology at its purest. We have to accept that there is trash already in nature—nature itself is not recycling in this sense. Namely, what is the basic idea of recycling? It is simply to abolish trash. All trash will be somehow refunctionalized. A very idealist notion. No wonder that the archbourgeois thinker, utilitarian Jeremy Bentham, in his panopticon—the first architectural project of totalitarian central control—also involved an idea of recycling. His problem is how to use all the waste. For example, there are some crazy moments there concerning human waste, that is to say, urine and excrement. Excrement is obvious: we use it in the prison garden. For urine he has an incredible idea, that the walls of this panopticon building should go a little bit towards the inside, curving inward, so that prisoners should urinate on the walls, keeping the walls warm in winter. You know, this idea that every piece of trash, every bit of excrement should be reused, is ideological. So I think, again, the thing to accept is simply that trash is original in the sense that there is irreducible trash in nature itself. Again, the very idea of recycling is ideology at its purest.

But I really hate this. I read somewhere that some of the ecologically correct congresses and symposiums happening today try to promote themselves as ecologically clean at the level of recycling. The idea is that when you are filling out some form you have to list what kind of transportation you used, and then people try to make an estimation of how many trees you ruined with your trip, and then you have to pay to plant that many new trees, and so on. It sounds nice, but I think, first, it's also ideology at its purest because it individualizes all the problems, with its typical bourgeois individualist utopia. If all of us would be erasing our sins this way, somehow the cycle would be reconstituted. This is another obvious reason why re-cycling is ideology. Even the big official figure like Al Gore makes the good point you mentioned, that this strategy of the big companies is to spread the guilt, as it were, to make us all responsible. You know, like did you recycle your newspaper and so on, to make us all guilty to cover their big crimes.

On the other hand, what always fascinated me—and this doesn't mean that I have any doubts about ecology, but it's good to know what uncertainties we are dealing with here—if you are old enough, you may remember perhaps some twenty years ago there was in Europe, especially in Germany, a big obsession with the forests dying. What we learn now is that precisely as the result of pollution, because forests thrive on carbon dioxide, forests are flourishing. There are more forests in the world today than twenty years ago. I am not a Bush conservative who says ecologists are crazy hysterics and nothing's going on. I am not saying that the situation is not serious, but that it's even *more* serious, that we really don't know what we are dealing with. If I may refer to a well-known but now a little bit forgotten already American philosopher named Donald Rumsfeld, his famous ideas apropos the Iraq War, of the "known knowns," "known unknowns," and "unknown unknowns," there are things we know that we don't know, like I don't know how many cars there are behind this building; I know that I don't know how many cars. But there are things that I don't even know that I don't know because they are simply unimaginable.

And of course ecology is—this is why it's so difficult to deal with—in the field of "unknown unknowns." We are dealing not simply with things that we don't know but with things that we don't even know that we don't know. Maybe through some ecological measures we are causing, at a different level, more disturbances. Because the mystery of nature—I am not a New Ager here, it's just the complex causality—is that things which may appear as trash or surplus can have a function that we are not aware of. So, in a way, by disposing of something that we perceive as trash we may trigger another catastrophe.

It's a well-known story. For example, the Chinese Communists, when they took over in 1949, in the early '50s, there was a big campaign against sparrows, those birds who eat too many seeds in the fields, and all the women and children, everybody, were obliged to kill birds. There were even campaigns where thousands of people were supposed to go to the fields hitting drums all the time, making noise so the birds wouldn't land and then, at the end, would drop down in exhaustion and be killed. But they didn't know that the birds were not only eating the seeds in the fields but at the same time were cleansing the fields of parasites and animals. So it was a catastrophe because half the crop was much more destroyed by these worms and animals than what was eaten by the birds. So at the end—the ultimate irony—China had to import millions of birds from the Soviet Union to reestablish them.

OK, it is a very simple example, things are more complex today, but this is where I see a problem with recycling. On the one hand, "unknown unknowns," things that we don't even know that we don't know, and on the other hand, the fourth category not mentioned by Rumsfeld, "unknown knowns." The reason we don't take ecology seriously is not that we don't know, but that we don't know what we know. We don't know the ideological prejudices that determine us.

These are the two fields where ecological struggle is crucial, I think. With the "unknown unknowns," we keep our mind open. Of course, it's not so simple that you look at the product, you make judgments, what are the costs and so on. We don't know; we must accept this marginal uncertainty. And on the other hand, "unknown knowns." It's very difficult to get rid of all the false knowledge in you, and I don't mean the ideological knowledge in the sense of belief in technology and so on, but, on the contrary, in the ecological dangers that dwell in our most elementary daily sensitivity, in our practically half–biologically ingrained prejudices, attitudes. In order to cope with ecological crisis, we will literally, in some sense, have to denaturalize ourselves, to get rid of nature.

TAYLOR: So by getting rid of nature also denaturalize ourselves, in the sense of examining and challenging our own prejudices and preconceptions and instincts. Let's change topics a bit. What about ecology's relationship to economy? I'm sure you have something to say about this. But first [*gesturing to the ground*], don't step on the porn!

ŽIŽEK: Porn! Where? My God. This is serious now. [*Picks it up.*] No, you call this porn? My God, I want real porn. Is there any here?

TAYLOR: Obviously porn shouldn't be trashed.

ŽIŽEK: Why do they always get these guys with the tattoos, as if they have to get some poor sailors or something?

TAYLOR: You mean they should hire professors? [*Laughs.*]

ŽIŽEK: Like professors of philosophy?

TAYLOR: Exactly. [*Laughs.*] OK, economy.

ŽIŽEK: I think ecology is the limit, or rather one of the limits, of capitalism. Capitalism is, as we all know, infinitely plastic, so it can accommodate any—almost any—crisis. So we should not expect there will be this great ecological catastrophe and then people will suddenly realize we cannot afford this endless capitalist expansion. Capitalism can turn any new critical domain, ecological catastrophe, health catastrophe, whatever you want, into simply a new field of capitalist investment. Let's say the entire climate of the earth were to change because of global warming and that the whole of humanity would have to move much further north because the whole equatorial region had become too warm and uninhabitable. Can we only imagine what kind of an incredible new field for capitalist investment this presents, starting from real estate speculation on Arctic and Antarctic coasts?

Again, the underlying illusion is that when we talk about pollution and ecological problems, we are dealing with what Rumsfeld called "known knowns" or at least "known unknowns." We know, or we can at least learn, what the ecological consequences of certain measures are and then try to counterbalance them through additional taxes or whatever, through market mechanisms. But problems start when we begin dealing with much larger radical catastrophes that are not only quantitatively much larger but where we are dealing with "unknown unknowns." And there humanity cannot even afford a failure, a mistake.

So I think that ecology is such a threat that we will not be able to solve it by using simple market mechanisms themselves like, for example, including environmental costs in the cost of commodities as part of so-called externalities. Because if we are talking about really big catastrophes, much larger even than Chernobyl, that method works only when you have a certain breathing space. We cannot do run-and-try procedures, the "let's try this" approach, "let's try that" approach. That's the market approach, where ten companies compete to satisfy the same demand, nine companies go bankrupt, and one succeeds. Simply put, the stakes are too high. This is not affordable. Let's say an ecological megacatastrophe threatens the whole east coast of the United States. Some say, "No problem, why don't we constitute a megainsurance company in that region?" But that's meaningless. Market mechanisms do not work at that level.

Now I am not idealizing state intervention here. I am not saying that the traditional form, the one we have, of state intervention will do. But I want to emphasize one thing: many ecologists are distrustful of politics. One of the commonplaces of the standard form of ecology is the emphasis on corrupt politics, playing this naive antipolitical stance. But I think that politics with regard to ecology is the same as democracy. You know Winston Churchill's famous quip, "Democracy is the worst imaginable possible system; the only problem is that there is none which is better"? Yes, politicians are the worst imaginable, corrupt, demagogic, inefficient, and so on, but nothing else works. Who will do it? The deep ecological lesson would have been we all should do it. We should all change our daily lives. OK, OK, but somebody has to direct it, to organize it. Who? Experts? Scientists? They are too naive. They are too intelligent, and for that very reason too naive. They think in too simplified, rational terms. You shouldn't trust scientists making big social decisions. Who else? Radical ecologists, priests, New Agers, and so on? Even worse: they are too full of ideologies. So I think that we need politics more than ever in order to cope properly with ecological threats. But we do urgently need a new breed, a new kind of politician. I know that this sounds utopian, it is maybe utopian, but it's an even greater utopia to think that either the existing type of politicians or anybody else can do it. Ecology must be approached as a political problem.

TAYLOR: Let's take a break for a minute and go to the other side of the depot. I like the scenery over there. You can think of some more words of wisdom while we walk.

ŽIŽEK: You know, in *What's New, Pussycat?* with Peter O'Toole and Peter Sellers, they had this ironic thing, that whenever there was some deep thought a star blinks on the screen and says, "Warning to viewers: A deep thought is about to happen, listen carefully." [*Laughs.*] I love this; I am a total Brechtian here. I hate that idea, that a good film should give you the lesson between the lines. No, I like to be given lessons explicitly. I like films that tell you, "Be careful, now comes the moral lesson." I want to be told directly.

TAYLOR: Perhaps I should do that with this sequence: "Watch out, here comes a deep thought from Slavoj."

ŽIŽEK: But you know that deep thoughts are total shit. I played this game in one of my books. I think I demonstrated it, that any shit can pass as a deep thought if you can formulate it properly. No, no, literally, I took the example of a relationship between eternity and temporality. Look, if somebody looks into your eyes and says, "Forget about this terrestrial temporal life, eternity is there [*gestures to sky*], not this vain driveling." It sounds deep. Now somebody looks you deep in the eyes and says exactly the opposite thing. He tells you, "Forget about the dreams of eternity, life is here, real life, use it." It sounds deep. Now a third person comes and tells you, "Don't go into extremes, neither eternity nor temporal life, find the right balance between eternity and temporal pleasure. That is the true wisdom." It sounds true, and then another guy comes and says, "We humans are tragic beings, half animals, half angels. We are forever split. No way to escape it." Now you see my point. Any shit you say, if you say it with the proper tone, sounds like a deep thought. This is why I am totally against wisdom.

We have this in Slovenia—whatever happens, there will always be a wise man saying a wise thought, explaining it. Let's say I have to do something now which is a little bit risky. If I succeed, a wise man will say, "You see, that's it. In order to succeed you must not be afraid, you must take a risk." OK, if I fail, then you have dozens of proverbs. In Slovenia, we have one that's wonderful: "You cannot pee against the wind," meaning, "Don't try too much." Whatever happens, there is a wise guy.

TAYLOR: Ah yes, we have that proverb too. I never really thought about its meaning before.

ŽIŽEK: But you know, this was my nicest linguistic mistake. It happened in Paris. I was making the same point about wisdom, but my French was weak and I made a mistake. I wanted to translate it into French, you cannot urinate or pee against the wind. I confused the verbs and said, "Vous ne pouvez pas chier contre le vent," "you cannot shit against the wind." And then, here, Jacques-Alain Miller was great. He looked at me and said, "The wind must be really strong in Slovenia." This was one of the great moments with Miller, I must say.

TAYLOR: That should be a proverb: "You can't shit against the wind."

ŽIŽEK: Yeah, but it is a little bit eccentric, like what's the point, no? [*Laughs.*]

TAYLOR: But as you said, it can mean anything. It's how you say it!

ŽIŽEK: Well, that's true. But my first reaction was maybe not against the wind, but if I were to shit, I would like to shit in the wind because, you know, the smell. What do you want? To shit in a closed room so that everything smells there? It's a very good idea. It's like natural ventilation.

[*We return to the central mountain of garbage. A framed photograph of two lovers in the surf, the woman suggestively straddling the man, catches Žižek's eye.*] What's this? Is it?! No, it's not. I thought this was Burt Lancaster and Deborah Kerr in *From Here to Eternity*, that famous movie. This was considered, in '53, a big deal, the first time in Hollywood when you find this explicit representation of an illicit affair. It's exactly this scene. You know where I used this shot? Did you see *Deep Impact*, that shitty science fiction film? You remember, there, at the end, the daughter embraces the father and there's this megawave. So that's my reading. A small illicit affair—you get small waves, like in this image. For a true incestuous passion, you get a much larger wave!

TAYLOR: OK, I just have one question about—

ŽIŽEK: You see how she does that! Rhetorically it implies that it's the last question, but of course it's not.

TAYLOR: Almost the last one. I promise. I have to make sure I have everything I need before I release you. Let's try to keep the answers succinct from here on out. You spoke about our inability to face the looming environmental crisis, but at the same time ecological issues seem to be omnipresent. For example, all the big corporations green-washing, working to appear green in their advertisements, etc. So ecology is very trendy, we're hyperaware of environmental issues, but at the same time there's this disavowal of the catastrophe that may be upon us. I'm wondering if you could speak on that seeming contradiction.

ŽIŽEK: You're right, there is an obvious paradox in our attitude to-wards ecology. On the one hand, we hear from all sides calls to finally awaken, we cannot ignore the problem any longer. On the other hand, isn't ecology one of the few topics where everybody agrees? It's chic to be green, it's almost an obsession. The richer you are, even the upper classes—even they are obsessed with it.

How to read these two aspects together? I think that as a philoso-pher, I can give an answer. It is so-called pseudoactivity. Often we do things not so that something will change but to make sure that noth-ing changes. For example, imagine a group of people. They have to approach some traumatic point, and then usually some of them can't stop talking—I often play this role, I nervously talk too much all the time, why? Because I know the moment I stop talking, somebody will touch that sensitive topic. You are active all the time just to prevent some traumatic thing, the real thing, from happening. And I think it's a little bit of the same here if we look at these trendy forms of ecology, buying green—or even trendy forms of charity, because I think with ecology it's a little bit the same as it is with charity. It looks very nice if you pick a boy there in Africa, you send him some $20 or $30 through the bank every month, and we know the game. Every year you get a letter of gratitude with a photo. Why are we doing this, those who are doing this? I am not. You are. Pure, feel-good moralism where you are paying not so much to help the boy but to make sure that the boy will stay there. It's a kind of bribery to make sure that you really do not have to change your own lifestyle here.

I think it's a little bit of the same with ecology: let's eat healthy, let's buy green, let's recycle, and so on and so on. Let's do all these small things just to postpone the moment when we really have to do something. I think ecology today is the main field of pseudoactivity. I think a much healthier attitude is a more cynical one, which I have. Whenever I see the so-called "green" apples, apples grown organically, the first thing you notice about them is they look much uglier. They are half-rotten and so on. So I cannot contain this cynical reaction that probably some big food industry manipulator does this. They harvest all the apples. They pick out the beautiful ones, sell them at a certain price, and then the ugly ones they sell at double the price as green, as ecologically correct.

TAYLOR: The politics of food is something we definitely don't agree on. [*Laughs.*] I like my organic, vegan, hippie food and my ugly apples.

ŽIŽEK: Ah, but if you go a step further—Patricia Highsmith wrote a wonderful story based on the premise that some people claim that very complex trees have some murmurs of their own and communicate. And there are some vegetophilic—opposite of vegetophobic—animal-loving radicals who claim that, through some exquisite measuring instrument, you can measure these murmurs. So if you go to the end of this road, you end up just drinking water and eating nothing. Now I am talking serious things—serious in the sense that I really read them somewhere, I am not saying that they are serious—they made some kind of experiment even proving that plants must have some kind of memory.

TAYLOR: You don't believe this, right? Animals have central nervous systems; plants don't. It's obvious animals have the ability to suffer and feel pain, which is why I don't eat meat.

žižek: Sorry? No—God. But wait a minute. I am a good liberal hypocrite. I eat meat, but only abstract meat. Like, you know, this pure steak so that I can sustain in my imagination that this was dressed and produced in a factory of direct meat, like a sausage, and was never a part of a living animal. So I absolutely cannot eat anything that reminds me directly of an animal—chicken should be abstract. Chicken to me is McNuggets. To me it should not be combined with bone or whatever. It is absolutely impossible for me to eat kidneys or brain or these concrete parts.

taylor: Isn't that another example of disavowal? And what about factory farming's impact on the environment? I read a report from the UN that said the meat industry produces more greenhouse gases than all the world's planes, ships, trucks, SUVs, and cars combined. It occurs to me that one ecologically beneficial way to become more artificial would be to stop industrial meat production and grow protein substitute in vats, which scientists are trying to develop—you know, actual flesh but not connected to a thinking, feeling animal that has to eat and shit and be pumped with antibiotics and all that. But we should move on. You said something earlier that I think would make a good conclusion to the sequence, the part about idealization and loving garbage. But I'm thinking about how we will get to that point once I'm in the editing room. So I want to ask you this: What does it mean for an ecologist to love trash when its production—the production of greenhouse gases and toxic waste— is putting humanity in peril? What does it mean to love something that has the capacity to cause the ultimate catastrophe?

žižek: OK, I see what you mean. Trash is by definition toxic. Trash is that which threatens us all. It is polluted material. If we continue with this crazy production, we will some day be drowned in it. So why should an ecologist love trash? I would like to turn around the perspective. I think that what is truly threatening is not trash as such, it is separating trash, it is throwing trash out. I think that the ultimate horror is, again, a nice green pasture or whatever where trash disappears. I think that an ideally balanced (environmentalists use this term) ecological society would have to be a totally chaotic space where trash is simply part of our environs, not discriminated against.

TAYLOR: I must say, I'm not so sure about that. Again, I feel we have a good ending—

ŽIŽEK: But. Go to but!

TAYLOR: —but we need to somehow segue from the explanation of the ideological myths concerning ecology to your thoughts on aesthetics and love.

ŽIŽEK: Let me try a totally different line of thought, briefly, and then you will see what you can do. OK?

Accepting trash does not mean that we should love trash, that we should dwell in it, embrace it, enjoy it. I'm not for masochism. Accepting trash means accepting our hatred of trash. I think maybe I'm more and more convinced the solution is to accept our— what appears to our immediate perception—antinatural attitude, to accept that there are things in the world that we hate. We don't have to accept the world. The function of humanity is not to reconcile itself with the whole of nature. The function of humanity is to draw a line of distinction. I accept this part, I reject that part. What we should accept is our imbalance. We are not the focus of the universe where we have to worry, are all the accounts settled? Are we disturbing some balance? Instead we should accept ourselves as imbalanced monsters, as beings whose activity introduces imbalance, and as such we are part of nature. So I think we should accept our hatred, our aggressivity, our imbalance. We should accept our hatred. The true ecological attitude is to hate the world: less love, more hatred.

TAYLOR: Just the opposite of what you said earlier!

ŽIŽEK: Yes, the opposite. You'll see what works! [*Laughs.*]

TAYLOR: I'm going to torture you for a few minutes more. Again, quick questions, quick answers. Give us an idea of what ecology without nature looks like in practice. What would this attitude toward trash—now you say hate the world, earlier it was based on the idea of loving and embracing trash—what would this idea of ecology without nature look like in action, not just as an attitude?

ŽIŽEK: So what does this idea of ecology without nature amount to not only as a mental spiritual attitude but in practice? How does it change our practice? Of course we still fight pollution, dangers and so on, but I am tempted to say that we do it as open warfare. It's like in open warfare where you are aware that every firm position you get you have to fight for. You are aware that you do not rely on anything. You are aware that you are in an open process where the consequences of your acts are ultimately unpredictable. You know that in the end you will lose. To accept this radical openness of the situation means accepting that there is no final solution, we are just temporarily buying time. And I think that in a strange way accepting this open warfare situation is the only true respect of nature.

TAYLOR: The ecologists you are talking about currently function by organizing around the idea of pure nature that must be preserved, so their rallying cry is "save the earth." What is the slogan of a true ecologist in your mind?

ŽIŽEK: If the cry to rally people, the slogan of standard ecologists, is pure nature—reestablish the natural cycle, redeem plants of human pollutions and so on—what should then the model of a truly progressive ecology be? I think the first one should be it doesn't have any meaning. Natural catastrophes, even human-caused catastrophes, are a totally meaningless part of life. There is no meaning in it. Nature is neither good nor bad. Nature is blind, stupid. Point two: I think that what we have to be aware of is that the only way to approach the ecological crisis is in a ruthlessly egotistic way. Let's face it, if we were to follow the so-called natural course of events, humanity would probably have disappeared long ago. We should shamelessly intervene in nature by artificially creating conditions with which we will be able to buy time. So my paradox would be a plea not only against nature, in the sense that there is no nature, but even a plea for violating nature.

I think that we should paradoxically become aware of the very fragile status of humanity. We are violating nature in the sense of imposing on nature things that would never happen without human intervention. But we should accept this with gladness. Yes, we are violating nature. We are, as it were, running against the current. We are buying time. I think that we should proudly admit our self-centeredness. Why should this be unnatural? The paradox is that precisely by admitting our attitude against nature, we can reconcile ourselves to nature. That is to say, not caring about what happens with the global universe; there is no global universe. It's just an endless multiplicity of elements, no meaning in it.

TAYLOR: Final question—and this time I mean it. So what of meaning? Or the lack of it you just mentioned? Isn't that what philosophers are always asked about, the search for meaning, the meaning of life? You spoke about the temptation of meaning earlier. Why is resisting that temptation such a challenge?

ŽIŽEK: Why is resisting the temptation of meaning so difficult? It's incredible how we philosophers, even when so-called ordinary people approach us, ultimately the question is always the meaning of life. Why are we here? Does it have some meaning? My position here is pretty radical, of course. Searching for meaning is a kind of a natural temptation of human nature, but I think that meaning as such is a lie. There is no true meaning, no false meaning. There, is a mystification in meaning as such. It's not that we have two types of meanings: scientific meanings and ideological meanings. Truth has no meaning. Quantum physics is maybe true, but it has no meaning literally. You cannot even translate it into the terms of your daily reality. So I think meaning is an escape from meaninglessness. Paradoxically, meaninglessness comes before. Meaning as such is a defense, and I think it's the duty of a philosopher to allow us not to get rid of meaning but to see it as what it is: a defense, a fundamental lie of the human condition.

JUDITH BUTLER WITH SUNAURA TAYLOR

Interdependence

This dialogue is unique in that it appears on camera as a conversation between two subjects. During one of my preliminary meetings with Judith Butler, I introduced her to my sister, Sunaura Taylor, a graduate student at Berkeley who uses a wheelchair because of a congenital physical disability. After a long conversation over coffee, Butler suggested Sunaura participate in the filming process, rightly suspecting they would have many interesting things to talk about. The exuberantly muraled streets and graffitied alleyways of San Francisco's Mission District provided their walk's setting.

JUDITH BUTLER: Maybe I should start by saying why I thought this was a good thing to do?

SUNAURA TAYLOR: That sounds great.

BUTLER: All right, Sunny, so I thought that we should take this walk together, and one of the things I wanted to talk about was what it means for us to take a walk together. When I first asked you about this, you told me you take walks, you take strolls—can you say something about what that is for you? When do you do it and how do you do it and what words do you have for it?

S. TAYLOR: Well, I think I always go for a walk, probably every day I go for a walk, and I always tell people I'm going for walks—I use that word even though I can't physically walk. I mean, to me, I think the experience of going for a walk is probably very similar to anybody else's: it's a clearing of the mind, it's enjoying whatever I'm walking past. And my body is very involved even though I'm physically not walking. I have my own ways in which I engage my body, my balancing. But yeah, I use that term: walking. And most of the disabled people that I know use that term also.

BUTLER: So you move when you walk, but you also have motorized movement, and it's a combination of movements, no?

S. TAYLOR: Yeah, it's a combination of movements. And it's very subtle movements also: moving my hand very subtly, movement of my back. I'm always moving though I'm not walking.

BUTLER: It makes me wonder whether any of us move without techniques of movement. Everybody has to learn how to move in whatever ways they can.

S. TAYLOR: Well, we're very culturally ingrained early on to move in certain ways, to walk in certain ways, to gesture in certain ways. And for me it's very interesting to think about what it means to be born in a body that can't physically move in the culturally accepted ways, and you have to design your own movements. I would say that many culturally accepted movements are also restrictive on some level.

BUTLER: It seems to me that there are two ways of thinking about this. One way of thinking about it is to say that when you walk you're supplemented by a chair, by wheels—they assist you in walking—and that differentiates you and other people in chairs from those who are not in chairs. On the other hand, it seems to me we could think that there's a more general condition, maybe a shared condition, that we could even speak to.

I mean, it seems to me that we're all supported in our movements by various kinds of things that are external to us. We all need certain kinds of surfaces, we need certain kinds of shoes, certain kinds of weather, and even internally we need to be ambulatory in certain ways that may or may not be fully operative in all of us. And I'm just thinking that a walk always requires a certain kind of technique, a certain support. Nobody takes a walk without there being a technique of walking. Nobody goes for a walk without something that supports that walk, something outside of ourselves. And maybe we have a false idea that the able-bodied person is somehow radically self-sufficient. I think there's an idea of self-sufficiency that might be a fantasy and kind of an ideal norm that doesn't actually suit any of us or help any of us think about how we move or why we move as we move.

S. TAYLOR: I think that idea translates also into so many other, different fields, this idea of independence. That an able-bodied person can take a walk independently without anything else is sort of a myth. They do need certain ground, they do need shoes, as you said, they need social support. And I think that's something that definitely affects the image of disabled people. That somehow disabled people are perceived as more dependent, or that they are the ones that are dependent, when in actuality we are all interdependent, that is, dependent on different structures and on each other. There's also just the way that we are affected by other people's opinions when we're taking a walk and other people's views of us when we're taking a walk; disabled people are impacted by people's discomfort or by people's lack of knowing how to interact or react. But I'm sure that's similar for all people in some ways.

BUTLER: So what seems clear to me is that we're always conditioned to take a walk. Certain conditions have to be met. We need means of mobilization, we need support, we need surfaces. And it seems to me that having the use of your feet is not a necessary condition for a walk. That's one of the things that becomes most clear when you talk about taking a walk or taking a stroll. Feet can be one means of mobilizing the body, but certainly not the only one, and not even a necessary one. And that means we get to rethink what a walk is in terms of all the things that power our movement, all the conditions that support our mobility.

S. TAYLOR: And I have many friends who don't have feet who go for walks.

BUTLER: Let's talk about this: Which environments make it possible for you to take a walk? What does the environment have to be like in order to support your mobility?

S. TAYLOR: Well, disability really dramatizes all these conditions that affect us, that affect both disabled people and able-bodied people. For example, a real physical condition for me would be if we're taking a walk and then suddenly there's no curb cut. Then I would literally have to stop taking my walk. And so the physical environment for a disabled person—at least at this time in our history, in our culture—makes the effects of the environment much more obvious when in fact even the movements of able-bodied people are influenced by similar factors. I've been in suburban environments created for cars and where there are no safe spaces to walk, where walking can be very hazardous. So the existence of sidewalks and paths show that able-bodied people also depend on spaces designed for them. Does that make sense?

BUTLER: Yeah. Are there curb cuts in San Francisco?

S. TAYLOR: I moved to San Francisco, to the Bay Area, largely because it's the most accessible place in the world. And partly what's so amazing to me about it is that the physical access, the fact that public transportation is accessible, there are curb cuts most places, most buildings are accessible, leads to a social acceptability. That somehow because there's physical access, there are simply more disabled people out and about in the world, and so people have learned how to interact with them and are used to them in a certain way. And so the physical access leads to a social access and acceptance.

BUTLER: It's great. We can say, where there are curb cuts, there will be increased populations of people using chairs and that that will change the demographic of an entire city.

S. TAYLOR: Or, for example, in my hometown, in Georgia, I was always very nervous about going out and buying things because I do things differently. Here I don't have to explain to anybody how to help me because they are so used to working with, and figuring out, and being creative with, disabled people coming into their stores. Here almost always people will say, "Can I bring that coffee to you?" or "I'll bring you a straw." And so there's this knowledge of this whole way of physically interacting with people who are different, and that really results from physical access. But that's always been a dilemma within the disability community: How do you demand physical access first if you can't get out into society to demand it?

BUTLER: Yes, that's a big question, the access to even get the population together who can then make the claim in an effective way.

S. TAYLOR: Yeah, and it's really only just within the past fifteen to twenty years that that's really been taking place.

BUTLER: So you talk about going into stores or dealing with people who are able-bodied but who've had experience dealing with disabled people and trying to figure out creative ways to meet their needs or have whatever exchange they're having. Well, first of all, I just want to say it must be nice not to have to always have to be the pioneer.

S. TAYLOR: Yes. Definitely, definitely.

BUTLER: To be the first one—

S. TAYLOR: —to be the first disabled person they've ever seen.

BUTLER: To say, yes, I do speak and think and talk and move and enjoy life and suffer many of the same heartaches that you do. But anyway, what I'm wondering about is moving in social spaces, right? All the movements you can do and which help you live and which express you in various ways. Do you feel free to move in all the ways you want to move in social, public space? And to what extent are there social restrictions on you, kinds of stigmas or forms of socially acceptable movement that are restrictions on you—not your disability, but rather the social restrictions on what a "disabled" person should do?

S. TAYLOR: Well, to use going to a coffeehouse as an example, at first it was just the embarrassment of asking for help. Because of these independence issues we've been talking about, it takes a lot to be that pioneer and to ask for help and to watch someone as they're nervous trying to figure out how to help you. But I think, after I sort of went through that, I realized that actually it was strange because a lot of the time I might not even need help. For instance, I could go into a coffee shop and actually pick up the cup with my mouth and carry it to my table, but that becomes almost more difficult because of the normalizing standards of our movements and the discomfort that's caused when I do things with body parts that aren't necessarily what we assume that they're for. That seems to be even harder for people to deal with. So this is something that I'm very interested in: How disabled people can creatively redo or reinvent those movements. Or how they have to create their own concepts of what a movement is and what their body parts are for. I think that we're sort of taught that hands are for giving things, picking things up, they're for shaking hands, that mouths are for drinking, for kissing, for talking. And when I go into a coffee shop and mess those up—when I, with my mouth, pick up a cup instead of using my hands—it's sort of undoing this assumption that people just take for granted. It's not even something that people usually think about, that there may be a socially constructed way of using your body.

BUTLER: Right, I mean, I don't know if you ever go to baseball games, but . . .

S. TAYLOR: Not often.

BUTLER: Not often. OK. But it does occur to me that if you were to look at even so-called normal eating habits of people at baseball games, they use their mouths in all kinds of ways, uncorking and spitting and putting their mouths into their bowls of whatever. And I mean, nobody says, "Oh my God, that's completely unacceptable." And yet maybe it is unacceptable, according to a certain propriety or class mores or a sense of correctness. It makes me wonder why people don't get really upset about that. When an able-bodied person maybe uses their mouth in an unconventional way, it's OK, but if a disabled person does, then there's some kind of challenge to our idea of what human functions are or what certain body parts are meant for.

S. TAYLOR: Well, I think it's one thing if it's a choice, if it's a choice to eat the hot dog in a messy, different way. Forget the hands—they're too busy holding the big beers or whatever. However, I actually think that while it is more acceptable, people do feel all of those restrictions in more subtle ways. And maybe it's allowed at a baseball game, but if you're at a relatively fancy restaurant, that wouldn't be the case. I guess if you're even walking down a street and you're wearing something funny, you may feel judged. It seems to me able-bodied people feel a lot of self-consciousness about their movements and presentation.

This makes me think of an experience I recently had. It's pretty rare unless I'm hanging out with a lot of other disabled people. I was flying back home and I was sitting next to this man, this French man, and he was very frustrated about something and I couldn't understand him. But he kept trying to communicate with me and there was something kind of off and I couldn't tell what it was. And then I realized that he had a big, fake, plastic arm. It was like a prosthetic that tried to look like a real arm so I didn't notice it until probably halfway through the flight, and then we kind of bonded even though we couldn't understand each other. I kept noticing that he would do things with his mouth a lot because he only had one hand, so he was always doing things with his mouth. So then finally, near the end of the flight, our ears were popping as we were going down and he got out this pack of gum and he offered me some, and the only way for him to get out the gum and unwrap it was with his hand and his mouth. His real hand was full or something, I don't remember exactly, but basically the only free part of himself to offer me the gum was his mouth!

BUTLER: Yes, that's very sweet! So did he?

S. TAYLOR: He did! And I was just like, well, when else am I randomly just going to be in contact with someone else who does everything with their mouth? So I took it and it wasn't weird in terms of being, like, oddly sexual or too close or anything. In fact, I was really quite blissed out by the fact that this guy did things with his mouth too, you know? It was just really kind of a wonderful moment of just sharing intimacy because of the ways that our bodies worked.

BUTLER: Yes, that's wonderful.

S. TAYLOR: It was very funny.

BUTLER: Well, I'm thinking that what's kind of exhilarating about this story is that you could both do this somewhat improper thing together. And of course it's fully proper, it's fully appropriate, and it's actually quite wonderful. I mean, imagine if you had not taken the gum because you had no way to get it or because you were too embarrassed to exchange it in that way. That would be terrible. I think this sort of thing happens a lot at these microlevels of exchange. Like, how do you say hello to somebody? Usually they offer you their hand. And I remember when I first met you, I offered you my hand and you offered me your shoulder. And then my hand went on your shoulder and that was our contact. But I had to learn, and my first thought was, well, I don't know her very well, is it OK to put my hand on her shoulder? Yeah, that's fine, right? But whatever that formality is that suggests that bodies shouldn't have too much contact when they first meet each other unless they've—

S. TAYLOR: Or only contact through the hand!

BUTLER: Only contact through the hand! These protocols are highly structured, but sometimes they break down. For instance, a friend of mine who's nearly transsexual—she's very, very butch, nearly transsexual—every time she goes to use the bathroom (and she uses the women's bathroom still for whatever reason), she gets yelled at the minute she walks in the door. And everything about her body is inspected by people who have never met her. They want to know whether those are her breasts; they want to figure out whether she's in the wrong place. In her case, a kind of invasiveness takes place. People feel like they can say anything to her, that they have a right to know about her anatomy or they have a right to know about her gender in a way that respects no privacy whatsoever. So that's a different case in which the social protocols are not about keeping separateness, which always assumes we know who each other are and what's appropriate, but where the kind of invasiveness seems to know no boundaries.

s. TAYLOR: And that happens a lot within the disabled community also, especially with people who can pass as able-bodied in some circumstances. Some people seem to think that they have the right to ask questions, to be overly intimate. But I think there are positive levels where these different ways of moving or being can lead to freedom of touch and freedom of intimacy in different ways, and those moments are really lovely. And I know that when I have participated in events or in settings where there are a lot of people with different embodiments, part of my favorite thing is just being completely confused about how to greet someone. Not knowing how to give that physical contact or how to even say hi, or wondering how someone is going to say hi back to me. And I think that those experiences are just so important, almost as a reminder of all the walls that we've built.

BUTLER: Yes, ways of expressing acknowledgment or welcoming somebody—those are actually really crucial acts. How do I make contact with this other human?

ASTRA TAYLOR: Sunny, maybe you could tell the story about how you became aware of disability as an intellectual issue, as a topic that could be theorized about—how disability studies fostered your political consciousness, which eventually inspired you to participate in those events you just mentioned, and how that changed your life.

S. TAYLOR: So it wasn't until I was in my early twenties, about twenty or twenty-one, that I became aware of disability as a political issue. And that happened largely through discovering the social model of disability, which is basically this: In disability studies they have a distinction between disability and impairment. So impairment would be my body, my embodiment right now, the fact that I was born with arthrogryposis, or what the medical world has labeled as arthrogryposis, that basically my joints are fused, my muscles are weaker, I can't move in certain ways.* And this does affect my life in all sorts of situations. For instance, there's a plum tree in my backyard and I can't pick the plums off of it. I have to wait for them to drop. And so there's that, there's that embodiment, our own unique embodiments. And then there's disability, which is basically the social repression of disabled people. The fact that disabled people have limited housing options, we don't have career opportunities, we're socially isolated, and in many ways there's a cultural aversion to disabled people.

BUTLER: So would disability be the social organization of impairment? [*The shot is momentarily interrupted as we clear the sidewalks for passersby. "Can you make us famous?!" they ask.*] I was just trying to figure out what a good formulation for understanding the distinction between impairment and disability is. And would it be fair to say that disability is the social organization of impairment? The way impairment is addressed or fails to be addressed by social means?

S. TAYLOR: Yes, yes. Exactly. The disabling effects, basically, of society. That's what it would be.

BUTLER: That seems extremely important. So what happened when you realized that disability is a political issue? At what point did you recognize that and what facilitated your understanding?

---

* To learn about the environmental causes of Sunaura Taylor's impairment see "Military Waste in Our Drinking Water," Alternet.org, August 4, 2006.

S. TAYLOR: Well, I think all the feelings that I had grown up with—that my body was abnormal, that I was deformed, that it was a tragedy—all these sorts of things that I'd really sort of internalized as being my own personal problem suddenly blasted open and then I just realized how much they're political and they're civil rights issues, so it made me more determined to figure out a way of interacting physically with the world.

BUTLER: What happened? Did you come in contact with disability activists or did you read certain things?

S. TAYLOR: I read a book review, actually. But it was also definitely very hard because when that happened I lived in Brooklyn. And I would really try to just go and order a coffee by myself. And I would sit for hours beforehand in the park just trying to get up the nerve to do that. Because it was a matter of asking for help, which in this society is just looked down upon.

BUTLER: Well, and there's no guarantee that someone's going to help.

S. TAYLOR: That too!

BUTLER: Or that they're not going to disdain you for needing help.

S. TAYLOR: Yeah, yes. Or that it just won't be a very awkward moment. They won't know how to help you and you'll have to explain to them how to help . . . though it's never, never as awkward as one thinks it will be. But then I sort of had the epiphany that actually, in a way, it's a political protest for me to go in and order a coffee and demand help simply because, in my opinion, help is something we all need. And it's something that is looked down upon and not really taken care of in this society when we *all* need help, when we're all interdependent in all sorts of ways.

BUTLER: I think that's true and it *is* a political act to ask for coffee—I mean, you are intervening in social space in a particular way, you're challenging the protocols through which certain kinds of items are asked for or help is asked for, and you're asking for that social world to open, not only to you personally, but to all the people who are in your situation. And so I think your asking for coffee *is* political.

S. TAYLOR: Yeah, I agree. And I think it becomes more political when it involves me actually showing the ways in which I do things. Or asking other people to interact with the different ways in which I do things. Because I think it can help make people aware of the ways in which they are entangled in this web of normalcy.

BUTLER: Can we go back for a moment to moving or eating in public and what kind of challenge that is both for you and for able-bodied people who are around you or with you? I'm struck by the fact that the able-bodied population has certain feelings of anxiety and stigmatizes impairment precisely because there are things you are perceived not to be able to do, you are perceived as helpless or dependent. But, in fact, it seems to me that when you do things in the way that you want to or can—if you move in the way that you want to, if you needed to move on the floor or if you needed to eat something or drink something or move something with your mouth or paint with your mouth, and you do paint with your mouth—then it's the form your ability takes that is stigmatized at that moment. It's very peculiar.

S. TAYLOR: It is very peculiar.

BUTLER: If you're disabled, you're not supposed to be able to do those things, but your means of doing them, instead of being applauded and being understood as kind of the creative acts that they are—

s. TAYLOR: They freak people out.

BUTLER: They freak people out.

s. TAYLOR: They totally freak people out. And that's why I've been thinking a lot about how wheelchairs, actually, as wonderful as they are, as liberating as they are, they are actually tools to keep my body in a certain acceptable space because I'm not moving. I'm not interacting with the world physically as much as I would if my body was moving naturally on the ground without a wheelchair. Without my wheelchair I would be walking, but in a very different way than you walk. I'd be scooting. Both are movements that would make people much more uncomfortable because of—what would be the right word—the transgressive nature or something of—

BUTLER: Your transgressive movements, yes.

s. TAYLOR: Yeah, my transgressive movements would freak people out.

BUTLER: Right, well, there's a norm of what—not even what the body should be like and look like, but what parts should move and what those movements should be like. But you see, I guess I would maybe gently contest you a little bit because you're in a chair—you're moving in a chair, you are moving. And I wonder, sometimes when we say, "I move" or "I'm moving by myself," we imagine completely self-generated movement, as if the body is completely independent of an apparatus, of a machine, of even nutrition, of all kinds of things that one needs to move. So I guess I want to go back, you know, remind us that maybe that idea of the self-sufficient body, moving by itself—

s. TAYLOR: Doesn't exist.

BUTLER: I don't think so!

S. TAYLOR: Yeah. But I do think, just in terms of wheelchairs, they are a signifier of what disabled people are supposed to be. They're supposed to be helpless. And we're not supposed to be able to do things. Because if we get out in the world, then the world will have to change to some extent. So I think it's easier for society to have us be helpless, to, you know, stick us in nursing homes.

[*As we turn down an alley we notice a lone sneaker.*]

BUTLER: Someone's missing their shoe.

S. TAYLOR: I wonder if they can walk without it?

BUTLER: I wonder! I think that as I'm listening to you I'm hearing several things at once. That, on the one hand, there's a social expectation that if you have an impairment, you should remain helpless. There is also anxiety and stigma that many able-bodied people have in relation to that helplessness; they get freaked out by it. They don't know what to do about it. So they require you to be helpless, but they're also freaked out about your helplessness.

S. TAYLOR: They also like it sometimes.

BUTLER: They also like it; it makes them feel . . . virtuous. I'm sure there's lots of virtue-tripping.

S. TAYLOR: Lots of virtue-tripping. Lots and lots of pity.

BUTLER: Lots of pity and virtue-tripping. Just what we need. But the other thing I hear you saying is that when you can do things, and you do them in your own way, that that's also stigmatized, right? So the use of your mouth, the use of your body in ways that are not conventional, freak people out, which suggests that they would rather you not be able to do things than to do things in ways that challenge their idea of what human body parts, how human beings, move; what they look like when they move, what bodies are supposed to be like, how they're supposed to appear in social space.

s. TAYLOR: I think we should add to that how people smell in social space and how people sound. Because I think that both of those things have a lot to do with disability too, the random noises people make or random smells disabled people might emit. So there's many different levels of perception.

BUTLER: That's right. We've been talking about mobility, morphology; vocalization is clearly huge. So that just makes me think about what kind of norms people live with regarding what their body parts are for. Like, what do you use your mouth for? What's the proper use of your mouth? And it just strikes me that there's a broader kind of morphological politics that we could talk about that would include gender, people who live with intersex conditions, disability, race . . .

s. TAYLOR: Even just different cultures. Yeah.

BUTLER: Racialized ways of walking, speaking, gesturing. All the ways in which we have very restrictive ideas about what body parts are for and how they should appear. So when you can use a body part to paint, since you paint with your mouth, that challenges people to think what the mouth is and what the mouth can do . . . or what painting is! What the act of painting or drawing is. All of those ideas have to be rethought, but it's amazing what the resistance is. But I think we could find similar kinds of resistances to gender and to morphological issues that merge with gender. You know, the biological females for whom a certain kind of walk is obligatory. If they don't walk in that way, their femaleness is called into question.

s. TAYLOR: Yeah. Or their able-bodiedness.

BUTLER: Or their able-bodiedness is called into question. And both can be called into question at the same time, right? I mean, if there are dimorphic ideals of what a man is like or what a woman is like, there are also able-bodied ideals, right? So able-bodiedness is a presupposition of gender norms.

s. TAYLOR: And I think just the words "strength" and "weakness" have a lot to do with this too. The idea of being weak or of looking weak seems definitely to be associated with the idea of being feminine. So those words, "weak" and "strong," also sort of link gender and disability.

BUTLER: Right. So you'd say there's kind of an extrafeminization of the disabled body, if weakness is associated with feminization?

s. TAYLOR: For males, definitely. There's been a lot of research and work on what it means to lose strength if you're a disabled male. But then, for a disabled female, what does it mean to not be able to walk in that way that you were just saying the ideal female should walk or women in general are supposed to walk? [*The weather has suddenly become chilly. We pass by a vintage clothing store.*] Should we stop and get me something warm?

BUTLER: Yeah. That's what we're going to do. [*Butler pauses at a rack of garish dresses.*] I don't know, honey. Let's go find something. . . . Oh look, these are really warm. These are warm.

[*A red sweater catches Sunaura Taylor's eye and Butler helps her try it on.*]

s. TAYLOR: I think this would be fine. And I like it. It's stylish.

BUTLER: It's very stylish. It's kind of, you know, sporty and fancy.

s. TAYLOR: It's gonna be a new show: "It's shopping with Judith But-ler!" [*Laughs.*]

BUTLER: For the queer eye!

[*Butler and Taylor approach the cashier.*]

BUTLER: We put the sweater on.

CASHIER: It's priced by weight . . .

BUTLER: Can we guess?

CASHIER: I can give it to you for $4.50.

s. TAYLOR: Great. [*Hands money to the cashier.*] Can you give me the bills first, and then the change? I can't hold both at the same time.

[*We head back onto Valencia Street.*]

BUTLER: There's an essay by the philosopher Gilles Deleuze on Spinoza, speaking to the question: What can a body do? And the question is supposed to challenge the traditional ways in which we think about bodies. We usually ask what is a body or what is the ideal form of a body or what's the difference between the body and the soul and that kind of thing. But what can a body do is a different question. . . . It isolates a set of capacities and a set of instrumentalities or actions, and we are assemblages of those things. And I liked this idea because it's not like there's an essence and there's an ideal form, but there are just different kinds of assemblages.

s. TAYLOR: So by assemblages do you mean ways in which we put together the use of our bodies?

BUTLER: Our capacities, our instrumentalities, also what we feel, what we respond to, zones of passivity, interdependency, and action. All those come together in some way or another. But what I mean— I'm not really Deleuzean and I don't even know if I'm a Spinozist, maybe I am a little bit—but it seems to me that it goes against certain ideas of ideal morphology and what a body should look like. It's exactly *not* that question. Or what a body should move like. And one of the things that I found in thinking about gender and even violence against sexual minorities or gender minorities—people whose gender presentation doesn't conform with standard ideals of masculinity and femininity—is that very often it comes down to how people walk, how they use their hips, what they do with their body parts, what they use their mouth for, what they use their anus for or what they allow their anus to be used for, how they handle being in a relationship to other people's orifices, which orifices you can enter and how and which you cannot, which orifices can be used for certain actions, which cannot, right? All those things are very highly regulated. So I remember at the beginning of the queer movement, there were straight men who thought, well, if they enjoyed anal intercourse, no matter what the gender was of the person who was penetrating them, they were made gay by the act. Why are you "made gay" by the act? Why should that have to be just gay? But people got confused about acts and orifices and body surfaces and what they could be used for and if you used them one way or another, then your identity was called into question. So people, I think, had to work against certain stigmas that body parts could only be used for certain purposes and that's how gender got constituted. So I'm interested in this. I think gender and disability converge in a whole lot of different ways. And one thing I think both movements do is get us to rethink what the body can do—what are its abilities and what are its actions and what are its modes of receptivity—and free up our understanding of how we can make use of what we have and for what purposes. But it does mean challenging certain very entrenched ideas of how those things are supposed to line up.

S. TAYLOR: I've always seen the body as a creative tool and that we're sort of taught how to use this tool in certain ways. And I think that's probably, really, one of the benefits of being disabled or of being born into a situation where you have to realize this creative capacity. Or else you won't be able to do anything, you know? Just to think about mouths, my mouth is put in all sorts of places—because I can't use my hands—that are just totally socially unacceptable. I put my mouth on doorknobs, which I know people think is highly disgusting! Or I put my mouth on pens. I'm constantly putting things in my mouth.

A. TAYLOR: I want to interrupt you and see if Judith could talk about that young man who was killed because of his feminine walk. It seems related to what you were both just talking about.

BUTLER: I tell this story, when I'm trying to explain gender violence to people, about a guy in Maine who, I guess he was around eighteen years old, and he walked with a very distinct swish, hips going one way or another, a very feminine walk, a conventionally feminine walk—I would say not even conventionally feminine, I would say hyperbolically feminine. And he was teased by his classmates on the way to school and he got used to it and he just walked, and I think he even walked a little more outrageously the more he was teased. Maybe there was a little bit of a "fuck you" in the walk. But one day he was walking to school and he was attacked by three of his classmates and he was thrown over a bridge and he was killed. And the question that community had to deal with—and, indeed, the entire media that covered this event—was how could it have been that somebody's gait, that somebody's style of walking, could engender the desire to kill that person? I mean, what is it that's so threatening in that social space? And I think, if that young man could show that gender was that variable or if he could cross over to another gender so effectively, it really raised the question for everybody else—and especially for those that attacked him—of whether their own genders were also perhaps not quite as stable or quite as fixed as they thought. And I think it also evoked sexual panic because, if he's a girl, if he's girling himself on the street, then, those boys in relationship to him, are they in a heterosexual encounter? Is this an encounter with a girl? And does that make them homosexual? Does that make them heterosexual? I think the panic around all those issues led to a desire to obliterate this person from the face of the earth because they could not handle the challenge. And that makes me think about the walk in a different way. I mean, a walk can be a dangerous thing. If you go for a walk, you're also vulnerable socially. There's no question about that. You assert your rights of mobility and you take a certain risk in public space.

s. TAYLOR: I'm just remembering when I was little, when I did walk, when I would walk places, I would be told that I walked like a monkey. And I think that for a lot of disabled people, the violence and the sort of hatred exists a lot in this reminding of people that our bodies are going to age and are going to die. And in some ways I wonder also, just thinking about the monkey comment, that it is also—and this is just a thought off the top of my head right now—where our boundaries lie as a human and what becomes nonhuman. You know?

BUTLER: Well, it makes me wonder whether the person was antievolutionary? Maybe they're creationists. It's like, why shouldn't we have some resemblance to the monkey? [*Laughs.*]

S. TAYLOR: Well, the monkey's always been my favorite animal, so, actually, quite a lot of the time I was flattered.

BUTLER: Exactly!

S. TAYLOR: But when in those in-between moments of in between male and female or in between death and health do you still count as a human?

BUTLER: Right—or animal-human-machine. Right? Animal-human-machine. You know, those boundaries, they make up the complex environment for all of our lives. There's no way that we can distill the human out of those relationships.

S. TAYLOR: And I think what's ultimately threatening about it, about all these things, about the way in which someone moves or the way in which someone uses their bodies or the way in which someone speaks differently, is that it's a threat to our most basic categories that we've built our systems of power on. And maybe that's why it hits people at such an emotionally uncontrollable level.

BUTLER: I think so. And these are really restrictive ideas about what the human is. I have to have a fixed gender in order to be a recognizable human, I have to be able to be human and not animal, or to be human and not motorized by metal, I have to be somehow extracted from all these things and stabilized, able-bodied, fully capable according to various standards.

S. TAYLOR: I'm just thinking about the eugenics movement. I mean, that is a very clear, physical thing that happened very recently in history where it was: this human doesn't count enough as a human to be allowed to breathe, basically.

BUTLER: Well, I think this leads to the question of how we conceive of human lives that are worth protecting, worth sheltering, worth supporting in their capacity to flourish, however they might flourish, and I think that's also true in our contemporary war effort. For example, the way Iraqi civilians are consistently presented by the media—theirs are lives not worth preserving. They're not even human lives that we've destroyed. They're threats to the human. They don't look human enough to protect from war. I think that we're all very confused and cruel when it comes to thinking about the category of who is human.

A. TAYLOR: Can we dig even deeper into the perceived threat that the populations you are discussing pose? Why the aggression and fear towards them?

BUTLER: Well, I think there are a lot of different reasons for social violence toward people who are perceived to be on the margins of gender, the margins of able-bodiedness, the margins of racial normativity, and a lot of it has to do with fear of contact and contagion, that maybe somebody else's vulnerability will become one's own. I think the thought of another person in a state of dependency, in a state of social marginalization, makes some people want to assert their centrality and their power as a way of evading any feelings they might have of their own limitations or dependency or permeability otherwise. So in a world in which we are all subject to violence, where we could all be violently impinged upon against our will, people manage that sense of precariousness. They want other people to embody it for them so they can feel protected or immunized from it.

But, in fact, my own sense is that a lot of what we've been talking about brings us to a recognition that lives are precarious, fragile, dependent, but also capable in very specific kinds of ways. And that gets organized differently for different people. But I don't think that there's any evading either side of that territory. I guess the main point that I want to make is that, as bodies, we're vulnerable. I mean, that's the thing about bodies. They're not just self-motored, they're not just self-sufficient, they're always vulnerable to being looked at, to being called, to being touched. They're also capable of touching or sexual love or intimacy, to other forms of physical contact, right? And none of us get to fully control the way in which that happens. So I would say one feature of human bodies is permeability. We can be contacted, we can be impinged upon by others, and sometimes that's great and welcome and sometimes it's horrific. But there's no way to get rid of that aspect of the body. And I sometimes think that the social violence that affects people who look more permeable, who look more dependent, who look less defended, is a way in which impermeability on the side of the people who are violent is managed: *you* be the permeability of the body, *you* stand for the vulnerability of the body, and *I* will be the impermeable. So it's a way of managing and allocating that permeability so others stand for it and one gets to feel through one's violent acts that one's exempt. But no one's exempt.

[*We take a short break and move to a different part of the Mission District.*]

I was thinking about these ideals of self-sufficiency that people have about bodies: that bodies should be self-sufficient, that we worry when they're not. And one thought that I've had about gender, for instance, is that nobody has their own gender. That is to say, no one gets to have a gender all on their own. That's because we're embodied; we fundamentally depend on other people to recognize who we are and to help us figure out who we are in a social world. We can't—we don't, actually—make radical or self-sufficient decisions about who we want to be or how we are perceived or recognized. I mean, one of the struggles for gender and sexual minorities has been to get recognition for who one is. And if one doesn't have recognition for one's gender presentation or one's gender identification, then there's a certain kind of suffering—one doesn't get fully constituted socially, one doesn't get a place in the social order. So that's a kind of dependency, right? If I need someone else or some group of people or a social world to recognize me in my gendered reality, then I'm going to petition the law or I'm going to petition medical establishments or I'm going to petition educational establishments to allow me to be whatever gender it is I'm petitioning to be. But I can't really do it on my own. In other words, we're all dependent on social vocabularies, on the availability of recognition, on institutions that will give us the acknowledgment we need in order to live the lives that we have to have. So, in my view, none of us simply makes up our gender on our own or lives it as a radical individual, self-sufficiently. We're constantly negotiating to gain certain kinds of recognition or to produce the social world in which we can live. And that means gender is kind of constituted socially, interrelationally. It doesn't generate from me, it's not an expression of my individual personhood; it's my effort to negotiate a social world on which I'm radically dependent.

[*At this point we realize that we're stranded on a stretch of sidewalk that has no curb cuts. We have to stop filming as Sunaura's chair and the camera, which is mounted on a dolly, are lifted onto the street.*]

I'm interested in that moment where you picked up that article at the age of twenty or whatever it was. I wonder what the language was that allowed you to recognize that disability was not a purely personal issue, that it was socially constituted, and what kind of empowerment is involved in that recognition? And it's hard because it means there's a limit to individualism, although each of us are obviously negotiating our individual solutions to the problems of ability, disability, gender normativity, all these issues, we can't do that as radical individuals. We can only do it by entering social space, demanding different kinds of recognition, producing certain kinds of bodily scandals in the world, and, also, acting in concert with other people as a way of changing what is normative and what is not.

Again I think underlying all of this is the idea that we are interdependent as we try and attract certain social transformations that affect us at very personal levels, right? How I can love and how I can move and how I can eat. I think this also links to the idea that the body is itself—whatever else it is—a site of dependency. None of us come to the world independently. Infants are radically dependent. We're all radically dependent, and if we're not cared for by others, if we can't rely on that care, we cannot thrive, and even what we call our self-sufficiency, whatever that might be, can't come into being without a certain kind of well-met dependency, a dependency that got addressed and continues to be addressed. And it's not as if any of us, no matter how able-bodied we are, overcome that dependency when we become adults. We might posture as if we do, but think about the systems on which all of our bodies depend. It's quite astonishing if you think about health care or you think about systems of shelter or any number of things like that.

s. taylor: The disability community sort of has this distinction between what people think of as being independent and actual individual physical independence. Because, the truth is, in our society right now it's really about being in control of services. It's being able to be in control and choose. I think this way of understanding independence is helpful.

butler: Yeah, but even if we take that formulation, right?—to be independent is to have the ability to choose certain kinds of services—that depends on a world of services being in place. That depends on Republicans not controlling the universe and the social-service economy not being decimated by the effects of capitalism. There are so many things we are dependent on in order to exercise what we call our autonomy. My sense is that what's at stake here, both in the kind of gender politics like we've been talking about and the disability movement, is really rethinking the human as a site of interdependency. I think that there are certain notions of autonomy, of self-sufficiency, that have actually led us astray, that have made us think about individuals as self-motored, and, in fact, individuals are never self-motored, no one comes into the world self-motored. And to the degree that we find ways of moving, of living, we do so because we've been cared for by people and we continue to be cared for by people. Systems of care are essential to human relationality and they don't ever cease to be. And that becomes especially true with illness, it becomes true with aging, but I think it's true within every phase of life.

s. TAYLOR: Yeah. I do think it's important in this conversation just to think about economics and capitalism and how that has affected and created, in a lot of ways, this myth of self-sufficiency and of independence. And also how capitalism in so many ways treats some human beings as . . .

BUTLER: Expendable?

s. TAYLOR: Expendable, because they're no longer efficient in the workplace. And I think that has a lot to do with aging and weakness and disability. To put it really simply, certain bodies can't be good workers, and all bodies at a certain point in the process of aging won't be good workers.

I guess the question is, what do we want from society? What do we want a society to be? Do we want a society that only values people for the ways in which their bodies are efficient or fit these norms of productivity and profit? Or do we want society to value the sort of dependency that all people share?

BUTLER: Well, of course one of the problems of capitalism is that it exploits precisely that dependency, right? It offers a certain prospect of survivability to those who can comply with its work norms. And it does actually have a stake in keeping a working class dependent in that way. The question is, what would dependency look like if it weren't being exploited under those kinds of conditions? And I think when you walk into the coffee shop, if I can go back to that moment for a moment, and you ask for the coffee, or you even ask for some assistance with the coffee, the question of asking for assistance is also a question in which you're basically posing the question: Do we or do we not live in a world in which we assist each other? Do we or do we not help each other with basic needs? And are basic needs there to be kind of decided on as a social issue and not just my personal, individual issue or your personal, individual issue? So there's a challenge to individualism that happens in the moment in which you ask for some assistance with the coffee cup. And hopefully people will take it up and say, "Yes, I too live in that world in which I understand that we need each other in order to address our basic needs. And I want to organize a social and political world on the basis of that recognition!" It's no less than that kind of challenge.

But I think what we're also seeing these days—and we see it in Europe with the decimation of the social welfare state, I think we see it in the U.S. under the conditions of neoliberalism, which I don't want to get into too much—but we see the systematic production of precarious populations, populations that are always living on some edge, whose survivability is not guaranteed, it's not guaranteed by anyone, and the retraction of that obligation to imperiled populations, to refugees, to the poor, to those who are without health care. We're seeing a heightening of that precariousness under contemporary conditions. And I think it really poses the question of whether we still conceive of the human community as a system of necessary interdependency. And I think there are people who really want to say no, who really want to break that and let certain lives go, for the purposes of maximizing profit or even a kind of theory of the survival of the fittest.

s. TAYLOR: Disabled people make up the largest minority in the world and we have the lowest employment rate. There's also, for instance, the nursing home industry, which has a vested interest in institutionalizing people, and different movements throughout history that have aimed either to do away with people who have disabilities or to stop them from breeding. Considering all that, I think we are definitely a very strong example of a precarious community.

BUTLER: Of a precarious community, yes. And I think some of what we've been talking about in terms of who constitutes an intelligible human or who's recognizable as a human being—what are the norms that constrain our conceptions of who is human and who is not—that these, what seem like intellectual issues or conceptual issues, are actually profoundly economic ones as well. Those lives considered precarious or not worth sheltering or protecting—

S. TAYLOR: Even giving birth to.

BUTLER: —not worth giving birth to, not worth mourning when they die, not worth attending to when they're ill, not worth providing the conditions under which they might flourish—we see more and more populations differentiated along those lines. I think the question of whose lives are worth protecting, valuing, furthering, really gets to the heart of the issue.

ACKNOWLEDGMENTS

Since these interviews were initially conducted for a documentary and filmmaking is a profoundly collaborative medium, many more people were crucial to the creation of this project than would have been the case if it had been devised solely for print.

My deepest thanks go to the subjects who allowed me, in the ambiguously sarcastic words of Slavoj Žižek, to "ruin their afternoons." They were all incredibly generous and gracious, allowing me to walk them in circles while asking variations of the same question over and over again. I particularly appreciate their attention to the chapters presented here and patience with any follow-up queries I posed.

This project also wouldn't exist without the incomparable Ron Mann, whose infectious enthusiasm and faith in this effort convinced me that it was possible. He, in turn, brought steadfast producer Bill Imperial on board, as well as Michael Boyuk and the rest of the Sphinx Productions and FilmsWeLike family.

Given the fact they're responsible for some of my all-time favorite documentaries, it has always been my dream to work with the National Film Board of Canada. Producer extraordinaire Lea Marin was sublimely Socratic in her approach, and the movie benefited greatly from Silva Basmajian's incisive commentary. It was an honor to work with TVO's Jane Jankovic and Linda Fong, whose comments helped the movie find its proper form. Credit also goes to Rudy Butignol, who initially commissioned *Examined Life* and later brought it to Knowledge Network, as well as the Ontario Media Development Council for supporting the project at various junctures.

My brilliant and helpful brother, Alexander Taylor, provided practical support, intellectual backup, and much-needed encouragement and criticism at every stage. My crew—cinematographer John M. Tran, camera assistant Scott Burton, and sound recordist Sanjay Mehta—were pros. Over the course of a brutal winter, editor Robert Kennedy and I pruned down hours of footage into a manageable formation, taking great pleasure in a process that would have driven most people mad. I am also indebted to the many others who gave their time, attention, and skill to the movie at different stages, especially Heather McIntosh.

A few others were so essential in the development, creation, and release of *Examined Life* (often unbeknownst to them) that I must recognize them here: Laura Hanna, Bill Schroeder, Aaron Levy, Polina Malikin, Gavin Browning, Jim Miller, Michelle Ballif, Ronald Bogue, Emily Russo, Nancy Gerstman, Clemence Taillandier, Jonitha Keymoore, Cathy Hsiao, Colin Robinson, Mary Ann Rodriguez, Simon Critchley, Colin McGinn, Rebecca Solnit (without her wonderful book *Wanderlust: A History of Walking*, the project's peripatetic motif never would have crossed my mind), and, in particular, Lawrence Konner.

I'm truly fortunate to have a relationship with The New Press and all the people who make it such a unique and necessary institution, especially Ellen Adler and Sarah Fan. I am relieved these intelligent and gifted women agreed to work with me given my notorious tendency to miss deadlines. The chapters benefited immensely from Sarah's conscientious editing, a task she approaches with appropriate, and much appreciated, levity.

For aiding in the transformation from screen to page, gratitude is due to Charlotte Sheedy and Meredith Kaffel of Sterling Lord Literistic. Anna Grace and Jeremy Varon provided valuable commentary on my meandering preface. Giving freely of his (limited) time and (seemingly limitless) talents, Jeremy, in particular, pushed me to a greater clarity, insight, and eloquence than my meager abilities could have achieved alone.

Finally, I want to acknowledge my family—Will, Valarie, Sunaura, Alexander, Tara, and Jeff—all coconspirators in examined living. My parents, who raised their children as autodidact question-ers of authority, no doubt bear some responsibility for the unusual path I have chosen, though any wrong turns or missteps I make on it are all mine.

THE PHILOSOPHERS

Kwame Anthony Appiah was born in London (where his Ghanaian father was a law student) but moved as an infant to Ghana, where he grew up. A philosopher, cultural theorist, and novelist, he is Laurance S. Rockefeller University Professor of Philosophy at the University Center for Human Values at Princeton University and the author of many books, including *The Ethics of Identity*, *Cosmopolitanism: Ethics in a World of Strangers*, *Thinking It Through,* and *Experiments in Ethics.*

Judith Butler, Maxine Elliot Professor in the Departments of Rhetoric and Comparative Literature at the University of California, Berkeley, has contributed to the fields of feminism, queer theory, political philosophy, and ethics. Published in 1990, *Gender Trouble: Feminism and the Subversion of Identity* has sold well over 100,000 copies internationally, becoming one of the most cited contemporary philosophical texts. Her other books include *Bodies That Matter: On the Discursive Limits of "Sex",* *Precarious Life: Powers of Mourning and Violence*, and *Giving an Account of Oneself.*

Michael Hardt is the co-author, with Antonio Negri, of *Empire*—an international bestseller dubbed the "the *Das Kapital* of the anticorporate movement" by Naomi Klein—as well as its sequel, *Multitude.* He is a professor of literature at Duke University.

Martha Nussbaum, Ernst Freund Distinguished Service Professor of Law and Ethics, holds appointments in the Philosophy Department, Law School, and Divinity School at the University of Chicago and is a board member of the university's human rights program. She holds thirty-two honorary degrees from universities around the world. Her research and writing covers a broad range of subjects: philosophy and literature, ancient philosophy, liberal education, social and political issues, and philosophy of law. Her many books include *Frontiers of Justice: Disability, Nationality, Species Membership; Upheavals of Thought: The Intelligence of Emotions;* and *Liberty of Conscience: In Defense of America's Tradition of Religious Equality.*

Avital Ronell—literary critic, feminist/deconstructionist, and philosopher—received her PhD from Princeton University in 1979 before continuing her studies with Jacques Derrida and Hélène Cixous in Paris. University Professor at New York University and Jacques Derrida Chair of Philosophy and Media at the European Graduate School in Switzerland, she is the author of *The Telephone Book: Technology, Schizophrenia, Electric Speech; The Test Drive;* and *Stupidity,* among other works, and writes regularly for *Artforum, ArtUS,* and *Vacarme* (Paris). She is a 2009 guest curator at the Centre Pompidou, where she offered a "rencontre" with Werner Herzog, Judith Butler, Laurence Rickels, Jean-Luc Nancy, and others.

Peter Singer, called the "most influential" living philosopher by the *New Yorker,* is Ira W. Decamp Professor of Bioethics in the University Center for Human Values at Princeton University and Laureate Professor at the Centre for Applied Philosophy and Public Ethics (CAPPE), University of Melbourne. He has written many books, including *Animal Liberation,* a seminal text of the animal rights movement; *Practical Ethics;* and, most recently, *The Life You Can Save: Acting Now to End World Poverty.*

Sunaura Taylor is an artist, writer, and activist living in Oakland, California. She is disabled due to U.S. military pollution, a legacy that has affected all aspects of her work. Her artworks have been exhibited at venues across the country, including the Smithsonian Institution and the Berkeley Art Museum. She is the recipient of numerous awards, including a 2004 Sacatar Foundation Fellowship and a 2008 Joan Mitchell Foundation Grant. Her published work includes the *Monthly Review* article "The Right Not to Work: Disability and Capitalism" and "Military Waste in Our Drinking Water" (with Astra Taylor), which was nominated for a 2007 Project Censored Award. Taylor is currently co-editing a book on disability and animal rights. She received her undergraduate degree in disability studies from Goddard College and holds an MFA from the University of California, Berkeley's Department of Art Practice. Her website is www.sunaurataylor.org.

Cornel West, the Class of 1943 University Professor at Princeton University, has been heralded by *Newsweek* as an "eloquent prophet with attitude." In his latest book, *Hope on a Tightrope*, he offers courageous commentary on issues that affect the lives of all Americans; themes include race, leadership, faith, family, philosophy, and love and service. His other books include the *New York Times* bestsellers *Race Matters*, which won the American Book Award, and *Democracy Matters*. West has won numerous awards and has received more than twenty honorary degrees. He also was an influential force in developing the storyline for the popular *Matrix* movie trilogy.

Slavoj Žižek is a Slovenian philosopher and cultural critic. He is a professor at the European Graduate School; International Director of the Birkbeck Institute for the Humanities, Birkbeck College, University of London; and a senior researcher at the Institute of Sociology, University of Ljubljana, Slovenia. He has published

南懷瑾 講述

我說參同契

上冊

老古文化事業公司

我說參同契（上冊）

南懷瑾　講述

封面題字：南懷瑾

國際標準書號：ISBN 978-957-2070-88-8

己丑 2009(98)年三月臺灣初版一刷
庚寅 2010(99)年三月臺灣初版六刷

有版權・勿翻印　● 局版臺業字第一五九五號 ●

發 行 人：南懷瑾・郭姮妟

出 版 者：老古文化事業股份有限公司

地　　址：台北市100信義路一段五號一樓（附設門市）

郵政信箱：台北郵政一一七―六一二號信箱

電　　話：（〇二）二三九六―〇三三七　　傳真：（〇二）二三九六―〇三四七

郵政劃撥：〇一五九四二六―一　　帳戶名稱：老古文化事業股份有限公司

香港出版：經世學庫發展有限公司

地　　址：香港中環都爹利街八號鑽石會大廈十樓

電　　話：（八五二）二八四五―五五五五　　傳真：（八五二）二五二五―二二〇一

網　　址：http://www.laoku.com.tw

電子郵件：laoku@ms31.hinet.net

定價：新臺幣三二〇元整

宋儒朱熹化名鄒訢註

參同契是大笑話

昔年為講此書亦一大
笑話

劉雨虹翻舊稿整理又
一笑話

仙佛不可見不可知是
一大笑話

生不知所來死不知所
去豈不笑話

要我衰老之年校閱此
書豈不笑話

姑且留待高明者自有
慧目看清楚即是

去更是笑話

戊子臘月杪
南懷瑾

楔子

宋儒朱熹化名鄒訢註
參同契是大笑話
昔年為講此書亦一大
笑話
劉雨虹翻舊稿整理又
一笑話
仙佛不可見不可知是
一大笑話
生不知所來死不知所
去豈不笑話
要我衰老之年校閱此
書豈不笑話
姑且留待高明者自有
慧目看清楚即是
去更是笑話

戊子臘月杪
南懷瑾

出版說明

這本書是南師懷瑾先生講解《參同契》的記錄，時為一九八三年在台北十方書院。

《參同契》一書，自來被認係丹經之鼻祖，為超凡成仙的修煉寶典，是徹底轉變肉體生命而成為壽與天齊的神仙。用現在的語言來說，就是真正的生命科學了。

作者乃東漢時期的魏伯陽真人（約西元一〇〇年—？），距今已一千八百年了。魏真人出身浙江上虞官宦望族之家，不喜仕途而愛好修道，後入神仙之列，並將修煉經驗寫出這本《參同契》，當時佛法尚未傳入中國。

清朝初年，有道家北宗龍門派道士朱雲陽，因早年由此書入門，又三山五嶽遍參諸方後修煉有成，再窮十年之功，註釋《參同契》，於康熙八年己酉（一六六九年）刻版印行，書名為《參同契闡幽》。此書一掃千多

年來對《參同契》的錯解、邪見與誤導，而正視聽。此次課程所採用的書本，即自由出版社所印的這本書。

惟讀《參同契》猶如讀天書，即如雲陽真人這本闡幽，亦為三百多年前的古典文章，加以一般人對《易經》、陰陽五行等缺乏研究，欲懂《參同契》太不容易，如無真實修養者解說，實難入其堂奧。其實，連入門都不可能。

《參同契》共分三篇，上篇與中篇讀之令人有重複之感；其實不然，上篇為綱要原則，中篇再作深入微細解說，以免曲解而流入旁門別庭。

南師懷瑾先生，當時選講這門課程，旨在引導學人進入中華重要典籍的初步研討，所講僅上篇及中篇之重點（包括十八、二十、二十一、廿二及二十四章一段），因下篇為總結，學人應可自己研究了。

南師講解後，有行者逐漸發現，在工夫修持過程中，道家的著作如《參同契》一書，解說具體而周詳，且有對治方法。有人甚至說，仔細研讀了南師的講解，才對佛法的修持較為明瞭，尤其對東晉初期傳來佛家修

煉禪定的十六特勝法門，才有真切的體會。

另有人說，略知《參同契》，才了解什麼是正統道家，什麼是邪說亂道，這世界上的誤傳和歪曲修法太多了。

《參同契》是在佛法傳入中國之前的著作，之後佛經翻譯常採道家的遣辭用字。朱雲陽真人由習禪而轉道家，故而常以禪法解說。朱氏認為，《參同契》「向來埋藏九地，而今始升九天之上」，乃指《參同契闡幽》一書，令原著轉暗為明。

也有人說，《參同契》不止是丹經道書，而是古哲學，古典文學之作，其中包含了中華民族最高深承天接地的文化‥是一顆明珠，因深奧而埋藏，經朱氏闡幽而出土；更因南師深入淺出的講解而閃發光芒。

吾人何其有幸，生為炎黃子孫，有祖先璀璨光輝的文化留傳，豈能不繼續努力以發揚先祖的智慧成果！

再說這本書的出版，頗為偶然且有趣。緣香港佛教圖書館的親證尼師，發覺南師所講《參同契》錄音帶，保存不易，故而率同圖書館數位同

修加以記錄，再由石宏君將文字略加清順。稿子帶至廟港後，歷經我等八

個多月整理，將所涉及種種問題，請示南師加以釐清、修訂、補充，務使

儘量明白易懂，以便利讀者。

《參同契》為兩學期的課程，每週一次二小時，共八十講，所講內容

涉及廣泛，舉證既多，更有南師親身諸多奇特經歷的人與事。全部整理後

八十餘萬字，故分上中下三冊，計劃三個月內出齊。

此次配合工作，除張振熔查證資料外，更有宏忍師自二〇〇六年起即

搭配相助，晝夜辛勞，因緣特殊，特誌之。

又，書中小標題為編者所加。

劉雨虹　記

二〇〇九年一月

目錄

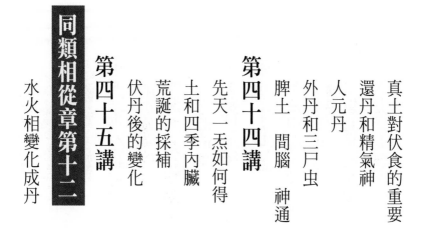

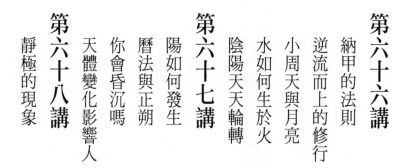

第七十九講

關鍵三寶章第二十二

第一講

　　我們書院有關道家哲學思想的課程，從《老子》《莊子》到《列子》，是一系列連貫下來的。現在要研究的是《參同契》，這是最難研究的一本書。我本人對《參同契》的理解不一定是全對的，這並不是謙虛，我只能把自己的一些心得提出來，貢獻給諸位做參考。這一本書在中國整體文化裏，佔有非常重要的份量，古人更直指《參同契》是千古丹經之鼻祖。古今以來，尤其是講修道的神仙之學，要煉丹法，要返老還童求得長生不老之術，這是一本非讀不可的祕密典籍。不僅如此，它可以說既是哲學又是科學，很多有關學理，都來自這本書。現在西方人研究中國古代科學發展史，也把《參同契》看成是化學、地球物理、天文等等學問的重要源頭。只是我們自己中國人往往忽略了這一本書，原因之一是這本書實在很難研究。

驚人的學說

書名為什麼叫做《參同契》？「參」就是參合，「同」就是相同。怎麼樣叫做「參同」？簡單的說，就是參合三種原則相同的學問，融於一爐。這三種學問就是老莊、道家的丹道，還有《易經》的學問。我先聲明，我是沒有做到返老還童長生不死；假使做到了，我應該是個童子，結果我還是個老頭子。不過這裏提一件事情希望大家注意，據我所瞭解，世界上人類都在研究追問生命的來源，也在追問是不是死後有個東西可以存在。全世界人類由宗教開始，一直到現在的科學，都在繞著這些問題打轉。宗教家說有一個東西在人死後還存在的，到天堂那裏，或者到了別的世界，像極樂世界。這種說法是不是能兌現，我們不知道，不過教主那麼說，信眾當然那麼信。只有中國文化沒有提這個事情。

但是中國文化提出來，人的肉體生命與天地一樣，是可以永遠存在的。我們標榜人的生命可以「與天地同休」、「與日月同壽」。中國文化

把人的生命價值，提得那麼高，並不靠上帝，不靠佛菩薩，也不靠祖宗、鬼神。每一個人都有這個資格，每人都可以作上帝，可以成聖賢、成仙、成佛，只要能找到自己生命中真正的東西。我們現在活著，真東西沒有發展出來，都是假的部份在維持著生命。

所以中國文化大膽地說，人的生命可以與天地同壽，只要太陽月亮在宇宙存在，我就存在，與日月一樣的長久。我們研究世界各國的文化，不管是宗教是哲學還是科學，沒有敢這樣大膽吹牛的！可以說世界上吹牛吹得最厲害的是我們中華民族。即使只是一種假設，也只有中國文化敢這麼講。其次，道家提出來，可以利用自己肉體的生命功能返老還童，長生不死．；外國任何文化也沒有敢這樣說的。將來有沒有不管，至少過去沒有。

所以講到中國文化的特點，只有道家的思想具有這一種特點。比較接近的是印度佛家的文化，但是佛家在這一方面是不願多提的，只是偶然露一點消息。在釋迦牟尼佛的許多弟子當中，他特別吩咐四個人「留形住世」，把肉體生命留在這個世界上，等到下一次地球冰河時期過去，另一

個劫運來了，世界太平的時候，才交代給下一位成佛者，然後他們四人才可以入涅槃，離開這個肉體。

據我所知，只有佛家有這麼一個說法，有一點接近中國文化這一方面的消息，這是其他人類文化所沒有的。所以我們站在自己中國文化的立場看來，這一點很值得炫耀。

可是千古以來，究竟有沒有不死的神仙？我們從小讀的小說，聽的傳聞，乃至丹經、道書、神仙傳上都說有不死的神仙；甚至現在還有朋友來講某某地方的山洞裏有神仙。問他見到過嗎？不，是聽某人說的，某人又聽他表哥說的，一路追蹤下去連影子都沒有了。世界上說神仙說鬼，多半都是如此。

龍代表的意義

前幾年有年輕人提倡所謂龍的文化，這是很有趣的一件事，年輕人當然有他的理想，可是這樣提法是不大妥當的，因為中國遠古文獻並沒提到

龍的傳人。《易經》上再三講所謂的龍，不過是我們所用的一個標誌而已。孔子是非常佩服老子的，弟子們問他，老子在你心目中究竟如何評價呢？孔子說：鳥，我知道牠能夠飛；魚，我知道牠能夠游；獸，我知道牠能夠走；至於龍，我知道牠能乘風雲上天，而老子他就像龍一樣。

我們古代所講的龍不是西方神話的龍，更不是已經絕種的恐龍。我們這個龍是四棲動物，能夠飛，能夠游泳，能夠陸地上走，能夠鑽山入洞，能夠變大，變成宇宙那麼大；能夠變小，比一根頭髮還要小。所以龍所象徵的就是「隱現無常，變化莫測」，也可以說不可測。古人畫龍沒有畫出龍的全體，所謂神龍見首不見尾，見尾就不見首。這個動物在古代究竟有沒有我們不管，至少是民族表達自我的一種象徵，就像有些民族用獅子，美國人用的是老鷹。

《參同契》提出來的，是老莊的思想觀念、《易經》的變易法則、丹道的修煉方法。三樣的原理相同，只要懂了某一面的道理，對於生命真諦就把握住了，這是《參同契》書名大致的來源。歷史上相傳，作者是東漢

魏伯陽先生，道家稱他魏伯陽真人。我們講《莊子》的時候提到，這個名稱是莊子所創，得道的人叫真人。所以後來道家道教的神仙都稱做真人。

那麼相反的呢？我們沒有得道的都是假人。所謂假人，道家的名稱叫做行屍走肉，把我們人類罵慘啦！沒有得道的人走路，只是屍體在走，其中無物，其中無道，中間是空洞的。

歷史上這位魏伯陽，學術地位很高，官並不大。很奇怪，中國歷史上學問好的人，官大的並不太多；官大的，學問又不一定成比例地好。不過，中國上古的文化，事業功名與學問是一路的，文武是合一的，後世把文武分途了。魏真人對後世的影響很大，道家神仙傳上稱他火龍真人，一條渾身帶火的奇怪的龍。可是在東方我們曉得，龍都是帶雨帶水的。

宋儒口中的異端

過去的中國文化，由於儒家是學術的正統，對於佛家、道家的思想都有一點批判的，所以舊的觀念稱佛、道兩家文化為「異端」。「異端」是

孔子《論語》裏頭一個名辭。後世像宋朝以後的理學家——我叫他們理學家，並不一定承認他們是正統的儒家——他們排斥佛、道兩家，稱兩家為異端之學，好像就是我們現在講的旁門左道。但是孔子並沒有罵佛、道兩家異端，是宋儒擅用了孔子的名辭，自己又不懂這兩家的學問，就是普通說「吃不到葡萄，嫌葡萄酸」同樣的道理。

所謂異端就是偏見，孔子罵一般有偏見的人為異端。「異」就是不同，「端」就是另一頭，另一頭當然是偏見了，當時並不是指佛道兩家。

後世宋儒理學家，共有五大儒，最有名的朱夫子朱熹，我們中國文化受他的影響有數百年之久，實在太大了！宋朝以後的儒家變成朱夫子的儒家，招牌雖打的是孔孟老店，老闆換了朱夫子。本來另外有一個股東合作的，後來被朱夫子趕出去了，就是陸象山陸夫子，所以孔家店後來換了老闆。

朱夫子註了四書，從宋元到明朝，要想考功名做官的話，非用他的思想解釋四書不可，否則是考不上的。假如我生在幾百年前，人家問我《參同契》看過沒有，我說看過，那我就是異端，也就不能考功名了。

整個明朝三百年，朱元璋朱和尚當了皇帝以後，要拉一個有名氣的同宗，光宗耀祖，就認了朱熹先生，他所註的四書就成了國家標準版，致使中國文化染上了重症。朱熹的觀念對與不對，我們暫時不加討論，那是儒家學術範圍。但是朱熹雖然拚命地反對道家與佛家，卻偷偷研究《參同契》，而且他還化名空同道人鄒訢，作《周易參同契考異》。他研究《參同契》很多年，但卻搞不通，到晚年都鑽不進去。當然鑽不進去！他也不打坐，不修道，怎麼鑽得進去！

朱熹與白玉蟾

朱熹為什麼要研究《參同契》呢？據說朱夫子在福建武夷山講學的時候，剛好有一個道家南宗的白玉蟾，也在武夷山修道，有很多徒弟，後世稱他為南宗祖師。既然稱他祖師，差不多也是神仙了。一個道家，一個儒家，二人門下都有大批弟子。人類的好奇，古今中外都是一樣，這些儒家年輕讀書人，每天都聽子曰、子曰，聽了半天，沒有怎麼樣。可是看到人

家那邊修煉神仙丹道工夫的，不是紅光滿面就是臉上發青發烏，覺得總有一套，奇怪呀！就偷偷跑過去聽。

朱熹總是講那是異端，你們不要亂去聽。後來弟子們告訴朱夫子，白老師那裏是有些怪事情，他有先知之明，是有道之人。朱夫子說，他「偶中爾」！也就是說瞎貓撞到死老鼠，給他碰巧碰對了。這個話當然是在他自己的補習班裏對自己學生講的，可是那個白玉蟾老師，也沒有出門就知道了。第二天白老師就叫學生來約朱夫子，兩校同學歡去郊遊。朱夫子也很高興，就同意了。一去郊遊，這可好了！下起雨來，大家沒有帶雨傘都淋濕了。可是白老師雖在雨中，他走過的地方四面沒有雨，身上也不濕。朱夫子忍不住了說：「白老師呀，你這個是什麼道理呀？」白玉蟾笑笑說「偶中爾！」這一個「偶中爾」，朱熹臉面就掛不住了，心想我昨天說給學生聽的話，他怎麼知道？而且今天馬上回敬我一個耳光一樣。這個很奇怪，因此朱熹開始研究《參同契》。

朱熹經常偷偷研究佛、研究道，這是公開的祕密，誰不想活得長命，

誰不想變成超人？只是面子上死不肯承認。所以我對宋儒不論哪一位，始終有一點不認同。學問道德宋儒沒有話講，就只有一樣不好，明明借用了佛家道家的學理，來說明儒家的道理，然後翻臉批評他兩家都是異端，都是騙人。宋儒搞的這一套，叫什麼聖賢之學呀！

說到朱熹批評佛道兩家的話，似乎內行又很外行。譬如他作了道家與佛家的比較，講了很內行的話，在朱熹文集裏頭都有。他說道家修道是「形神相守」，這個對道家就超過普通的了解，這是說修煉神仙之道，可以修到返老還童長生不死。怎麼叫「形神相守」呢？道家認為這個身體是形體，等於是個機器，這個機器的電能是道家所稱元神，是我們靈魂生命的根本，那是電能，就像電燈有了電能才發亮。所以只要我們這個肉體存在，那個元神就在我們身上。身上每個細胞每個地方都通元神的，人老形體衰了，這個機器用壞了，神也不通就離開了。道家所以能夠返老還童長生不死，他做的工夫就是把形與神凝結在一塊，這就叫煉丹。

佛家不同，佛家講涅槃，生死都是空的嘛，時間到了，打個坐就走

了。所以朱熹說佛家是「形神相離」，學佛的人求空，把肉體都看空了，使神和身體分離，這是朱熹的批評。表面上一看，佛家、道家都駁他不了，他不簡單的呀！道家佛家的修煉工夫和學理，他還是作過研究的。

朱熹的學問沒有話講，但他對於白骨觀沒有深入研究，批評白骨觀不是究竟。他說學佛的喜歡修白骨觀，所以覺得這個世界是痛苦的，沒有意思，不想留戀，而想到西方極樂世界。他不同意這個觀念，又認為白骨觀在佛家工夫是下層的，當然他沒有寫他認為高的工夫是什麼。其實他沒寫的下一句，就是認為人的生命是可以留在這個世界上的。不過他老兄同我們一樣沒有留住，他下意識承認，人的壽命是可以修的。

朱熹在他的傳記裏有好幾條是他對《參同契》、對道家學問研究的結果，他下意識承認，人的壽命是可以修的。

第二點關於儒家與佛道的關係，我常常提一句話，讀書人都愛好仙佛。尤其中國過去一般的讀書人，你查他一生的歷史、文章、詩集，都記載有幾個和尚道士的朋友。好像不交幾個這種朋友，就沒有學術地位。也像很多現代人，要認識電視電影明星，才表示自己交際的廣潤一樣。當

年想認識和尚道士，是表示自己清高，所以文集詩集裏，幾乎每一個人都談到與佛道人士交往的事。知識份子都好仙佛之道，但是知識份子永遠修不成功，因為學問好，欲望就多，煩惱就大。叫他打坐放下來修道，想是想，辦不到。可是反過來看歷代神仙傳《高僧傳》，我們卻得出一個結論，就是仙佛的學問都很好。所以如清代詩人舒位有句詩說：「由來富貴原如夢，未有神仙不讀書」，這是真正的名言。青年同學要想學神仙的，書一定要讀好才有希望。

我曾經把這個詩第一句改了，寫了一副對聯送給一個喜歡喝酒的文人朋友，他是富貴中人，所以上一句就改成「由來名士都耽酒」，一般名士都喜歡喝酒的，下一句還是「未有神仙不讀書」，因為學神仙許多是愛讀書的。

參同契三大綱要

講了這麼多算是《參同契》的開場白，這一部書有歷代各家的註解，

書中主要的有三大綱要：第一是「御政」，第二是「養性」，第三是「伏食」。所謂「御政」，那包括很多了，上至皇帝下至一個普通人，想修心養性作人做事都是「御政」。怎麼樣作人呢？就是走一條正路，知道人生的正道，政治也同時包括在其中。所以一切有關修道與作人做事，天文地理，以及人世間各種各樣的正當法則原理，都屬於「御政」的範圍。

第二「養性」，我們普通人修道學佛，要夠得上第二步「養性」可難了。我經常說學佛修道是我們中國古時的一個科學，這一門學問是研究身心性命之學，它是有理論的，自己生命身體怎麼來？為什麼人有思想？要想得到答案，必須先把理論弄清楚，懂了理論再來修行。修行就是實驗，反求諸己，用自己的身心去做實驗的。自然的科學也是懂了原理理論，然後用物來做實驗的。

這個所謂「御政」的原理懂了以後，修養才叫做「養性」。但是我們一般學佛學道的，不管用哪一種法門，念佛也好，禱告也好，唸咒子也好，打坐也好，都是走「養性」的最初步路子，可是性仍然養不好！要

「養性」，首先就要認識性，也就是佛家所講的明心見性。常有人說某人個性不好，個性是什麼東西？還有中文把男女關係也叫做性，明心見性至高無上也用這個性。這個性究竟是什麼東西？這就牽涉到中國文化的本位了。《禮記》上提出來人有「性」跟「情」兩部份，所謂性情，我們老一輩子講話，這一個孩子性情不大好呀。這個性情的性是什麼東西？情又是什麼東西？所以「養性」是養哪一種性？這些都是大問題。

第三「伏食」，就是成神仙。「伏食」就是在「御政」與「養性」做到之後，最後那個工夫。這個東西不從外來，是從自己生命裏來。但是也不全然是從自己這個肉體生命來的，而是同宇宙有關係的。就是說有一個東西忽然會進入身體中來，但不是從嘴巴進去，而是由身體另外一個地方進去的。千古神仙不敢講，據說講了天打雷劈。不過我已經被天打雷劈很多次了，雷公來了我也跟他講理。

我認為道是天下的公道，既然是天下之公道，就沒有什麼可祕密的；不是我的也不是你的，也不屬於上帝。過去人為什麼要當祕密藏起來呢？

是怕人學壞了，因此把道法變成祕密，大部份是這個原因。好像一把刀一樣，壞人拿刀去殺人，可是醫生開刀也是靠這把刀。我素來不藏祕密，何必關起門來？不過有時候我也關門，因為我囉哩囉嗦講了半天，公道擺在那裏，你就應該懂，何必來問我，我就煩了。

這另外一個進入人體的地方，就是頭頂。我們曉得嬰兒頭頂上這裏砰砰跳，修道修得好，這裏一定開了，學密宗叫做開頂，不曉得你們諸位看過沒有？我是看過的，書上看來的不算數，我碰到過這種人。過去我在四川的時候有一位老師七十幾了，鶴髮童顏。

鶴髮可以有兩種解釋，一種鶴的羽毛是白色的，所以鶴髮是形容銀白頭髮；童顏是說面孔如嬰兒一般。但是另一種解釋說鶴髮是黑的，所以暫且不做定論。講到這位老師，他有四個特點，七十幾歲子孫滿堂，卻不跟子孫在一起，一個人住一個小房子修道。房頂瓦漏了，他也不用樓梯，自己拿幾片瓦，一跳就上了屋頂，補好了再跳下來，這是我們親眼看到的。

第二點，我們都曉得這個老師從不睡覺，我們年輕人頑皮都是第一流

的，故意輪班和他談話，一講一整夜。他有一個習慣，一到了正子時，他靠在椅子上不動也不說話，無論你怎麼說話他就是不答。大概要經過半個鐘頭，眼睛張開了，然後你剛才講的話他都答覆你，每天夜裏如此，我們屢試不爽。

第三個特點，他七十幾歲的老人，兩個乳房一擠，同女人一樣有奶水的。換一句話說，他修道到了這個程度，他的血已經變成白漿，當然不是什麼變成白血球，白血球過多是毛病。

第四點，他的頭頂上我們都去摸，砰砰跳的，同那個嬰兒一樣。別的稀奇古怪事我們不去管他，可這四點很不同，是別人稀奇古怪不來的，也是我親自見到的。這個所謂「伏食」，與頭頂有關，到了某一個時候這個東西就進來了。

後來宋朝南宗道人張紫陽真人，他著的另外一本丹經《悟真篇》，同《參同契》媲美。張紫陽真人既是禪宗的祖師，又是道家神仙。他那篇《悟真篇》就提到「伏食」的道理，他說「一粒金丹吞入腹，始知我命不

由天」，那也是牛吹得很大。他說人修道到了「伏食」那個境界，一個東西就進來了。「一粒金丹吞入腹」，腹是這個肚子，這可不是大家修道修的這個丹田，「始知我命不由天」，生命就可以自己做主了，這就是「伏食」的綱要。

三種丹

在這裏我要再介紹道家所講的「伏食煉丹」。在我們的甲骨文裏，也就是中國最古老的文字，丹字跟太陽的「日」字一樣，就是一個圓圈中間一點，空空洞洞之中有一個東西。後來把這個丹字中間加了一橫，有各種寫法，反正是代表有個東西在一個空洞的中間。

我們曉得道家的分類有三種丹，所謂天元丹、地元丹、人元丹。我們普通一般所謂打坐做工夫，打通任督二脈奇經八脈，煉精化氣，煉氣化神，煉神還虛，都是自己做工夫在身體中煉成了「人元丹」。現在一般練氣功的人還做不到，真正煉丹成功的還只是「人元丹」。

「人元丹」是根據道家的《高上玉皇胎息經》來的。這本經講到上藥三品，就是人本身的精氣神，我們後世一般打坐修道做工夫都在搞這個東西。這個就又要扯到明朝的大儒王陽明，他同朱熹對中國文化影響都非常之大。不過他同朱熹的路線相反，是走陸象山這個學派的路線，而且佛道兩家他都學過。在他傳記裏都有，能夠未卜先知，不過後來他放棄了。為什麼放棄？也就是書讀多了，官做大了，「道」就不容易修成功了。王陽明雖然最後放棄了學道，可是也吹了一句大話，依我們現在觀念看來是逃避的心態，他說道家也不必修，在那裏練氣功打坐，上通下來，下通上去，一天時間都浪費了，王陽明認為那是搬弄精神。

但是我們再仔細看看王陽明這一句話，他承認人的生命裏有一個東西叫做精神，他至少承認這一點。我們常常看到有恭維人精神不死，精神是什麼東西？精神是不是一個真東西？這是個問題！如果是真東西的話，就可以把握回來，把握回來就叫做「人元丹」。王陽明後來為什麼能夠搬弄精神而不搬了？我們休息一下再作報告。

第二講

想成仙的大人物們

剛才講到王陽明這個理學家，他也學過佛，學過道，打坐工夫很好。學佛走的是天台宗止觀這個路線，修道家走的是哪一派的丹法沒有資料可查。有一點在他的傳記裏記載，當時有一個道人叫蔡蓬頭，蓬頭是外號。因為修道的人把名利已經看得不值錢了，所以自己姓什麼、叫什麼沒有關係。這人道行很高，王陽明曾經專門去山中的道觀拜訪他。蔡蓬頭站在道觀的山門外面，王陽明老遠就跪下向他磕頭。這個蔡蓬頭居然拂袖而去，袖子一甩進山門去了，王陽明趕快站起來，跟他走進道觀大殿。

道家的大殿供的是「三清」，是太上老君的一氣化三清，據說太上老君就是老子搖身一變變出來的。反正這些宗教事情，事出有因，查無實據。這個三清是「上清、太清、玉清」，如果我們做比較宗教研究，這有

可能是從佛家來的。佛教大廟子的正殿供的三尊佛，代表了「法、報、化」三身；如果我們用道家的觀念來講就是「精、氣、神」。「精」是「化身」，生生不已；「神」是「法身」；「氣」是「報身」。

這個蔡蓬頭當時走進大殿，在「三清」前面一站，不理這個王陽明。王陽明一上大殿，又跪下來磕頭，蔡蓬頭又拂袖而去，向後面上了一個假山上的亭子，王陽明跟到亭子上，又磕頭。蔡蓬頭回頭看看他，對他說，你呀！前庭後堂拜了我三次，「禮雖隆」，你這個禮貌很隆重了，「終不離官氣」。他說你不能修道，功名還有份，將來官做得大，事業好。

我們讀書看道書，看到這個地方不要輕易放過去。一個人的習氣是很難變的，修道的人自然有修道人的習氣。這一點我們講兩句古人的詩，大家聽了不要灰心。古人說「此身未有神仙骨」，這個身體上沒有神仙的骨格，「縱遇真仙莫浪求」，就是看到神仙你也不必拜了，你求了有什麼用？王陽明雖前庭後堂三拜緊跟，蔡蓬頭接著掉頭又走，王陽明又在成功，可見仙佛是生來就有種子的。「莫浪求」就是不要亂求，你求了有

後面跟，但卻找不到人了。

我們再看漢武帝，這些歷史上的大人物和英雄，尤其是中國帝王、名士都喜歡學神仙，其實就是人性心中欲望的擴充。一個人到了事業地位的最高處，一切都滿足以後，唯一要求的是如何能不死。所以秦始皇、漢武帝都求神仙之術。漢武帝在我們中國歷史上可以說是雄才大略，這個稱譽，他當之無愧。一個二十幾歲的年輕人，在一個政治環境很複雜的情形下，登基做了幾十年皇帝，開創了一個盛世，真不容易。可是到了晚年就喜歡學神仙，他求神仙花的本錢太多了，甚至把自己的公主都嫁給一個騙子道士。像這樣荒唐的事情，他都幹得出來，明知道做了錯事還不承認，後來不能自圓其說。

漢武帝旁邊有兩個大臣，一個是汲黯，一個是東方朔。漢武帝是何等難伺候的帝王，在他左右的人講話就很難了，高明的意見很難提出來，因為他太高明了。但是我們看歷史，漢武帝有許多次因為有人犯了大錯，他要殺人，出場擺平的都是東方朔。此人專會說笑話，東逗西逗就把漢武帝

逗笑了，然後事情就作罷了。所以研究作人的道理，要多留意道家的精神。老子的話「曲則全」，一件事情走直線有時候是不行的。一個領導決定的事，明知他是錯的，挑明說決策有問題，那就糟了！人是有個性的，格老子！你說有問題，我偏要幹！所以老子說曲則全，轉一個彎，這個事情就圓滿了。東方朔走的是曲線的路，所以漢武帝碰上很多的問題，東方朔一來，往往就起了作用，把錯誤決定扭轉過來。

漢武帝身旁第二個重要人物是走直線的汲黯。我們大概可以想像這個人臉應該是方方的，一天到晚不帶笑容，講話是仁義道德，連漢武帝都怕他。漢武帝當時見這些大將軍、總司令，常常很隨便，跟他的祖父漢高祖一樣，在宮女幫他洗腳時也叫大臣進來報告，很不禮貌。但是漢武帝聽到汲黯一來，趕快更衣戴帽才敢見這個汲黯。我們現在的年輕人讀歷史要注意，一個人自己的人品、人格養成到真正高尚正直的時候，任誰都要尊敬他的。連漢武帝這麼一個嚴君，對於大臣要殺就殺，但是卻尊敬這個部下汲黯，自己衣冠不正還不敢見汲黯。所以汲黯是以敢批評漢武帝出名的，

換了別人講話，漢武帝非殺他不可，連司馬遷為李陵辯護，漢武帝一氣就罰司馬遷受宮刑。

汲黯批評漢武帝很直率的，汲黯講：「陛下內多欲而外施仁義，奈何欲效唐虞之治乎？」就是說你武帝內心欲望太重，外面好像做好事，如此怎麼能效法遠古的聖王之治呢？這雖然是在批評武帝的政治表現，但也間接指出武帝要學仙道是不會有成就的。一個人連人都沒有作好，還想做神仙！「內多欲」思想裏欲望太多了，什麼都要，錢也要，壽命也要，名利也要，兒女也要，反正好的都要。其實每人都是這樣「內多欲而外施仁義」，所以求神仙，做得到嗎？

這種話在朋友之間講都很刺耳了，對皇帝講更不得了。歷史上記載武帝聽了當然很不高興，不答覆他，但也沒有對他不禮貌，可是汲黯的官運也就到此為止了。有趣的是，漢武帝臨死的時候吩咐子孫，在我死了以後，為了太子的安全，還是要找汲黯這樣的人來護國才可。

我們引用王陽明跟漢武帝這兩段故事說明，是告訴大家我們研究神仙

之道可以，卻不要輕易想當神仙。這個神仙很不容易做的，是要放棄了一切，這個一切就包括很多了，我們放棄不了的。換一句話，我們每一個人都是「內多欲」，但並不見得能「外施仁義」，這樣豈能成佛成仙呢？這個話要自己提出來警告自己。

龍門派與成吉思汗

閒話少說，言歸正傳。我們研究的這個《參同契》，是採用清代朱雲陽道士所註的版本，尊重他一點可以稱他為真人。我們認為在所有的《參同契》註解中，他的最正統。朱道士是道家北宗龍門派的傳人。龍門派在道教裏是元朝以後開始的，創派的祖師就是跟成吉思汗非常要好的道士丘處機，又名丘長春真人。丘長春真人有一本書叫《西遊記》，不是孫悟空那個《西遊記》，這一段故事在我們歷史上也很特別。中國文化史上有兩個特別事件，一個是在南北朝時，為了爭取一個外國學者法師鳩摩羅什到中國來，派了幾十萬大軍消滅西域兩個國家。這個歷史是外國所沒有的。

另一個就在元朝成吉思汗西征，打到印度來時，他得知中國山東有一個有道的道人丘長春，就派大使到山東把丘長春請到印度邊境上見面。所以丘長春由山東到北京，由北京到新疆，一直到了天山南面跟成吉思汗見面。成吉思汗要拜他為師求道，丘長春告訴他少殺人，未來自然一統天下。丘長春早就知道，中國免不了一場災難，所以與他約定，萬一你打到中國來的時候，不要殺人。成吉思汗答應了，所以給他銅符鐵券，就是兩個人定了契約，兩塊鐵上面蓋了印。後來蒙古人打到中國北方的時候，每家門口只要丘長春道教的符牌一貼，元朝兵不進來，保存了多少人的生命財產。這個在歷史上也是一段奇跡。

現在北京的白雲觀，是有名的道教叢林，就屬北宗龍門派，這一派是出名的絕對清修派。南宗修道的人，許多道士是有家庭，有太太有孩子的。後世道教裏的道士，也大部份是北派丘長春的系統。我們手邊拿的這本《參同契》，是朱雲陽註解的，就是北派的鉅子，不過他也通南派的各種修法。他的註解實在很好，那是正統道家修煉神仙的學理，我勸大家自

己多看才好。

現在我們翻開《參同契》的本文第一章，就是「乾坤門戶章第一」。

下面低一格的字就是朱雲陽真人的註解，文字頂頭的就是《參同契》的原文。

乾坤門戶章第一

乾坤者，易之門戶，眾卦之父母。坎離匡廓，運轂正軸。牝牡四卦，以為橐籥。覆冒陰陽之道，猶工御者，準繩墨，執街轡，正規矩，隨軌轍，處中以制外，數在律曆紀。月節有五六，經緯奉日使。兼并為六十，剛柔有表裏。朔旦屯直事，至暮蒙當受。晝夜各一卦，用之依次序。既未至晦爽，終則復更始。

日月為期度，動靜有早晚。春夏據內體，從子到辰巳。秋冬當外

用，自午訖戌亥。賞罰應春秋，昏明順寒暑。爻辭有仁義，隨時發喜怒。如是應四時，五行得其理。

十二辟卦

《參同契》是漢代的文章，差不多都是四個字一句，很嚴謹的。我們講到中國文學史，由東漢文體演變了二三百年，形成南北朝的文學，對仗很工整，後世普通叫做四六文體。這第一章首先提出來「乾坤者，易之門戶」，是《易經》的綱要。研究《易經》也好，修煉丹道也好，「乾坤」是《易經》八八六十四卦的父母根本卦，就是「眾卦之父母」。除了「乾坤」以外，就是「坎離」兩卦。現在韓國的國旗就是「乾坤坎離」四卦。

「乾坤」這兩卦代表天地，這個宇宙天地就是兩個現象。什麼叫卦呢？古文字典上解釋，「卦者掛也」。宇宙的現象，像畫一樣，掛在外面看得見的就是卦，八卦是個代號。除了天地以外，其他的自然現象，日、月、風、雷、山、澤等等，都掛在那裏，這就是卦的道理。

「坎離匡廓」，坎離兩卦代表兩個東西掛在那裏，一個太陽，一個月亮。太陽月亮在天體裏頭走，「運轂正軸」，像一個車輪子在轉一樣。這個是什麼意思呢？車輪同我們有什麼關係？為什麼說《參同契》是千古丹經的鼻祖？這是什麼道理？

因此，為了研究《參同契》，第一步必須要瞭解《易經》的「八卦」。講到八卦又是個專題，現在各位手中這一張圖表，希望諸位每一次要帶來，至少在「御政」一篇隨時會提到；要瞭解中國文化的基本，也是要提到的。這一張表上面寫的一歲，就是一年十二個月，分為六陰六陽，這是說明天體形象，包括的內容非常多。

我們看一層一層的圈圈，共有六層，中間是空的，這個空的外面第一層是十二個卦，專門名辭叫做十二辟卦，「辟卦」也叫做「侯卦」。中國上古的政治，中央政府的皇帝曰天子，天子只有一個；地方的領袖是王，叫諸侯，「侯卦」的意思就是「臣卦」。在時間上說，一年是個主體，分十二個月，十二個卦名代表十二個月，叫十二「辟卦」。再外一圈是卦

一歲十二月六陰六陽之象

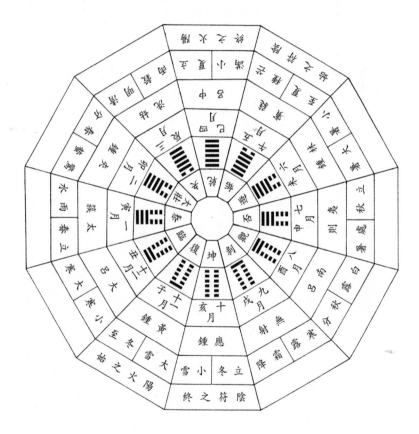

象，這個卦一筆一筆怎麼畫法？我們慢慢也要解釋一下。第四圈是中國陰曆十二個月份，每一個月另有一個代號，就是子、丑、寅、卯、辰、巳、午、未、申、酉、戌、亥。

當然還沒有加上亥是豬，戌是狗……這些十二生肖的來源，據我的研究是東漢以後，隨印度文化過來的天文觀念。所以一直到今日，從印度北部到西藏地區，你問現在是幾月啊？他說狗月，我們就曉得他講的是九月；他講羊月，就知道是陰曆的六月了。為什麼選這些動物代表六陰六陽？比如子月是老鼠，同老鼠有什麼關係呢？老鼠是五個腳趾，五是單數屬陽；；雙數屬陰。我們形容一個人膽子小叫「首鼠兩端」，剛爬出洞的老鼠，習慣走兩步，看一看前面，咚咚，又鑽進去了，再跑出來多走三四步又鑽進去了。首鼠膽子小，膽前顧後就是「首鼠兩端」，兩頭牠都要看清楚。丑月屬牛，牛的蹄是兩瓣屬陰的，所以一陰一陽這樣分開。龍啊、蛇啊等都有些道理，這是一種解釋，我們將來提到時再說，這是第四圈。

天文　曆律　氣節

　　這個第五圈麻煩了。這是中國文化音樂的樂律，與古代的天文也有關。中國文化以天上的星象變化判斷人事，非常準確。諸位同學要研究這個問題，順便告訴在大學研究所的同學們注意，先要讀《史記》的〈天官書〉，其次讀《漢書》的〈五行志〉。我們現在讀歷史都是通史，其實不大合理，因為歷史上重要的東西，真正的歷史哲學，歷史上都把他漏掉了。譬如《史記》中重要在〈禮〉〈樂〉〈律〉〈曆〉〈天官〉〈封禪〉〈河渠〉〈平準〉八書。歷代史書都有〈天文志〉，不叫〈天官書〉，司馬遷的《史記》才有〈天官書〉。我們每一代的歷史還有一個〈樂律志〉，在唐史、宋史，一直到明史，乃至現在出來的《清史稿》都有的。中國在科學上比任何一個民族國家發展都早，因為發展了天文科學，天文科學又是以數學為基礎的。不過很抱歉！那是祖宗的文化，你看故宮博物院，那是我們祖宗的，你的在哪裏？沒有呀，拿不出來，這不行啊！現在

我們連「天文，曆律」這些都搞不清楚了。

這個圖外面一圈是二十四個氣節。一年有十二個月，一個月有三十天，五天叫「一候」，三候叫「一氣」，六候就是「一節」。一年有七十二候，每個月有一個節，一個氣，一年十二個氣十二個節，合起來共二十四個「氣節」。現在有一個問題，民國以來用陽曆，老百姓是陽曆跟陰曆並用，這個習慣很難改，八九十年來，大家還是願意過陰曆年。民國初年湖南那個大名士葉德輝先生，作了一副對子：

男女平權　公說公有理　婆說婆有理
陰陽合曆　你過你的年　我過我的年

我經常很感嘆，這副對子九十年來沒有變。那麼你說是陽曆好，陰曆好呢？這個問題是科學問題，其實中國幾千年來已經陰陽合曆了。

我們算八字是以二十四氣節為標準，二十四氣節是以太陽為標準，我們的陰曆以月亮出沒同潮水漲落為標準。所以由廣東到東北的海岸，海邊

人就曉得，我們小的時候就會唸「寅申漲，卯酉平」。潮水漲落都在腦子裏，老祖宗就告訴我們，初一十五出門坐船，「哎呀！船開了沒有？」一算，「寅申漲，卯酉平」，沒有沒有，趕快跑去還趕得及，潮水還沒有退，可以上船。這個科學已經變成民間的習慣了，後人不用腦筋已經都統計好了。所以二十四「氣節」是一個天體太陽系統裏月亮系統的統計。這一個圖表裏頭東西多得很，我們中國文化大部份生活習慣的原理，都在這張圖裏。卦者掛也，就掛在這裏給我們看的。

易經的八卦與文字

要瞭解《易經》的「乾」「坤」這兩卦，我們先要瞭解，什麼叫「八卦」？什麼叫八八六十四卦？你不要把它看成死的，它是活的，是個代號。大家說研究了《易經》以後就發覺，我們祖先的文化思想、哲學科學，為什麼在上古時期就到達這樣高的程度？我的看法是，上一個冰河時期之前，人類文化已經發展到最高處了。一個學問越高明就越簡化，開始

發明都很複雜，到了最高峰反而簡單而明瞭，複雜的不算真學問。古人歸納一切法則畫成這個代號八卦，很容易懂。冰河時期，人類整個毀滅了，好在這個「卦者掛也」留了下來，就靠這一點卦，告訴我們宇宙天地的一些訊息。這些符號所表達的內容太多了，這是第一點我們需要瞭解的。

第二點講到《易經》的「八卦」，也是中國文字的起源。人類文明本來都沒有文字，文字是人為製造的。中國的文字是由象形文字開始，象形就是圖畫、漫畫，「八卦」也是漫畫開始的。所謂「伏羲畫八卦」，古人的卦是怎麼樣畫的？是不是我們現在這樣畫？八卦是否就是中國先古文字的開始？過去幾十年來，有些考古學家不大承認卦是文字的開始。我們卻認為《易經》是中國文化根源的根源，哲學裏的哲學，經典裏的經典，文化中心的中心，但是你在考古文獻上找不出有關八卦的東西。

譬如過去那位董作賓先生，我們的老朋友，他是甲骨文學家。我對他說要靈活來看，在甲骨上看到一條線的，幾條線的，幾個點的，那個就是卦。古人畫卦或橫畫、或直畫、或點一下，反正是代號。三直是「乾

卦」，或者打三點也是「乾卦」，都是代號。所以我們看到最古老的一本《易經》叫《易緯》，裏頭畫的卦不是橫的，而是三條直的。慢慢在甲骨上也找到了這些東西，可見我們中國文字文化來源很早。

《易經》為什麼叫「易」呢？這個「易」字為什麼這樣寫呢？上面一個圓圈加一點代表太陽，下面這個圓圈有個缺口代表月亮。甲骨文上有沒有這個「易」呢？是有的。換一句話，什麼叫《易經》？「日月之謂易」，就是太陽月亮天體系統之下的學問法則。

所以八卦從「乾坤」兩卦開始。可是還有一些基本的常識要向諸位介紹，現在我們這一本《易經》叫《周易》，這是由伏羲氏畫八卦，周文王的演繹，孔子傳述所謂「易更三聖」。我們現在這本《周易》，是經過這三位整理過的，實際上《周易》只是《易經》學問的一部份。《易經》的易學有三種，稱為「三易」：《連山易》、《歸藏易》、《周易》，現在流傳下來的是《周易》。《周易》是以「乾坤」兩卦為開頭的，所以現在《參同契》用的是《周易》的道理。

第三講

道家與禪宗的易學

關於《易經》學問的本身，所謂道家的易，觀念上同理學家們，尤其是朱夫子、程夫子他們所解釋的易，實有不同之處。道家的易差不多都是講應用的。

上一次我們提到《易經》的所謂「三易」，除了現在留下的《周易》，則是神農的《連山易》，黃帝的《歸藏易》。《連山易》以「艮卦」為首，「艮卦」代表「山」。《連山易》的意思是「如山之出雲」。《歸藏易》是黃帝時代所用的易，以「坤卦」為主，「坤」是純陰，一切陽能「歸藏」到純陰的境界裏去了。

到了周朝，經過周文王整理，就是我們手邊這個《周易》，一般稱它是我們五經裏經典的經典，哲學的哲學，也就是我們文字文化的起源。

《周易》以「乾卦」開始。傳統《周易》的學術觀念認為《連山易》、《歸藏易》是只有其名，沒有實際的東西。我們現在手邊拿的《周易》，上面許多圖案，包括八八六十四卦，什麼先天圖、後天圖這些等等，同幾千年流行下來的法則並不一樣。尤其我們卜卦用到的，或者在陰陽家用到的六十四卦的次序，「乾為天，天風姤，天山遯……」一路背下來卦的次序，同《周易》六十四卦所排列的次序也不一樣。

據我們所知這些卜卦用到的六十四卦的次序，以及《河圖洛書》等等，是宋朝以後才出現的。宋朝的邵康節是當時講卦的第一名人，據說邵康節的這些卦圖是一個鶴林寺的和尚傳給他的，這個和尚的法名叫壽涯。

但是這些傳聞在學術界是個疑案。據說邵康節能算過去未來等等，他不但幫我們中華民族算過，連世界的命運差不多也算過了。他又著了一部很難看懂的書，叫做《皇極經世》，這是用《易經》的「數理」推演法則，斷定過去未來歷史千萬年的事情，有個公式擺在那裏。我們大家都是諸葛亮的弟弟諸葛暗，屬於事後方知，事後一查《皇極經世》，他講的一點都沒

有錯，但是事先看不出來。所以道家的易學究竟哪裏來的呢？據我的瞭解就是《連山易》《歸藏易》的遺留，這個法則是《周易》之外的另一章。所以我們一般所應用的算命、看相、看風水，稀奇古怪的都是用這一套來的。

那麼這一種「易學」後來傳到哪裏了呢？傳到佛教的大禪師們手裏了。禪宗有五宗的興起，其中有一個大宗派叫曹洞宗，是以一對師徒而出名。師父是洞山禪師，徒弟是曹山禪師，兩個人是以他們住的廟子為名。

不過為什麼顛倒唸呢？因為我們的文化喜歡講韻文，洞曹好像不大美，曹洞就很美，所以倒轉來說，就成了曹洞宗。

曹洞宗的禪宗工夫，我們如果嚴格地講，就同道家有關，而且是丹道派的道家。丹道這一派的保留，就靠曹洞這一脈，所以研究曹洞宗的禪宗還必須要懂得《易經》呢！尤其是它取用「坎離」兩卦，認為與悟道修道做工夫有密切關係。唐代以後的道家，傳出來神仙丹法裏有「取坎填離」這個工夫，就與曹洞宗有關。所以依我的研究，曹洞宗這一脈到了宋朝，

五代的人物

南宋以後的道家就很難講了，他們也會佛家的道法，都很高明，而且比學佛的人還學佛。當然也比學道的人還學道，更通達儒家，但是這些人都走上神仙之路了。所以我們看歷史，五代共亂了七八十年，歐陽修奉命主編五代史，歐陽修有個感想，說五代七八十年沒有出一個大人物，沒有一個大帝王，也沒有一個了不起的將相。五代有名的一個宰相馮道，是歐陽修最頭痛的，五個朝代五個皇帝，都請他出來當宰相。歐陽修說他是中國文人中的無恥之徒，是無恥的代表，他活了八九十歲才死。可是呢，與歐陽修同時的蘇東坡跟王安石，卻認為五代有很多的人物，都是頂尖的。王安石說五代人才太多了，但都出家去了，不是當和尚就是去修道了，那

是他們對於時代的一種反抗，因為看不下去了！

所以我們講禪宗真正的興盛是在唐末五代，道家這些神仙人物也在五代最多。歐陽修認為馮道是最糟糕的！但是王安石認為馮道是位度眾生的大菩薩；蘇東坡更認為這些人是活佛！因為五代這七八十年的變亂，都是邊疆民族外夷來當皇帝。蘇東坡說，如果責備馮道不盡忠，請問他該為誰盡忠？但是他把中國文化保留了幾十年，那可是很困難的一件事。馮道在歷史上幾乎沒有什麼建樹，也沒有多講過一些話，也沒有著作，只是庸庸碌碌，可以說是鄉愿的代表。一切都是上面講了是，奉命照辦。但是他有時候也不辦，我們至少從歷史看出來，這樣一個變亂的政權沒有法律，也沒有正義，不對就殺掉你。他能夠讓所有上台皇帝請他來當宰相，那可不容易啊！至少這個人本身在公事、私事上，沒有什麼缺點被政敵抓到的，否則這條命也早就沒有了。

中國文化一個通俗的觀念是「宰相肚裏好撐船」，就是當宰相要包容一切好壞正反的意見，要有這樣大的度量。馮道一生一篇文章都不留，一

封信也不留，詩啊，勉勉強強找到幾首，有一首詩中最後一句是：「狼虎叢中可立身」，那是他的修養。五代他所侍候過的這一些皇帝，他認為都是豺狼虎豹，沒有把他們當皇帝看。

道家、佛家這一些學術思想，在五代這個變亂的時代，是非常昌明的。我們後來看的所謂修道的這一些丹經，多半是五代以後的著作。譬如說有位呂純陽，也是唐末五代的人物，我常常說，道家的呂純陽等於是佛家的六祖，屬於道家的一個革命派的人物。

道家與密宗的關係

我們回過來看手邊拿的這個十二辟卦，這個法則是道家的，也可以說是《連山易》《歸藏易》這個系統來的。這個用處可大了，我們的中華民族文化、生活思想習慣、乃至民間一切的風俗，都用得到它，這是大的方面。小的方面，我們學醫藥針灸的要懂得，至於要修道打坐做工夫，尤其想成神仙的──成不成不管啦，只要想修神仙，這個十二辟卦法則一定要

知道。這個法則對學密宗學瑜珈的人，比三脈七輪的法則還要準確。如果不知道這個法則，你修的氣脈，三脈七輪是沒有用的！

修密宗的人有偏見，認為道家不如密宗。這個問題我花了幾十年也解決不了，究竟是道家傳到印度，再傳回到西藏變密宗呢？還是印度的修持方法在周、秦這個階段進入了中國，與中國文化融會變成了道家？現在沒有定論。因為事出有因，查無實據，考據很難。至於說秦始皇那個時代，印度修煉成功的人早有來來過。歷史上記載秦始皇時來了兩個西域的異人，個子很高大，秦始皇把他們關起來，又看見他們在外面逍遙，關不住的！這文獻沒有寫明這些人是否為比丘，反正不是比丘就是婆羅門教的人物。這證明周、秦階段，中、印的文化已經在交流，尤其是修道方面文化交流得很早。所以說，有關道家密宗究竟怎麼樣認定先後，還不敢斷定。學術的立場要公正，不能有主觀的意念。

不過，西藏密宗有一個奇怪的地方，當然這個可能是宋朝以後的事，西藏幾乎沒有中國其他的神，但是有關公廟，也有八卦圖，這是很奇怪

的。今天有一位朋友問：「喇嘛與活佛有什麼關係？」我說喇嘛是個稱呼，等於我們稱呼佛教的出家人是和尚，喇嘛就是出家人，和尚、法師是總代號。活佛呢？由唐朝開始經過中國皇帝封過的叫「呼圖克圖」，當然不要唸成糊里糊塗。

「呼圖克圖」翻譯的意思是法師、大師、活著的佛，所以也簡稱活佛。並不是每一個喇嘛都是「呼圖克圖」，真正受過賜封為「呼圖克圖」的，宋元明清一直到民國都有。國民政府成立以後，封過的並不多，這個順便一提。在西藏許多喇嘛或者活佛，會拿唸珠卜卦，後來我知道，他是用《易經》的天干地支，所以就越看越奇怪了。

我們再查，唐太宗把文成公主下嫁給西藏王，陪嫁過去的有道士、儒生，都是全國選出來的菁英。至於說土木工匠百工等等，也配備了很多同去，是這樣開始文化的交流。這些道士到了西藏就在那裏落地生根，道家的文化，當然在那裏傳下去，漸漸又變成另外一套。所以研究西藏許多的沒有幾個。像章嘉活佛是受國民政府賜封的，他是蒙古人，西藏方面賜封的

法則，講氣脈至少並沒有離開道家的這個法則，這是站在學術的立場講

話。信宗教的人不大喜歡聽這些話，因為宗教不免被宗教情緒影響，產生一些偏見，那也沒有辦法了。我們現在的閒話好像與本圖沒有關係，其實確有密切的關係。

陽火之始

現在我們只講圖，先做個初步簡單的瞭解。在這個圖中，先把最外圈的「陰符之終，陽火之始」八個字找到。再找到內圈的一個卦名是「坤」。坤卦的隔壁就是「復」卦，這個卦象就是「地雷復」（☷☳）。畫卦是先從下面畫上來，下面三筆叫三爻，是內卦。復卦的內卦三爻是「震卦」，震代表了雷，雷就是電，意思就是發電震動的作用。復卦上面的三爻叫外卦，這三爻中間斷了，代表「坤卦」，抽象的「坤」代表了陰；實質的代表是大地，這個地球土地。所以「地雷復」六爻整個的卦名叫「復卦」。「復卦」是「坤卦」與「震卦」的結合，也就是「地與雷」的結合。

講到這裏我又要說一個故事了，曾經說了很多遍。有一年一位美國的教授來訪問，我們講到科學。我說最近看到消息，你們美國很了不起，現在已經研究到打雷了，科學家總想有辦法把雷裝起來，是拿什麼裝我就不知道了。為什麼？認為打了一次雷，地面上增加了幾十噸的肥料。我說我們中國老祖宗早就研究過了。他說哦？中國有這個，不是一種哦！有八種雷，而且又演變成十幾種雷！他聽了就愣住了，有這樣奇怪的事情！「水雷屯，澤雷隨，風雷益，天雷无妄，火雷噬嗑，山雷頤，地雷復……」每一種雷不同哦！夏天打的雷是在半空中下著大雨打的，那是「火雷噬嗑」啊！每年春天第一聲雷是「地雷復」，地下冒上來的。假如是海裏頭打的雷「水雷屯」，或者「火雷噬嗑」，就同肥料關係不大，最為重要是那個「地雷復」。

「錯綜複雜」是我們現在用的一個慣語，實際上這四個字是《易經》的學問。這個卦我們正面看是「地雷復」，如果把這個卦上下倒轉過來看，就成了「山地剝卦」（䷖）。上面這個「雷卦」倒過來是個「艮

卦」、「艮」為「山」。下面這個「坤卦」顛倒起來還是地。這一種就叫做綜卦，錯綜複雜。所以任何一個卦都有四面八面的看法，現象都不同。

復卦是什麼

「地雷復」卦，為什麼這個卦名稱為「復卦」呢？你看啊，這個卦上面五爻都是陰，只有下面這一爻是陽；陽能在下面發動，地下打雷了。這個卦所代表的同我們學道都有關係。拿現代人的觀念來說，就是宇宙萬物都在放射，譬如這個桌子也在放射，手錶也在放射，我們的生命也在放射，諸位也是在放射。太陽的放射被地球慢慢的吸收，復卦開始，地心吸收到的陽能漸多，所以冬天地心是暖的，地球表面上是涼的。冬天的井水，我們手摸進去是溫的，夏天井水是涼的，外面是熱的，這是地球物理作用。所以到了十月是坤卦陰極，十一月的大雪是節，冬至是氣。每月一個氣一個節，節等於這個圓的地球在虛空中轉動。氣是什麼？是地球本身內在的放射功能，太陽月亮跟自然界的放射配合的。到了十一月的「冬

至」，是「一陽生」，最下面一爻由陰變陽爻，代表一個陽能開始生長，所以這個卦叫「復卦」，這個就是「冬至一陽生」的道理，因此我們過冬至就進補了。

算命根據的二十四氣節，並不是用陰曆，是用陽曆啊！太陽星座準確得很。陰曆是一個月三十天，每月的十五月亮圓了，所以我們本來就是陰陽合曆。冬至這個一陽生不是生，是地球吸收太陽的熱能進入地球的中心，冬至以前是收縮到極點的狀態，「冬至一陽生」重新放射出來，地球的熱能放射慢慢上昇了。

在我們中國的律曆有一個東西很重要，順便提醒大家一下。講到中國文化，譬如說每一部歷史書上都有一篇很重要的律曆，「律」是指什麼呢？在這個圖上「黃鍾、大呂、太簇、夾鍾」都是音律，同宇宙的音聲、宇宙的法則有關的，也是音樂的原理，這個是「律」。一年三百六十五又四分之一天，這個是「曆」，每個朝代規定的曆不同。我們的「曆」，每年以陰曆十一月為子月，周朝就是以「冬至一陽生」這個月為歲首；殷商

以十二月為歲首；夏朝的歲首是正月，就是我們現在過的正月。

年輕同學們注意！過去國家政治改變的時候，對於不投降者，有個名稱叫做「不奉正朔」，就是不照你的律曆來做準則的，這個也有很多的道理。每月初一為朔，因為夏、商、周三代不同，可是現在我們用的陰曆正月過年，用了幾千年很習慣，用在算命陰陽五行方面的也是夏曆。

我們把這個表轉過來看，一年有十二個節十二個氣，叫二十四氣節。到了十二月「小寒」是節，「大寒」是氣。十一月這個卦是「地雷復」卦，十二月是「地澤臨卦」（䷒），第二爻也變成陽了，這表示地球陽能從地球的中心又向上昇了一點。所以「臨」就是快要來了。拿地支來代表月份，子月就是十一月，丑月就是十二月。

一月泰 二月雷

現在我們再轉過來看一月，月份的地支是寅。一月裏「立春」是節，「雨水」是氣，立春過後是雨水，要多下雨了，這是大陸中原氣候。這個

時候的卦象變了，下卦三個陽爻了，叫做「地天泰」（☰☷），又叫「三陽開泰」。有人說「三陽開泰」，過年要吃羊肉就殺了三頭羊，哪有這回事啊！「三陽開泰」是地球的熱能發展到地平面上來了，也就是陽氣上昇要到地面了。地在上，天在下，所以叫做「地天泰」。過年門口貼一個「三陽開泰」，不過這個陽字有時也寫成羊，因為羊字在上古的寫法代表吉祥的祥，所以正月過年也可以叫「三羊開泰」。

再過來就是二月了，卦名是「雷天大壯」（☰☳），外卦是雷，內卦是乾，「驚蟄」是節，「春分」是氣。什麼是驚蟄節？二月外卦的陰爻第一爻變陽，只有兩個陰在上面，四個陽在下面。陽氣由地球中心一路昇上來，到了二月陽能已經超過了地面，所以我們可以放風箏了。我們小的時候放風箏，沒有過驚蟄風箏是飛不起來的。可是南方不一定，冬天也飛得起來。譬如大陸中原地區，雞蛋在端午節才立得起來，在南方隨時可以立起來。

第四講

剛才我們講到二月裏的「驚蟄」，「蟄」這個字是執下面一個虫字，就是動物的冬眠。譬如蛇呀、青蛙呀這些小動物，到了冬天，地面上太冷不能生存，這些動物嘴裏含了一口泥巴，就進洞去入定了。所以西方人把打坐入定叫做是動物的冬眠。冬眠動物不吃也不拉兩三個月，要等到驚蟄節才出來。因為此時地球的陽能上升到相當程度了，地面上有陽氣變溫暖了，這不是靠太陽來的，是地球本身的陽能發出來的溫暖。到了這個時候，所謂驚蟄一聲雷，驚蟄的雷是什麼雷呢？剛才我講我們中國有八種雷，其實有十幾種呢！這個二月的卦象是「雷上天下」，就是「雷天大壯」卦。陽能在外面，冬眠的動物就醒來了，把嘴裏的泥巴吐掉，開始重新活動起來，所以叫驚蟄節。

我們鄉下農村光腳種田的人，從田裏回來，腿上莫名其妙紅一塊青一塊腫起來了，因為踩到冬眠動物吐出來有毒的泥巴。最好的治療就是抓把

土，混入人的口水，抹一抹就好了。

驚蟄後第一聲春雷「雷天大壯」，地面上才適合農作，開始農忙了。

在中國中原地區最準，驚蟄以前不適合農作。

氣象　春秋

我們常常聽朋友講，氣象台靠不住！其實不止國內，日本、美國也一樣。有人寫一首缺德的詩，我只記得中間幾句，「呼風風不至，無雨雨偏來」，預測不下雨偏偏下雨；「不如風濕病，風雨有準哉」，還不如風濕病的人，難過起來，知道明天就會下雨了，反而還準。實際上不怪氣象台，氣象台輸入的資訊是大氣之中的東西，沒有算進去地球本身的變化，而這個地球上的物理又絕對與天氣有關，但是很難搞通。你懂了《易經》就知道難搞了。譬如一個省，你要分南部、中部、北部，都不同。就算是一個城市一條路的南面，北面，東面，西面，各有一個不同的太極。把地球本身的放射能量再配上大氣物理，那就是另外一套學問了。

有時你還不如掐指一算，中國這一套，就像瞎貓撞到死老鼠，報個時辰算算看，憑心裏的靈感求一下，有時反而準。這是個氣象台，不是神通，也不是靈感，是根據《易經》這一套法則。但是這一套法則怎麼那麼靈呢？這個裏頭就妙了。學《易經》我們要記住孔子在《繫辭》上兩句話：「變動不居，周流六虛」，六虛就是東南西北上下；「變動不居」，應用起來不是呆板不變的。但是這個法則規律是呆定的，所以我們要先瞭解。

學《易經》不曉得活用那就完了，所以孔子把秘訣都漏給我們了。「周流六虛」，這個法則是呆定的，但是應用起來要活。

我們一年過得最舒服的日子在春秋二季，小的時候，老祖母都告訴我們，二八亂穿衣。就是二月八月時候，隨便你穿吧，身體弱一點穿厚一點，身體好一點穿薄一點都沒有關係。

我常常給同學們講，孔子著《春秋》，寫春秋戰國幾百年的歷史，他為什麼叫《春秋》，不稱冬夏呢？春天是由冷變熱，慢慢一點一點熱起來。秋天是相反，夏天的熱慢慢退掉，退到了秋天剛好涼爽，不算冷也不

六陽的上半年

三月間清明節這個陽氣上昇，五爻都是陽能，只有最上一爻是陰。這個卦名是「澤天夬」（䷪），這個夬字（音拐）是形容人有一點跛，腳不利便。實際上「夬」是有一些缺點的意思，因為陽太多，只有一陰。三月的氣是「穀雨」。

再過來就是四月了。四月「立夏」是節，「小滿」是氣。地球到四月它所代表的是純陽，六爻都是陽，就是「乾卦」（䷀）。陽氣昇到了最高，所以我們要注意啊！真正夏天那個悶熱，到陰曆四月陽曆五六月，這個地球放射陽氣昇到了極點，感覺白日又長。我們年輕讀書的時候最喜歡

算熱，所以春秋是持平也。不但氣溫如此，夏季白晝長，冬季白晝短，春秋兩季的日夜長短也是持平的。所以我們講「春秋持平也」，是個天秤。古今人物，對於國家社會有沒有貢獻，《春秋》在這個歷史上持平論之，所以「春秋」是持平之論的意思。

放暑假，「春天不是讀書天，夏日炎炎正好眠。等到秋來冬又到，收拾書箱好過年」。所以一年都不要讀書。

半年完了，這叫六陽上半年。我們先打個岔，陽能陰能一放一收，這之間代表了一年氣候。一年分成十二個月，一個月有三十天，地球繞著太陽轉，中間又加了一個月亮。一年太陽走多少度呢？從地球看太陽在虛空移動，簡單叫行度，在中國天文書上叫「躔度」。一年十二個月，共有三百六十五天又四分之一，多的四分之一天，擺在閏月，閏年，閏日，是這樣分配的，這個裏頭就很複雜了。我們幾千年史書上專門有一篇叫〈律曆志〉，從唐朝乃至到我們最近出來清朝的《清史稿》都還有。尤其清朝經過康熙親自參予編制，改進很多。康熙皇帝很用功，自己又愛讀書，拉丁文、梵文、蒙古文、滿州文都會，又學過術數，數學也很高，天文、曆法、數學他都會，所以這個律曆是他下令由學者一起整理過的。現在有些風水的書都要以康熙整理過的做標準。當然這一兩百年來沒有整理，現在又需要整理了，不整理的話這個天體運行的計算會有差度的。

一年十二個月，一月三十天，五天一候，三候一氣，六候一節。所以一個月當中有一個節一個氣，一年有七十二候，二十四個氣節這都是呆定的，這是一年。再講一天，一天有十二個時辰，這個時辰的代表就是這張圖的中間空心往外數到第四圈。四月是巳月，五月是午月，這些是「子丑寅卯辰巳午未申酉戌亥」十二地支。這個地支在一天的代表就是時辰。我們注意，下面研究到《參同契》有一個字，「簇」，「簇」年為月，「簇」月為日，換句話再加一句可以講「簇」日為時。這個法則是呆定的，用起來是活的。我們一畫一夜，十二時辰就是十二辟卦所代表的。一年的法則可以同樣運用到一個晝夜，晝夜之間太陽從早晨出來到晚上下去，這個運程變化是地球在自轉，使得地表的一半是亮的一半是黑的。這個地球的光明和陰暗，影響了地球上物理的生命法則，影響到我們人的生命。

醫病的法則

我們人自己以為了不起，在地球的立場來說，我們像是地球表面上的

細菌，我們的生命自然要受地球宇宙法則的影響，所以修道人講究時間的配合。學中醫針灸的同學，更要注意人體的氣血流行，因為氣血流行同十二經脈配合，與時辰的變化法則一樣。學針灸有一本「子午流注圖」，就是特別注意十二時辰的血脈流通，把天地的法則與人體內部十二經脈的運行，配合診斷。

針灸同中醫是相連的，不是分開的。我常給同學們講，我不懂，我只把學理告訴你們。古代中醫講「一砭二針三灸四湯藥」，屬於四個大的醫治手法，診斷病情是「望、聞、問、切」。

「望」，也是看病人走路的姿態，注意他的身材，看他的體質個子，然後觀察面上的氣色，就曉得病在哪裏。

「聞」是聽他講話的聲音，譬如感冒了，聲音變了鼻腔的音出來了，身體裏頭有其他的毛病，音聲都會反應；情緒激動，個性急的火氣大，就要注意他肝功能了。望、聞之後才「問」，他說感冒了，可是他是運動家或者是練拳的，你下藥的成份就不能那麼輕了。如果是坐辦公室的，背又

是駝起來的，弱不禁風，藥就要下輕一點，否則他受不了。「切」，最後把脈，才把這個病因病灶病狀找了出來。

一砭，我們這個刮痧拔火罐都屬於砭，就是這個病尚在表皮時，治療就容易好。不好的話，曉得這個病已深入，就要下針了。針不好時，曉得更深入了，就用灸了。古人用薑片在上面燒艾，拿現在觀念勉強講像電療，但同電療不同。艾是通氣，把那個熱能逼進身體經脈裏頭，把病趕出去。灸再不行，病已進入腑臟到腸、胃、心、肝、脾，就只好用中藥了。

所以這一套程序是分不開的，「一砭二針三灸四湯藥」。

我小時候最會生病，六歲到十二歲是藥餵大的，我什麼病都生過，所以對生病非常有經驗。幫我治病的那個老師很高明，問幾歲啦？哪一天什麼時間開始發這個病？都與十二經脈有關。他不管你頭痛不頭痛，先找病的來源，一天看不了幾個病人。

有一次他幫我開了藥還不回家，連第二副藥他也開好，吩咐兩副藥統統要煎。先告訴你第一劑藥吃下去，一個鐘頭後會難過得打滾，會吐的。

吃下去後真難過得打滾，家裏人也跟著慌啊，又不敢說。他就坐在前面，瞪著眼睛看著你，任你疼得叫死了，他也不管。後來我知道，他比我生病的人還緊張。看著你，哇！吐了！他把煙筒放下，知道藥用對了，所以換第二劑下去。然後放心了，洗洗臉才回家去。

中藥店以前是沒有禮拜天的，過年有病人叫門，如果不開門抓藥，地方上的人會打這中藥店的。現在不同了，又有禮拜天，又有禮拜六，等到禮拜一才能生病。所以我們要年輕人瞭解我們中國文化，這些你們都看不到了，我都是親身經驗過的。

所以學中醫對於這個十二辟卦要懂得。這個「簇」字就是拿這一年的法則串成一個月，一個月的法則串成一個時辰。講到人體上應用，也是子時，每人的身體不同，所發動生命陽能的子時也不同。一定的法則，不一定的時間。

二至　否泰

剛才講到六陽上半年，現在繼續下去就是「乾」卦以後的五月「天風姤」卦（☰），五月「芒種」是節，「夏至」是氣。「夏至一陰生」，陰起來了，所謂一陰生是什麼道理呢？我們拿現在觀念來說，地球放射功能此時達到了極點。夏至以後太陽又開始向南，太陽能的放射對北半球漸減，這就是陰生。夏至也叫做「長至」。我們讀古人的詩詞文章見到「長至為某某兄寫了一首詩」，就知道是那一年的夏至，這一天是一年中白畫最長的一天。五月地支排到「午」，就是我們吃端午粽子的午月。端午、中秋、七月半這些都是民間風俗的節日，不屬於二十四氣節，因為是民間風俗，我們也沿用了千多年。

這二十四個節氣，是中華文化，甚至說是東方人的文化遺產。一講夏至，民間在生活習慣上要注意什麼呢？夏至一陰生，潮濕起來了。尤其是住在南方，五月開始梅雨天，老式的房子發霉了，有些舊房子裏頭香菇都

出來了。香菇木耳都是腐爛木頭上長出來的，因為它是陰中之陽，所以白木耳有補肺功能。

夏至不久就是六月了。節氣有「小暑、大暑」。六月是未月，二陰生了，卦名叫做「天山遯」（）。外卦是「天」是純陽，內卦「山」，二陰了，內在的陰氣慢慢盛起來。「遯」者陽氣在裏面慢慢收縮了，陰氣盛了謂之「遯」。

七月是申月，立秋是節，處暑是氣，卦是「天地否」（）。否的對面就是泰，正月「地天泰」是好運氣，七月「天地否」是壞運氣。講到這裏我岔進來一個故事，當年講到《易經》，有同學們提出來問，老師呀，這兩個卦名好怪哦！「地天泰」，地在上，天在下，是泰是太平；天在上，地在下，就成了否，就糟糕了。天在上地在下才應該是太平啊！我說這對面就是泰，天下太平嘛！也沒有你也沒有我，也不要吵架了，也不要來聽課了，大家睡大覺，就是泰了。「天地否」，天地開闢了以後，人生才那麼多事嘛！你說這是笑話嗎？並不一定

是笑話，有道理的。陰在內陽在外，外表看是很好，內在陰氣就是糟糕的壞的，是不好的。所以「天地否」的意思，就是立秋之後處處有陰氣。

到了八月「白露、秋分」，內在陰氣更進一層了，四爻都是陰，外面只剩兩爻是陽了，叫「風地觀」（☴☷）。外卦是巽卦，巽為風；內卦是坤卦，坤為地。如果你們研究哲學、宗教的要注意！文王、孔子，在這一卦提出來宗教的定義，「聖人以神道設教」。這一句話多去研究研究，就懂得宗教哲學了。宗教是人為造成的，所以聖人以神道設教，就是教育的一環，這是講「風地觀」順便提到，你們搞宗教的同學們注意！

至日閉關與奇門遁甲

佛家道家打坐練工夫叫做閉關，這個「閉關」也出在《易經》上，「先王以至日閉關」。注意呀！「至」就是冬至和夏至。「至日閉關」這句話，如果老師們不傳，誰也讀不懂那些書。我是吃過苦頭的，很不願意你們也吃苦，所以我知道了就告訴你們。「奇門遁甲」大家都想學，學

了呼風喚雨，撒豆成兵，不做個諸葛亮也做個諸葛暗啦！這些學問都很高深，沒有那麼簡單的。像「奇門遁甲」，八卦不搞清楚，什麼陰遁、陽遁，都是迷惑！很難懂。我這個頭腦不喜歡數學，學得很痛苦，瞭解以後我就把它丟開，我知道了就行了。我有個好勝求知心，不知道的一定想知道，知道以後就算了。學奇門遁甲有一個口訣：

陰陽順逆妙難窮　二至還鄉一九宮
若能了達陰陽理　天地都來一掌中

「陰陽順逆妙難窮」，陰陽順逆倒轉，這個中間的巧妙，就是宇宙法則妙難窮，你永遠搞不通，只講第一二句就把我考倒了。一直認為自己讀書很聰明，不料被考倒了。「二至還鄉一九宮」，糟糕！我一宮都不宮，一個房子都沒有，哪裏來個一九宮啊。這還不講，「二至還鄉」又怎麼說呢？問起那些算命卜卦看風水的，不懂。有些懂的人只是笑笑，因為學這個口訣要磕頭拜門。有些人看看他的模樣，萬一是旁門左道總不大光榮

吧！就不肯拜，不肯拜書就讀不懂。什麼「二至還鄉」？其實就是冬至到夏至一陰一陽，一順一逆回到那個本位。

「二至還鄉一九宮」，一是陽數的開始，九是陽數的極點，一始一終了，可是你天地也拿不到啊，不是那麼簡單的！這一句話只是告訴你法則，陰陽順逆的確是妙難窮，你真懂嗎？所以我們現在先要解釋二至，冬至和夏至就是一順一逆。《易經》有句話，「先王以至日閉關」，這是中國古代文化。一個人閉關，每天一樣，每月也一樣，到了那個時候就要清心寡慾，齋戒沐浴，就是打坐修行了。拿佛法來講，就是六根六塵都關起來叫做閉關。「至」是一陽來復的時候，或者一陰初生的時候，如果這個時候把握住天地法則，你打坐一個時辰，也就是兩個鐘頭，等於你坐三個月的工夫。當然這是吹噓一點的，是鼓勵性的，但是把握時辰打坐的話，功效絕對等於你多坐幾次是真的。

所以說「陰陽順逆」，用在這一面也要知道。有人問每天子午卯酉

這可不簡單了。這四句話最誘惑人，但是我現在這樣一講，就算你們都懂

時，有人說要打坐，有人說不可以，答案是當然可以！這是我們講到「觀卦」補充提到的，我們簡單的把兩卦報告完了。

借東風之謎

到了九月，「寒露」是節，「霜降」是氣，是「山地剝」卦（䷖）。

這時陰氣的剝削只剩上面一點陽氣了。唸到《易經》這個卦，想到古文〈李陵答蘇武書〉：「涼秋九月，塞外草衰」，就是這個剝卦的意境。

再過來就是十月了，是個純陰的「坤」卦（䷁），節氣是「立冬」和「小雪」。天氣冷了，但是十月不算最冷，真冷還要到下個月。十月在陰曆來講是立冬，又叫做「小陽春」。所以每年十月北方，在冷的時候一定有個幾天，大概三天，當中會轉成暖的，雖然不像春天般暖和。這個是在哪一天呢？十月有三十天，是初一到初三呢？還是二十到二十三呢？每一年不一定。冬天是吹西北風的，但是十月小陽春可以在這三天當中轉為東南風，東南風一吹就轉暖和。

諸葛亮借東風就是在這個時候借的，你核對歷史就曉得周瑜被諸葛亮騙了，他騙周瑜會借東風，他不過把《易經》十二辟卦學通了，他懂得天文，告訴你不要擔心，等幾天我幫你借。他算定了小陽春時會吹東南風，他已經很篤定了。

曹操赤壁之戰敗北後，回去夜裏關在房中看書，忽然跳起來大笑，大家問丞相你五十萬大軍打得光光的，高興個什麼？曹操說我現在弄懂了《易經》上兩句話「先甲三日，後甲三日」，「先庚三日，後庚三日」，這個配合「天干地支」一定是小陽春轉成東南風。曹操雖懂，可是《易經》沒有學精，他想大概沒這回事，十月一定吹西北風，所以不怕諸葛亮。諸葛亮比他理解得透徹，所以這兩個人，一個是碩士班的，一個是博士班的。

第五講

占卜與神通

這裏有人提出來兩個問題，說佛家有一種木輪占法，可以占卜善惡。

其實木輪占法只是一種，佛家還不止這一種卜卦的方法。現在他問這一種方法，同上星期講到的《易經》的三易這個法則有沒有關係？這是第一個問題。第二個問題，像木輪占法等等，如果靈的話，是不是同上次所提到的《易經》法則的靈驗是一樣的道理？

這個問題，我想問問題的人已經自己答覆了。所謂占卜，占是占，卜是卜。占卦是另外一種方法。在我們的上古文化裏，卜法有很多，有用各種各樣骨頭來卜的方法，譬如牛骨、魚骨、雞骨等。占，是拿數理來推測的，後來就發展成筮法，用蓍草以算數理的方法來推測的。所以占是占，卜是卜。卜的東西比較多，現代考古學可以找到很多證據。譬如剛剛有一

位朋友拿本書給我看，寫的是我們中國的少數民族瑤族、苗族文化傳統占卜的方法，他這一本書上正好提到瑤族用雞的骨頭來卜的方法。所謂卜卦，乃至到廟子求籤，這些都是人為的。

《易經》的道理，天、地、人謂之「三才」，上是天，下是地，中間是人。我們人生的價值是什麼？人生的目的是什麼？依中國傳統觀念就是「參贊天地之化育」。這句話上面並沒有寫一個人字，但是誰在參贊天地之化育？當然是人。天地有沒有缺陷？有缺陷。人的智慧可以彌補天地的缺陷，所以「參贊天地之化育」是人的價值，人的智慧的價值，人的能力的價值，所以不要輕視了人為。

我常常跟一些好朋友說笑話，我說你蓋個廟子嘛，我給你負責作一百首籤詩。籤詩很好作，也最難作，因為籤詩的話全都不著邊際的。過後一看，真靈！壞的一看也對，好也不壞也不錯。

卜卦這些道理都是人為的，這是人的智慧，所以人修養到最高處就有神通。這些卜卦、算命等等都叫術，所謂術就是方法。在我們中國舊文化

裏頭，有個名稱叫術數。普通說佛家所講的神通有五種，一是「依通」，是靠卜卦等等這種術數，或靠一個法則，靠一個數學的統計，而知道一切事。譬如看相有時候看得很靈也是依通，是依靠身體五官來判斷。

一種是「鬼通」，就是給鬼迷住了，也可以說這個人有神經分裂，精神病，屬於鬼病的一類，可能有一些預知能力。三者是「妖通」，妖怪的妖。四是「報通」，這報通是生來就有的。前生有修持的人，這一生就有些眼睛能夠看鬼，心裏能夠預知一些事情。我過去有幾位朋友，天生就有報通。在抗戰時有一位朋友，他是名畫家也是個大學教授，我們在重慶成都經常在一起，日本人飛機來轟炸的時候，我們跟他跑警報。他一看，哎、哎，這邊不要躲，好多斷了手、斷了頭的鬼。那邊好，少一點。他只講少一點，沒有說哪個地方沒有鬼，在他看來滿街都是鬼。他說這個鬼，越鬧熱的地方越多，冷清的地方少，他說鬼也愛鬧熱，同人一樣的。他也不信什麼教，可是就看得見。大家熟朋友們邀他出去，先吩咐他，你到那裏不要作怪相啊！他坐在你家客廳裏，突然作個怪相……大家都嚇死了。這一

類的人報通是與生俱來的。還有第五種是「修通」，是打坐修定，學佛、修道，修成功發的神通。

其實所謂神通，是人的生命精神本有的功能，是智慧的成就，但不一定是得道的智慧，這個是有差別的。得道的智慧無所謂神通了，連神通都不用了，等於沒有了。這是答覆剛才這個問題，我想這個問題沒什麼重要，大致如此。所以我經常告訴大家學《易經》，不要求未卜先知。你們也不要學這些，一個人真有先知之明，活著豈不是很沒有意思！最好是糊里糊塗的活著。先知之明的人今天曉得明天的事，又曉得明年的事，這個人還幹什麼事呢？不要幹了。我們曉得明天上街會撞車，就擔心起來，不敢出門了。所以先知並不好！古人說「善於易者不卜」，真把《易經》學通了的人不卜卦、不算命、不看風水。同時古人也講過「察見淵魚者不祥」，一個人能夠精明到把水淵中的魚，都看得很清楚，那是不吉利的。頭腦這樣用是會壞的，所以還是糊塗一點比較好。換一句話說，得先知的人，能知過去未來是不吉祥的人，是不吉利的。你看那些所謂呼風喚

雨能知過去未來的大師，你查他一生，他又成就了什麼呢？他雖能知過去未來，那他自己呢？他的過去未來也不過給人家算命而已，所以用不著的啦！這些道理我們要懂。

干支 陰陽 消息

我們上次也曾從子月開始講，一年十二個月有十二個代號，子丑寅卯辰巳午未申酉戌亥，叫做十二地支。天干有十位，甲乙丙丁戊己庚辛壬癸。算命、看相、看風水都要用到的。古人解釋，所謂干就是樹幹，這一種解釋我不大同意。再查古書上，我們干支兩個字非常有道理。天干是由五行的金、木、火、水、土變化出來的。太陽系統的金木火水土五大行星，加上日月，在古代天文學叫做「七政」。我們小時候讀《幼學瓊林》要背的，「日月五星為之七政」。

子月就是陰曆十一月，它的節是「大雪」，氣是「冬至」。「冬至一陽生」，冬至是月中，所以一陽生就是中氣開始。這個中字就要注意啦，

中究竟是在哪裏？天上的中心，還是地下的中心？在我們身體是哪一個地方發動這個陽？譬如密宗講中脈，道家認為衝脈就是中脈，不過修密宗的人不承認道家講的衝脈就是中脈。這是意氣之爭我們不管，我們站在學術立場瞭解，它應該是一樣的。地區不同民族的文化不同，代表的名辭也不同。所以在中醫這個中脈叫衝脈，沖脈是簡寫。

這個衝脈同中氣很有關係，我們提到這個中氣，就要注意卦象，卦的陽爻是一橫，也就是一點，代表這個生命一個陽能，向外發展叫做上升，收縮回來叫做下降。一升一降、一收一放是講物理的現象，在生命就是一生一死，在學理觀念裏頭就是一消一息。「消息」兩個字出自《易經》。

什麼叫「消息」呢？這些觀念為什麼要囉嗦的講？這同我們修道做工夫有關。譬如十一月冬至一陽生，陽氣生命能剛剛成長，到十二月二陽上來「地澤臨」，到正月三陽開泰，看到的是陽氣的成長上升。

看到一個嬰兒剛生下來，我們很高興。可是《易經》的道理，這個叫做消，消就是慢慢用，直到用完為止。依莊子的道理，生的那一天就是開

始死亡的一天，所以生下來是在等死。就算是活了一百年、一千年，「不亡以待盡」，不過是在等最後一天的到來，所以生命的過程是消。那麼死亡了以後，是真的沒有了嗎？不是沒有了，那叫「息」，休息去了，休息是充實充電，所以息的時候不是沒有生命。我們習慣了把消耗、活動的時候當成是生命，不知道那個息，表面上看到是死亡，實際上是在充電，是新的生命正在開始。所以叫一消一息之間，換一句話說是一動一靜、一善一不善、一是一非等等。

這個我們瞭解了以後，十二辟卦從子月開始計算，走一圈到陰曆的十月，就完全變成純陰之體，純陰的卦是坤卦。這個過程就是一消一息之間，代表了這個天地運行，以及生命運轉自然的現象。這十二辟卦的作用，十二個圖案就是兩個東西，以一陰一陽兩個為代號。一個是陽能一橫，代表了生、生命、生發的力量。這一橫在《易經》有專門名字叫作「爻」。這一爻中斷的就是陰爻，不中斷的就是陽爻。就是這一陰一陽，說明宇宙之間的相對性，也就是兩個相對的力量。這不是愛因斯坦的相對

論啊！這是《易經》的相對原理，講宇宙一切萬有生命相對的作用。常有許多年輕人學《易經》，以為同愛因斯坦的相對論一樣，不要亂扯了，是兩樣！愛因斯坦的相對論，我說他有些道理，但是不一樣。不用把科學拿來給自己撐門面，也用不著把老祖宗跟近代人愛因斯坦排排站！如果說老祖宗的學問同愛因斯坦一樣，等於說祖父長得跟孫子一樣，這是不通之論。

宇宙間有一陰一陽，就是兩股力量。我們的動作也好、說話也好，任何生命都有兩個作用，這兩個作用是生滅的，消息的，所以《易經》講消息，就是佛學講生滅法。有成長就有衰弱，有衰弱就有成長，一邊高另一邊就低了。那你說一個高一個低不能均衡，這個宇宙豈不就沒有均衡了嗎？說這個宇宙有均衡的話，是假定的，那是形而上的，也要看你如何定義均衡。形而上是不是這樣？不知道，暫時不管。

乾坤 天地

這個一陰一陽在宇宙的作用由兩個符號代表，就是乾坤兩卦。《周易》的乾坤兩卦，乾代表天，坤代表地。講到這個天字，在我們中國文化裏頭可以有好幾層意思。所以讀古書讀到這個天字非常麻煩，有時候同一個句子，這個天字出現兩次，第一次講的天是形而上，理念世界的天，是個代號。第二次是講物理世界這個天體的天。有時候這個天就是西方哲學家本體論的概念。還有一個天，性理上的天，是把理性兩個字倒過來，就是我們說天理良心這個天。這不是有太陽月亮的天，也不是上帝住的地方，這個天是在我們自己的心中。所以這個天，在同一個地方就有不同的用法。在《周易》裏頭的這個天，首先是代表自然界的天體，可是有時候又用到性理方面，有時候又用在形而上的本體方面。

現在看乾坤兩卦，每卦三畫。這兩卦三橫的畫法，在唐宋以後有一個名稱叫做「先天卦」，只有三爻。把三爻卦再加上三爻，那叫「六爻

卦」，是後天的用法。為什麼先天卦只畫三爻呢？等於老子說的一個道理：「道生一，一生二，二生三，三生萬物」。三以後不談了，已經發展到不曉得多少數了。所以先天卦也只畫三爻。

六爻卦是後天的用，講到後天用，這裏有一個奇妙之處，《易經》講宇宙一切法則，它只畫到六爻，沒有第七爻了。但是古人將第七層叫作「遊魂卦」，第八叫「歸魂卦」，這個很有意思的。我們人類的文明到現在為止，不管是宗教、哲學、科學，你看沒一個東西到過第七位，只有六位。你看化學的公式化出來只有六位，第七位那個東西是死的。所以我們的老祖宗當年就知道，宇宙之間一切的應用法則只到第六位，第七位變了，到了第八位是歸魂返本還原。雖然是還原，但與原來還是不同，已經變了，所以叫歸魂卦。

坎離　日月

說了乾坤，再講「坎卦」跟「離卦」。坎離兩卦也是畫三爻。坎離兩

卦代表什麼呢？離卦代表太陽，代表火，也代表熱能。在人體上，離卦代表眼睛，代表很多了。坎卦代表月亮代表水，在人體上是代表耳朵，甚至代表腎，都是代號。

乾坤代表天地，坎離代表日月。韓國的國旗就是這乾坤坎離四卦，也非常有意思。我們曉得周武王革命推翻了暴虐的殷商紂王，然後建立周朝。商朝的貴族箕子，是紂王的親戚，他帶著中國的文化逃到了現在的韓國，保留了一部份中國文化在那裏。這是一段歷史淵源，交代一下。

現在我們看這個坎離兩卦，坎離是乾坤卦中間一爻變動來的。剛才講到中氣，我們說一件事情要變化，是自己心裏頭先動了念，中間中爻一動就變了。乾卦的中爻一動，陽爻就變陰，變成離卦，叫做「離中虛」

（☲）。如果畫一個圓圈象徵太陽，太陽那麼亮，太陽裏頭有一點黑點，太陽裏頭有黑點，這一點謂之「至陽當中有至陰之氣」，是中氣。乾卦的中爻一變，就變成離卦，所就是那個陰。所謂離中虛，是陽中有至陰。這是拿中國文化解釋太陽，不是用現在科學講《易經》的物理觀、宇宙觀。太陽裏頭有黑點，這一點謂之「至陽當中有至陰之氣」，是中氣。乾卦的中爻一變，就變成離卦，所

以太陽是代表天的乾卦變來的。

坎卦是坤卦變來的。坤卦的中爻一動，陰極就陽生，變成坎卦（☵）。

坎代表月亮，我們的古人早就知道，月亮本身不能發光，它是吸收太陽的光能而反射，才有這個光明。「坎離」兩個卦是陽中有陰，陰中有陽。

因此《參同契》頭兩句：「乾坤者易之門戶，眾卦之父母」，這是《易經》的關鍵所在，是入門之處。第三句話，「坎離匡廓」，這個天體空空的，中間有兩個圓球在轉，一個月亮（坎）一個太陽（離），變化出來萬有的生命。中國的文學有時候稱太陽跟月亮為雙丸，像兩個彈丸一樣在轉動。這個天地的運行，地球的轉動，就靠太陽月亮推動的力量。「運轂正軸」是像車輪子一樣在這個太虛、在這個宇宙裏頭轉動，有規則的動。而且它的中心一定是中正，等於車輪那個軸心一樣，不能歪的。

在十二辟卦的十二個月當中，半年屬於陽卦，「冬至一陽生」，陽氣在上升就是剛才講的「消」。半年屬於陰卦，「夏至一陰生」，陽消陰長是「息」。陽氣陽能慢慢向地球中心回收來休息了，這個是息。一消一息

之間好像是兩樣東西，實際上就是一樣東西，我們拿現在觀念講就是生命能。能把握到這一股生命能，就可以成仙成佛，超凡入聖了！現在只拿坎離兩卦做例子，太陽月亮的運行法則，說明宇宙有個總的生命能，就是一消一息之間那麼轉，形成了一年十二個月，四季春夏秋冬的現象。實際上一年沒有四季，只有二季，就是一冷一熱。春天是熱的開始，到夏天是熱之極。假使用陽代表熱，「陽極陰生」，秋天是冷的開始，所以涼爽，到了冬天是冷之極，這就是一陰一陽的來往消息。

干支 氣血 點穴

這十二辟卦再用十二個地支來做代表，所以天干是天的干擾，地支是地球本身的放射，支持自己的生命能轉動，天干地支之間變成兩重活動。

古人講：「天道左旋，地道右旋」，一正一反，所以我們看到太陽東邊上來西邊下去，好像太陽是圍著地球那麼轉，實際上是地球永遠向一個方向轉的。天道左旋，地道右旋，兩個方向不同在轉。把它縮小時間，十二辟

卦就對應一天十二個時辰。

時辰是中國古代的說法，一個時辰等於現在兩個鐘頭。十二辟卦中，一天的子時是夜裏十一點起到凌晨一點鐘，這兩個鐘頭是子時。轉過來午十一點鐘到下午一點鐘就是午時，就是這個十二辟卦的陰陽。十二辟卦的時間代表一天十二個時辰，太陽月亮與人體生命是有密切關係的。譬如我們曉得武功裏頭有一門點穴，武俠小說描寫用指頭一點，這個人就站在那裏不能動了。

點穴不一定是用指頭，如果用指頭點穴，這個指頭就要練成鐵棒了，骨節都粗起來，會武的人一看這人的指頭，哎呀！小心會點穴的！普通是用拳來點穴的，也有用腳尖來點穴。點穴的人非要記住十二個時辰不可，我們人體的穴道，哪個時辰氣血剛剛通過，點穴把這個關鍵的地方一堵塞，就把人體氣血的過道閉住了，就是這個道理。所以聽說有些朋友一下子死了，我問怎麼死的？沒有什麼，他就是扭了一下而已。在我的觀念，他當時扭撞的地方，恰好是氣血正通過的穴道，他本人只覺得輕輕碰一

下，年紀大的人氣血衰了，雖然只輕輕一碰，卻像鐘一樣停擺了。

所以人體的法則，在一天之中與時辰的關係一定要知道。中國道家講修道、打坐、做工夫，子、午、卯、酉四個時辰非常重要。子時與午時剛才說過了，卯、酉就是早晚五點到七點之間。有些人傳說，子、午時不能打坐，會走火入魔，把人嚇死了。又有些人專門勸人在子、午時打坐，所以搞得中午飯也不敢吃，夜裏不敢睡覺。子午打坐有沒有道理呢？非常有道理，這是我們先民老祖先們，根據自然法則安排起居飲食，太陽一下山就睡覺了，睡了差不多五六個鐘頭，正子時醒來了，半夜正好打坐。順其法則，日出而作，日入而息。我們現在畫夜顛倒，所以子時同午時就要活用了，不能死照這個法則。照這個法則並不是不對，效果是不同的。道家有個法則叫「子午抽添」，子午兩時辰做工夫是抽添，卯酉兩時辰打坐做工夫叫做「沐浴」。「抽添」跟「沐浴」稍稍不同。

第六講

沐浴的人

　　剛才講到用十二辟卦代表一天十二個時辰，就是二十四個小時。每一分每一秒，這個天地宇宙萬物都在變。我們學《易經》要懂這個道理，宇宙、天地、萬物、人事，沒有不變的。在佛學叫無常，無常是講他的原則，不永恆叫做無常。《易經》講的法則是變，一切皆在變化，沒有不變的事。《易經》也告訴我們，一切的變，都是漸漸地變，不是突變，突變是不可能的。我們人看不清楚，認為宇宙間有突變的事，因為對前因後果不瞭解，感覺是突變，實際上都是漸變而來。

　　宇宙、天地、萬物必變，所以人、事、物理一切皆在變動。因此諸位學打坐的，覺得有時境界很好，或者是放光了動地了，下一刻你既不放光也不動地。所以它必然要變的。變不是壞，是變了一個現象，懂了這個道

理，你可以修道了。有時說現在很清淨，等一下算不定很煩躁，也是必變的法則。所以我們每一分秒都在變，都是配合宇宙變的法則。道家告訴我們，要把握這四個時辰，子午卯酉，也叫「四正」，四個正的時間。我們畫一個十字，上下左右就是四個正。其它的叫四隅，四個斜角方向，一共是八方八卦。

這個四正時間用處又不同。子午抽添，抽就是把東西抽掉，把它減少；添就是增加，把它加上去。卯酉這兩個時辰沐浴，沐浴就是洗澡。講到這裏我又要岔進來一個故事。當年年輕喜歡四處訪道，我曾碰到一兩個奇人，這都是親身經歷，向諸位報告，做一個參考。

那時在湖南有一個學道家的，一天洗四次澡，以前家庭的衛生設備不像現在，每一次洗澡要熱水好麻煩。好在他家裏有錢，他早晨跟晚上一定洗澡，每次要泡個把鐘頭。他修道就是卯酉沐浴啊！這個人當年是六七十歲，望之如三十多歲的人。他的儀表很好，氣象也很光潤，後來我想想那是洗澡洗出來的（眾笑）。他用這個工夫對不對呀？那也是卯酉沐浴，不

過做到外表去了。

還有我在峨嵋山閉關的時候，來了一個修道的人，這個人跟廟子的當家師吵架吵得很厲害。原來峨嵋山用的水，有些廟子是靠下雨靠雪溶化積存起來，水池子有我們這個房子兩倍那麼大，很深，聚藏的水要用上半年。可是這位修道的老兄，每天要卯酉沐浴，他先跳到廁所裏洗澡，大陸上當年的廁所是個大坑，他要跳進去洗澡，不曉得嘴巴露不露出來（眾笑）。洗完了以後再跳到清水池裏洗澡。和尚們拚命拉住他，他就跟和尚吵得一塌糊塗，後來吵到我這裏來。我正在那裏閉關，我問他「你是不是遂寧人？」四川遂寧當年有一個有名的法師叫瘋師爺，同濟顛和尚一樣瘋瘋癲癲，是有神通得道的。我們當年要去訪瘋師爺，不要說拜他為師困難，你連找都找不到他。不過他經常坐在廁所，他的禪堂在廁所，不是現在的廁所，是當年那個毛坑，臭得不得了！瘋師爺就在這毛坑邊上打坐，你要拜他當徒弟要準備在廁所跪上三天三夜，不怕臭不怕髒。可是當時我就做到了，我曉得你有道，我把你廁所當成極樂世界，跪不了兩個鐘頭，

他跑過來找我了，「起來，起來！」他那時又不瘋了。可他沒有收我做徒弟，我也沒拜他為師，不過很敬仰他。

所以我就問這個學道的人，「你是不是瘋師爺的徒弟呀？」他說：「是呀！那是我師父。」瘋師爺的師父叫顛師爺，一瘋一顛（眾笑）。我說：「是嗎？你師父是我朋友啊！」我先把資格拉得老老的，也是真的，我沒有說假話。雖然我跪他，但沒有拜他為師。我說瘋師爺他可不教人家這樣啊！據我所瞭解，他走的是正路的佛法。他裝這個樣子，是要拜他做徒弟的太多了，他煩得很，就故意搞得一身髒。所以大多數人怕髒愛乾淨的，就不敢找他了。我說：「你不要冒充，我問你為什麼跳到廁所裏洗澡？」他說：「莊子說道在屎溺」。我跟他講了半天，後來總算把他說服了。你看講到卯西沐浴，我親身經歷，再加鹽加醋就是很好兩篇小說。這個世界的人物，有很多有趣的故事。

子午卯酉的作用

實際上子午抽添，卯酉沐浴，講老實話不是這個道理。但是配合宇宙法則打坐是對的，子時同午時真有作用。我曾經做了一個科學的實驗，這裏有一位科學家朱文光博士，他把金字塔的圖案尺碼弄來，用金紙做一個金字塔模型，完全依照尺度比例製作，差一點都不行。如果戴在頭上打坐，身心都特別定，是真的。他說國外曾經做過實驗，把這個紙做的金字塔做得小小的，夏天最熱時把一塊新鮮的豬肉放在金字塔中，不要冰，一個禮拜後豬肉拿出來也不會臭。這個是什麼作用？很難講。假使刮鬍子的刀鈍了，刮不動了，把它擺在金字塔的正中間，一個禮拜拿出來，刀又可以刮了。所以我跟朱博士講，你做些帽子賣，專門賣給人家打坐的（眾笑），一打坐就得道。他光說不練，到現在一頂帽子也沒做出來。這個事就是說明宇宙間的自然法則同人體有莫大的關係。

所謂子午抽添，子就是在添，你自己不用再去添它啊！子時就是復

卦，你夜裏十一點鐘開始打坐，陽氣自然上升，這是依自然法則。以前的人晚上六點鐘睡覺，睡到半夜子時醒了嘛，子時醒了陽氣正在上升，這並不是地球影響你，而是人體內的自然法則，並不是說太陽地球特別照顧你啊！我們人體生命運行的法則同這個法則一樣，你照自然的法則生活，到子時陽氣一樣升起的。所以子午抽添，子時陽氣上升，就是添的時候。你讓它自然上升，不用管它。但是你要注意身體上，譬如說氣脈發動了，這就是添。氣脈發動也同這個層次一樣，一步有一步的工夫，一步有一步的境界。我們引用《心經》上的話：「照見五蘊皆空」，你就照著它，由它自然添長。

我們到了午飯過後，人有一點悶悶想睡覺，因為陰氣生了，就是自然在抽在減。減的時候你不要硬把它拉回來，你只照住它，讓它清淨，好像要睡眠，其實並不一定睡著，只是順其自然。這就要做到「順天者昌，逆天者亡」。這個天並不是宗教，是天地自然的法則，生命的活動配合宇宙的法則規律，就是順天者昌。違反了，那自找麻煩，自找短命，就是逆天

者亡。可是我們現在的生活都是晝夜顛倒，都是「逆天者亡」啊！所以這件事，只能說子午絕對可以打坐的，但是這是一天的子午，我們還沒有說代表一生的子午，將來再說。

怎麼叫卯酉沐浴呢？不是去洗澡，而是我們學佛的道理，要你放下、清淨、不動念，身心內外有無比的寧靜、安詳之感，這就是沐浴道理。所以卯酉兩個時辰打坐，清淨自在；不是刻意去清淨，你真要造一個清淨，已經很不清淨了。這是我們看到道書上「子午抽添，卯酉沐浴」的一個原則。諸位要注意啊！我所講的只是我的意見，提供給諸位參考，我可沒有道啊！我是教書的，吃開口飯的，對與不對你們自己去研究。

採補　奪舍

因為道書有「子午抽添，卯酉沐浴」，就有許多人認為子午抽添是道家的旁門左道，叫作「採補」。採補是一個道家的名稱，你不要聽到採補就害怕！什麼採陰補陽、採陽補陰，沒有這些鬼話！採補有很多，道家的

採補有採日月的精華。這個方法，並不是邪門，而是一個很好的方法，是個大採補。採日月精華的修煉方法就很多了，這個裏頭又分得很細，所以修道這一條路很艱苦，不是你以為的悠哉遊哉。採太陽的精華，每月只有陰曆初一初二初三，初四初五就差一點，勉強可以用，過了五天就不能用。萬一碰到初一到初五都下雨，這個月就修不成了。

至於採月的精華，只有每月的十四十五十六三天，到了十七十八已經不能用了。採月亮的精華也很難的，中國許多小說上寫那些妖怪狐仙修道，是專門吸收日月精華的。但是「人生幾見月當頭」啊！人活一輩子，幾次看到月亮在頭頂上？一年只有十二次，有半年天冷你不願出來看月亮，有時碰到下雨或者月亮給雲遮起來，所以採月亮精華也很難，除非到非常高的山上，避開雲層霧氣。

我們在第一講提到過道家的「天元丹」，天元丹在佛家密宗的修法，是修東方藥師佛真正的灌頂法，可以使你長壽。「長壽法」在密宗是一種修法；「不死法」是另外一種修法。修密宗的長壽法一定跟不死法配起來

修的，而且長壽法不死法又一定是跟往生「頗哇法」配合起來修的。現在在座的，大概有很多人都修過。「頗哇法」是藏文，就是往生法，也叫轉識成就法，修成時頭頂上開了竅可以插草，插了草就像是買了保險，死後就可以往生西方。

一般學佛的人走淨土路線的，這一生可能修不成功，就要往生到阿彌陀佛那裏去留學，但是很少人有把握一定能往生。其中另有一個方法，就是道家的修法中有保存，密宗的修法已經沒有了。

當年我問我的師父噴噶活佛，藏密裏頭這個法有沒有？他說藏密這個法已經失傳了。我說中國道家有個法叫「奪舍法」。至於這個法究竟屬於道家還是密宗還是由印度傳來，說法很多，我們在此不論。道家修行人曉得此生還沒有希望，靠這個肉體修不成功了，來生再投胎又沒有把握，就趕快修「離神法」，也有叫它是「離合神光法」，離開這個身體，把這個肉體快一點丟掉。其實這個法門後來我才知道，佛說白骨觀的密法裏頭也有，不過佛說的都很隱晦。

離神法修完以後就變成陰神了，這個人離開肉體，靈魂自己可以做主。奪舍就是侵佔，要找到一個個把月剛夭折的嬰兒才好，嬰兒靈魂剛剛出去，你就進入嬰兒的身體，這叫奪舍。其實這已經犯戒了，道家這叫罪犯天條，需要有很大的功德，不然是不行的。你更絕對不能妨礙人家，不可以搶嬰兒的肉體去住，去搶的話，那是罪無可赦的。

所以我們要懂一個道理，佛家跟道家一樣絕不准自殺，也絕不准隨便投生，就是要還業報。你前生所做的善與惡業，應該要受完才可以走的。等於法院給你判了刑，你刑期沒有滿就想辦法逃出來，這是犯法的，所以奪舍法是逆道而行的。不過是有這種方法，所以修神仙、修佛，都是一個道理，大家不要隨便希望啊！修這個法門以前要「三千功滿，八百行圓」，三千功德善行要做滿，救人一命算善行一件，想做仙佛的要救多少條命才行啊！大概別人已經救過我們很多次了，欠的都是賬，所以想成仙佛太難了。

日月精華與日輪觀

由採補的道理引伸下去，岔進這一段，奪舍也屬於採補的旁枝，也屬於天元丹的一個很小的流派。採煉日月精華有些是道家的理論，引用了莊子所說「與天地精神相往來」。關於這方面，我不妨跟你們講一講，因為過去有老師父們傳過我。我一輩子都是喜歡研究，但是學了就不用，我也曉得我做不來，成不了佛，也成不了神仙。不下地獄已經很好了，一天到晚亂講，都犯戒的。真正的採日月精華很不容易的，必須很有定力，也不是對著太陽月亮看的。沒有經過老師指點不要自己看了這些書亂來，太陽月亮的精華怎麼會讓你吸進來呢？那是借用太陽月亮在宇宙間放射的功能，與你自己的氣配合起來。那麼這個氣是什麼氣呢？開始的氣粗的是呼吸，這個不是氣，真的氣是意，所謂意氣，在密宗的道理就是觀想。所以什麼是觀想？就是意氣。觀想也是第六意識的「妙觀察智」。

宇宙的精華本來跟人體是相溝通的，這個意氣自然可以作用。在佛家

來講，釋迦牟尼佛把這些方法都說了，可是一般人讀經就讀不懂。佛法的採日月精華的方法，還用不著跑去看太陽、月亮，你坐在房間、坐在地下室、坐在鐵籠裏都沒有關係，仍然可以跟太陽、月亮、宇宙的精華往來。因為太陽的放射功能，並不是牆壁可以擋得住的。如果你能夠拿意識跟它溝通的話，也就是「與天地精神相往來」。所以佛家有「日輪觀」，修淨土《觀無量壽經》也要修日輪觀，而且戒律規定所有出家的弟子，睡眠的時候心中要做日輪觀睡，這是什麼道理？所以我說釋迦牟尼佛一點祕密都沒有保留，都說了，可是一般研究經典沒有看出來。這是顯教，不是密法。有些人拚命去求密宗，實際上密宗所有的方法，顯教裏頭都有，你又看不懂，那是真密宗。

我說的是有憑有據的，我現在提出來，你們諸位看佛經就懂了。其實經典上都明明告訴你了，他沒有祕密保留，所以我一再強調，道是天下的公道，真正三教或者五教的聖人、教主沒有保留祕密，他希望一切眾生個個成功，他明明告訴你了，是你自己看不懂！道家說的：「得訣歸來好看

書」，經過老師指點，得到口訣懂了，然後自己求證一番，才把這個書看懂了。只好「掩卷一嘆」，把書本合起來嘆口氣，「古人不我欺也！」古人沒有欺騙我，是我們辜負了古人。古人把好的東西都留給我們，我們自己看不懂，只好到處去找。所以我常常說，學佛的同學們你不要感嘆找不到老師，多得很！善知識在佛經裏頭啊！佛的教法，即使是末劫的時候也還在啊。你自己修證到了，翻開經典一看，臉紅啦，為之汗顏！原來他老人家講過的，可是不到那個工夫境界，你還真看不懂！

劍仙的話

　　我們剛才講「子午抽添，卯酉沐浴」，因為講抽添，提出來採補之一種，所謂「採補日月精華」。關於修道，我再告訴諸位一個經驗，在我大概只有十幾歲，還在杭州念書的時候，聽說杭州城隍山上有一位老道士，是劍仙啊！我那個時候神仙也不想當，佛也不想成，只想當劍仙，兩手指一比，一道白光就射出去了！所以一聽說有這個老道，就想辦法去看他。

聽說他還是清朝的皇室出身，到城隍廟那個道觀修道。你們諸位杭州朋友應該還記得，城隍廟是很大一個道家的叢林，他是方丈，見他可不容易了，我跑了八趟，影子都看不見。後來總算找到一位佛教法師，見他跟這個老道有點交情，才算見到，那可不容易喔！我看他出來那個風度，可惜我不會畫，當年也沒有照相機，所謂白襪雲鞋，白的襪子，黑的鞋前面繡個雲頭，走出來大袖那麼一揮，那個樣子我看到都醉了。這就是神仙啦！那真好看，氣象萬千呀！然後一坐，很客氣，「為什麼一定要找我呀？」我趕快跪下了，我說「求道呀，師父。」「不可以叫師父，哎，請起，不要客氣，不要客氣。」他馬上把我扶起來。

然後我問他這個劍術，他說：「這個我不懂，這個不懂。」他一口否認懂劍術，然後告訴我兩件事，我一輩子記得。他說：「我們的這個心呀，只有拳頭那麼大，你看這一件事情也裝進來，那一件事情也裝進來，裝了多少事情！會迸開來的！你年輕人，什麼劍術呀，都不要裝進來，什麼事情這裏一過就丟出去，永遠丟出去，你一輩子受用無窮了。」其實這

個就是道，心裏不裝事。

他還告訴我：「哎，你也不要來求什麼，我也沒有道，也不懂劍術。

你啊，眼神不要那麼露，年輕人眼神要收斂。你會不會看花呀？」「花怎麼不會看？當然會看呀！」「唷，你不會看花的！」我就問：「那要怎麼看？」他說：「一般人看花，看任何東西，眼睛的精神跑去看。錯了！要花來看你。」我說：「花怎麼來看我呢？」他說眼神像照相機一樣，一路照過去，把花的那個精氣神吸到心裏頭來，那個時候他不講腦。花、草、山水、天地的精神用眼光把它吸進來，不是拿我們的精神去看花，要把它們的精神吸回來。

我跑了幾趟求見他，光這兩段話，這一輩子就受用無窮了，到現在我都很感謝他。他修煉精神的方法，也是與天地精神相往來，就是這個原理。那個時候聽了雖然很佩服，可是不覺得是方法。我又跪下來：「師父，你總要傳我個秘訣嘛！」我賴著不肯走，然後他旁邊那個道僮，等於佛家的沙彌，來催了他好幾次，是真的有事假的有事，我不知道，反正我

不走的，在門外跪三天三夜我也要跪。

他後來給我逼得沒有辦法，說：「你把你的劍法練給我看看。」他叫那個道僮把劍拿來，然後我就老實不客氣，把平生所學的本事都使出來了。他看了只笑這一些，都是花拳繡腿，他不好意思講跑江湖賣膏藥還可以。他說：「不要搞這些啦！時代用不著了，你劍術再高，一顆子彈就完了。」他又說練劍不容易，要人站好，一隻手叉腰，一隻手拿劍，是真的劍，是鋼鐵打造的很有份量。你要手腕用力，手腕的力氣到了劍尖上。他說晚上在房間裏點一炷香，一劍下去，香劈成兩半，兩頭都有火花，這是第一步。第二步，黃豆抓一把在手裏，丟一顆，憑空一劈就對開。然後再劈綠豆，綠豆比黃豆還小，你都劈得開時再來，我再教你。這一下我也不想再跪了，也不想再來了，沒有這個時間，永遠練不成。

我把這一些故事給諸位報告，說明修煉的這些法子，道家、密宗方法很多，但是基本原則是一樣。所以研究《參同契》第一步先把這一個圖案，配在一年，配在一天，配在身體上，配在心理上。這個法則統統把握

住了，不用向人家求方法，你自己會懂方法去修持了。今天對不起我插了很多小說一樣的故事來說明這個原則，耽誤了很多時間。但是我這個插進來的故事不是亂說的，都是配合這個道理。

第七講

四卦的作用

我們用了很多時間介紹十二辟卦與《參同契》的關係，在座的同學有人有意見，認為《參同契》的原文沒有講太多，自己不曉得怎麼研究。但是《參同契》基本上離不開所介紹的這些，譬如原文的「乾坤者，易之門戶」，就要研究《易經》乾坤坎離這四卦的變化，它所代表的法則是研究《易經》入門的綱要。乾坤是眾卦之父母，八八六十四卦都從乾坤兩卦來。這個《易經》卦理是講變，前面已經說過，雖然我們介紹十二辟卦時，看見變化是從下開始往上走，但是一切變化以中爻為主。等於一個人內心的中心思想一旦有變，慢慢外面的事實也變了。

又乾坤兩卦的中爻一動，乾卦純陽之體，中爻一變為陰，就變成了離卦，就代表了太陽。坤卦純陰之體，中爻一變就成了坎卦，坎卦代表了月

亮。至於人物的話，離卦乾卦都代表男性，坎卦是代表女性，不過以人事來應用又不同。這個道理有很多了，我們沒有時間再多談。所以眾卦「坎離匡廓」，都靠天地太陽月亮，也就是這乾坤坎離四卦做為一個大綱。

「運轂正軸」，等於一個車輪的中心點，一個轉動陀螺的中心點。

「牝牡四卦」，「牝牡」二字在《道德經》裏常用到，牝字代表母性，牡代表了公性。所以在古書上，公牛就稱牡牛，母牛稱牝牛，也就是代表陰陽兩個字。乾坤坎離這四卦，四個符號，乾代表陽性，男性，正面；坤代表陰性，母性，反面。坎兩卦，離代表陽性是公的、正面，光明面；坎代表陰性的，母性，黑暗面。「以為橐籥」，這是老子《道德經》裏的話，老子講：「天地之間其猶橐籥乎？」這個宇宙形成與滅亡了又形成，不是誰能主宰，而是自然共有的一股生命的力量。

「橐籥」兩個字分開來講是兩件東西，「橐」是布袋子，我們小的時候都看過，鄉下人做生意的，出門揹一個布縫的袋子，中間塞進衣服錢財。「籥」是七孔或九孔的笛子，竹管做的。「橐籥」合起來代表風箱。

以前打鐵或爐火，有個木頭做的手拉風箱，手一推動，拉起來咔嗒咔嗒響空氣就來了，一關一開吹風，代替人來搧火。所以「橐籥」就代表一動一靜、一開一合、一來一去之間這個動能。在靜態的時候，什麼都沒有，空的；一動之後，一開一合就有一股動能出來。

這就是中國道家哲學，包括儒釋道三家最高的哲理，並不像西方文化那樣，認為宇宙是有一個主宰創造的。東方文化是科學性的也是哲學性的，所以老子講宇宙之間其猶橐籥乎！

「牝牡四卦，以為橐籥」，它就是宇宙之間這個生命的大象。《易經》叫做「大象」，大概的現象，是說原則不變的；不是小象，沒有詳細分析。大象就是乾坤坎離。乾坤代表了宇宙天地，坎離代表太陽月亮，「牝牡四卦」就是這陰陽四卦，「以為橐籥」，就是太陽月亮一切在運轉，所以形成我們人世間有白天、黑夜；有動相、靜相。這個動能在中國道家就叫做氣，所以古人的詩說到宇宙萬有生物的生命，「悟到往來唯一氣」，悟到生與死就是一股氣的作用。「不妨吳越與同丘」，活著為了爭

一口氣，大家鬧意見也是這一口氣的作用。吳越是敵對的國家，死後這一口氣不來了，就算埋在一起都沒有關係了。

氣與物

古人所講這個氣以及道家所講的這個氣，千萬不要誤解為空氣或者大氣層的氣。所以研究中國道家哲學，對於這個氣字一定要搞清楚。我經常介紹氣有三種，我們現在寫的氣字，是中國文字自然的演變，這個氣中間有個米，代表米穀之氣，是吃了東西以後的呼吸，營養進去的這個吸收功能。至於空氣的氣，過去寫法中間沒有米字，就成了气。那麼道家原始寫法那個「炁」，中間是沒有連著的。那個古代炁字，就是兩橫。現在這個「无」字，是中國古字的無，下面有四點，中國字四點是代表火，无火之謂炁。我們勉強的借用現在觀念只能說，生命的本能是這個「炁」，但是我們一點也沒有發揮這個炁。

發揮這個炁字道理還很多，大家打坐做工夫，開始都是用鼻子呼吸。

有人問氣功究竟有多少種？據我所知有二百八十多種，都是由這兩個鼻孔玩的花樣，人真會玩。真達到所謂氣充足了，神凝氣聚，精神專一，達到這個境界的步的工夫。但的確可以利用呼吸之氣來修煉身體，這是最初氣已經不是呼吸的氣了，同呼吸就沒有多大關係了。這是做工夫方面，我們會再討論到。

「牝牡四卦，以為橐籥」，實際上這兩句的意義，就是生命的功能那個東西。這個東西宗教叫它是菩薩也好，上帝也好，但在道家文化學術裏，沒有這些名稱，因為無法給它一個名稱。老子叫它道，也是假名，所以「道可道，非常道，名可名，非常名」。這個東西，叫它什麼都可以，它不是唯心也不是唯物，但是心物都是它的變化。

老子同莊子的道家觀念，認為宇宙之間這個功能就叫做物化，但是這個物，不要認為是現在唯物思想的物，春秋戰國時候沒有什麼唯物、唯心的分別。所以讀那個時候的古書，常常讀到這個物，有時候這個物是實體的東西，有時候這個物是代號。等於我們現在罵人，你是什麼東西？我說

我是學哲學的，我真不知道自己是什麼東西。東是東，西是西，但是它構成了一個通用的觀念，這樣你就能懂這只是個代號。

所以研究春秋戰國時候的《老子》，看到一個物字，不要認為老子是唯物思想，那就錯了。那個不是現在的心物觀念，譬如老子說「其中有物」，這個裏頭有個東西，這個東西他勉強取一個名字，就是我們中國老祖宗叫做道，叫做天，叫做乾卦，也都是代號。表示宇宙中有一個生命，它在動靜、生死之間看得出來。這個體，形而上的體在哪裏？西方哲學和宗教，專門討論研究這個體，宇宙萬有生存之體，死了也就看不見了。在東方文化，體雖然看不見，仍然是有。體在哪裏見？在用上見，在相上見。有用有現象，體的功能在其中矣！

譬如人會講話，但能夠講話的不是言語，也不是嘴巴，是人的生命會講話。在哪裏看見呢？就在他講話上，講話是他的相，現象是體的用，所以體是在相和用上見的。離了相和用，雖然有體，卻不可見，不可知，不可說，無形無相。所以東西方哲學有時候把人思想搞得很混淆，往往有些

人講體，其實只是在講相，有的只在講用，他又牽涉到本體，於是就搞不清楚了。實際上體、相、用是一個東西。

還有，大家都以為打坐是在修道，打坐只是做工夫，不是道，不過是修道的一種方法，一種作用，本身不是道。道不在你打坐上，也不在你做工夫上。如果說修道，打坐應該叫做修腿，不叫做修道，因為打坐有兩隻腿在坐。用鼻子吐納，那也不是修道，那叫做修氣。道不在這個呼吸的氣上，氣也是它的相，是它的作用。有人說守丹田，或守個什麼地方叫做修道，那只能說你很愛惜你的肚臍眼，把它守得牢牢地，那不能叫做修道。道不在肚臍眼這裏，如果光是肚臍眼、丹田這裏是道，難道我們別的都不用了嗎？

四卦與修道

所以這個道理一定要搞清楚，「牝牡四卦」，天地日月這四卦，是代表生命往來興衰這個作用的現象。「覆冒陰陽之道」，「覆」就是蓋，包

括的意思。只要懂得《易經》的「乾坤坎離」四卦的真實作用，這個法則瞭解，就是已經「覆」了，整個宇宙萬有生命的功能也都會瞭解。「冒」就是放在頂上。「覆冒陰陽之道」，把乾坤坎離四卦作用，十二辟卦等等搞清楚了，就把宇宙陰陽、生死、生發之際、動靜之用，整個把握住了，然後可以懂得修道了。

這是漢代的古文，內容包含有那麼多，我們簡單地介紹。懂得了「乾坤坎離」四卦與宇宙萬有中心的法則，也懂得了修道，就是「猶工御者」像一個會駕車的人——「工」就是代表專家，「御者」是駕車的人，騎馬的人。「準繩墨」，繩墨叫做墨斗，古代劃一條線，是用一個裝墨水的斗狀物，把一條線拉過墨水，線兩頭拉住，中間一彈，一條直線就印下來了。要能「執街彎」，御馬的人把馬的韁繩拉住，馬就聽指揮了。「街彎」是馬嘴的兩邊繩子，「正規矩」是說做工程的人，要想準確畫直、圓、三角，必須要用繩墨來「正規矩」。「隨軌轍」是車子走路，一定要遵循軌道。

我們這個宇宙的自然，並不是亂來的，要注意啊！這一點我常常跟同學們提，像中國畫的山水，庭院藝術的建築，都喜歡自然的美。自然美看起來像是沒有規律，但是不規律中有絕對的規律，不可以變動。這就是東西方藝術的不同觀點，相同當中有不同之處。所謂自然的東西，它自然而有規則。沒有研究清楚，認為亂七八糟就是自然，這個觀念就錯了。

宇宙的法則是很呆定的，自然的法則是很嚴謹的，不可以有絲毫差錯。譬如說今年下雨特別多，大家都很煩，好像覺得下雨毫無規律，其實它是有規律的。為什麼今年，尤其到這個季節，和過去不同呢？假使研究中國傳統的天文，就應該知道是必然如此。因為下元甲子要到了，它同天文氣候都有一定的關連。

「處中以制外」，這一句話特別重要。我們大家修道，一切都是你心的觀念，心念一動，身體感受和生理都會起變化的，所以修道講「處中」。道家講的「中宮」，畫上下兩個連環圓圈，代表了身體。上面一個圓圈，肚臍下面一個圓圈，「中」就在這個中間，所以叫做「守中宮」，

這個是有形的，也是方法之一。「處中以制外」與道家的「守中宮」有關。道一動，外相就變了。相就是現象，現象變了作用也變了，像乾坤兩卦，中爻一動變成坎離，所以我們瞭解修道就在中心。中是個什麼東西？這是個大問題了。譬如儒家有《中庸》，佛經裏有龍樹菩薩的《中論》。道家是非常注重《中庸》的，所以「處中以制外」。

數是什麼

「數在律曆紀」，前面說過《易經》有三個重點：理、象、數，加上通、變，實際上有五個。變就是用，通了才能曉得應用。理就是哲學的道理，理字也代表《易經》講宇宙萬物本體。象就是現象，用就是作用。所以研究《易經》每一個卦，每一爻都有它的體，都有它的作用，它的現象也都不同。再進一步講，任何宇宙萬物有現象有作用就有「數」，譬如我們這個手那麼動一下，或者一秒鐘，或者半秒鐘，就是數。數在中國大家習慣也叫「運」，所以算命問運氣。運就是動，在動態當中，一動必定有

數，所以有數的理。學西方數理哲學到了極點，也懂了道，那也是一樣的。所以萬物皆有其數，是呆定的東西，一步一步來的。

剛才我們講過，天下沒有一個東西是突如其來的。突如其來它也有數，它突一下多少數，修道做工夫自己要懂這一個道理。所以你說，我修三年五年了，為什麼沒有進步？你才三年五年，用佛家的話，只吃三天素，你就想生西天，沒有這回事！況且你修了一輩子，有沒有合這個規律？真的懂了沒有？否則都是白搞了。所以一年的天候，太陽月亮同宇宙地球的關係，每月每天的時間，都是呆定的，不能說現在是傍晚，卻希望下一個鐘頭就是明天早晨，那是做不到的。

一個現象有它的數，這個數就在「律」表達。我們再拿十二辟卦的圖來說明，由外圈數進來的第三層，這個「黃鍾、大呂、太簇、夾鍾」等等是講「律」。在中國的音樂哲學叫做「十二律呂」，是中國音樂哲學的最高點。我們歷代史書上都有〈律曆志〉，屬於中國文化的重點。現在先解釋這個「律」，「律」就是曆法，就是這個圖外圈第三層，十一月叫子

月，十二月叫丑月，陰曆同陽曆配起來用。

「十二律呂」代表了太陽的行度與我們地球的關係，這個「呂」字代表了月亮，太陰。月亮同地球有一定的的關係，這是曆法。我們中國幾千年來，都是陰陽合曆用的，但不是現在這樣亂用。我們中國古代所謂以農立國，還沒有氣象台，但是民間對氣候變化的掌握就是靠這個。譬如說過幾天是清明了，清明、立秋，這個用的「十二律」是陽曆的作用，至於說每月初一到十五，用的是陰曆，所以是陰陽合用的曆。

「律曆紀」，「紀」是什麼？十二個月為一年，擴大一點，十二年就是一紀。三十年叫一世，這是中國文化的科學與哲學。可是現在的青年大部份都不知道了，嘴裏天天叫中國文化，你問他什麼是「律曆紀」，他就莫名其妙了。這些都是中國文化精華所在，所以外國人寫到我們中國科學史，就非常佩服。

什麼是自然

回轉來講，這個宇宙運行的法則，一步有一步的現象，一步有一步的作用，每一個現象也不是亂七八糟的。所以修道要懂這個，「處中以制外」，把握那個中心。我們人為什麼衰老？衰老是一定的，因為生來必有死。生老病死四大過程等於乾坤坎離，從天亮到夜晚，呆定的，誰都免不了。但是道家文化認為可以免得了，不過一定要懂得這個法則。所以老子講「人法地，地法天，天法道，道法自然」。「法」就是效法，人要效法這個地球運行的法則。人靠地球而生活，地球生長了我們，也把我們收回去了。「人法地」，就是效法地球這個作用。

地球靠什麼？「地法天」，這個天是代表太陽系統，這個天又是哪裏來的？這就是哲學問題了。生命哪裏來的？上帝造的。上帝誰造的？上帝外婆是誰？姓張的，姓李的，一路要問下去。「天法道」，道就有這麼一個作用，這個功能，在宗教叫做神啊、主啊、上帝啊，叫做什麼東西不管了，在中國文化只是天效法道，不可以違反道的規律。那麼道效法什麼呢？老子講「道法自然」，我們現代人讀《老子》，認為自然就是自然科

學的自然，古文不是這樣讀，我們現在的自然科學是借用老子的觀念。自然兩個字原來不一定是合在一起的名辭，道法「自」「然」，是說它自己當然如此，它的自體當然是如此，不要再問了，不能問下去。等於宗教講的一樣，上帝是誰造的，信就得救，不要問，再問下去問不到底了。

所以道法是「自」「然」，自己當然如此謂之自然。我們現在讀《老子》的人，因為受了幾千年後日本人借用《老子》的自然觀念，翻譯自然科學名辭的影響，所以我們一提自然，說這個風景那麼好，那是自然的，人要到自然裏頭走走，於是自然就代表空氣、代表了空間。人怎麼會到自然裏頭走走呢？這一些自然的觀念同老子的自然毫不相干，名稱給他們借用錯了。所以老子說「道法自然」，「道」效法誰？道就是道，它自己本身必然一定是如此，有一定的規律。

所謂自然不是盲目，剛才再三強調，自然非常有規則，一步不能違反。所以魏伯陽真人在《參同契》告訴我們，道家修煉神仙之道，如科條之不可違。等於法律、科學的定律沒有辦法違反一樣。我們現在的年輕人

做工夫，說是這裏動，那裏麻，就認為任督二脈一下子就通了，那是超越了自然，不可能的，那是假通。氣脈假通是很容易的，因為那是感覺不是真通。真正的通有它的相，一步有一步的象徵，一步有一步的作用。所以「體」「相」「用」是不能違反的定律。就像一個孩子剛生下來，就想會講話走路，那是不可能的。我們先報告到這裏，這還牽涉到人體生理生命的關係，先休息一下再說。

第八講

我們講傳統的道家是指秦漢以前，那時儒道諸子百家並沒有分家。換一句話說，傳統的道家在秦漢以前的，就是中國文化的根。所謂儒家孔孟思想是「道」的一部份；其他如名家、法家乃至於兵家、軍事哲學，都出自道家。連醫家、農家以及諸子百家，都是由道家而來。所以到清朝時，紀曉嵐奉命搜羅中國的書籍編成《四庫全書》，關於道家的這一部份，他有八個字的按語：「綜羅百代，廣博精微」。「綜羅百代」是所有中國文化的一切，都包含進去；「廣博」形容非常大，非常淵博；「精微」等於是科學的，是嚴謹的，微妙的，這就是道家。

生命的卦變

剛才我們提到，在醫學方面必須要懂十二辟卦，以及乾坤坎離的應用。我們上其他課的時候也提到過，現在再重複一次。人的生命，由母親

第一天懷孕開始，一直到出生，是屬於乾卦。乾卦是個符號，代表生命的完整性，沒有男女之分。我們講《易經》的六爻卦，下面三爻稱為內卦，上面三爻稱為外卦，這個六爻卦的應用是很妙的。我們老祖宗知道宇宙的應用法則，「用」只在六位的範圍，到第七位要變去了，第八位是返本還原，還原就變另外一個東西了，這些前面也提到過。

生命的開始是以乾卦做代表，然後這個數的問題來了，男性以八為基礎，女性以七為基礎。雙數謂之偶數，也就是陰數；單數謂之奇數，就是陽數。《易經》之中，數的道理只在十個數字範圍打轉，一增一減，就概括了一切。單數的一、三、五、七、九，這五位是陽數，五在中間；雙數倒數回來，十、八、六、四、二，也是五位，六在中間。《易經》的數理裏頭有很多的東西，我們現在不是專講這個，以後再單獨的介紹。那麼為什麼說男性的生命用八來代表？假使男性屬於陽，為什麼他的數又變成陰呢？女性屬於陰，為什麼數又變成陽呢？

這些道理牽涉很多，就是陰中有陽，陽中又有陰的道理。一個東西到

了極點就要變化，所以陰極就陽生，陽極就陰生。宇宙萬有的現象界都是相對的原則，就是「道」。現象和用互變，所以陽極陰生，陰極陽生。但是萬變中間有個相對互用，這個變化在《易經》有一個名稱叫互變。

男性外表看是陽，其中又有至陰之精；女性應該屬於陰，但其中有至陽之精。《易經》講「陰陽坎離」，這些道理都不是呆定的。我曾經向諸位介紹過，孔子在《易經繫傳》裏講過，「變動不居，周流六虛」，所以研究《易經》學問的，千萬記住不能把一個法則呆板的用，不要認為是不能變動的。事實上，其中的變化太多了，陰中有陽，陽中有陰，重重無盡。

人的生命在出生以前，屬於內卦的範圍，內卦也叫先天。生下來以後，女性以七數為基礎開始計算，男性以八數開始計算，就是後天。中國醫學根本的一本書，就是《黃帝內經》，其中講到「女子二七而天癸至」，什麼叫「天癸」？癸就是中國文化天干最後一位，五行裏頭屬水。譬如今年是癸亥年（一九八三），這個亥字在十二地支是最後一個，也屬水。所以有人隨便講陰陽八卦，把今年下雨特別多講成是因為癸亥年的關

係。這倒不一定，但是不能說完全沒有關係。二七而天癸至，是說女孩子十三四歲第一次月經來，就開始不算童子了。男性要到二八，十五六歲這個階段，開始變成少年，這個時候男性童兩個乳房會發脹發痛，起碼有兩三天之久，但是生理的轉變男性沒有女性的明顯。此外，女性的生理週期為什麼叫月經呢？因為它是像月亮圓缺一樣有週期的，以四七二十八為一個週期。

女性到了二七，十四歲前後天癸至，乾卦破掉了，先天的生命變化，開始了後天的生命。當然這個六爻的卦象也變了，上面三爻還是乾，下面三爻最底下的一爻由陽變陰，就變成了巽卦（☴）。這個六爻合起來是天風姤卦（☴☰），就是純陽裏頭第一步開始變，陰來了。接著以七年為一個週期，三七二十一歲再變，把第二爻又變成陰的，就是變成天山遯卦（☶☰）；四七二十八再變一爻，變成天地否卦（☷☰）；五七三十五又變了，變成風地觀卦（☷☴），這時外形也變了，人已到了中年。我們中國文學老句子，人到中年萬事休，到中年就差不多了，走下坡路了。到老年要

普通變化（受物理現象的限制，生命逐漸消耗。）	名象卦	齡 男	年 女
	坤		
	地山剝	56↑49	49↑43
	地風觀	48↑41	42↑36
	地天否	40↑33	35↑29
	山天遯	32↑25	28↑22
	風天姤	24↑17	21↑15
	乾	16	14

修道昇華（突破現象界的限制，奪天地之造化）	名象卦	方 法
	乾	1. 由生理着手，藉吐納、藥物等方法，煉精化氣，煉氣化神……
	澤天夬	
	雷天大壯	
	地天泰	2. 由心理着手，致虛極守靜篤，或等而下之如守竅……是。
	澤地臨	
	雷地復	
	坤	

◄生命的兩種變化（長生或不亡以待盡），▤▤代表生命中生生不息的功能，▤▤表示生命已受的損害。

趕緊修道，不修來不及了。

六七四十二山地剝卦（▤▤），身上的陽氣，由父母稟賦帶來的生命能只剩一點了，像銀行裏的存款已經用得差不多了，是後天用的。這個卦上面只剩一點陽能，一個陽爻了。在男性就是相當於六八四十八。人到中年痛苦悲哀經驗多了，看得多了，沒有時間煩

無根的樹

到了七七四十九，經期就要停止了，現在醫學叫做更年期。男性也有更年期，男性是七八五十六歲。以前有一位上將，他現在過世了，好多年前，有一次見到他，我說我看你身體好多了。他說，老師啊！你曉得醫生把我怎麼治啊？他給我打雙性荷爾蒙！他當時還罵這個醫生亂搞，都七十幾了還有什麼荷爾蒙不荷爾蒙！醫生說，報告長官，你就聽我這一次，打一針試試看好不好？結果他就打了，這一打下去覺得好舒服，精神好了百倍！男女性的稟賦中間有些不同，所以以道家來講，女性修道要在卦氣未盡，七七四十九以前就要下手修持。所謂下手修持，並不是說明天報名學打坐，自己就算修道了，好像盤盤腿或者唸唸佛就會把卦氣拉回去了，沒有這回事，不是那麼簡單，修道可不容易喔！所謂「天元丹」，是要懂這

惱，也沒有時間高興了，就要學莊子講的：「喜怒哀樂不入於胸次」。只有一陽還留著，以道家來講，趁這個時候趕快修，不然就不行了。

此法，「地元丹」就要瞭解一切醫藥，「人元丹」則在自己本身。

道家有位祖師爺叫張三丰，我看過他親筆寫的東西，在成都的青羊宮，碑有七八個吧！我看了佩服透頂！那真叫做神仙筆跡，每一個字不是橫，不是直，那個筆劃都是圓圈，真像是太極拳，可是都看得清楚。他的文學著作好得很，寫過一本《無根樹》的詞。《無根樹》是比喻我們的生命是沒有根的，隨時會死亡，所以必須要把根栽起來，這是修道的工夫。

他中間有一句，「下手速修猶太遲」，勸人趕快修道。他說年輕人早早求明師下手修都恐怕來不及了，等到卦氣完了再來修，更來不及了！這樣一講，我們就都很悲哀了，到了一定年紀以後怎麼修道？不是說不可以，一口氣沒有斷以前都可以；但是比卦氣沒有完的人困難，需要多加兩倍的工夫。所以在卦氣未絕、沒有斷，還沒有到更年期以前，就要開始專修。不是說打打坐唸唸佛叫做修道，這個聲明在先。

因為道家這一套修持的方法太不容易了，所以學道家的有個術語，叫做「得訣歸來好看書」。其實神仙丹經道書上，修持的路線、方法都教

了。等於我常常告訴學佛的同學們，佛把修行的方法，在《大藏經》裏毫無隱藏地都教給了我們，顯教裏頭都是密教！就是大家看不懂而已。所以道家的書你也可以看啊！不過我有個主張，近一百年來關於道家修煉的著作不能看，尤其是現在有些三年輕之輩寫的，問題太多了。我必須要向諸位抱歉，因為我好像很狂，也可以說傲氣，我年輕時候非秦漢以上的書不讀！就那麼傲！好像後人見解學問有點靠不住。再到後來更狂了，非周秦以上的書不讀！因為發現周秦以後的人，有許多見解也靠不住。花了那麼大工夫讀了一部書，結果是錯的！你說這個多痛苦呢！所以非周秦以上之書不讀，尤其是佛道兩家的書。最近出版也發達了，亂寫書，害死人不要本錢的。這個要注意因果啊！像我們一輩子寫文章不敢亂寫一個字，這是傳統文化精神，老師和父兄都嚴屬地告誡我們，文字殺人不見血，但犯的殺戒比害死十條命都厲害。乃至叫我們教書都要小心，怕斷送人家的慧命，比殺人家性命還要可怕。

父兄告誡我們還有一件事，不要做官。「一代贓官九代牛」，如果做

貪官，九輩子都要變牛還債，所以不敢做。我們小時候背的〈朱子（柏廬）治家格言〉：「讀書志在聖賢」，並不是為了做官；既然做了官，「為官心存君國」。所以我都叫你們背來，你會背的話一輩子都有用。最後的兩句話就是「為人若此」，知識份子作人做到上面所講的標準，「庶乎近焉」，差不多勉勉強強算一個人了。這是中國文化教育的目的，上至皇帝下至討飯，那只是職業不同，和事業沒有關係，這多難啊！

人欲能平嗎

　　講到作人難，現在作人是不太容易，不過這個生命也是來之不易，因此說，「下手速修猶太遲」。可是老年的修，超過這個卦氣怎麼辦呢？只有加倍工夫了。因此道家幾乎沒有一個不通醫藥的，也沒有一個不懂軍事的，都懂！你要修道，在莊子的觀念稱為「心兵」，是天理人欲之爭。人的欲望非常大，把這個欲望淨化了，才走上道業的路。所以佛經有句話，「染緣易就」，這個欲望一旦黏染住了，越來越嚴重，道業就難成。所以

修道做工夫，心裏頭有干戈之相，天理人欲之爭，只有人欲平了，那個所謂天理，道的境界才能出現。

我常跟青年人說，我們有些錯誤的情緒思想，不完全是心理的，而是生理的變化限制了人。所以道家的方法與佛家不同，第一步先要把生理變化了，也就是從物理開始轉起，把你轉過來。有些密宗講氣脈也是走這個路線，先改變了血肉之軀的生理氣質，然後打坐得定就很容易了。當自己心中對自己不再鬥爭時，在佛家講是妄念平息。儒家的理學家也引用來講理，但我們經常說，理學家的名辭很好聽，但只是空話，能做到很難。

理學家得什麼道呢？儒家孔孟之道是「人欲淨盡，天理流行」，妄念雜想平靜淨化了，就達到道的境界。這是把佛道的主旨用孔孟的觀念思想，講成「人欲淨盡，天理流行」。這個人欲談何容易淨盡，天人合一境界是人欲淨盡了，天理才能流行。理學家也用道家、佛家、禪宗的方法靜坐，從靜來入手，可以達到「人欲淨盡，天理流行」的境界。不過他們是不盤腿的，打坐就是正襟危坐，這是儒家坐法。

以前我們小的時候家裏有老師教書，去找老師時一看老師坐在那裏，大家不敢動了，為什麼？因為老師在入定，不是老僧入定，他們是靜坐，每天也規定時間。那麼「人欲淨盡」何以能夠做到呢？所以理學家講變化氣質，這個變化氣質也就是從佛家、道家裏頭拿出來的。氣質就是這個肉體生命實際的東西，怎麼把它變得過來呢？道家所謂真正修道要修到自己脫胎換骨，整個肉體都轉換了，這也就是變化氣質。

道家把七歲做一個單元，這裏就告訴諸位要懂中國醫學的兒童保健了。要培養小孩子身體健康，七歲到八歲是一個階段。二七十四到十六，所謂少年的煩惱時代，身體變化這個階段要注意。女性是七的數字，男性是八的數字，所以我們講：你這個人七七八八的，亂七八糟，不三不四，都是《易經》數理的觀念。不三不四，因為第三爻第四爻最難辦，這是由內卦到外卦；亂七八糟，是說七不能亂，八也不能糟，七七八八就形容糟亂了。所以這些俗語俗話，都有很多的哲學道理在內。

男女兩性的保養觀念，可以從七年縮小至七天一個變化，再縮小至七

個時辰，也就是十四個鐘頭，乃至於七秒鐘都變一次。我們現代醫學也知道，一個人七年之中身體大部分都換新細胞了。十二年一紀，從內到外沒一個東西沒有換的。我們今天坐在這裏，你是你還不是你？這個生理的變化有它的法則，我經常說修道學佛是個科學，先要把理論搞清楚才能下手修。有許多人以為這個修道做工夫，打坐就是了，何必懂那些理論！不懂理論叫做盲修瞎煉，盲修瞎煉有沒有用處？有用處，那等於是保養一個機器一樣，你少用一點，經常給它抹抹油，經常把它包起來，也就可以拖長一點才壞，但是，那可不叫修道！

逆流而上

修道的工夫，是硬要鬥天地之造化，是跟上帝、玉皇大帝、宇宙、閻王爭命呢！我不聽你主宰，要聽我自己的！這是道家的工夫。就像張紫陽真人在《悟真篇》裏頭講：「一粒金丹吞入腹，始知我命不由天」，要到那個境界，修道才有些基礎，有點把握。

我常常說你看一個家庭，兩夫妻年輕相戀，愛得要命，幾年以後就變了！交變，卦變，他倆都變了！尤其到中年變得更厲害。老年也變，但年老以後也沒得可追了，只有爭看電視吵吵架。所以注意這個數字的變。為什麼？生命自己做不了主，受物的影響，受生理的影響。所以修道不懂這個法則，光學了一招半招怎麼修啊！修道關鍵就在這裏。「順為凡」，你照自然法則去走就是普通人；「逆為仙」，掌握生命的自然法則而修為逆行。懂了十二辟卦法則，就懂得一天十二個時辰生理的變化，把握好才能改變，也就是逆為仙。

修道要懂配合時辰，乃至地區環境。譬如在南中國用的方法同黃河以北的不同。所以我常常告訴年輕學醫的同學，現在你們在這個濕度大的地方，按照《傷寒論》絕對沒有問題。《傷寒論》是張仲景在湖南地區的經驗累積，你如果到黃河以北，《傷寒論》有些病可以治，到了西北或大北方，如果用南方這一套方法用藥，也許會醫死人的。萬物各有一太極，每一個地區各有一個太極，隨便用就不對，常會用錯，而且每一個人不同。

修道也是一樣，每人身體稟賦不同，有人身體質弱，有人生來體質弱，有人生來特別強，有人生來肝臟不好，有人肺臟不好，有人腎臟不好。你這些法則懂了才可以去修神仙，所以說想做神仙談何容易！

一個仙佛無所不知，無所不曉，大家天天坐在那裏屁都不懂，還想成神仙，還想成佛，不可能的！生命往來就是這股氣，真的！我剛才講的話，你們年輕人還笑，有些人說老師經常講屁都不懂一個，這是真的。有許多修道的人，屁也不敢放，也不敢洗澡，怕漏了元氣。所以一天到晚提肛，把肛門夾住，結果搞得一臉烏氣，那是大便中毒，因為那個氣是瓦斯，是濁氣，要放掉才行。清氣要留著，身體內部什麼是清氣？什麼是濁氣？同樣是個屁，也有很多學問；同樣，卻反應出身體內部不同的毛病；同樣是呼吸，呼吸的學問更多。

能把這些瞭解了，把握這個法則才能談修道。不是說兩腿一盤，學個一天半天工夫，就算開始修道了。我經常說，看了幾十年，各地所謂的仙啊、佛啊，看了很多了，最後呢？據我所知不是心臟病、血壓高就是老人

症，也同我們大家一樣，茫茫然而來，茫茫然而去。我還沒有看見過一個真能修養到心理、生理絕對健康的。真能達到身心絕對健康，雖然不能成仙，也已經夠得上是地仙，大概可算是半仙了。

第九講

南宗北派有別

目前最耽誤時間的就是《易經》這一部份，但是我們也沒有時間詳細的講，只能說一個大要。這一部份記有道家的術語所謂「內金丹」，就是人修煉自己性命的方法。這個原則非常重要，所以一定要瞭解這個理論，然後做工夫就很確實了。道家這一方面偏重於工夫修證的程序，而佛家講修定很空洞，只講了四禪八定的大原則，但是由初禪怎麼樣證入？初禪基礎所謂得定得止與生理心理的關係，究竟在哪裏？佛家是完全不談身體方面的事，只要你能夠徹底把它空了，一路就到底。事實上這個身體擺在這裏空不掉的，處處都是障礙。所以老子也說，有這個身體就有障礙。

《易經》法則的十二辟卦同天地運行的法則，與修道有絕對的關係。所以我們現在多耽誤一點時間，後面就比較好辦。如果前面馬虎了，後面

反而難辦，這是第一點要交代的。第二點，我們現在採用的本子，是清代朱雲陽這位道人註解的本子，也有人稱他祖師，他是北派的。據我個人所瞭解，所有《參同契》的註解有幾十家，也有朱熹註的。朱夫子的我們暫時不談，那比較外行；內行的註解以朱雲陽的最好。另外有些註解是屬於南宗的，南宗是雙修派，不必出家，是夫婦可以同修成神仙。這一派在道家叫做南宗或是南派。南派裏頭又分了很多家，在大陸有些南派道家的道觀中，是有道人帶了家眷的，像是日本的佛教。這一類的修道人就是「火工道人」，就是說自己在火裏頭修；用佛家的術語是在火裏頭種出蓮花來。這個本事大啦！單修、專修比較容易，修道有家眷又不離世俗法，那就太難了！

古代有些《參同契》的註解完全是採南派的觀點，說法又不同，卻也是言之成理。能講一套很嚴謹的理論也不簡單的！諸位把這些書拿到手裏一翻，就曉得是屬於哪一派哪一宗的說法。南派在中國的道家歷史有多久呢？也許有三五千年，春秋戰國時候就有了。到了兩晉的時候，出了一位

很大的神仙叫做許旌陽真人。在座江西的朋友都知道，江西南昌有一個萬壽宮，那就是他的道場。他那一派在道家是屬於淮南子的哲學思想，歷史上除了黃帝、許旌陽拔宅飛升全家修成神仙之外，再沒有他人。他們房子都帶走了！文學上形容：「犬吠雲中」，連他家裏養的雞狗，受了丹藥影響都帶上天了。吳梅村寫過個句子：「我本淮王舊雞犬，不隨仙去落人間」，講他寧願做神仙的狗，一下子就帶上去了，也用不著打坐做工夫。

南派走所謂雙修的路子，在東漢魏晉之間影響很大，後來都歸併在道教裏。實際上它是另外一個教派，叫做「淨明忠孝教」。根據中國文化的道理，一個人想做神仙想成佛，先要把人作好。道家說，世上天上無不忠不孝之神仙，一定是忠孝節義俱全的人，才夠得上成仙成佛。你查中國道家神仙的歷史，確實個個都是如此的人。

有些《參同契》的註解，古怪的很多。有一點我再次告訴青年同學們，佛道兩家近一百五十年以來的著作都要小心，絕對不能看，不光是佛道兩家的，隨便那一家都不能看。只有一些考據學說的，晚清以後的倒值

得一看。至於現代著作我就不知道了，因為我這個人活著等於死了，這個要向諸位交代的。

朱雲陽道人的《參同契闡幽》，在我認為是屬於第一流的註解。文字好，道理也透徹，非常好！那是真正最正派的說法，道家所有工夫道理都放進去了。以我讀書的經驗，這一生讀他的註解配合《參同契》，大概讀了一百多次。想起來又把它重新讀一次，一次有一次的體會，次次不同。所以不能說這些書已經看過了，不用再讀了。很多人對學問方面不大注意，也就會對自己做工夫應該走的路搞不清楚，以致工夫到了某一階段，就不知道應該怎麼樣才能再進步，所以唯一的辦法是求之於古人。古人都是我們的老師，不管他是正派、邪派，就算是邪派的，有時候還會啟發我們正的思想，這個諸位要特別注意。

月節 中氣 剛柔

現在看本文，「月節有五六」，五六就是三十天。根據十二辟卦這個圖，一個月有兩個節氣，一年共有二十四節氣，用的是太陽曆，太陽行度。我們是太陽曆太陰曆幾千年來合用的。譬如一年十二個月，一個月三十天，這個我都向諸位報告過，這是以太陰為標準，表現月亮圓缺潮水漲退，與女性生理的週期的關係，所以女性生理週期稱為月經。至於二十四節氣，再說一遍，五天一候，三候就是一節。每一個月，有一氣有一節。哪個是氣？哪個是節？希望諸位在圖表上都記住。每一氣叫做中氣，節就是過節，也就是過程。做工夫有時中氣發動，注意這個中氣發動，等一下我們要討論打坐做工夫是怎麼一回事。現在修密宗的人很多，要打通中脈，又是在海底又是在頭頂，搞了半天，中氣究竟在哪裏？究竟是個什麼東西？這都要搞清楚才行。

「經緯奉日使」，直線謂之「經」，橫線謂之「緯」，這個「經緯奉

日使」是以太陽在天體的行度為標準。「奉日使」是用太陽曆，所以我們上古就使用了。「兼并為六十」，以一個月來講，每天一半是白天一半是黑夜，合起來就有六十個作用。如果配合上《易經》的卦來講，六十四卦真要研究就麻煩了，因為《易經》是根據天文來的，要把中國的古天文學都拿出來，二十八宿的星座在哪裏？北斗七星在哪裏？那個牽涉太大了。

所以真正學《易經》，要規規矩矩地走中國文化基本的路線，先把中國天文學學通。現在難啦！過去我們一個朋友高炳梓先生，他是懂得的，當他在世的時候，我求一班青年同學們做一點好事，到高先生那裏學。我跟高先生講，你只要能教出三個學生就行了，把中國文化的根留下來，否則你死了就沒有了。那些學生呢？好！好！老師我去！結果拖拖拉拉不肯去。現在他過世啦，有些學生要我來講，哎呀，我比他差遠了！而且我不喜歡搞這個，太麻煩了，還要配上現在的天文學，才可以瞭解一些道理。

《易經》原圖六十四卦，為什麼把乾坤坎離四卦拿開？因為乾坤兩卦代表天地，天地在那裏不會動的；坎離兩卦代表太陽月亮也是呆定的。天

地是個假設的名稱，我們能夠看得見天地的作用是太陽月亮。把這四卦拿

開，剩下六十卦配起來就是一月卦，也就是「兼并為六十」的道理。「剛

柔有表裏」，每一卦有它的陽面，陽裏頭就有陰，陰裏頭就有陽，陽是

剛，陰是柔，所以要注意剛柔。

我又岔進來講句話，二十多年前在一個朋友家吃中飯，他客廳掛了一

副對子很正派，字也好，寫的是「柔日讀史，剛日讀經」。朋友曉得好，

就是解釋不出來。其實柔日是陰日，不是指陰天，也不是指干支陰陽，所

謂柔日，是一個人心裏有煩惱，事情複雜解決不了，這時陰柔之氣在心

中，最好多讀歷史。讀歷史啟發人的氣魄，勇氣眼光就起來了。剛日是精

神特別好，思想特別清明的時候，要讀經，讀四書五經，讀佛經，讀基督

教的聖經都可以。讀經需要思想，哲學思想必須要頭腦精神夠的時候去研

究。精神不夠的時候，看看《紅樓夢》，看看什麼彩虹藍天那些小說也可

以。如果你人不舒服，頭腦昏昏的還來研究《參同契》，那只會睡著啦！

當安眠藥來用蠻好！所以剛柔就是代表陰陽，《易經》裏的陰陽兩個是物

理代號，這個觀念要懂得。

「剛柔有表裏」，「表」就是外面，「裏」就是裏面。也就是說，每天的氣候，從夜裏十一時開始，一直到第二天上午十二點，都是陽氣；下午屬於陰氣。現在都市生活很多年輕人，都是陽氣不夠。上午起來昏頭昏腦，一點精神沒有，到下午睡一個午覺起來，精神慢慢好，到夜生活一來，精神越來越好，這些人都是陰氣很盛，學中醫看病就要知道了。

譬如咳嗽，有些人半夜子時陽氣上來，非咳嗽不可，比鬧鐘還要準。因為他那個肺被痰包圍了，就像是垃圾堆裏有些東西出不來，半夜一到，陽氣要往上沖痰出來，就咳起來了。道理就在這裏，曉得這個病源就曉得用藥了。你說涼藥應該屬陰了，熱藥補藥是屬於陽了吧？不一定哦，涼藥也有陰陽，涼藥熬久了以後物極則反，陰中生陽。你說大瀉的藥吃下去就拉肚子，你買個三十斤熬它三天三夜，吃下去就便秘，瀉不了！為什麼呢？物極則反，這就是《易經》的道理。西醫大多是不管這個的，我們有大西醫在座，對不起呀！不過他現在研究中醫了。中醫藥有特別多物極必

反的狀況，所以補藥吃多了反而出毛病。有些熱藥很可怕，熱藥蒸過就是化學作用，起一個變化就變成涼藥。為什麼講這些呢？做工夫也一樣，你這個原理不懂，打起坐來，有時候坐不住，怎麼辦？這個裏頭就是「剛柔有表裏」，早晨屬於陽卦，下午屬於陰卦。

每月六十卦

「朔旦屯直事」，你看這個古書多難讀呀！每個月初一叫做朔，旦就是早晨，這就是指每月初一的早晨。十五叫做望，所以朔望要搞清楚，退回七十年前，讀小學的都懂。以前做官朔望是大事，縣長朔望要穿上禮服到城隍廟行禮，陽間的縣長去向陰間的縣長打招呼，恐怕有些冤枉案子，我陽間的縣長管不好，陰間的還要幫個忙呀！當皇帝的朔望也要祭告天地，這是中國古代政治所謂神秘性、宗教性的一種制度。

初一的早晨「屯」卦在「直事」，這個怎麼講？這是另外一個圖啦，因為現在主要的不是講《易經》，那個圖就沒印給各位。《周易》有一

個「上下經」次序，這個要背來。我們現在研究的《易經》是周文王整理的，它同《連山易》《歸藏易》不同，是從乾坤兩卦開始，第三卦就是屯，第四卦是蒙，第五卦是需……所以是乾、坤、屯、蒙、需、訟、師……這個是周易六十四卦的次序。我為什麼提到這個？現在我們碰到這個「朔旦屯直事」，一個月是三十天，把「乾坤坎離」四卦拿掉了，每月初一早晨屯卦直事，「直」就是值班。講到這裏我很感慨，現在你一聽我說就明白了，可是我年輕時也不懂，請教這個老師那個老師，有說大概這樣，有說大概那樣，我一聽曉得老師沒有懂，還是向老師行個禮，走了。

我自己很辛苦摸了幾十年才懂，知道每月初一的下午，是蒙卦當班。

「水雷屯」（䷂），水的下面是雷就是屯卦。你看這個卦，假定把上下倒轉你們看看變什麼卦？不是屯，而是「山水蒙」（䷃），成了蒙卦。

所以《易經》一個卦是八面玲瓏地看。有人說《易經》的道理同黑格爾的辯證法一樣，我說你真是亂講！黑格爾是什麼年代的人？我們老祖宗是什麼年代的人？硬把老祖宗拉來跟外國的小孫子比，怎麼那麼沒有出息！況

且《易經》講的不是三段論法，是八段論法，可以說十段論法。一個卦要十面看，這個道理就是，立場不同觀點就兩樣。能懂得這個卦理，看一切的事就能真正客觀。這個「水雷屯」卦，把它倒過來變成「山水蒙」，這樣叫做綜卦，綜就是相反。

初二的早晨是「水天需」（☵☰）卦，晚上反過來，成了「天水訟」（☰☵）。那麼你說懂得這個和我修道打坐有什麼關係？關係大啦！如果你不懂，工夫到了某一個境界，你就不知道下一步怎麼樣走。就算你工夫做到放光，老停在亮光裏也沒有什麼好玩，玩一陣總要到黑暗裏玩玩吧！所以你下一步怎麼動呢？你就不知道了，對不對？

這個原理，《易經》現在這裏告訴我們大象，大象也叫天象。「朔旦屯直事，至暮蒙當受」，到了初一的下午，蒙卦當班。所以「畫夜各一卦」，白天算是一卦，夜裏算是一卦。

「用之依次序」，所以我說當年讀這個是照《周易》六十四卦次序來的，六十四卦拿了四卦出來，剩下六十卦。「既未至晦爽」，「既未」是

六十卦的最後兩卦「水火既濟」及「火水未濟」。一個月分三段，初一叫朔，十五叫望，三十叫晦。「晦爽」是三十早晨起來朦朧有點亮。每個月用六十卦，但是有時候小月是二十九天，這個是配合太陽曆的氣節來的。

「終則復更始」，這六十卦在一個月裏頭應用是這樣，用完了重新第二個月初一又是屯卦開始。六十卦配月份，乾坤兩卦變出來配年份，十二個月是這樣配的。

你們拿到的《易經》那個書本上有個方圓圖，外面有一圓圈六十四卦，中間四方塊又是六十四卦，方圓都是六十四卦，作用不同。這一個圓圖的六十四卦是配一年，排列方法又不同了。所以我常常感嘆中國文化了不起，一個是中國人會做菜，第二個是會搓麻將；麻將就是從《易經》學問變出來的，同樣這個牌玩來玩去各有不同。我經常鼓勵同學研究《易經》時，把六十四卦做成一個麻將牌亂擺，你慢慢就會發明東西了。算不定你成為愛因斯坦第三，這個裏頭發明的原理多啦！

孔子任何書都教我們讀，但他沒有教我們讀《易經》，因為《易經

是「玩索而有得」，要去玩這個卦。當年我學《易經》，就用六十四顆棋子，每一個棋子貼一個卦名，就是亂擺，慢慢就擺出道理來了。《周易》圓圖六十四卦，你曉得五天一候，每一卦分配到五天多一點，剛剛一年三百六十五天有多，這是圓圖。方圖配合整個的中國，或者配合歐洲的地圖，或者是配合世界地球的地圖，每一卦裏頭都可以找出道理來。譬如你到了法國，不用電腦，我們把方圖這樣一擺，太陽出來這一面是東方，一擺就曉得這裏南方，那裏北方，這是西方。然後六十四卦一擺，這個房子要不要就知道！走運的房子方向對了就要，不是房子蓋得好不好！就那麼簡單。所以《易經繫辭》講「易簡，而天下之理得矣」。

《易經》真搞通了，就覺得這個原理非常高深，但是天地間最高深的學問到了最高處非常簡化，因此叫作簡易。所以說，《易經》的法則非常簡單，懂了的話，這個手掌就成了電腦，指上一節一節跟你畫好了，掐指一算，天地都在一掌之中，就是這個原則。古代佛教的講經叫做消文，把文章先消化了再說；消化了文字，才能明白其中的意義。

第十講

日月運轉的影響

「日月為期度」，「日月」是指太陽月亮，「為期度」，每天每月每年的運轉都有週期性。在我們中國曆法上，十天叫做一旬，一個月有三旬，這些數字大概記一下，都是中國文化，實際上現在民間還在用。「動靜有早晚」，這個天象，宇宙的氣象，在理論上所謂早晚就是一動一靜之間。夜裏睡覺休息是靜態，白天醒了以後一切是動態，動靜代表了早晚。

「春夏據內體」，現在講到大的範圍，一年之中春夏秋冬四季，我們也曾經說過，實際上只有兩個現象，一冷一熱。冷的開始叫秋天，冷到極點叫冬天，所以秋冬是一個系統，春夏又是一個系統。一年十二個月，三個月為一季，譬如春天是正月二月三月。在文學上每季第一個月叫做孟，譬如春季正月叫孟春，孟是老大。如果古代有人叫王孟湘，我們就曉得他

理學，也可以叫做法律哲學的根據。所以幾千年的帝王政治，一個死刑犯

「賞罰應春秋」，這是中國古代制度的刑法原理，用現在的話講是法

「秋冬當外用」，秋天冬天當外面用，「自午訖戌亥」，就是上半年。拿一天來講，每天從午時開始，直到戌亥時，就是下半天。

「從子到辰巳」，拿一天來講就是夜裏子時陽氣發動，子、丑、寅、卯、辰、巳，六個階段，直到上午十一點鐘；拿一年來講是上半年。

血球來啦，把裏頭的細菌用高溫殺死，再來治療這個傳染性的病。

醫都曉得發燒並不一定是壞事，有時候讓它燒一下再來治療。發燒就是白覺，被子蓋不住。所以學中醫也要懂這個道理，有時候發燒是病象，中西人說手發暖，坐起來出汗了，熱得不得了，衣服都要脫掉，或者睡不著

這裏說「春夏據內體」，同我們做工夫有關係了！就像打坐時，有些

平」、溫和、不冷不熱，剛好！

季夏也都可以用的。一年當中春秋的道理，講十二辟卦時也講過是「持是家中長子；二月叫仲春，仲就是老二；三月叫季春。夏季孟夏、仲夏、

不到秋天不殺，尤其春天是不准殺人的。春天生生不已，死刑都不處理，寧可把他關在大牢到秋天再講，所以叫秋決，有秋收冬藏的意味。

「昏明順寒暑」，我家鄉的土話，晚上叫黃昏，天晚快要進入黑夜了。所以唐宋一些詩詞，許多寫黃昏的文學，很有味道。講到文學，李後主的詩詞是好：「無言獨上西樓，月如鉤」，月亮像鉤一樣彎彎的，「寂寞梧桐，深院鎖清秋」，寫得好！如果他寫：無言獨上西樓，月如盤，那就沒有意思啦！又如「姑蘇城外寒山寺，夜半鐘聲到客船」，如果是夜半鐘聲到酒家，就沒有什麼道理，更沒有什麼味道了。「昏明順寒暑」是晨昏順應冷熱，以氣候來講一個冷天，一個暑天，寒暑代表了一年。

講了半天同我們打坐做工夫有什麼關係呢？先把文消了，現在只解決文字問題。這些書就是中國文化的密宗，它都告訴你了，你懂不進去，就通通沒有用；懂進去，全都是修道的法則。做工夫，不管是佛家、道家、密宗、顯教，哪一家都違反不了這個原則。這就如同天地一樣，你工夫再高道再高，也沒有辦法把早晨的太陽拉到晚上來用，你做不到，上帝也做

不到。所謂「道法自然」，是呆定的。至於說你道修成功了，超越自然，那是另外一回事，已經不是這個肉體生命了，肉體生命是沒有辦法違反這個天地法則的。

「爻辭有仁義，隨時發喜怒」，後天卦每一卦六爻，六個次序構成的。這一劃叫做一爻，什麼叫爻呢？爻者交也。交通的交字就是爻字變的，爻就是交的意思，彼此相交，互相交換的關係。《易經》每一掛有卦辭，每一爻有爻辭，是卦和爻的註解。我也提到過一句話，「善於易者不卜」，《易經》學通了的人，不看相不算命不看風水也不卜卦，自己都知道啦，好壞都清楚。《易經》的八八六十四卦，沒有一卦絕對好，也沒有一卦絕對壞。都是好中有壞，壞中有好。譬如有一卦說「厲无咎」，好呀！好呀！其實一點都不好。「厲无咎」的意思，你小心就不會出毛病，不小心當然出毛病！只有一個「謙」卦，涉及作人的道理，比較起來是六爻皆吉。其他都是有好也有壞，上一爻好，下一爻不一定好；昨天好今天就壞。同我們人一樣，昨天精神旺得不得了，到了今天忽然煩悶起來；昨

天胃口好，今天消化不良要吃胃藥。人的身體同天氣和卦象一樣，隨時會變，你有辦法能夠做到不變嗎？行住坐臥都是那個境界不變，你做得到嗎？做到就差不多啦！所以「爻辭有仁義，隨時發喜怒」，等於我們的情緒變化一樣，沒有一定的。

四季五行和人體

「如是應四時」，這樣對應一年春夏秋冬四季。「五行得其理」，五行就是金木水火土，五行配合五臟，我們要講一下啦，尤其學中醫的要瞭解。肺屬金、肝屬木、心屬火、腎屬水、脾屬土。提到腎臟要注意，中醫講腎臟，不光是西醫講的兩個腰子，而是包括甲狀腺、腎上腺的荷爾蒙，乃至生命的元氣，發動整個生命系統的動力。腎臟屬於水，屬於坎卦，換一句話說，腎虧就是荷爾蒙生長分佈不平均。土是脾胃，講脾胃就很嚴重了，因為我也不是醫生，所以亂講不負責任的。中醫注重的是脾胃能夠消化的那個動力。有些人消化不良，說自己有腸胃病，腸子是腸子，胃是

胃，要分清。胃消化了就到腸子裏去，如果這個腸子水管推動不得力，水管不通，大便就堵塞在那裏。所以學道家的人為什麼都學醫而且必然懂醫？因為他自己做工夫，與書本上讀的醫學知識不同，他每一步走到哪裏，五行起的變化清清楚楚。

譬如有些同學跑來告訴我，老師啊，我有心臟病！我問，你做過檢查了嗎？哪裏痛？他們指胸口。我說心臟在那裏嗎？沒有人心是在正中間的，世界上人心都是歪的，這裏痛很可能是食道和胃消化不良的問題。這個食道管看起來簡單，但是我們平常人不容易通的，這一節氣脈完全通了，這個人就沒有雜亂妄想，隨時都可以安定清淨。這個道理像玻璃杯盛牛奶，喝完了以後，玻璃杯還是沾了牛奶。我們食道管吃了豬肉、牛肉、青菜、蘿蔔，嚥下去都有些沾住的，但是一般人不會有感覺。如果這個管道完全乾淨，妄念就沒有了，思想就清淨了，這是絕對有道理的。

因此中國道家以及學瑜珈術做工夫的要洗胃，洗胃有各種方法，一種是內洗，每天把舌頭向上向後捲，練習向內舔，舔到小舌頭就會嘔了，這

是一種洗法。還有一種瑜珈洗法，把舌頭拉到外面，能夠把舌頭舐到鼻子，那工夫練得很苦。據說佛的舌頭可以舐到髮際，我們普通人舌頭都很短。你問為什麼要練這個？我告訴你，年紀越大舌頭就短了僵化了。你問老先生吃過沒？他回答……吃！吃！吃過了（眾笑），他舌頭短了，是不是啊？要死的時候，噎！噎！他就死掉了，那個舌頭就封鎖住了，所以練這個舌頭同健康長壽很有關係的。

舌頭為什麼硬呢？你去看殺豬就知道，我們小的時候鄉下殺豬，殺豬的把喉嚨這裏一刀切開，肚子拉開，把食道管一把抓，連舌頭五臟六腑一串提出來，如果發現舌頭僵硬，這豬就有問題。所以一個人身體要自己知道，有時候舌頭發苦，舌頭沒有味道，早上起來鏡子裏一看舌苔白的、黃的、紅的顏色，不同的顏色就曉得哪一方面有病。所以中醫的診斷要看看舌頭，就診斷出來病在哪裏，那叫做舌診。有些舌頭一吐出來，上面像鍋巴一樣一條一條，那很嚴重，裏面在嚴重發炎。不只是舌頭，連眼睛、耳朵也反映五臟六腑的情形。高明的中醫跟西醫科學診斷下來相同，人體就

是表裏動靜之間相應，也就是「五行得其理」。

瑜珈術還有另外的洗胃法，要弄一塊紗布，唉！你們不要亂學呀！我可不負責，這裏只是講學，我沒有工夫我也不懂道，我只講學術性的給你們聽。用一塊很長的紗布慢慢吞下去，吞滿了拉出來，那個味道很難聞，等於現在到醫院照胃鏡。我們這個人有什麼漂亮啊？看到拉出來的布你鼻子都要挾住。學瑜珈的人一禮拜起碼要洗一次胃，不然學瑜珈也走禪定路線，一個禮拜有一整天不吃飯光喝水，清理腸胃。這很衛生，這個方式你們可以用。不過你們吃慣了的，很難熬了，半餐不吃就受不了，三餐不吃，二十四個鐘頭不吃坐在那裏簡直要叫外婆啦，還不是叫媽！像我們搞慣了無所謂，越不吃越舒服，吃了就想睡覺，昏沉嘛！不吃東西頭腦就清醒，這是一種。

給大家講了瑜珈術，我這個人素來唱反調的，人家講外國的東西好，外國月亮圓，我就罵，中國月亮不圓？不大？你們也不懂！中國的洗胃方法呢？是用葛根清理食道。葛根是一種草，四川很多，把葛根外面綠皮剝

掉，裏頭雪白一節不軟又不硬。有一定的長度量好，這個長度我忘記了，由喉嚨管開始，等於現在照胃鏡一樣，把那個白的葛根慢慢吞下去，那個很軟，不會傷到喉嚨，不過有點青草的味道。我都自己試過了，因為雖然學會了，我不親自試過不相信，危險我也不怕。我忍一下，硬把它嚥下去到胃裏，如果不抽出來，它會給消化了。

當這個胸口感覺有東西，下也下不去，上也上不來，到時間發冷，到時間發燒，那麼治療的辦法很簡單，吞葛根。吞下去你硬是感覺到有個東西咚！就掉到胃裏去，馬上就舒服了。抽出來之後，也不發燒也不發冷了，一身微微汗出來，痛快得很。打坐做工夫，有時候也會到這個程度的，因為本身生命有這個功能。世界上的文化都一樣，都是人類老祖宗們幾千年經驗來的。說真的，現在的青年們，不知道祖宗留給我們的文化，是幾千年多少人犧牲了生命得出來的經驗，你不經意的丟棄就是罪過！我從小專門搜羅古的東西，我總覺得古的東西有它的道理，不能隨便輕視，結果自己一研究下來，都是很好的。我從小是一路反對新的東西，現在老

了反而接受新的，因為古的我差不多都瞭解了。

你愛吃補品嗎

把這個文字消了，下面的註解叫做玄談，玄談就是發揮討論。我們現在又回到這個十二辟卦，諸位把手裏這個表好好搞清楚，將來會很有用處的。譬如你研究起來，復卦冬至一陽生，冬至是氣，大雪是節。冬至是一陽初生處，冬至要吃湯圓，吃湯圓是假的，叫你注意這個時候可以配合補品了。但是有傷風感冒的話，一點補藥都不能吃，有其它毛病也不能隨便吃補喔！只要身體內外有一點不清爽就不能吃補，一補就把它封鎖住了，病就好不了，所以要特別注意清補這個道理，清理就是補。有些人非常莫名其妙，「唉呀，老師啊！這個清補不算補。」所謂清補，不是說輕微的補藥叫做清補，完全搞錯了。譬如這個房間，你說牆上破了把它補一補，表面補好了，實際上裏頭還是破的。還不如乾脆把破的清理乾淨，倒是個新的局面。所以真正的補是把內在的病完全清理乾淨，因為我們的生命功

能自有生生不已的力量，生命自己會補助自己，這就是清補。

過去有一位很有名的老西醫，他去世好幾年了，四五十年前德國留學的，是蔣介石的醫療顧問。他懂中醫也會打坐，因為忙得沒有時間，抓住一點時間就打坐。那個時候沒有計程車，一般人出門坐三輪車，他就坐在三輪車上打坐。有一次我有點頭痛，打電話問他，他就幫我開藥。實際上他是學醫理學的，是醫生的顧問，回到國內來他反而變成看病醫生了。吃了他的藥以後我對他說，你到底是學理論的，藥不靈。他說，我本來醫術就不好，你何必相信我？後來我別的藥試試也不對，又再吃他的藥，吃了以後又好了。我又打個電話給他，喂！你的藥還是對的；他說，本來就很對。他這個人就那麼可愛。

又一次我家裏人病了，我說你弄一點什麼補血的給他吃。他說，你怎麼搞的，別人可以講這個話，你怎麼講這個話？哪有補血的藥？我說，怎麼？中醫當歸總補血吧！女人血虧吃當歸。他說，你能把當歸裏擠出來一滴血，我的頭給你！真補血就是打血漿，十毫升的血你能吸收到兩毫升就

了不起，其餘都排泄掉了，吸收它好困難。他又說，如果要吃補血的藥，你多吃三塊肉就夠了。不管中藥西藥，都沒有補血的，所謂補血的藥都是刺激你肝臟的功能，自己生出血來。

生命的功能，只要你一口氣沒有斷，把內在清理了就是補，你不需要飲食補啊！亂吃補藥被藥補死的，我看了很多，所以絕對補不得。以前有一個老朋友住在醫院，已經病危了，他太太端來餵他東西，我一看是燕窩！我說：「拿開！不准，這個時候可以吃燕窩嗎？」「不行啊！好久沒有補了。」我說：「不准！湯都不能喝，補不得啊！」「燕窩不算什麼補吧？這是清補。」我說：「他都快不行了，寧可留一點氣多講幾句話，有什麼事情沒有講完，快講吧！」

其實只要一口氣在，裏面清理了就是補。懂得修道的人，年紀大了到那時不要怕死，充其量是死，就完了嘛，除了死還有什麼可怕的！對不對？又要死又怕死，你看多可憐！修道人先要懂這個，隨時準備死，算不定你還死不掉呢！上禮拜天我夜裏上山去，又下雨又崩山，既然上就上

了，車開上去，崩山也不管，開！我說有護法神保祐，結果沒有事，不知是否真是有山神保祐。既然來了就是一條命，如果咚隆滾下去，就算報銷了！早死遲死一樣，這有什麼怕的呢？怕是在你要去不去的時候，已經決定去了還有什麼前途好考慮？後途都不管，還管到前途嗎？要有這個勇氣才可以修道。

關於一陽來復

你懂了這個原理，只要把自己心念平息下來，聽其自然念頭一空。念頭真空掉，一陽來復，復卦，氣就來了。念就是氣，氣就是念。我們常教訓人一句話，你這個小孩不要意氣用事啊！這就是道家工夫了，對不對？意就是氣，氣就是意。所以道家講無火之「炁」，那個不是呼吸了。在佛學裏頭，那不叫做氣，叫做「息」。拿中國字看看，什麼叫做息？你們看看，自心謂之息。中國字都告訴你了，自心謂之息，自己這個心就是。結果拚命坐在那裏搞氣，還記數字，我今天已經數了三千下了。你數三萬下

心念也沒有息呀！你真做到心念息下去，神就凝結了，氣就聚了。神凝氣聚就一陽來復，復卦來了，你還怕什麼病？

可是你要注意哦！任何人的身體，不管男女老幼，復卦一來陽氣剛剛發生，麻煩得很，病人的病表面上看起來會加重，一點都不怕，這個加重是好事。我常常告訴人，一個人跌傷了，尤其吩咐你們年輕女同學做媽媽的，孩子跌倒在地上，沒有哭之前不要抱起來，你一抱算不定這個孩子閉氣死了。所以看到孩子們跌倒，老太太們就叫旁人不要動！不要動！等一下！等到孩子哇一哭，好，可以抱了，他氣通過了，一陽來復。剛跌下去時精神受了恐嚇，身體的氣脈各部份不順了，你一去抱，氣岔斷就危險了。成年人也一樣，看到別人跌倒在地，不能馬上去拉他，先過去看他鼻子呼吸慢慢調整好了，才能起來。尤其照顧老年人要特別注意，怎麼樣？痛吧？唉，很痛。他能夠開口就是他氣通了，你大膽可以扶他起來。真的跌傷了是不曉得痛的，等到藥下去慢慢曉得痛了，有救了，這個傷快要好了。

這個就是一陽來復的道理，陽氣的來復這個卦屬於子月。生理上的復呢？男孩子很清楚，嬰兒睡到半夜，其實不一定到半夜，我們現在先講半夜，嬰兒生殖器就翹起來，曉得要屙尿。這時嬰兒絕對沒有男女的欲念啊！絕不會是想到異性才有這個現象。所以老子說，「未知牝牡之合而朘作」，這個朘作啊，講一句你們覺得很難聽，我覺得很文雅，就是小孩子的小雞雞翹了，當母親當爸爸，就知道這個小雞雞要屙尿了。老子講的是，這個嬰兒不曉得有男女兩性的分別，可是到那時候自然舉起來。有時候不一定是屙尿，是冬至一陽來復。生理上變化男性看得很清楚，女孩子也是一樣，自己不大覺得，實際上她胸口會發悶、發脹，像是女性有些經期來以前的感覺。這個陽氣發動的時候要能夠把握得住，怎麼把握呢？有些修道的人趕快把氣控制住，那就完了！佛家講心空一念，只照住它，看它發動，有病的病就更加重，實際上是好消息。如果咳嗽的話，這個時候咳不停了。

子時一陽來復，到丑時不同了，就變啦！安詳一點了。陽氣上來，在

身體的內部從哪裏上來呢？所謂的海底，現在有人講海底在肚臍下面，或者肛門前面睪丸後面。其實海底是個形容辭，海底，海深而不見底。身體的海底是在下部沒有錯，但是，這個是「正子時」「活子時」的道理。

第十一講

本篇開始的題目叫「御政」，就是說修道先要把天地與我們生命的法則把握住。懂了這個原理以後，修起來就容易了。這個法則就是《易經》的法則，然後配合道家老子、莊子等等的思想。

坎離二用章第二

天地設位，而易行乎其中矣。天地者，乾坤之象。設位者，列陰陽配合之位。易謂坎離。坎離者，乾坤二用。二用無爻位，周流行六虛。往來既不定，上下亦無常。幽潛淪匿，變化于中。包囊萬物，為道紀綱。

以無制有，器用者空。故推消息，坎離沒亡。

言不苟造，論不虛生。引驗見效，校度神明。推類結字，原理為

徵。

坎戊月精，離己日光。日月為易，剛柔相當。土王四季，羅絡始終。青赤黑白，各居一方。皆秉中宮，戊己之功。

修道先要了解的事

「天地設位」，就是說這個宇宙之中，我們人在中間，上有天下有地，這就是《易經》的法則。乾卦是天的代號，坤卦是地的代號，天在上，地在下。「設」就是假設，初定了這個位子，「而易行乎其中矣」。

什麼叫作「易」？日月謂之易，太陽與月亮這個系統叫作易。中國文化解釋《易經》最清楚的，就是《參同契》。所以這個易字的古文寫法，上面是太陽，下面是月亮。後來講到《易經》的學問道理，前面已經講過包括了三易，簡易、變易、交易。第一簡易，是說易經的道理看起來複雜，真懂的話非常簡單容易。第二變易，它告訴我們宇宙萬有隨時隨地都在變化，沒有不變化的時候。第三交易，任何一個變化，與前因後果、內外、

左右、上下、彼此都有關聯，所以叫交易。

到了宋朝以後，有些學者另加一個法則，交易變易是現象，在現象之間有一個本體不動的叫做不易，這個是不變的，所以以不變應萬變。為什麼以不變應萬變呢？是說那個本體有一個基本的原則，它始終不動的，變的是它的現象，不變的是它的本來。比如我們這個房間是本來，今天就做為我們研究《參同契》的課堂之用，明天可以開會用，後天可以當倉庫用。現象是變易的，但是這個房間，這個空間不易，它沒有變動。這是順便解釋一下這個易。

「天地設位，而易行乎其中矣」，一個太陽一個月亮構成了我們人世間，以及地面上各種生物生命的法則。下面它本文的解釋說，「天地者，乾坤之象」，「象」就是現象，「天地」是乾坤兩卦的現象。「設位者，列陰陽配合之位」，「設位」意思就是變化，宇宙間萬事萬物總是相對的。一靜一動也是相對的，有陰必有陽，有陽必有陰。陽到了極點就陰生，陰到了極點就陽生。所以講陰陽就要配合太陽月亮運行的法則；在我

們身體上，這個生命能變成氣血，要配合它的部位。所以中醫針灸有一派非常注重子午流注，就是因為「列陰陽配之位」。如果真通了這一種原理，用起針灸來效果也特別好，這是一個事實。

下面他解釋「易謂坎離」，這個《易經》的易字所講的是代表坎離二卦，坎離就是日月，離是太陽，坎是月亮，這是講天地的大象。「坎離者，乾坤二用」，乾坤代表的是天地，但是乾卦（☰）中爻一變，變成了離卦（☲），就變成了太陽，所以太陽代表天。坤卦（☷）中爻一變就變成了坎卦（☵），代表月亮。所以乾坤二用的意思，就是有這兩個作用。我們仰頭看虛空，我們叫它是天，天在上面，踏在腳下面的就是地。這兩個精神的代表就是太陽月亮，一冷一熱這兩個作用。

下面這幾句千萬要記住，尤其在座的大概很多都是修神仙的。「二用無爻位」，這個坎離兩卦就是太陽月亮，在天體「無爻位」，沒有固定的位置，而是永遠在那裏轉，一分一秒都不停的在轉。所以說認為坎離兩卦或者太陽月亮固定在哪個方位上，那是人為觀念，事實上不是如此。宇宙

的生命永遠在動態中，沒有靜態。所謂靜態是非常快速的動，在我們的感覺上反而覺得沒有動，所以叫做靜。譬如說我們坐飛機，速度很快，自己卻覺得沒有動。或者坐汽車在高速公路上走，太快了，只感覺外面東西在動，實際上是自己在動，不是外面。

這個宇宙的動態就是太陽月亮的流轉，「周流行六虛」，它是圓滿的，四方八面上下無所不到。六虛是中國文化所謂六方，莊子叫「六合」，就是東南西北四方加上下。所謂六合之內就是講這個天地之間。地面也可以講八方，東南西北加上四個角就是八方。八方再加上下就是十方。但是上古沒有用十方這個名稱，這是中印文化交流以後所產生的，所以古代說太陽月亮「周流行六虛」，是說它無所不到，它的光芒和精神無所不在。

「往來既不定，上下亦無常」，日月流轉不是呆板的，不是固定的，天體的法則，太陽月亮永遠在轉，東西半球、南北半球都有。我們現在是晚上，別的地方剛好天亮，有些地方是半夜，不是月亮在那裏當家就是太

陽在那裏當家，無所不在，所以是「上下亦無常」。

「幽潛淪匿」，這個非常重要了，尤其講修道，我們不管是學佛修道，或者是學顯學密，都離不開這個法則。我們為什麼要打坐？是為了要使生命精神回歸到最初的境界，就是「幽潛淪匿」這四個字。也就是先把我們在外面活動的精神收回來，「幽」是半明半暗的，非常深遠。「潛」是沉伏下去沉潛下去，像魚一樣沉到海底最深處。「淪匿」，好像光明看不見。我們修道靜坐的人，如果坐在那裏能耳朵不聽，眼睛不看，不知道身體，忘掉自我，就達到「幽潛淪匿」的境界了。

「幽潛淪匿」是基本的，譬如現在到了晚上，大地上的東西都看不見了，就是「幽潛淪匿」陰的境界。修道初步先用陰，所以老子是以陰柔之道為基本。陰不是壞事，陰極了才能陽生，所以「幽潛淪匿」是初步。

「變化於中」，修養達到了「幽潛淪匿」的境界，生命的功能才發動，身心才起大的變化，這是「幽潛淪匿」的道理。別的星球我們不去討論，單說這個世界上，植物也好動物也好，生命的開始都是所謂靜的狀

態。在靜到極點時就是「幽潛淪匿」的現象，什麼都沒有了，那正是生命功能的開始。

關於這方面，還會仔細的討論，現在先解釋文字。「幽潛淪匿，變化於中」，靜極當中才能求變化，這個一動一靜之間「包囊萬物」，一切萬物，不管動物、植物、礦物等等，乃至於精神世界、物理世界的，都離不開這個法則，無法違反。「包囊」就是裝進去，萬物都在這個法則原理之內。「為道紀綱」是說，這是修道首先要瞭解的。「紀綱」是綱要。

守丹田的問題

我們瞭解這一段之後，再回到前面，我們已經曉得坎離二用日月兩卦的重要。這個日月兩卦，我們上一次提到它是配合我們這個生命的。所以道家認為人身就是一個小宇宙。反過來講，整個的天地宇宙就是一個大生命，我們不過是大生命分化出來的小生命。如果我們講宗教哲學，拿西方的宗教來講，上帝照他自己的樣子製造了人，這個是宗教性的講法。但是

升了。當然面帶桃花色又是另外一種了，那是好事。如果臉漲得通紅，皮膚發亮，算不定忽然無疾而終，也算得道了吧！其實是血壓高腦充血。

但是這個部位是不是可以守呢？可以的，某一種身體適合某一種工夫。譬如有人神經特別衰弱的，就可以叫他守這個上丹田，但是也要看他的氣血流行夠不夠，否則守這個地方也會出毛病的。

據我所知，外面很少有人初步叫你守中丹田，倒是守上下丹田，毛病出得少一點。但是也有問題，有時候搞久了有些人覺得心窩痛，不是心臟痛，是食道和胃消化不良，或者呼吸氣管或者肺部有問題。

這個三丹田順便講一下，也是修道的常識。

管住耳朵和眼睛

剛才講到坎離兩卦，這一派修道的，在道家正統的觀念，秦漢以上的古書，都把眼睛所代表的神光返照叫做存神，也叫做存想。在密宗叫做觀想。這兩個名稱有差別，當然方法也有差別，但都是運用思想。存想久

了，就是古人所謂存想飛升，人可以飛起來，這是一個原理，真正幾個人做到呢？可以說沒人修到過。換一句話說，你存想也好，神照也好，照到身體必須要達到「幽潛淪匿」，身心沉潛下去然後起變化。當變化一來時，就要懂得講過的這些法則，走到那一步一定顯現那個原理，詳細的我們慢慢再報告。

實際上，打坐時把眼睛收回來，或者照到哪裏，行不行呢？還是不行。你把離卦雖轉入內境界，還是沒有完全「幽潛淪匿」，因為我們坎卦耳朵，歡喜向外面聽聲音。要把眼睛耳朵收回來沉下去，簡單的說就是收視返聽，也就是佛家修行的觀音法門。以道家的看法，觀音法門是利用坎卦耳根起修。用觀音法門的好處在哪裏呢？我們這個耳通氣海，換句話說，兩個耳朵與這個生命腎氣相通。所以一般年紀大的，耳朵聽不清了，就是腎經的元氣衰弱了。眼睛也老花了，那是肝經閉塞出了毛病。所以這一派道家用的方法，是在身體上轉，把眼神收回來照到肚臍，要耳朵不聽外面，慢慢使氣歸元，到這個時候，就是真正的「幽潛淪匿」了。

這一派的道家，他的道理是以八卦代表人體。所以乾卦是頭部，為首；坤為腹，坤卦是整個肚子。艮卦為背、離卦為目、坎卦為耳、兌卦是嘴巴、巽卦是鼻子、震卦為雷是身體。這是以有形身體來代表，詳細的道家又另有分類。所以道書之所以難懂，它沒有統一過，千古以來讀書最討厭讀道書。拿眼睛來講，離卦另有一個配法，左眼屬離卦，右眼屬坎卦。同樣的道理，每一部份他又把它再分化，這豈不是很複雜，不是亂套嗎？

不亂套，有它的原理，因為宇宙萬物各有一太極，各有一個天地。等於講我們人體整個是一個生命，如果在醫學上分開來研究，每個分開的再分開又是一個單位。這個單位用八八六十四卦的法則來研究，又是一個系統，都合那個規律，都合那個法則。所以我們要特別注意，這都是歸納性的講法。如果呆板的分析這是哪一派哪一家，分類起來太多了，所以我們不詳細的分類。

精神與魂魄

正統的道家，在解釋坎離二卦日月二用的道理就很準確了，說：「日出沒比精神之衰旺，月盈虧比氣血之盛衰」，這就把坎離二卦所代表的內在意義告訴我們了。現在我們要解決一個哲學問題了，中國道家處處提到精神，精神是個什麼東西？很難下定義，精神就是精神。我以前常常當笑話講，學校規定要對學生精神講話，我說這不合邏輯，因為講話本來就用精神在講話，講話就是精神。如果精神以外還有一個精神講話，我說不要變成神經講話了！

所以精神還是先要下定義，它是個什麼東西？它所代表的又是什麼？

你說這是個抽象的，那就沒有話講了，抽象就不談。但是在中國文化中，精神確實是一個東西。所謂精神就是魂魄，就是魂與魄的變化。換一句話說，魂魄是精神的變化。那麼什麼叫魂魄呢？心理的狀況是魂，屬於神的；生命的能量旺盛是精，是屬於魄。我們普通講，這個人很有氣魄，這個氣魄硬是物質的身體所暴發的。一個三期肺病的人，或者癌症到了最後階段的人，再也沒有氣魄了。

精（魄）—生命的能量

神（魂）—心理的狀態

魄字是白字旁邊一個鬼字。什麼是鬼？一路研究下來，先要認識中國字，所以先要認識部首，這個鬼字從田字為主。為什麼呢？我們是地球的文化，人都在這個地面。田在古代的寫法，一個圓圈一個十字就是田，不是方的。這個田上面，中間一筆出一點點頭就叫做由。由字就是草木在土地上生出一點苗。所以由來就是有一點苗頭。上面通下面通就是申，代表電。這個鬼字上面上不去的，你看那個鬼字寫法，專門向下面走的那個就是鬼。至於神字，上下通的叫作神。

這個魄字是白色的鬼，白代表陽氣，有陽氣有實質的這個精神部份叫作魄。沒有實質的，人死後肉體實質已經完了，就是鬼旁邊加個云字，那就是魂。云就是天上的雲，有時聚攏來看見了，有時散了看不見了。所以魂魄是代表生命的死亡與存在兩個階段。

那麼精神是哪裏來的呢？歸納道家的說法，分為兩部份，神屬於性，本性；精和氣屬於命。道家早就把身體分成兩個宇宙，我們這個肉體存在是我們的命，所以身體是命。至於那個性呢？那個就是神，不屬於這個身

理，是一般修道人的第一錯誤。相反的，他說「但修祖性不修丹，萬劫陰

身體，在身上轉河車，轉來轉去，不瞭解心性的道理，不懂一切唯心的道

道家有一句重要的名言：「只修命不修性，此是修行第一病。」光煉

修心養性的原理，也是不行的。

種。所以只修命，不修性，光煉身體，不懂佛家的所謂明心見性和儒家的

氣功啊，煉身體啊，在身上搞來搞去玩弄精神。王陽明所批評的就是這

元明以後的道家同時也反對一般修道的道家，認為他們光是修命，只是練

心理入手，對身體一點辦法都沒有，所以仍是生老病死，很痛苦。但是宋

家的，認為他們都不會修道沒有用。他說佛家跟儒家光修性不修命，只從

宋元明以後的道家，也就是正統的道家，老實講是反對佛家也反對儒

表的，性命雙修就是兩樣要齊頭併進。

同，認為修道的人必須要「性命雙修」。性命就是陰陽，也就是坎離所代

燈泡壞了就不能通電，也不起作用了。因此道家的理論同佛家或其他的不

體，但身體也是性的部份。比如電，這個電是通過燈泡發亮而發生作用。

靈難入聖。」只曉得在心性方面入手，在明心見性的學理上參，這個空了那個空了，但身體氣質變化不了。他認為這是陰陽沒有調好，永遠不能證到仙佛的果位。

所以正統的道家主張性命雙修，對佛法也是非常恭敬的，認為佛是修成功的。普通一般學佛修道沒有成功，因為不是偏在修性就偏在修命。這個主張拿佛學來講合理不合理呢？非常合理。研究了佛學唯識，研究了般若就懂了，這個身體是阿賴耶識的一部份，身和心各一半。所以修道的認為一定要半斤八兩，要兩個齊頭而併進，也就是要性命雙修。最後身體由衰老變健康，由健康變化氣質，由變化氣質到達脫胎換骨。再配合上心性的修習，這個道就修成功了。

性命雙修成功了以後，道家稱為無縫塔，修成一座無縫的寶塔一樣。佛學的說法就是證得無漏果，得漏盡通，一切都成就了，沒有滲漏，沒有遺憾，沒有缺點，這個生命是個完整的。

第十二講

一陽初動無陰陽

前面我們提到正統道家講「性命雙修」，是從宋元以後開始的。講到這個法則就要先瞭解一樁事，瞭解什麼呢？就是「一陽來復」。「性命雙修」之說，是把性跟命也就是心理生理兩個合為一體。西方柏拉圖的哲學思想，世界分成二元，精神世界和物理世界，實際上兩個世界是一體。因為這兩個是一個功能所產生的兩面，一陰一陽。有關精神世界，就是心性這一面的修養，我們先要了解如何把握「冬至一陽生」的法則。在這個十二辟卦中，一陽初生之處最為重要。

宋朝五大儒之一的邵康節（雍），他是研究《易經》的專家，他的成就是跨越時代的。他把易學整理出來一套法則，是前無古人後無來者，後面的人到現在為止，能夠真正超越邵康節的還沒有。講到冬至一陽生的道

理，他的見解後來的修道人沒有不用的。他的名句是：

冬至子之半　天心無改移
一陽初動處　萬物未生時

這個也是「冬至一陽生」的原理，是《易經》最高也是最基礎的原理。冬至是子月（陰曆十一月）下半的氣，子月是復卦，一陽來復的意思。此時天地間陰極陽生，開始了一陽，運用到人的生命上，就是子時，從夜裏十一點到次晨一時。所謂正子時正好是十二點正，正子時是子時的中間。他說「冬至子之半」，在每天時間上來說，十二點是子時一半，上一半的子時屬於當天夜裏，下一半的子時是次日零分開始。

邵康節說「冬至子之半」，冬至是子月一半的時候，宇宙萬物到了一個不屬於動態也不是靜態的時刻。「天心無改移」，平穩極了，這中間是真空狀態。這真空的狀態是一陽之氣初動之先，也就是「萬物未生時」。

所以佛家講修到無念，真正空了，才是陽氣來之前的境界。

講到這裏順便提到一件事，在今天這個二十世紀的八十年代，講到中國文化，尤其講儒家宋明理學家的思想，我站在學術立場看來，不管政治不論地位，蔣老先生是真正通達理學家的。如果他現在仍在世的話，我不會提他，不過，百年之後，歷史上看他有關儒家的學術成就，會超過他功業的成就。現在可以講，他在世的時候一天靜坐三次，每次大約兩個鐘頭。他不盤腿坐，就是平常這樣坐著打坐。他有一句名言：「窮理於事物始生之際，研幾於心意初動之時」，這是他老先生對於理學的境界，對於心性修養，尤其對於邵康節的研究，屬於他自己總結的心得。他在傳記裏提到過，二十幾歲時替母親抄寫《楞嚴經》《維摩詰經》，佛經看過很多，靠老太太的督促，對於佛學有一點瞭解。老先生這一副聯語，就是邵康節的「天心無改移，一陽初動處，萬物未生時」的引伸，比理學家東說西說的簡單扼要，說得很明白。

我們再回來看邵康節這一句「冬至子之半，天心無改移」。道家所謂「天心」就是佛學講無念真如這個境界。這個時候「天心」叫做天心正

運。運就是運動的意思，就是這一剎那之間，指南針剛停在那裏，對著南北極最準的這一剎那。所以有些算命看風水地理的，要想懂天心正運就很難了，那是極微之間，剎那之間。所以「天心」也就是佛家講明心見性那個階段，是萬緣放下一念不生時。「天心無改移」這個時候，陽氣將要發動，道家叫無陰陽之地，不陰也不陽。也就是佛家講非空非有即空即有，所謂止的道理。

品性 理性 工夫

我希望年輕同學們注意，中國文化在周秦以前是儒墨道三家。儒家以孔子代表，墨家是墨子，到唐宋以後所謂三家才是儒釋道三家。這三位都是我們所謂根本上師，根本的大老師，但是三家的文化各有偏重。佛家是從心理入手，達到形而上道。據我的知識範圍所及，世界上任何宗教哲學沒有跳過如來的手心的。當然我的知識範圍並不一定對的。道家的思想偏重於從物理及生理入手，而進入形而上道。那麼我們也可以說，講物理生

理入手的修持方法，任何一家無法跳過道家的範圍，跳不過太上老君的八卦鑪。所以《西遊記》上描寫孫悟空進了太上老君的八卦鑪，一身毛都燒光了，只好躲在爐角裏不動，兩個眼睛被薰得紅紅的變成火眼金睛了。儒家則偏重從倫理、人文、道德入手，而進入形而上道。

因此我常常告訴青年同學們，我們三位根本的老師，加上後來兩位外國的，耶穌和穆罕默德，都是我們的老師，都不錯，各有各的一套學問。他們五個人坐在一起，一定是很客氣，彼此相互敬酒。可是他們的徒弟太差了，彼此打架。當然我不是五貫道，也不是三貫道，純粹是公平的學術立場。所以我說今後的中國文化，要學儒家的品性，我們作人做事不能不學儒家的道理。儒家就等於佛家大乘菩薩道的律宗，講究戒律，所以儒家非常注重行為。

除了學儒家的品性還要參佛家的理性，你要想明心見性，直接領悟成道，非走佛家的路線不可，否則不會有那麼高，不會成就的。同時還要配合道家做工夫的法則，不管密宗顯教，都跳不出這個範圍。但是道家的學

問不止修道這一方面，中國歷史有一個奧密之處，每逢天下變亂的時候，出來救世所謂撥亂反正的，一定都是道家的人物。等天下太平了，他們多半走老子的路線，功成身退，天之道也，隱姓埋名，什麼都不要。等到盛平的時候，又都是儒家人物出面。

我們懂了「天心無改移」，就懂得陽氣真發動的狀況。當一個人睡覺打鼾時，實際上沒有真睡著，腦子還有思想；當他真正睡著時，原本吸啊呼啊，忽然有一個短暫的不呼也不吸了，動都不動，那是真睡著了。等一下他又吸氣了，身體也動一下。所以懂得佛家禪定修止息的，就知道息的境界就是不呼也不吸。在密宗或瑜珈術就叫做寶瓶氣，停止了呼吸。這個境界配合心理的「天心無改移」，到了呼吸真正不來不往的時候，思想心念絕對沒有了，這個是空靈，要從這個地方起步修道。

修性就是心理方面達到無念，雜念妄想都沒有，完全空靈，連空都不存在。這樣的清淨境界，心理上就是子時，一陽來復要開始來了。生理上拿呼吸來講，就是剛才說真正睡著，不呼也不吸那一剎那，也就是生命上

一陽將動之處。這兩個一定是配合的，一半一半。半斤八兩合起來就是中國度量衡十六兩，叫做一斤。所以道家術語問你，工夫做得怎樣？噢！十二兩。十二兩就還差一點，完全成了就是一斤。這個道理研究起來很有趣。佛家有沒有呢？你看《法華經》上提到的大通智勝佛有十六子，另有什麼八方佛等等，這個數字很多，有很多數理的奧密在裏頭，同修道都有關係的，這是第一個要瞭解的。

你經驗過一陽生嗎

第二個要瞭解的，修道的人要把握子時一陽來復的陽氣。據我幾十年來所看到的修道人，把握子時陽氣多半都注重在身體上，心理方面不大注重。修道以什麼為陽氣？什麼是一陽來復？以男性生理上來講，陽舉的時候就是。所以睡醒的時候，陽一舉就嚴重了。有許多學佛的修道的人也問，這個時候怎麼辦？我常常提佛家的規矩，其實當年道家也是這樣，每個廟子差不多天一黑就打鐘睡覺，尤其在深山古廟，太陽一下去，現在

講六七點鐘就睡覺了。早晨早一點是三點，遲的四點，修行人都起來上殿了。為什麼那麼早？他配合自然法則這個時候陽氣剛剛發動，起床做工夫了。唸經的唸經，打坐的打坐。做工夫不會漏失。像青年男性的遺精，什麼時間最多？如果晚上八九點鐘睡的話，遺精差不多都是四五點鐘快天亮的時候。一覺睡醒了，醒一下再睡，實際上腦子並沒有睡著，那個陽氣一動配合生理的慾念，就遺漏了。女性這個生理的現象沒有男性明顯，但也是有，女性在這個時候精神、生理都有變化。

所以道家就把生理上這個變化認為是精氣發動，但是有個觀念錯了，把有形的精蟲當成精，錯得一塌糊塗。因此有些人忍精，在要漏精的時候點穴道把它忍住，這是很嚴重的問題。這一類修道的人一望而知，面孔像豬肝色發烏，烏的外面有一層油光，東一塊西一塊，兩眼愣愣的，憨憨的，都是忍精所造成的，最後或者是吐血，或者是大小便中毒。像這種已變成有形的精，本來是身體的新陳代謝，在要排洩出去的時候，你把它堵住了，最後多半是攝護腺（前列腺）出大毛病，嚴重的會腦神經出毛病。

實際上所謂精之回轉，以男性來講，沒有經過睪丸以前還是氣，氣才可以收回。那麼怎麼收回呢？一般人就是打起坐來把它提上來搞了半天，叫做「運轉河車」。什麼叫河車？講到氣脈的時候再詳細告訴你們。這些人搬運河車，運到腦上面又轉下來，轉來轉去認為身上氣脈通了。我常常問他們，轉到什麼時候為止呢？這是說要有一個限度，哪個時候才不轉？轉到什麼程度？都是問題。

所以一般把這個時候當成子時，陽氣發動了，回轉來轉運河車，打通氣脈。轉河車之前你先去檢查檢查有沒有遺傳的毛病，假使有先天性的梅毒就很嚴重了，運轉河車一到腦子就瘋了。所以先要把身體上潛伏的病清掉，不可以亂玩的啊！我是吃開口飯教書那麼吹吹的，我不是仙也不敢成仙。過去我看見許多學神仙的，但我沒有看到成功的，而遭遇痛苦後果的我看得太多了。他們就因為學理不通，把這個當成活子時，就修搬運轉河車。實際上身體上的氣脈河車，「天地設位」「坎離二用」，是自然的任運，哪個人奇經八脈不通呀？如果不通就死亡了！血液一定是循環在流通

的，這是呆定的法則，不要你去幫忙它，你幫忙反而把它幫壞了。

修道的人要懂得活子時，剛才我們已經提到過，我們身體是個小天地，精神氣血流行的法則，同太陽月亮天體的運行是同一個原理，同一個法則。但是每人稟賦不同，胖的瘦的、男的女的、老的少的各有不同。這還不算數，心理的狀況不同，古人講人心不同各如其面，世界上沒有兩個人面孔相同的。同樣的，世界上沒有二人思想是一樣的。

換一句話說，高明看相的人，看了面孔就曉得這個人的個性思想，以及他一生的成就與失敗。這就是「卦象」，掛在臉上，你不高興時就掛出來了，你高興哈哈大笑，臉上也掛了出來，所以一個人心理的現象表現在每人身上。一陽來復，每人陽氣的發生，時間不同際遇不同，所以叫活子時，要活用。也就是剛才所講的「幽潛淪匿，變化於中」，「二用無爻位，周流行六虛」，這個是陽氣真正的發動。

源頭活水

說到陽氣發動，照道家這個規律，一定要從下面發動了極點，而一陽生為復卦。密宗叫海底，中醫學就是會陰穴。譬如說男性的陽舉，女性的生理變化，都是陽氣發動。修道學佛許多人因為搞不清楚道理，自己陽舉時，心想糟糕犯了淫戒，有罪了。這個錯誤到極點！陽舉只是生理變化，如果沒有配上男女的慾念，它本身並沒有善惡，它只是生命力的現象而已，犯什麼戒啊！犯不犯戒是根據心理狀況而定。這個生理變化是個活子時，是生命的來源，沒有這個還不行。道家也認為這是源頭活水，是生命力。大家唸過理學家朱熹一首詩：

半畝方塘一鑑開　　天光雲影共徘徊
問渠那得清如許　　為有源頭活水來

不過朱熹那個源頭活水不是道家這個源頭，真正的源頭活水是生命的

來源，這時陽氣發動不一定是子時來的，不一定是身體下部來的，每人因身體不同而有異。所以有些青年打坐，忽然手心足心發燙了，這也是一種象徵呀！道理是什麼？「二用無爻位，周流行六虛」。但是有沒有理由呢？有理由。譬如這個人身體非常虛弱，他今天學道是想救命治病，所以學打坐。能不能當神仙不管了，至少打坐這個修養現在醫學比做冬眠治療，對身體是有好處的。學動物一樣靜下來，也就是物理生理自我治療的一種方法，所以打坐對治病對身體健康，只有幫助而沒有壞處。說打坐壞了，什麼神經失常了，那是他自己亂搞，自己打坐想變成神仙，又想得眼通又想得他心通的，那已經是神通的二號，就是精神有病，當然搞壞了。

如果說打坐會出毛病，那睡覺也應該出毛病啊！

打坐是一個休息狀態，休息怎麼會出毛病呢？那只是心理上出毛病罷了！所以你說打坐靜下來忽然左手發熱，忽然這一邊肉咚咚咚跳起來，忽然肚子裏面也攪動了，有些人就嚇死了，怕出毛病了。你不是還坐在那裏嗎？裏面跳動你怕什麼？許多同學拿這些事來問我，我一聽就生氣，你是

怕有蚯蚓進去，還是怕裏頭觸電？這個雖然不是活子時來，也是氣動的一種，只要不去理它，慢慢氣脈就發動了。至於說它為什麼在這個時候發動，你仔細研究道理就多了。譬如說，左邊屬陽右邊屬陰；又如五個手指也不同，這屬於心臟，那是肺臟。所以要想真正懂中醫，你還有得學呢！

過去大陸上沒有所謂小兒科醫生，但是我家鄉有一位老太太，她幾代行醫，婆婆傳給她，她再傳給媳婦，不傳給女兒的。那個時候鄉下沒有西醫，每一家小兒生病非她來不可，她一來靈得很。好在我還看到過，所以可以告訴你們。老太太一到，把那個嬰兒手抓來，指頭掰開一看，喔……肝氣，吃一點藥就好了。或者餵一點點藥，或者她拿三個指頭在這個嬰兒的身上東一抓西一抓，就退燒了。那個時候覺得不可思議，後來才懂這個原理。大人也一樣，身上有了病，指頭的氣色變化就看得出來，臉色也不同了。

我現在是隨便就講出來，假使在當年想求人家告訴你，這個指頭管什麼，那你準備五萬塊錢，人家幹不幹還是問題，那可是祖宗不傳之秘呀！

過去中國人就有這種觀念的，不像我在這裏什麼密宗什麼法都公開，因為我認為這個文化不能再秘密了，否則都失傳了。學針灸的跟這個都有關係，我再講一遍，你們每人都欠我五萬（眾笑）。每一個足趾也一樣，分陰陽左右，中年以上的人哪個指頭不靈光，就曉得哪個內臟出問題了。

所以學中醫真難，除了看指頭，還要看手心的青筋，看手心的脈。手心這個部份還分八卦，分五臟六腑的部位，一看顏色就曉得了。看耳朵也能診病，現在都知道叫耳診，從耳朵的氣色就可以斷定了，跟醫院照Ｘ光一樣。看眼睛也可以，叫眼診，在中國都有的。有一個老頭子懂眼診，他看病不用按脈，就叫你眼睛張開這麼看一下，就知道哪裏出了問題。現在都分開了，還有手診，我看過一本關於替小兒抓筋的書，這三根指頭要練過才抓得好。

這都是說明一陽來復活子時的時候，氣脈在身體上什麼部位發動也不一定，要懂得這個原理，才能夠真把這個陽氣修長。陽氣一發動是第一步性命雙修之道，欲知後文如何請聽下回分解。

第十三講

中國的文字文化

由東漢到魏晉南北朝，大致上文章都是四個字或者五六個字的短句，並不特意講求對仗。梁武帝的昭明太子，把漢代以來到魏晉南北朝之間，所有這些大文豪的著作集中起來，編成了有名的《昭明文選》。之後到隋唐之間，變成駢體文，所謂四六體的文字，非要對仗不可。比方我們大家唸過〈滕王閣序〉，唐代王勃的作品：「南昌故郡，洪都新府」，這一類都是四六駢體文的著作。每字每句都要對得很工整，意義還要表達得很好，這是中國文學的特色。

可是有一個問題，也是很大的感慨，到了隋唐之間辦公文就很麻煩了。因為要寫作公文，程度不好沒有辦法當公務員，不像現在的公務員，寫白字乃至亂七八糟條子都寫不清楚。我經常看到一些公文頭都大了，只

好投降，要去跟他們做徒弟去了，不然看不懂。

古時候公文太高深了，出一張佈告老百姓看不懂。到了唐太宗李世民，他本身是個才子，文武雙全，中國也安定統一了，他下命令公文要改過來，拿現在話講是變成語體文。因此，才有唐代的這個文章。這個大家要注意，三四百年之間一個美麗的文體，一下也改不過來。尤其中國人特別喜歡文學。大家講到文人都提到韓愈，韓愈已經是中唐的人了，他就極力提倡所謂古文。這個古文就是中國上古的文字，是長長短短的語體，但是把話說清楚了。當然不止韓愈一個人，不過他名氣大，所以後人推崇他「文起八代之衰」。其實韓愈提倡的古文，在我們現在看起來真是古文，越來越古老了。現在的白話文更嚴重，這句白話文是講什麼東西，很難了解，一百年以後會比古文還古，大概要很多考據學家來考據了。

現在不是講文學的問題，我們再回頭來看，像魏伯陽真人，他寫《參同契》的這個文字，是一種漢體的文字，非常清楚，四字一句。所以在中國文化歷史上，大文章或是代表一個政權最高的文告，多半是這一類文

章。這種文章，簡單明瞭，幾個字一句，可是很難寫的，字愈少意思愈清楚，這是工夫。等於電報體，每多一個字價錢就多了。

魏真人的說明

現在為了我們研究的方便，先跳過一段，看下邊一段，「言不苟造，論不虛生」，他聲明這一篇文章，不是隨便亂寫的，討論這個問題也不是空口說白話，而是有事實根據的。懂得了這個理論，身體上心理上做工夫要有效驗，所以「引驗見效，校度神明」，校就是校對，要把理論跟事實比一比。你說我懂得了這個理論，《參同契》研究過了，結果做起工夫來碰到什麼境界，或者身上氣機跳動搞不清，你這就白修了。不要動不動就問老師，老師不會跟著你，神仙是你要做的，不是老師做的，所以自己一定要弄清楚。「校度」，度就是度量衡的度，一步有一步的工夫尺度，一步有一步的象徵。「神明」，神而明之，要你的真智慧真精神來明白道理，才求得到功效。

現在有許多人修道做工夫，求老師給他一個辦法，再不然指頭把他一摸，奇經八脈打通了！打通了怎麼樣？自己也不懂什麼叫做通，什麼叫效果，第二步又不知道怎麼走。況且是不是真通還不知道，都是盲目迷信。

修道這個東西，拿我們現在的語言，用個漂亮的名字叫做生命的科學，就是人類研究自己生命的一個科學。普通的科學是靠人的智慧，從物質、物理上去求證。這個生命的科學，修煉神仙丹道之術，同普通科學不同，是要拿自己的身心，整個生命投進去求證的。所以他說「引驗見效」，一步就有一步的效果。但是求證不是亂來的，是有次序的，搞錯了法則就不行了。我們一再講，這一部《參同契》是《易經》、老莊、還有神仙丹法參合起來的，不是光說空洞的理論，它是實際的實證指導。

「推類結字，原理為徵」，古人最早是沒有文字的，大概一個原始的民族，沒有文字以前都是結繩記事，這叫「結字」。以前到高山或落後地區的部落還有見到。這個繩子打結不是亂結的，哪一種事情打什麼結是有一定的，這是人類的聰明。後來進步了，伏羲出來開始畫八卦，八卦就是

文字的開始，用圖畫的，比結繩記事又進步一點，慢慢就有我們今天的文字。現在已經到了電腦打字的階段，連書法都不要練了。這個結字的意思就是形成文字著作，他把這些道理告訴你了，後面我們要「原理為徵」，把這些東西融會貫通，懂得這個法則才可以修持。

魏伯陽說真空妙有

我們再回頭看這段前面的一行：「以無制有，器用者空，故推消息，坎離沒亡。」我們講中國文學要注意，千古文章一大偷，不是一大抄哦，是一大偷，不過要偷得好。我經常講這個故事，國外國內我常常接到各方面寄來要我審查的文章，拜讀後輩年輕人這些大作，實在很痛苦，尤其看到寫得不通的，那真痛苦。所以我不希望有這個榮耀，可是有些地方實在推不掉，那麼怎麼辦呢？當然就拜託我的學生這些高足、矮足們看看吧！看完了提意見。

話說有一篇美國來的論文，請一位同學看了，他說老師呀，這篇非常

好，而且一定要給高分數的那種。我說那不錯啊！很多年沒有看到好東西了，很好，很好。他又說，不過你看了不要罵哦！我說這是什麼意思？他說因為全篇都是你的，每字每句照抄不誤。我說有這種事？我這個人有個毛病，寫完了東西自己腦子不記得了。我就告訴他，不高明！千古文章哪個人是創作？都是偷，看怎麼偷得好，偷得妙就對了。

這「以無制有，器用者空」八個字，魏伯陽偷老子的，他偷得好得很，只用八個字就把他偷完了。老子說了一大堆道理：「三十輻，共一轂，當其無，有車之用。埏埴以為器，當其無，有器之用。鑿戶牖以為室，當其無，有室之用。故有之以為利，無之以為用」。老子說的是什麼道理呀？這不只是中國文化，包括印度文化的佛家，都講空能夠生有。佛學講真空妙有，妙有真空；一切存在的東西最後總是歸空，空並不一定是沒有。佛學翻譯成中文叫做空，中國道家叫做無、叫做虛，不叫做空。兩個用字不同，但是道理完全一樣，表達方式不同而已。

老子說天地間，威力最大的是什麼東西？是空，就是無。「三十輻，

共一轂，當其無，有車之用」，這是講車輪子，我們中國古代春秋戰國早就用車了。一個車上十個戰士都是長矛，前面五匹馬拖一部車子。那車子很大，假使五部車子並排走的話，這個馬路就很寬了，那時土地不像現在有限制，所以馬路開得寬。你看秦始皇的阿房宮，拿十丈高的旗過城門，騎馬就過去了，那個建築很高哦！可惜現在看不到了。那個時候的車子是木頭做的，中間一個檁子兩邊套著車輪子，這個車輪子中間是空的，外面一條一條的叫輻，是輻射狀的。你說這個三十條的支柱，每一條都互不相干，缺一條都不行，而每條著力點都在空的這個中心點，中空啊！所以「當其無，有車之用」。

「埏埴以為器，當其無，有器之用」，陶器原本是泥巴所做，沒有什麼方圓，捏成一個圓的或者方的模型，把它拿火來燒了就變成陶器的碗啦杯啊，就是空中生有。「鑿戶牖以為室，當其無，有室之用」，還有我們蓋房子，屋子裏面一定要有空間才叫房子，開了窗門才可以通空氣，才可以住人。所以老子的結論是：「有之以為利，無之以為用」。所以有無之

間要搞清楚，我們人是用慣了有，覺得生命是有，一切有，有就喜歡。我們講佛學已經講過，人要看通這個道理，這個有，一切萬有，包括我們的身體，我只有使用權。等到有一天它罷工了，不願意再勞動了，我們就沒有辦法指揮它，因為它畢竟不是我的所有，死了也帶不走。活著時它是它，我是我，也是兩回事。我們現在的有，認識到生命「有之以為用」，就要把握現時的作用，不要認為沒有生命就感到可憐就哭了。不要哭，「無之以為利」，愈空愈好，空了有大利，真到了空的境界就另外產生了新的東西。

所以老子講了一大堆，我們這位魏真人八個字把他偷完了：「以無制有，器用者空」。你們青年同學寫白話也好，寫文言也好，文章要會偷，人家的好句子原班不動搬上來很可恥。像我們小的時候寫文章偷用古文，老師看到就罵，過來！沒有道德！年輕人用古人的文句，好事！但是要註明出處！然後就在我們頭上嗝一敲，那個叫吃爆栗子，這是輕微處罰。如果忘記了是什麼人的原句，可以寫是借句。這是我們當年的教育，當年的

道德標準，連偷死去的古人都不行！現在就亂搬還盜印，然後把名字都拿掉。我的是我的，你的也是我的，搞成共產或無產！

現在人亂搞，但是不肯用腦筋，其實你偷人家的文章只要變一兩個字就不同了。中國古人每個都是詩人，凡是讀書都會作詩，再不然會作歪詩打油詩。你看詩，都是風啊花啊水啊月啊，可是幾千年來那麼多詩，有幾句相同過！順便給大家看看偷文章的做法，魏真人的「以無制有」，中間加了一個東西，就是這個「制」。像我小的時候，如果我能用出來這個字，先生一定說，你這個孩子了不起！然後拿起紅筆在字旁邊圈三圈，好！好啊！這個字用得好啊！一定這樣大加讚嘆。

制就是伏，控制的意思。空可以控制有，有不能控制空，是這樣的關係。所以修道做工夫是有，就怕你空不掉。學佛也一樣，修道打坐在道家講清虛，結果一般人修道是坐在那裏搞氣脈，這裏動那裏動，這裏守那裏守，然後嗯！還要打通它。都是在那裏搞有！所以搞了半天沒有效果。愈空時它的功能就愈發起來，你打坐修道沒有效果，因為你心不能空啊！心

空了，身體感覺都空得掉的話，這個效果就來了。所以這個「制」是重點，他把老子道理拿到這裏只用八個字，而且自己換了一個字「制」，就把道理講出來了。「以無制有，器用者空」，「器」是東西工具，一切工具能夠起大作用的，都是空的。現代物理學家，分析物質到原子電子……最後是空的！絕對空的，你絕對找不出東西來。因為空，它就有無比的威力，無比的功能。所以「以無制有，器用者空」。

日月二用與結丹

「故推消息，坎離沒亡」，「消息」兩個字出在《易經》。消不是沒有，消是成長。譬如說一個人從生下來開始，一路上來叫做消，這個功用把它消散掉，所以消是代表「有」的階段。息是代表「無」的階段，人死了並不是沒有，是個大休息，這個大休息以後重生了，所以消息是這個道理。很多人不懂消息出在《易經》上，把道理搞錯了，以為通信叫做消息。消就是消耗放射；息是歸納、培養回來。譬如太陽早晨出來，傍晚

下去，這個階段十二個鐘頭謂之消。晚上太陽下去了，到明天早晨剛剛上來，這個十二個鐘頭謂之息。息充滿了新的生命，又出來了，然後新的生命又消了，所以叫做一消一息。後來不用這個名稱，改為「消長」，消就是消耗，長就是成長。

「坎離」是兩個卦代號，後天以「坎離二用」為主。他說「故推消息，坎離沒亡」。你懂了一消一息，一有一空，互相成長之間，然後對於宇宙生命這個法則，所謂「坎離」兩卦所代表的身心作用，所代表這個太陽月亮的作用，就「沒亡」，就隱沒了。

道家到什麼時候才可以結丹呢？後頭章節會講到，真的得到神仙的丹藥時，則「日月合璧，璇璣停輪」，日月合璧是太陽跟月亮兩頭掛在那裏，彼此對照。你們諸位有沒有碰到這個境界？我在西康、西藏、雲南看到很多。有一次到晚上太陽沒有下去，月亮又上來，這邊太陽那邊月亮，這個天地是另外一個境界。都說多少年難得碰到一次，我一到昆明就碰到，所以運氣好。璇璣停輪，璇璣代表北斗七星中央指揮轉動，停輪是現

在不轉了，停掉了。所以這個氣脈通，是為了最後達到氣住脈停，呼吸停掉，沒有身體感覺，身上氣脈也沒有在轉動，心臟都不動了。在佛家瓊璣停輪叫做定，寧靜不動了。修道要到這個程度才談得上結丹。做工夫到這個時候才符合這八個字：「引驗見效，校度神明」。這才叫難呢！不是說打個坐，坐到這裏痛，那裏氣血流動跳動，以為有工夫了，那是憨夫，不是工夫！是靠不住的。

我們上一次提到過上中下三個丹田。有些道家傳工夫傳你一個地方叫「泥洹宮」，過去道家並沒有泥洹宮這個名辭，這是漢朝的翻譯來的，實際上是人頭頂的頂旋這裏。當然沒有一個人的頂旋真正是在中間的，這是一個秘密。大概的說，譬如一個人來算命，時辰不知道，那就看你頭頂頭髮的旋在哪個位置來判斷。子午卯酉是四正，其它時辰各有偏向，什麼時辰是兩個旋的？可惜我忘了，你們去研究吧。

學經絡的就知道頭頂這裏叫百會穴，可以扎針的。講一個事情很有趣，當年我到西康，看到他們修「頗哇法」，七天唸咒子，唸得大家臉紅

耳漲的，然後坐在那裏每人頭上插一根草，草插得很深，能夠插進草就代表死時一定往生西方極樂世界。我到那裏一看就跟朋友說，今天可好了！我們去學，我們要插草為記了。插草為記，中國人講起來是販賣東西或人口。他們修道很痛苦的，有些修不成功，插不進去。我說，我來保你們每一個都能夠往生西方，都插得進去。只要懂那個穴道的道理，手法懂了，一定就插得進去。但是藏人是難插進去的，他們不洗頭，頭皮厚得很。西藏那個地方也洗不得臉的，頭髮和皮膚還常常抹牛油保護，不然雪山的風一吹皮膚就吹裂了。這些油在頭上堆起來，那個草怎麼插得下去嘛！你懂了以後，先把油和這個頭皮渣子摳一下，咚！就把草插下去了！

泥洹宮究竟是什麼呢？就是佛經「涅槃」兩個字翻譯。頭頂穴叫百會穴，下面叫會陰穴。在密宗這個會陰就叫海底，海底就是會陰。學瑜珈的就不叫海底，叫靈蛇，也叫做靈熱，也叫做靈能，有時候這個地方發暖。據說這個生命的能是深深埋藏在下面，沒有一個人真正能發動。上天給了我們一個身體，我們沒有把這個身體的功用發揮出來，作人幾十年，

都是用假的外表一層。這個身體的生命的功能，它的會陰和百會，上下這一消一息，一升一降之間，有無比的功能在內，這個也就是「故推消息，坎離沒亡」。一個人活一輩子沒有把它發動，真發動起來這叫陽氣發動，要把握住。把握住做什麼呢？「校度神明」，一步有一步的效驗、效果。這個生命的威力大得很，功用也大得很，所以能夠修到袪病延年長生不死，也就是靠這個靈能、靈熱的功能。

第十四講

前三關　後三關

　　道家說，「道者盜也」，好像不做過小偷不能修道！事實上怎麼叫修道？是要盜天地之精華，硬要用偷盜的辦法，把天地的精神偷到自己身心上面來，使自己能夠永遠存活下去。所以修道是天下的大盜，所謂「小周天」就是這麼一個情況。我們人體前面都很好，樣樣都很周到，有眼睛有鼻子，呼吸的吃飯的都擺在前面，後面什麼都沒有。實際上後面屬陽，前面屬陰。人體很奇怪，所以修道都要懂，更要懂中國的古代科學、物理學。古代的科學也自成一個系統，叫做博物，現在有些學校還有一科叫博物。七八十年以前翻譯物理學叫做格致之學，是出自大學「物格而後知致」，日本、中國都是這樣翻譯，現在乾脆就叫物理。

　　古代這些道理，譬如說女性懷孕了，老太太們一看，哎呀！生男孩子

居多！懷男孩子肚子尖的，懷女孩子肚子圓的，因為嬰兒在娘胎裏頭「陽仆陰仰」。男嬰是面對著娘，背脊骨朝向肚子外面，女孩子相反。投水而死的男女也不同，男性的屍體浮起來是趴著的，女性的屍體浮起來是仰著的，所以一陰一陽不同。為什麼講這些呢？「男仆女仰」是呆定的，都同修道有關係。道家講身體有前三關後三關，前三關是從上到下，眉毛中間的印堂，兩乳房中間的膻中，肚臍下面的下丹田，這樣是前三關。後三關呢？背上尾閭是一關，還有兩關是夾脊和玉枕。從肛門這裏上來，這個骨結像算盤子一樣，一個一個的，第七個骨節的上面的地方，關係到腰痠背痛等問題，尤其是女性。

　　說到這裏我們順便岔進來一個禪宗公案，唐代有個文喜禪師，他三步一拜，拜上山西的五台山，要去見文殊菩薩。中國的四大名山，四川峨嵋山是普賢菩薩的道場，山西五台山是文殊菩薩，浙江普陀山是觀世音菩薩，安徽九華山是地藏王菩薩。過去大陸上有些人宗教的情緒很強，有些鄉下人用一個鐵條，從臉頰這裏穿過去用嘴咬住，兩邊掛兩個香爐三步一

拜，拜上山來。結果把鐵條抽了不會留疤，這個是菩薩靈驗！不過我曉得他還是要用藥的。有些女的手上穿一個洞，掛個繩子吊個香爐，就唸起佛來，好多天把香爐掛著，睡覺也那麼掛著。人類那個宗教的力量，那個熱情很奇怪的。

話說文喜禪師拜到了五台山下，碰到一個老頭子帶一個小孩。老頭子問，你從南方來，南方的佛法佛教現在怎麼樣？這個文喜禪師答覆得很好，他說，南方的佛教佛法「龍蛇混雜，凡聖同居」。就是說，有真修道的也有假修的。反問老先生，這個五台山上，一般出家人怎麼樣？老先生說，五台山文殊道場，顯教密宗的廟都有，我們這裏「前三三，後三三」。後來那個老頭子還帶他到茅蓬請他喝茶，茶吃完了後，老先生說你趕快上山吧，就把他趕走了。文喜離開了再轉頭一看，老頭子沒有了，原來是文殊菩薩化身，那個童子是文殊菩薩的獅子變的。他拜了好幾年想見到文殊菩薩，當面見到卻又不認識。

後來文喜禪師多年以後悟道了，就在廟上做飯。有一天文殊菩薩騎著

獅子現身，在廚房的大鍋上轉。文喜本來是要求見文殊菩薩，這一下他反而拿起鍋鏟要打文殊菩薩，他說，文殊是文殊，文喜是文喜，你來這裏搗個什麼亂呀！文殊菩薩就升到空中說：

修行三大劫　　反被老僧嫌

苦瓜連根苦　　甜瓜徹蒂甜

文殊菩薩是古佛再來，七佛之師，修行了三大阿僧祇劫，今天來看他，還被這個老和尚嫌，挨了一鍋鏟，就騎著獅子跑了。

後世修道的人引用「前三三，後三三」，就是文殊菩薩告訴文喜禪師，修行還是要注重「前三關，後三關」，這是大的。這是用道家解釋禪宗，不一定對！不過文殊所講的前三關後三關，這是大的。實際上拿針灸穴道來講，關口就多了。所以我們看道書所謂「玉液瓊漿」，下十二重樓，直達絳宮」。當你打坐坐得好的時候，這口水源源而來，是清淡清甜的，在道家叫做「玉液瓊漿」。從喉嚨的骨頭一節一節軟骨十二重下來，是「十二重

樓〕，「直達絳宮」，下到心臟這個地方。口水不是像吃糖吃飯那麼嘸，舌頭要提起來一點，口水就一直這樣下來，口水越來越多，身體越來越健康，至少可以幫助消化，胃功能增強了。所以人老了嘴巴會乾，甚至會發苦，就是因為這個功能衰弱了。

尾閭關　夾脊關　玉枕關

一般人打坐修道，不管你走甚麼路線，最重要的第一關「尾閭關」就通不過。所謂煉精化氣，打通奇經八脈就更別說了。老實講，三關真通了的人我還沒有見到過，這就是《參同契》上所謂「引驗見效，校度神明」。不要亂吹，真的每一關通了，內行人一看就知，當然這個內行就很難找了。「尾閭」這一關，打通也很痛苦哦。所以你們修道打坐想身體健康，結果反而腰痠背痛，各種難過都來了，這就要明白道家說「弱者道之反也」的道理。在恢復你的健康以前，是會有一度感覺很衰弱，比沒有做工夫之前還要差。「弱者道之反」，也就是老子說的：「弱者道之用」。

這個原理等於西方人的諺語，黎明以前的黑暗。所以每過一關都感到身體不適，並不是打坐把你坐出病來了，是身體內部本來已經有問題，因為打坐幫你恢復，在恢復的時候，反而有痠痛麻的現象。然後就被嚇得不敢打坐修道了，神仙這一條路也就走不下去了。所以你本身沒有神仙的骨格，碰到真的神仙，他就算把方法告訴你，你也不會！

我們從粗的觀點來講，人的脊椎骨有很多骨節，一層一層，當陽能的氣向上升，等於太陽上升一樣，要經過海底爆出來。陽氣要走通這個背骨是很困難的，尤其是年紀大身體衰敗的人，都是透支過多，尾閭關沒有打通。又因為煉精化氣做不到，有形的精力到這一關早就漏了，所以年輕人修道的搞成漏丹，到了色慾這第一關都撐不過。就算能撐過關，以後又垮，垮了再來，永遠衝不上去這一關，這是講有形的哦！這還不算是正統的道家，只是講身體方面「引驗見效，校度神明」。

第二關「夾脊關」，影響到胃，到了背脊兩個肩胛骨的中間這一關，更難打通。當年我看到有個修道的人，都七八十歲了，紅光滿面兩眼非常

有神，可是背是駝的，跟畫上的神仙不一樣，所以我後來才懂這些畫家沒有看到過真神仙。這個老頭子是修道的，佛也懂，精神奕奕，身體也很健康，但是他坐在那裏好像一隻鴨子一樣。我們年輕人都叫他老師，反正當徒弟的人都是「道者盜也」，你愛聽我們叫老師，我就叫得特別勤快一點，你愛什麼都幫你弄，心想你這個道就傳給我了。後來跟他熟了就問他，師父，你這個背是從小就彎還是做工夫彎的？他說是做工夫彎的。我說，那修行先要做這個工夫啊？他說是的，然後帶我去看他怎麼打坐。他人彎起來像個球一樣，鼻孔對著肛門，這個本事大了，你們練過芭蕾舞瑜珈術的不知道做不做得到。我一看他是一個肉球嘛！等一下他出定了，慢慢起來也蠻端正，面帶紅光。

我想這些人都有道，就像是《蜀山劍俠傳》一樣，每個都有一套專門工夫！不過我總懷疑道是否這樣！像這種道我也不大喜歡。這個人也講出一套道理來，他說白鶴和烏龜是長壽的動物，白鶴的脖子很長，睡覺的時候把脖子捲起來，鼻子插到屁股這樣睡覺的，牠的呼吸在自己內部通的，

所以能夠長壽。烏龜會深呼吸，我曾親自抓烏龜觀察過，大的烏龜次數少，小烏龜多一點，牠會慢慢把頭腳都伸出來，旁邊要很靜，你才聽得到牠吸氣的聲音。吸進來以後它把頭向裏頭縮，過了兩個鐘頭都不動，這口氣保持在那裏，這個工夫就叫做「服氣」，修瑜珈術和氣功都有這種修煉的方式。孔子也講過「食氣者壽」。不過孔子又講一句話，「不食者神明而不死」，所以孔子也曉得有神仙，這要看《孔子家語》（編按：有些資料不同）才知道。這個「食氣」道家叫做「服氣」，也叫做「伏氣」。

這些奇怪的人物不曉得有多少，都是我親眼見過的，等哪一天寫回憶錄也許會把他們都記錄下來。那個人講的理論好像是對的，但我就覺得不對，人到底不是普通動物，人體是直立的，為什麼練工夫打坐要把鼻子對著肛門這樣通氣？他們一家人都修道，他家裏頭沒有椅子，舖蓆子大家一起打坐，要出定以前，他和太太、兒子、女兒五六個，就像幾個肉球在房間內翻觔斗，翻過來翻過去，鼻子對到下部，大概滾了五六分鐘，然後再坐起來，人再慢慢直起來。他們的理論就是「伏氣」，用自己的「元氣」

營養自己，使人體達到長生不死。實際上我後來研究結果，他的夾脊一關就沒有打通，四川話講這個人就成鑼鍋了，背就彎起來氣憋在裏頭，胃呀肝呀都受影響。可是他們是有一套工夫的，都不簡單的。

還有一個人，我要跟他學，他不許我叫他師父，要叫他老師。他的頭是搖動的，很有意思，因為他「玉枕關」的氣走不通。我們假使把人體分成三節，這個「精、氣、神」三大關要把它打通很難，尤其是「玉枕關」的氣，好難走通啊！你們說，自己是學佛的，四大皆空，何必管這些！你啊，一大都空不了！不管道家佛家，這個生命肉體的法則是呆定的，等於太陽一定是這個行度。至於說學佛的可以不管它，可是你受它左右就空不了，所以道家密宗非要把身體搞到絕對的健康不可。絕對健康就是「日月合璧，璇璣停輪」，身體的感受障礙沒有了，才可以談修道。

但是光打通氣脈這一步工夫就很難了，規規矩矩修也要十幾年。至於說你們諸位，又想賺錢升官又想得道成神仙又成佛，世界上好事給你佔完了，哪有那麼便宜的！你來磕個頭，老師呀，你要傳我！做了三天工夫就

想飛到西天去，然後來說，老師，沒有效果。去你的！你樣樣都想，好事不做一件就想自己成佛得道，那我從小到現在幾十年，都沒有得道，我不是白玩了！我多冤枉呀！所以不簡單真是不簡單，我講的都是實際的經驗給你們聽，平常很少講，不過你們記起來都可以成為賣錢的文章。

難下降的前三關

現在修道的沒有一個是真正道家的人，學佛的也不懂做工夫的重要。

我們看龍樹菩薩，這位菩薩是中國八宗的宗祖，不論禪密都是他。他懂得醫藥又知道自己哪個經脈穴道的氣不通。雖然經脈穴道同修道沒有多大關係，但是經脈走通身體不會搖動，才能真正入定。你要看到真正佛菩薩的相，他一定是很端正的。隋唐以前西藏塑的佛菩薩像是對的，一個真正有工夫的人，他的身體到腰部是越來越細，肚子會收進去，小腹越來越充實。不是說這裏鼓出一大塊就是丹田了，那是肉彈，不是丹田；你看一個人肚子大大的，你用兩個指頭去碰卻是鬆鬆的。真正修道的人這裏是硬實

的，並不用力，元氣是充滿的。當然也不能太瘦，像我抽煙太多，是靠不住的，不要以我為標準。你們看佛像身體圓的，那是有他道理的。

我們把這個「前三關，後三關」講了，把這個法則配到人體上，「冬至一陽生」，由海底尾閭背上一直上來，子月丑月一直到乾卦到頂。這個由下面上來叫「督脈」，學醫的更要懂了。為什麼叫「督脈」呢？督者督導也，是總的、督促的意思。我們人體五臟六腑都掛在這個「督脈」上。

五臟六腑從這個喉嚨之下，肺、肝、心臟、胃，一直到腸子都這樣掛在這個背脊骨上。人和畜牲不同，畜牲的身體是橫的，五臟六腑掛在背脊骨不同。所以佛經裏畜牲道叫旁生也就是橫生。

人這個五臟六腑掛在背脊骨這裏，所以這個「後三關」其實不止三關，在沒有走通以前，身體很難完全健康。而走通到頂乾卦的時候，多半修得紅光滿面，這個叫做「進陽火」。陽火上升，陽氣上升還沒有到「退陰符」呢！上升以後必定要下。到這個時候你不想睡覺了，因為精神飽滿而不想睡覺。如果你不懂道理，有時候就會發神經了。

當這個陽氣到五臟六腑時，五臟六腑就發現毛病；到眼睛時，眼睛發出毛病。像我每一個機能都出過毛病，我都是親身嚐試了又嚐試。有時候為了試試是不是這個道理，我強拿自己的命開玩笑，我偏把它弄壞，弄壞了以後再來。工夫到這一步就要看看是不是這樣，三番幾次試驗確定是這樣才罷手，當然隨時準備眼睛瞎了耳朵聾了。譬如有一次我試驗氣到某個地方耳朵會聽不見，我仍然去上課講《孟子》，我講歸講但是我耳朵一點聲音都聽不見。如果把自己身體看得嚴重的話，一定不會去上課，先去住醫院檢查。我這個脾氣是，格老子充其量死！萬一倒下去了，你們諸位一定會為我哀悼，然後報紙登上這個人為學術而努力至死，大家一嘆然後把我燒了。還有一次也是講孟子，耳朵聽不見聲音，不是氣到那裏，是耳屎塞住了！有一次一個同學在這裏打坐，覺得身上東癢西癢，以為是氣脈打通了，結果搞了半天是個蟑螂在身上爬！

剛才說到「前三關」很難降下來，降下來會怎麼樣？你過了這一關，眼鏡要重配了，你本來假使是四百度，現在減輕成兩、三百度，可見這個

生命的功能強得不得了。到鼻子，鼻子出毛病，並不是鼻子眼睛原來是好的變壞了，而是本來有毛病，這一股生命的力量要通過堵塞的地方顯現的。我相信就算是有癌症的話，你工夫真到了，這一股力量道家的名稱叫做「丹」，到了那裏，像鑽六十照射，什麼癌細胞細菌都非殺死不可，這個身體所有的障礙都給你打通。這個氣降下來就走「前三關」，降下來以後周流，叫做「小周天」。

第十五講

穴道與針灸

上次講到十二辟卦的「周天」這個法則，一般所謂的道家講的兩個名稱，一個大周天，一個小周天。元朝明朝以後，道家的修煉方法演變成強調小周天是人體的「任督」兩脈，就是背部的督脈，和人體前面的任脈。中國的醫學提出來人體有所謂奇經八脈。

提到中國醫學，前面講過，在古代整套的治療，就是：「一砭，二針，三灸，四湯藥」。因為熬湯藥麻煩，也有把湯藥變成膏、丹、丸、散的形狀，那是後來的進步。像傷科的膏藥是熬出來變成膏的，丹是一塊一塊、一片一片的，丸子是搓成球狀，散是粉狀的。以前中藥店請一個師傅，第一就要考他這個膏、丹、丸、散是不是都會，這個技術可以說是中國古代醫藥的手工製藥業。

所謂針灸是要下針入穴道的，這個人體的穴道是中國老祖宗獨特的發現，很早就曉得有三百六十幾個穴道，就是配合道家和《易經》的思想。

太陽在天體的行度一天一度，這個躔度一年有三百六十五度多一點。事實上，我們現在發現穴道有四百多個，甚至不斷還有新的發現。除了在哲學上配合太陽系的行度以外，我們古代也有實際的人體解剖。我在講中醫學的時候常常說個笑話，西方醫學的發展雖然比較遲，可確實比我們的準確多了。但是他們的解剖學是拿死人來解剖的，所以他們的生理學我說不能叫生理學，而是死理學。

中國古代用解剖來發現穴道是很殘忍的，是拿活人解剖的，就是把死刑犯做解剖。歷史記載殷朝的紂王非常殘暴，因為他也好奇，就讓醫生解剖犯人來找穴道。王莽時候也做過同樣的事，把判死刑的囚犯拿來當場解剖，太醫院的醫生都站在那裏對證，看有沒有這個穴道，是不是這個穴道，位置是否準確。到了元朝，成吉思汗的宰相耶律楚材製作了準確的銅人圖，把醫學沒有求證完備的這些穴道都補起來。元朝這個宰相實際上是

遼族人，這個人是滿蒙種族裏了不起的一個人物，天文、地理、政治、軍事無所不知，同時也學禪宗也學道家，樣樣都懂得，醫學尤其好。他很多的醫療經驗是在戰場上就地診治受傷戰士摸索出來的。

這個針灸的穴道，要配合十二經脈。在座的年輕同學現在一窩蜂學習針灸，真正要懂十二經脈的哲學原理就要瞭解《易經》的十二辟卦。上次我提到過「子午流注」，這個是氣血流動的道理，武術裏的點穴就要配合子午流注。依我一點點經驗，如果把點穴同針灸原理配合起來，治病可以不需要針灸，一個指頭煉好就可以治病。可惜這一門功夫現在幾乎失傳了，這些學問很多流散到民間，甚至到海外去了。我們中國的醫學留傳到韓國與日本，這一派漢醫普通稱為「東醫」。有一部《東醫寶鑑》，是韓國日本關於漢醫的書，很值得一看。

經脈與醫道

上次提到古代的小兒科，為嬰孩診病，不是摸脈，只是拿指頭來看，

從指頭手心的顏色就可以判斷病情。又譬如刮痧，也是一個專學，很多病拿塊石頭刮一刮，或者是在皮膚放血，病馬上好了。有一位朋友患血壓高，他就自己放血，方法是拿個針在頭頂百會穴，咚！一下，只有一點點血出來，人就舒服了，血壓馬上下降了。這個話我是講給大家聽，你們千萬不要去試。這個朋友不懂醫，是自己亂搞碰巧成功了。後來我告訴他不如在腳部放血，在頭頂上放血畢竟危險。

當年鄉下這些所謂放血，有一種民間古老的「挑」法，叫做「挑羊毛疔」。我現在很後悔，當時不肯學，認為這些是迷信，真可惜！有些老太太不一定識字，看她在病人背脊骨一塊一塊地摸，哦！在這裏！隨便拿針這裏一挑，只是挑破一點點，一抽就有一根白白的毛，抽出來病人就舒服了。這個東西有些地方叫做發「羊毛痧」，也有些生瘡的叫「羊毛疔」，一挑就好了。看起來好像很土很俗氣很古怪，實際上是人類文化幾千年的經驗累積的結晶，原理不需要知道了，也不懂，但是它實用。

在十二經脈以外，有「奇經八脈」，這個「奇」，不是奇怪的意思，

這是《易經》的一個名稱，雙數為偶數，單數為奇數。奇經八脈就是單數，不屬於十二經脈，十二經脈是六陰六陽相對的。所以講針灸的道理，「病在上者，其治在下」，治療的時候不一定頭痛醫頭，腳痛醫腳。「病在左者，其治在右」，換句話說，「病在下者，其治在上，病在右者，其治在左」。什麼理由呢？因為人體的神經以背脊骨為中心點，是左右交叉的。人體的神經為什麼這麼古怪？因為人體有骨節，我們手要扭動，所以經脈會這樣轉彎。

這個道理在《易經》上有一句話：「曲成萬物而不遺」。老子發揮這個道理，說了一句名言：「曲則全」。人體是一個完整的，它的神經左右交叉，不只左右交叉，還上下交互，同畫卦一樣。因此中醫才講「病在上者，其治在下，病在下者，其治在上」。為什麼老年人兩腿沒有力氣，走不動了？光醫腿還是成問題，他的腑臟不健康了，荷爾蒙分佈不平均了，或者是自律神經，或者是某一部份系統有了問題。光是頭痛醫頭、腳痛醫腳是不通的。所以中醫原理同道家、《易經》、老莊、修道有

密切關係！因此必須要熟讀《黃帝內經》，其中包括〈靈樞〉〈素問〉兩部份。再要瞭解《難經》，「難」就是問難，一個一個問題提出來，提了「九九八十一難」，討論最難治療的病在什麼地方，都是醫理學的問題，所以《難經》讀了不一定能醫病。

這些都同奇經八脈有關係，所謂奇經八脈，指獨立於十二經脈以外的一個系統。普通所講督脈都認為是背脊骨一直上來，從尾椎骨開始，一路上來到後腦這個地方。其實不止上到頭頂，也從後面頸部轉到腦內。所以上次提到過，同善社演變到現在的一貫道點竅，乃至很多的旁門左道守竅等等，它的基本理由是督脈的頂點在眉間這裏。實際上是不是如此，在醫學上還是個問題；離開醫學，光講氣脈之學也是問題。所謂任脈就是從小腹開始，下來到男女的生殖部份會陰，一路上來則到咽喉。還有中間環腰的這個帶脈，女性要特別注重的是帶脈。

這裏有好幾位同學要想考中醫，我是很反對的，因為照現在的考試方法，你們都行，都很高明；但是照我的標準，你連《黃帝內經》都讀不

通，也解釋不了，然後去考醫，那是不應該的。所以有一兩位同學考試通過，聽我的話不敢給人看病，寧可開藥店算了。因為有幾次看病開藥，病人吃了以後沒有好，處方拿來我看，他方子開的都對，不過我說不能那麼用的，因為有年齡、性別的不同，你不曉得活用。

我說帶脈對女性重要，大家聽起來以為是笑話，學醫的修道的都要注意，因為女性的生命能在上身。剛才講的陰陽相反，只要看媽媽和祖母她們那個長頭髮，要坐在梳粧台梳個把鐘頭再盤起來，上肢並不覺得累。可是你叫男性學女性兩手伸直拿報紙，半個鐘頭不准掉下來，他絕對受不了；女性就沒有關係，受得住。

男性的生命能在下半身，你叫他立正站一兩個鐘頭站得住，你叫女性立正站一個鐘頭，那要她的命！女性站不住的。所以你看男人走路，是膝蓋頭在動的走。年紀大的男人，膝蓋頭不大彎得動，走路就不是那麼靈便了。女性走路是臀部搖動走的，這是兩性的不同。所以中醫「望聞問切」，病人一進來已經看出來了，這是知識。我有時走在朋友後面，看

到這人走路兩個手不甩動，我會說注意哦！心臟可能有問題，去檢查檢查吧。因為大部份心臟有問題的人，手臂就不動了，你們走路感覺一下，兩手是不是平均甩動。

生活習慣影響氣脈

實際上外形出問題就是因為內部出了問題，面相就看得出來。譬如鼻子歪了，或嘴歪了，那是習慣一邊睡，他應該反過來睡幾年，鼻子慢慢就會正了。這雖是笑話，但要注意，一個小動作有時可以治大病。我們的健康自己都知道，尤其到了中年以上更明顯。所謂「五十肩」也叫「肩凝」，肩膀這裏肌肉神經凝結住了。中年這兩個肩膀難過，走路時兩個手就不大甩動了，走路就像戲台上的曹操一樣，脖子也僵了，頭不能隨意轉，也經常會痛。所以自己要曉得運動，曉得調節，才保持健康。

我舉幾個例子引伸「前三三與後三三」，現在還沒有離開這個題目，這一條一條發揮起來都與用功修道有密切關連。講回女性要注重「帶

脈」，有時候勸我們這些中年女道友，把肚子練小一點，腰粗了就表示你生命的能力不凝聚了。譬如看到一個年輕朋友肚子很大，愛喝啤酒，他還自稱練過氣功，我在他肚皮上一抓有兩坨肉，這就不好了，因為氣不「凝聚」。真正修道也就是「神凝氣聚」。

你們學醫的同學，好好立志去研究，把東西文化融會起來。學醫是為了對人類生命的學問做貢獻，假使學醫只為了容易賺錢，那不值一談，動機就不對了。佛經有一句話：「因地不真，果招紆曲」，動機不正確，不會有正確後果的，所以我再三強調這一點。

例如督脈就是中樞神經系統，人體以這個背脊骨為中心，我們五臟六腑都掛在上面。任脈是自律神經系統。有時候年紀大的人肌肉歪了，講話會抖動，在醫學上就是自律神經失調。所以任督二脈也就是兩大神經系統。現在醫學歸納人體有七大系統，骨骼系統、神經系統，荷爾蒙內分泌系統，有腦下垂體、甲狀腺、腎上腺等等多得很。還有消化系統，呼吸系統，各有不同。科學及醫學的進步，對我們舊的東西有新的幫助和瞭解；

對於現在研究道家的學問，研究生命的道理也有幫助。

但是到現在為止，世界上真能貫通中外古今醫學的人還沒有，因為辦醫學教育的人多半都偏重一邊，不大瞭解溝通的重要。我相信道家與中國醫學的東西配合了西方醫學，對人類保健和疾病治療的貢獻會很大。有時候我發現有些很嚴重的病，只要懂了這些病理，兩毛錢就治好了，乃至不花錢。再嚴重的病，常常一個動作就治好了。

所以我常說，西醫救命，中醫治病。有些急症，例如胃出血了，你不相信西醫，不趕快去打針，偏要去看中醫，那你自己找死。你認為三個指頭把脈非常準確，我卻覺得不大保險。中醫摸脈叫做三指禪，這個不是禪宗的禪，不要搞錯。憑三指真能夠判斷到內部的全體嗎？那太難了。除非你打坐工夫已經到了二禪以上，或到了「心物一元，自他不二」的境界，那時你這個指頭把脈並不是光靠脈，是靠心靈的電感，自己與病人的身體合一了，才能體會出來病症。幾十種脈象，要靠三個指頭去感覺，粗細浮沉長短遲速，還算容易感覺，有些脈就比較難體會了。三個指頭摸人家的

脈，嘴裏還跟人家講話「股票今天怎麼樣？美鈔多少錢啦？」如果碰到我，趕快把手抽回來，寧可自己去抓藥。再看老前輩把脈的時候，眼睛一閉，叫他都不理，那是真把脈。有時候遲疑十幾分鐘手不拿下來，皺眉頭去體認。現在是隨便摸摸就開藥方，這種醫生不看也罷。

我們再講回任督二脈，常常有人找上我，我也不認識他，「想請教老師一個問題，我的任督二脈打通了。」還有的說「我的奇經八脈都通了，下一步怎麼樣？」我只好說：「對不起，我的任督二脈在哪裏我都還沒有找到，我沒有辦法答覆你。關於奇經八脈，我聽過這個名稱，你都通了的嗎？我就更沒有辦法貢獻你。」很多人認為自己打通任督二脈奇經八脈了，我說你這個叫做「凡氣通」，是凡夫感受的狀態，不是真正的打通任督二脈，為什麼？這個裏頭要研究了。

我們把背脊骨這個叫做督脈，背脊的這個骨節是一節一節這樣套上去，四面八方都是神經系統，像電纜一樣。所以有些人胃痛難過，在背上那個骨節穴位針一針，灸一灸，通一下電，他胃就好了。因為胃的微細神

經系統掛在那裏，那裏通了，胃蠕動的功能就好起來了。這是一個簡單的例子，詳細的還不止如此。這個背脊骨節電纜一樣的神經系統，這樣絞包下去，請問這個督脈假使通了，是骨節外邊這些神經系統電纜通了呢？還是骨節裏頭？我們的骨科大夫周院長，他是正牌的西醫權威，坐在後面監視我，我講錯了他會笑我的。骨節裏頭有骨髓，這個骨節中心是空的，如果骨節外面氣走通就是你說的氣通了，那只是神經系統的感覺來的。骨節裏面骨髓的氣不是那麼容易感覺到的。將來我們有機會請周院長來給我們上一課，講解這個骨節裏頭外頭的細部結構。

我講一個自己的經驗，我有一個孩子在七八歲的時候，有一天夜裏上吐下瀉高燒，我這個土郎中束手無策，醫生對自己的家裏人不敢下手，趕快就叫車子送醫院。一進去，掛急診還等了半天，來了個年輕醫生，很神氣派頭變大的。來了以後也不問，就把這孩子的衣服拉起來，說要抽脊髓化驗是不是腦膜炎。我說，不准！我心裏想你們都是實習醫生，就算是真正醫師來抽脊髓也不准！我問他有別的方法嗎？他說沒有，我就說不看

了。我曉得小孩子抽了脊髓將來問題多得很，非常嚴重。我有個小師弟，學問好，工夫好，當年抽過脊髓，到現在總是腦力不夠、散漫。所以我不讓他們抽脊髓，就抱起孩子去找我認識的一位余醫生。他一看說很嚴重，開了美國新到的一個特效藥。我讓太太把孩子抱回家，自己上街去找藥房，半夜十二點多，敲開幾間大藥房都沒有這個藥。

我只好再掛個電話吵醒余醫生，告訴他這個藥買不到，能不能換別的藥？他說最好是這個藥，但是現在這個情況，你回去買一瓶汽水給他喝喝再講啦。我一聽曉得他很疲勞了，高明的醫生也很可憐的，晝夜不得休息，要體諒人家。我想想自己的孩子嘛，生死有命，聽天由命吧！我就把余醫生當菩薩，買汽水回來給他餵了半瓶，結果他也好了。所以脊髓千萬不要輕易抽的，抽不得呀！脊髓抽掉非常難長回來。這個不是道家煉精化氣，脊髓雖然不是真精，但的確是精的重要一部份。後來我這孩子在美國讀到大學，回來說他跑步運動都是第一，我說你還第一呢！七八歲時候我如果放鬆一步，你這個脊髓一抽，你現在的背就是彎的。這就是經驗，要懂得這個道理。

第十六講

各家各派的氣脈說

現在西方世界很流行瑜珈術，印度的瑜珈術淵源久遠，同佛教本師釋迦牟尼佛是一個時代，都是印度文化的支流。現在普通講瑜珈術是指身瑜珈，是運動，身體的動作。身瑜珈也很高明，同中國武術的所謂南派的工夫，武當派的都有關連。唸咒子是音聲瑜珈，另外心瑜珈是心理方面，在印度已經失傳了。我們中國翻譯的佛典中，很重要的一部是彌勒菩薩的《瑜伽師地論》，有一個學派叫瑜珈學派。瑜珈是中文音譯，「瑜伽師」是學瑜珈專門修道的人，「地」則是一層一層的程度。《瑜伽師地論》是唯識學派所講的，是如何由凡夫求證成佛之道的著作，可算是印度的哲學宗教修養方法。它分成十七地，不是講程序，不是講成就的階級，是把這一套修持的學問規範成十七部份。

現在世界上好幾個瑜伽大師都是印度人，有的是三歲就有神通，譬如你們年輕人喜歡看的一本書《大師在喜瑪拉雅山》，他就是一個。這一類走的是印度教的瑜珈，他們傲視一切，認為天上天下唯我獨尊。他們是有些神通，各種各樣，都稱教主了。前幾年禪宗在美國歐洲不得了，後來又風靡瑜珈。現在歐美有一個新趨勢，就是極力崇拜中國的道家，不過沒有幾年也會下去的。你們要注意，不要看到人家一窩蜂，認為我們中國人了不起，不是你了不起，那是中國的祖先們啊！雖然道家開始流行，但是瑜珈術這個新生的氣象還沒有下去，并且影響越來越大。譬如天主教基督教很多也在研究打坐，都是受瑜珈術影響。瑜珈術也有打坐，也有禪定，所以禪定是共法，學過佛法的要知道，不要自己閉門稱王。

瑜珈術後來演變又進入佛家，與密宗在修法上合在一起，講三脈七輪。根據奇經八脈的說法，我們人體是立體完整的，就是沖脈（衝脈）、任脈、督脈、帶脈、陰蹻、陽蹻、陰維、陽維這八個大方向。瑜珈術沒有管奇經八脈，它將人體從中間剖下來，垂直平行的有三個脈，下面到上面

有七輪是七個部位。學密宗的人一定碰到這個問題，正式學密宗不是光唸咒子、灌頂一下，這些不算數啊！正式講到密宗的修持大法，不管紅教白教任何一教，非以這個三脈七輪為中心不可。所以在修法上，就是先修氣，後修脈，再修明點拙火，等於中國道家講煉丹。這樣修下去，這個色身才會成就。

三脈是中脈、左脈、右脈。七輪是海底、肚臍、心輪（心窩處）、喉輪（女性不明顯，男性有喉核）。喉輪在道家叫做生死玄關，我們摸摸喉骨，是兩個扣住的，修成了會打開，內部就打通了。所以有些人講氣脈通了，只要在前面一站，連我這個外行大致看看，就知道生死玄關打通了沒有。如果打通了，儘管有這個骨頭在，它的形象是兩樣的。喉輪上來是眉間輪、頂輪，外面還有梵穴輪，一共七個部份，但是中脈是最嚴重的。

有一派學密宗的人，攻擊中國的道家是外道，只有密宗才是正的。我這個人素來喜歡打抱不平，當著西醫我就說中醫好，當著中醫我說西醫對；當著密宗我說道家比你們高明，當著道家說密宗比你們完整。所以我

一輩子四方八面都挨罵，反正不討好。我覺得偏見很可怕，因為各家有各家的道理，是你沒有融會貫通。這個三脈七輪是以中脈為主，有的學密宗的，認為中國奇經八脈沒有中脈；我說奇經八脈有中脈，中脈在《黃帝內經》叫衝脈，內經上這個「衝」，實際上也就是這個「沖」。

瑜珈密宗所講的中脈是由海底起，通頭頂梵穴輪，打通了就和宇宙相通，等於莊子的話：「與天地精神相往來」。很多人，不論學佛學道的，都認為自己的中脈已經通了，這是不能開玩笑隨便說的，現在我先把學理根據告訴諸位。我必須要先聲明，我沒有通哦！真正脈輪通一節一節通了，這是一定有一節一節的象徵，有一節一節的作用。脈輪通了他本身的神通智慧一定俱備，那不是開玩笑的。你身上發脹了，不要自認為氣脈通了，這是個科學，不是憑你自己的想像。

我常常問人，氣脈通了轉河車，要轉到什麼程度為止？他就不曉得必須要轉到「日月合璧，璇璣停輪」，最後沒有身體的感覺，身體好像融化了。融化了就不談氣脈，沒有氣脈問題了，所以最起碼要能忘身，忘掉身了。

體。前天幾個老朋友做新鞋子穿，我也陪他們做了一雙羅漢鞋，大家穿起來腳痛。我說慢慢來，鞋子穿到舊了才會舒服。莊子有一句話：「忘足，履之適也」，穿鞋子忘記了自己有腳，那是鞋子穿得最舒服的時候。可是這時候鞋子也快要破了，新鞋子固然值錢，穿下去忘不掉腳啊！就是不舒服。

同樣道理，我們打坐還覺得有身體在，還有氣脈的感覺，就說奇經八脈都在通啊！放光動地啊！證明你還沒有忘身。就算是你忘掉了身體，還只是初步，這個肉身還沒有脫胎換骨。能脫胎換骨變化了以後，就算是老人的身體，也會骨節柔軟得像嬰兒。有些學密的人，不承認督脈與中脈的關係，但是瑜珈術不同，瑜珈術認為中脈在背脊骨這個骨髓的中心，細如牛毛，講得有形有象。真正脈輪通了的人，不要閉眼，自己身體內部都看得清清楚楚。那叫做「內照形軀」，也叫「內視」。「內視」就是反轉來看自己，透視自己的血液流動，以及內部各個地方，都看得清楚。

神光落地的人

中國講修道還有一個名稱：「長生久視之道」，所以這幾年我叫你們趕快修「白骨觀」，釋迦牟尼佛傳的這個密法有很大的深義證驗。我們一般人，年紀大了眼神神光落地，所以魂魄就向下走了，這並不是說神仙墮落了。因此我們附帶講到禪宗，禪宗的法門素來不談工夫，因為談工夫就不是禪宗了。可是禪宗處處是工夫，譬如說雲門祖師講，「我有一寶，秘在形山」，又譬如臨濟祖師說，「人人有一無位真人，天天從面門出入」，這些都是在講工夫，可是一般人不瞭解。

說到眼神，我們提一個公案，與這個是連起來的。宋朝有一位宰相叫張商英，在禪宗裏很有名，他是大徹大悟，在家人成就的，臨死的時候威風凜凜，真了不起。他苦讀出身，考取狀元，開始是反對佛的。他的太太是富人家的女兒，喜歡研究佛，學問也很好。他看到太太讀的佛經就很生氣，因為古代佛經所謂「裝潢嚴麗」，裝訂的非常好，用布包起來。他對

太太說，我們聖人孔子的四書五經就馬馬虎虎，那個外國人釋迦牟尼，他的書卻包得那麼好！他氣不過，要想寫一篇無佛論來反佛。太太說相公啊！既然沒有佛，又何必論他呢？他聽了就把筆放下了，對呀！這一棒打得很厲害，所以會當太太的用不著跟丈夫吵架。有一天他太太在看《維摩詰經》，他跑到後面看看，這個太太就抓到機會說，相公，你也看看人家講些什麼嘛。他一看就放不下來啦，從此信佛修道了。

與前面有關的是唐朝一位儒家的李翱，韓愈的弟子，寫過一篇《復性書》，講心性之學大大有名。李翱最初也是跟著老師反對佛的，他後來被派到湖南當太守，就是湖南省長。他聽到有位禪宗祖師叫藥山禪師，名氣很大，所以就去看他。唐朝的太守比現在的省長權大多了，有生殺之權，是一方的諸侯。他到了山上廟子裏，這位老和尚坐在太陽下面看佛經，太守站在後面，老和尚頭都不回，故意不理。李翱個性很急躁，站了半天看他頭都不回很生氣，拂袖而去，講了一句話：「見面不如聞名」。等於我們現在人講「久聞大名，如雷貫耳，今日一見，不過如此。」

這時老和尚回頭對他說話了，太守啊！你何必「貴耳而賤目」呢？老和尚反擊他一下，太守你何必把你的耳朵看得這麼寶貴，看不起你的眼睛呢？這個李翱一聽，吃驚了，趕緊回頭請教，談了很多，就向他求道。藥山禪師沒有講話，手向上面一指，下面一指，就完了。李翱不懂，只好問了，師父啊！這個不懂，你明白告訴我好不好？藥山禪師就講：「雲在青天水在瓶」。看起來一個文學句子，這個裏頭就是工夫境界了。

藥山禪師講了這句話，李翱就懂了，當時就寫了悟道的偈子…

我來問道無餘話　　雲在青天水在瓶

鍊得身形似鶴形　　千株松下兩函經

我來問道無餘話

鍊得身形似鶴形

「鍊得身形似鶴形」，由這句詩瞭解藥山禪師人很高很瘦，是脫胎換骨了。「千株松下兩函經」，松樹下面擺了經書在那兒看，好一幅畫面！「我來問道無餘話」，藥山禪師指上又指下，因為李翱不懂，師父只好在文學方面引導他，「雲在青天水在瓶」。我們大家不要給他騙了！藥山禪

師真的只講這個意思嗎？不完全是這個意思，「雲在青天水在瓶」，差不多，還不是那個道。

李翱認為自己悟道了，所以寫了這首詩給師父，然後問藥山，師父啊，假使悟到這個程度，後面還有事沒有？後面還有工夫沒有？然後藥山禪師又吩咐李翱兩句話，是說下山以後如何修持：「高高山頂立，深深海底行。」後世道家認為人身這個海底，究竟是不是禪宗祖師講的這個海底呢？這是個大問號。禪宗不給你說明，非要你參不可，所謂要自證自肯，那是靠悟得到的，不然沒得力量。以普通的道理來講，「高高山頂立，深深海底行」就是儒家中庸所講的「極高明而道中庸」。見處要高，可是工夫要踏實，要從作人做起，從戒定慧基本做起。這兩句話同後世的道家，佛家密宗、顯教做工夫有密切的關係，諸位可以自己去研究。引用王陽明的一句詩，「道是無關卻有關」，你說是不相關嗎？有相關；你說有相關嘛，不一定相關。藥山禪師又告訴李翱：「閨閣中物捨不得便為滲漏」。換一句話說，男女情欲這一關不過，永遠不成功。等於《楞嚴經》上說，

淫根不除要想得道，是像蒸沙成飯一樣不可能。

相隔差不多兩百年左右，宋朝的張商英悟道了以後，看禪宗的書看到這一段，認為李翱沒有大悟，沒有得道，所以他寫了一首偈子：

雲在青天水在瓶　　眼光隨指落深坑

溪花不耐風霜苦　　說甚深深海底行

我們講了半天就是為了引用這一句話，所以費了很多時間。「眼光隨指」，眼光跟著指頭「落深坑」，落在深深的坑裏頭，落下地獄去了。張商英的詩很高明，批評李翱沒有證道。「雲在青天水在瓶」，一般人把這個境界當成與氣脈通相等，有人打坐學佛到達這個境界，念頭空了，「萬里青天無片雲」，想永遠定下去，以為對了。張商英認為這真是笑話，是「眼光隨指落深坑」。

人要死的時候是眼光落地的，因為神散了。修道要神凝氣聚，如果神凝不住，氣就散了，所以「眼光隨指落深坑」，可見神凝不住收不住了。

自己神不凝氣不住，道沒有修成功，就沒有辦法出來弘道。所以我經常說修道容易成道難，成道容易行道難，行道容易弘道更難。所以張商英說「溪花不耐風霜苦」，你經不起那個魔障，像百花碰到秋冬天氣，生命就萎縮下去了，你有什麼資格說深深海底行！

氣脈真通和假通

關於這個氣脈的通暢，三脈七輪如何打開，七輪打開以後就是中脈通了，密宗認為中脈通了是第一步成功，不算是道哦！今天就是給你小周天、大周天、奇經八脈、三脈七輪都搞通了，也不算道，這只是助道品的初步，才有個基礎而已。換一句話說，學禪學佛的人這樣才可以進一步談禪定了。不然你定不了，你身體的障礙化不掉，不能脫胎換骨。所以「溪花不耐風霜苦」，你有什麼資格「說甚深深海底行」！

很多人在感覺上通了，認為氣脈真通了，到時間不打坐就難過，然後講這是工夫來找我，說得神乎其神。真是可憐，因為你那是個病態啊！你

身體不能輕靈，始終被身體感覺狀態困住，到那個時候有週期性的難過一來，你非要坐一下不可。你不能夠意念一定，神凝氣聚就把它化掉！你做不到，這叫做工夫嗎？這不是自欺欺人嗎？所以我說這個叫做凡氣通，只是身體的感受而已。

昨天還有一個朋友講身上的氣自己轉起來，這是氣脈，不過非常粗淺。我們如果把它歸類，這是道家講氣脈之道的導引工夫。導引工夫發展下來的有五禽戲，後來的八段錦，乃至各種內功氣功的修煉，還有我經常講的天台宗。天台宗是中國正統的佛家，是隋朝智者大師在浙江天台山創宗立派，山內山外之學。山外就是在家居士們也可以學的，修止觀法門，六妙門及呼呵噓等六字訣。慢慢發展下來的氣功有三十六步的工夫，流到日本還保存了一部份。我認為這一類的氣功都屬於導引。導引也是幫助修道的基本鍛練，先把身體鍛練到健康無病，再來下手修道。否則修道工夫是為治病在做，求祛病延年而已。

現在一般把這個感覺轉來轉去叫做小周天，把人體前後的任督脈配

十二辟卦，一陽來復的復卦，從後面督脈到頂是乾卦，前面下來配到坤卦，認為是小周天，這個還勉強可以。但是我們要千萬記住，根據十二辟卦，五天為一候，三候為一氣，每個月十五晚上，圓滿的月亮從東邊上來，這叫「中氣」，十二節氣這裏叫中氣圓滿。六候為一節，節是階段，越過另外一個階段，所以一個月叫小周天。在身體上那麼轉，因此有所謂「進陽火，退陰符」的說法，這是元朝明朝以後的講法，是身體修道的解釋法，我沒有下結論說對不對，如果真正瞭解了這一面也可以。退一步來講，你們同學打坐，有時候精神很健旺，今天坐得很好，境界很好，心境很清明。沒有念頭，心情又愉快，可以說是陽火充沛，下一步一定大昏沉，要想睡覺了。那個昏沉也不錯，那是退陰符，悶極了以後陽能又起來了。陰陽謂之道，有正面也有反面。所以我叫大家記住這句名言：「日出沒，比精神之衰旺；月盈虧，比氣血之盛衰」，可是這還只是講到後天小周天的道理。

第十七講

伍柳派的大小周天

我們討論到一般道家流行的所謂小周天、大周天這些觀念，普通認為小周天就是以我們這個身體為準，所謂前三關、後三關，甚至打通任督二脈轉一圈，這個叫做一周天。特別注重提倡這個說法的是元明以來，道家有所謂伍柳派；伍沖虛是老師，柳華陽是弟子。伍沖虛的著作《金仙證論》，柳華陽的《慧命經》，都是很有名的著作。伍柳派是過去道家最流行的一個支派，講神仙之道、修煉長生不老之道。事實上，《慧命經》和《金仙證論》是引用佛道儒三家合一的。中國文化幾千年來有個大重點，從南北朝以後，所謂三教合一，到現在還在爭論中，也沒有統一過，但是也沒有分化過。這兩本著作，反映了中國文化特點，就是經常引用佛經、儒家、《易經》、老莊等等。不過有一點，所引用佛經的觀念都錯了，而

且所引用的所謂《楞嚴經》的話，卻是根本沒有的。

所以在學術上，許多道家的書，不能使人引起興趣，不能生起信心，因為他們經常靠執筆扶鸞的東西來引證。扶鸞是扶鸞，扶乩是扶乩，所以真正一講學術，伍柳派的立場就垮了，因為無所根據。《參同契》不同，那是有所根據的，不管修道與否，其學術價值始終是留傳萬古的。清末民初的印光法師，是佛教四大老之一，本是儒家秀才出身，後來學佛，專門提倡淨土，是這一代淨土宗的祖師。印光法師對伍柳派的這些修持方法罵得很厲害，經常罵他們是魔子魔孫。這一點我覺得老法師言之太過了，不免還有一些宗教情緒在裏面，欠缺一點客觀。實際上伍柳派這些著作，印光法師大概沒有完全研究，假使深入一點，還是會敬佩他們的。

伍柳派是絕對禁男女之欲。所謂漏丹不漏丹，這個名稱你們注意，我看有些同學們寫筆記寫成「落丹不落丹」，不是落，是漏掉的漏。這些都是從伍柳派以後成為道家的觀念術語，佛家也照樣用。伍柳派認為男女破身了，或者男性有其他的猥褻的行為，當然犯戒，修道不能成功，就是有

遺精也不行。等於《楞嚴經》上說的，淫根不除，要想得到真正的禪定，如蒸沙成飯，意思是說，修道也是白修。

伍柳這一派修法講大小周天道理，是強調了不漏。它的工夫也強調從這裏起手，所以注重在「一陽來復」，就是生理上氣機發動的時候，也就是陽氣發動的時候，開始下手修，一直修到斷欲，才能打穩基礎。伍柳派認為，男女之間一百天不漏，這是以身體來講，叫「百日築基」。一百天不漏丹，差不多普通人也能做到，二三百天不漏丹的也有，這個裏頭是另外的問題。能永遠繼續達到色身絕對不漏，當然先要「煉精化氣」，才有後來「十月懷胎」的修煉。懷胎是根據道家的話，就是張三丰祖師在《無根樹》上提到，「男子懷胎笑煞人」。他們認為，男人有懷胎的現象，當然不是中年發福肚子大起來，是從入定生出了身外之身。道書上畫的頭頂上一個小嬰兒出來，一般人看了都是想像在打坐時，頭頂上出來一個我，叫做出陰神。伍柳派並不一定是這樣講法，不過那些道書上，下手畫時觀念已經錯了，所以會引出來這些誤解。

「十月懷胎，三年哺乳」，一個嬰兒養大要三年哺乳，然後「九年面壁」，這麼一算，由一個普通人開始修道，修成神仙要十二三年時間。我經常算算這個賬，你看我們六歲開始讀小學，十六年辛苦讀到大學畢業，然後可憐兮兮的找老輩寫封介紹信，拿個履歷找工作，頭都碰破了不過只拿幾千塊，除了房租吃飯以外，大概買兩件衣服剛好夠用，如此而已。算算這個賬，十二年的辛苦可以做神仙，太划得來！但是幾人能夠做得到？伍柳派這些書都很容易買到，現在有些地方把這些道書叫做《伍柳仙宗》，不叫做道家，稱為仙學。這也可以，反正巧立名目無所謂的，等於現在大學學科分得很多一樣。

伍柳派的小周天修法，有一個名稱叫做轉河車，在道書上就叫做河車運轉。大家都知道這是道家的修法，可是講句老實話，過去我在大陸上訪問很多的和尚，都是很有工夫的，深入一談發現，原來修的是道家的這個法子。可見在文化思想來講，伍柳派的修法非常普遍，各宗各派都是走這個路線。究竟這個小周天是不是這樣？我們真正研究正統道家之學的人就

要特別留意。有許多學佛的認為，這是道家跟我不相干。你不要糊塗了，我常說不管佛道、顯密，修行就靠一個工具。這個工具就是身體，這個心。這個生理身體和這個心，不會有別的花樣出來，它出來的現象是相同的，只是各家的解釋不同。

河車 周天 導引

許多人因為自己學佛就批駁了道家，有人因為修道家就看不起佛家，實際上是蠻可憐的。這又提到一件故事，差不多一九五○年前後，我認識一位朋友也是老鄉，他還年輕修道家的，佛也懂，自己認為有神通了、也悟了道，各種花樣多得很，玩了幾十年。我講這個人很可憐，將來會神經的。結果我的話又不幸而言中，去年果然大發神經，進了醫院，然後是上不見佛，下不見眾生，一切都罵完了，只有他對，結果還是神經而死，很痛苦的。他「得少為足，閉門稱王」，走上一個悲慘的結果。我跟朋友講，他儘管走錯了路，總是一個個修道人，就請同學們法師們給他唸了《地

藏經》，依俗禮盡心。

為什麼提這個故事呢？根據佛家的道理，叫做「發露懺悔」，寧可當著大眾說明，這就是見解不正確的可憐之處。學佛修道的人，陷入這樣歧路的為數不少，所以我們看了幾十年，不要說真的成仙成佛，就連能生死之間來去很自在的都很少。由此就可以瞭解古人說：「修道者如牛毛，成道者如麟角」的道理。

我們上次提出來真正小周天的道理，我是提供給諸位參考，我這個人光研究書本的，沒有工夫也沒有道，同諸位一樣，白髮蒼蒼、兩眼昏花、行將就木，靠不住的。現在根據學理告訴大家不要走錯了路，所謂小周天是一個月，以月亮的出沒為一個標準，用這個來比精神之衰旺，氣血之盈虧等等。這個標準要記住。

所以我們打起坐來，身體感覺背上通了，走到那一關了，這樣轉一圈叫轉河車小周天，沒有錯。所謂沒有錯，是因為人體血液流行的法則是這樣轉法，所以說沒有錯。可是我們把打坐做工夫的身體的感受，由背部轉

到前面又轉回到背部，然後加上意識，那只是用意念把它引下來而轉。在道家這是最粗淺的辦法，後來屬於內功練武功的，叫導引，就是拿意識去引導，引出來這個感覺的境界。道家的方法，導引屬於運動方面，所以華陀的五禽圖，後來的八段錦，乃至於瑜珈術等等，都是導引的工夫，都是由意識去導引。真正的道法、修道不是這樣。

如果在身體導引周流就叫做小周天，那麼我曾經問，這個小周天要轉到哪一天為止？這個轉轉轉，晝夜給你轉，一天轉個三百六十圈，你轉了幾十年，去檢查身體，骨頭還是老化的骨頭，神經還是老化的神經，並沒有改變，請問這個轉動有沒有作用？

導引的工夫對健康方面不能說沒有作用，是有袪病延年作用的。這個作用的道理在哪裏呢？不是修道工夫了不起，是因為我們人體有兩個作用，一個是外在的運動，一個是本身內在的運動，所以靜坐不加導引，它本身也在運動。氣血流行順著那個規律自己在流行，這是個運動，所謂「靜中之動」。因運動之故，慢慢身體當然健康，這是一個很簡單的道

理。譬如一個人生病了，感冒也好，重病也好，就需要睡覺休息，人得到充分的睡覺休息後，思想靜下來，氣血的流行就會順自然的法則走上軌道，所以能夠祛病，能夠延年。並不是說打坐或者修道有特殊的功效，因為人在靜態中時，健康的恢復乃至進步是當然的。生命有一種本能的活動，所以我們人病病來了，就要睡眠休息，以恢愎這個本能活動。所謂靜坐就是效法本能活動。常在靜態中則本能活動永遠在規律地轉，轉到一定時間，它要爆發了，爆發出另一種本能活動的作用。那個是有形的「真陽之氣」，是在生理現象上爆發的，那還不是無形之氣。

河車不轉又如何

真正的修道，這個所謂河車轉動，或者把人體當做一個小周天這麼轉，轉到不轉為止。什麼時候不轉呢？那就不簡單了，氣住脈停就是不轉，呼吸自然停止，脈搏及心跳寧靜下來，變得很緩慢，很久才跳一下。這不是心臟病，這是氣住脈停，自己都可以測驗。在道書上就叫做「日月

合璧，璇璣停輪」。「日月合璧」是指太陽月亮同時出現。

上次我給大家報告過，曾在昆明看到過這個現象，後來曉得中國西南一帶「日月合璧」是經常見到的。「璇璣停輪」就是當天體上北斗七星好像不轉動了，寧靜了，到這個境界差不多了。嚴格說我們修道，在我個人的看法──當然我的看法不一定對──修道到這個樣子的話，是「築基」成功。這個時候當然不漏丹了，這才算築基成功，還不能說是「結丹」，只算初步而已。那麼要多少時間築基成功？這個不一定，也許有人一上來就到達這個境界，也許三五天、六七天，也許修幾十年都到不了，這個中間有很多的問題。再說，這樣只是築基成功，是不是小周天呢？只是小周天的法則之一。

我們到達了所謂「日月合璧，璇璣停輪」，以佛家來講氣住脈停了，差不多到第三、四禪這個程度。這時我們就要提出一個問題，氣住脈停，永遠停在那裏嗎？這樣就叫神仙成功了嗎？我們的答案是否定的。剛才告訴大家，這樣只能夠算是築基成功，氣住脈停到相當的時間就是入定了。

這個假使叫入定，靜極必定會動。所以這個氣住脈停是陰極的境界，拿《易經》來講是坤卦的境界。如果在座有研究過《周易》的，翻開看一下坤卦上六的爻辭：「龍戰於野，其血玄黃」。陽數最高是九，陰數最高是六，陰到極點的坤卦，最上的一爻就叫上六。

什麼是玄？下面注解「天玄而地黃」，天是青蒼色，青色的。文學境界形容像漢魏時代的詩：「天蒼蒼，野茫茫，風吹草低見牛羊」，那是天玄，是塞外草原這個青天。我們家鄉那邊，晚上叫「玄黃」，就是黃昏的意思。詩人王之渙的句子：「白日依山盡，黃河入海流」，為什麼不講紅日依山盡呢？所以叫同學們注意，這是一個物理現象。早晨的朝陽是紅日，旭日初昇；快要落山時，太陽就白了，一點火力都沒有，所以「白日依山盡」。小時候唸書看古人句子，都另外做研究。例如李白的「床前明月光，疑是地上霜，舉頭望明月，低頭思故鄉」，我們就問問題了，這是李白初幾作的？而且他在房間坐在哪個位置？

「白日依山盡」是黃昏、玄黃。玄黃是陰極境界，在這個境界靜久

了，血液開始變了。用《易經》的辭句，血液要變橙黃色了。身體上氣機流行轉動的感覺，說是小周天，也可以承認是對的，因為氣機流行的法則有規律的，同小周天流行一樣。但是真正的道家所謂的小周天，是月亮的行度景象，是以地平面為準而看到的現象，跟現代天文學沒有衝突。天文學所講的是數，也是整個天體的運行。

築基成功了

所謂小周天是月亮之出沒，就是我們修到身體氣脈一部份一部份轉通了。轉通了以後，到達什麼程度呢？像十五的月亮一樣明，而且晝夜長明。工夫到這裏，當然所謂奇經八脈通了，不再有身體的感受，身體不是障礙了。譬如我們坐在這裏身體有感受，吃飽了知道飽，餓了知道餓，腰靠著東西覺得有個腰。到那一步以後，自己身體好像空靈了，沒有感覺，自己覺得這個身體像一片樹葉在虛空中飄一樣，晝夜長明，永遠是十五的月亮。不像我們打坐有時候昏沉了，坐到不昏沉時，精神剛剛來了，對不

實沒有睡著，自己覺得是休息一下，始終沒有睡著，可是這個肉體已經得

心一切都自然來了，不管打坐還是睡倒都一樣。而且夜睡無夢，好像睡其

話說的「晝夜長明，六根大定」。這時頭腦之清醒，智慧之開發，不必用

就是道家術語所謂：「精滿不思淫、氣滿不思食、神滿不思睡」。也是俗

他的意念就可以發動身心內外絕妙的快樂，人世間的欲自然就沒有了。也

「樂變化天」，到這個時候無所謂戒了，因為他本身「內觸妙樂」，

佛經其實把工夫都講完了，可惜一般人看不懂。

這是《楞嚴經》上說「於橫陳時味同嚼蠟」的境界，所謂「樂變化天」。

本身的快樂取代了欲界的男女之樂，看到男女之樂很低級，不值一顧了。

睡覺了；也用不著戒律了，也無所謂禁欲了，因為沒有欲了。為什麼？他

明，永遠身心清明的狀態。這時頭腦越來越清楚，不再睡覺，因為不需要

服，在樂感中；每個指頭、每個細胞，全身到頭頂都在快感中，是晝夜長

奇經八脈通了就不一樣，什麼腿麻不麻，不會麻的，一身都是快樂舒

起，兩腿發麻，只好下座了。自己說，也打過坐了，做過工夫了。

到了休息。

這樣是小周天的初步，假定氣住脈停叫築基——我是假定的，我不是神仙——接著下一步你會嚇住了，進入一個大定，什麼都不知道了，好像大昏沉。定多久也不知道，時間空間都忘了。這樣就像是月亮東升到圓滿，乃至到廿八，一點光都沒有。為什麼如此呢？這是自然的法則。因此大家學佛修道打坐有許多問題，其實都不是問題。許多年輕同學常講，老師，我這幾天睡不著。睡不著就睡不著！一天當兩天用，還划不來嗎！我們一輩子假使活六十年，三十年都在床上。如果三十年不睡覺，等於活了一百二十年，睡不著更好。

又有些人說，老師，我這兩天光愛睡。光愛睡讓它睡，我覺得睡是人生最享受的事，我也最愛睡，可惜我沒有時間睡，很可憐。我常常覺得「一被蒙頭萬事丟」，把被子拿來一蓋的時候，不空而空，不放下而放下，這是我詩裏的句子。所以我常常告訴同學們，碰到最困難痛苦的時候，睡覺去，睡醒了再說，有時候事情是會轉過來的。陰極又陽生，這就

是晝夜的現象，也就是一個月的現象，所以月的行度謂之小周天。

大周天不同了，伍柳派的道家把這個前後轉叫做小周天，幾十年來我也常常考驗人，大周天在哪裏？有些答道，大周天左右轉。如果就在肉體裏頭打轉，轉了半天，還是在肉體內，還是沒有修煉好。妄想了幾十年想成仙，結果就像是胡大川的幻想詩最後一句：「一念回腔子裏，依然瘦骨倚繩床」。這一念回頭並不是岸，依然還是一把瘦骨頭靠在床上，什麼道都沒有修成。因為我是個瘦骨，所以我常常想到這個詩。

第十八講

干支陰陽與方位

提到中國文化，有一套是屬於陰陽家之學，併在《易經》的學問裏頭，所以天干地支都要弄清楚。這張簡單的十二辟卦圖表很有用，外面第三圈，只有地支，天干沒有記上去。你把這個圓圈劃上去，簡單東南西北劃一個十字，定一下方位。諸位把冬至找到，「冬至一陽生」，冬至是子月，亥子丑是十月、十一月、十二月在北方。寅卯辰是一月、二月、三月在東方。巳午未是四、五、六月在南方。申酉戌是七、八、九月在西方。東方甲乙木，南方丙丁火，西方庚辛金，北方壬癸水，中央戊己土。剛剛提到的原文「故推消息，坎離沒亡」，坎卦在天體代表是月亮，離卦代表太陽。坎卦在人體代表精血，離卦代表神、氣。再回轉來說到有形的，坎卦代表腎、耳朵，離卦代表心

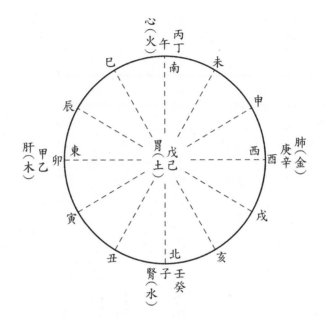

臟、眼睛。我們現在用的名辭是代表，這就是中國陰陽家所謂配卦。

現在看原文，「坎戊月精」，坎卦代表月亮的精華，卦中間一陽屬於戊。「離己日光」，離卦代表太陽，卦中一陰爻屬於己土。戊己兩個都是土，大家先要瞭解干支陰陽：

甲乙丙丁戊己庚辛壬癸，是天干。甲乙木，丙丁火，庚辛金，壬癸水，戊己土。古書上說甲木是陽木，乙木是陰木。甲木是木沒有成形的那個元素，乙木是成

形了的木頭。一個是有形的，一個是無形的。丙丁也是這樣，丙火是火之氣、火之源、火之能，是功能的能。丁火是有形的火。這裏頭陰陽家學問就很大，這是中國古代的科學。

譬如火，我們電燈的火究竟是陽火還是陰火？太陽熱能是陽火沒有問題，木材燒的火是陽火，瓦斯這個火是陰火。有一種電是陽火，有一種電是陰火，其中作用絕對不同。所以我們把瓦斯開了用手去感覺，是冰的，陽火陰火差別就很多。地支也是這樣，子丑寅卯辰巳午未申酉戌亥，這個北方亥子是水，東方寅卯是木，南方巳午是火，西方申酉是金，辰戌丑未這四個是土。

《參同契》這個地方沒有講地支，讀書就要另有眼睛了，這一段先講天干。「坎戊」代表了月亮，「離己」代表太陽。為什麼這樣配呢？我們修道做工夫就要瞭解，修道的話，日月兩個最重要，戊己這兩個都屬於「中土」，中間的土。所以他下面講「日月為易」，這是他對《易經》的解釋。以我個人的觀點，歷代學者只有魏伯陽《參同契》上這句話，所下

的定義是顛撲不破的。日月叫做易，上面是日，下面是月，就是甲骨文裏面日月的寫法。

「剛柔相當」，我們講《易經》時有陰陽剛柔，尤其孔子在《易經繫傳》中也用到這些。陰陽是物理的兩個代號，也可以說是正反兩個代號；剛柔是物質的兩個代號。物質沒有形成以前可以拿陰陽來代表，成形之後就叫剛柔；形而上叫乾坤，形而下變成天體就是坎離，就是日月。「日月為易，剛柔相當」，怎麼叫「相當」？是相對的意思，門當戶對，各有它應該的位置、應該的立場、應該的份量、應該的價值，這就是剛柔彼此相當。月亮跟太陽各有為主的時候，夜裏月亮做主，白天太陽做主。如果夜裏出太陽，白天出月亮，就天翻地覆了，不相當。

四象五行皆藉土

「土王四季」，中央戊己土，春夏秋冬都靠土，土也代表胃。你們學算命卜卦，還有學中醫針灸的，要特別注意這個問題。有關胃的穴道常常

針灸一下，把握這個「土王四季」，因為胃氣是與很多病有關聯的。譬如感冒，凡是感冒一定胃氣不好。胃氣不好不是講胃潰瘍或發炎，而是胃氣衰弱、寒了。所以你治感冒要隨時照顧胃，胃健康了感冒自然容易好。換句話說，胃衰弱了，感冒容易來。光治感冒不治胃，效果很差，你們學醫的可以試試我的老土辦法。

「羅絡始終」，「羅」就是周圍這一圈，「絡」就是脈絡，蜘蛛網一樣把它連起來，始終離不開「土」。所以道家乃至陰陽家，看風水算命以及學醫的，有兩句老話要記住：「四象五行皆藉土，九宮八卦不離壬」。道理是什麼？我們拿哲學的立場來講，土是地球，人類文化是離不開地球的，在佛學就是「欲界」眾生的文化是以地球為中心。宋元以後中醫分四大派別，北方的主張「四象五行皆藉土」，胃最重要，「胃土」健康了，百病就去了。所以北方一派，任何病都要先照顧這個胃。

南方一派反對。清朝以來，南方一派都出名醫的，他們主張凡是有病的人都是腎虛，要先補腎水，也就是「九宮八卦不離壬」的原則。把壬水

補足了，病就好了，事實上兩派都對。「青赤黑白，各居一方」，顏色代表方位，北方是黑，腎是黑；西方是白，肺是白的；南方是赤，心臟是赤；青是東方，肝是青，這就是「青赤黑白各據一方」的道理。南方北方飲食不同，氣候不同，土質不同。北方人大碗吃麵，包子饅頭大口吃，腸胃容易吃壞。所以北方「皆秉中宮，戊己之功」，胃很重要，夏天以泄為主，把腸胃清理。但是北方人到南方來，不要隨便給他泄，會泄虛的。南方人有些好吃懶做的，「飽暖思淫慾，饑寒起盜心」，腎虧的多，先補腎為主沒有錯。

　　壬癸水就是精水，老年人壬癸水沒有了，嘴巴張著看東西，實際上他嘴裏發乾沒有口水，早上起來發苦。所以道家說「玉液還丹」，打起坐來嘴裏的口水叫你直接嚥，這個才是「玉液還丹」，不是「津液還丹」。打坐坐得好，口水清涼發甘，有時候還帶檀香味，這個才是「玉液還丹」，久了以後，皮膚骨節都會變的。

顏色的作用

這裏順便告訴大家中國文化講顏色的作用，現在西醫也研究了，過去是絕對反對，認為沒有道理。現在曉得蔬菜的顏色，對人體營養都有關係。譬如我們過去講赤豆(紅豆)，大家發腳氣病，心臟不好可以吃，因為赤色入心。綠豆利水，青色入肝膽，黑色的入腎，白色的入肺。所以五色、五味同人體都有關係。過去中醫鑑別新鮮的生藥，乾的不算，生藥的葉子，有幾枝有幾個杈，開什麼花，就可以斷定這個藥對人體有什麼作用。這不是玄學，譬如中央「戊己土」是黃色，胃是黃的。有個藥叫「雞內金」，就是雞胃裏面黃色那一層，磨成粉是幫助消化的，胃的功能就在那一層。

有許多看風水陰陽的，以及搞密宗的都在玩這一套。我是無以名之，這些都是自欺欺人。一白二黑三碧四綠五黃，六白七赤八白九紫。他用來算這個方位，什麼方向好，什麼時間好，哪個座位不好，這個月在這個方

位，下個月在那個方位，搬來搬去，這些我全懂，但是我全不管。不好的方向我來坐，看它怎麼樣。我坐沒事，你們一坐就有事，因為你們自己怕了。見怪不怪其怪自敗，我就一正到底，當然有時拉肚子，有時多吃一點，人啊！隨時都會碰到好的事不好的事，你以什麼為標準啊？不要迷信！但是說迷信又不是迷信，它是科學，要善於應用。

因此古人講：「善於易者不卜」，真學通了《易經》是不算命不看相的。為什麼要看相算命呢？「有疑則卜，不疑不卜」，過去有句老話，心思不定看相算命。既然來看相算命就是心裏有懷疑，你怎麼說都靈。那些心思定的人，你拉他看相他也不看，忙得很，哪有時間搞這些！可是話說回來，這一套是科學，善於運用可以成道，不善於運用通通是迷信。我沒有做結論，結論諸位自己去做吧。

現在是介紹到「青赤黑白，各居一方。皆秉中宮，戊己之功」。青赤黑白都要靠中宮「戊己之功」。在身體內部，戊己就是胃，脾胃不是腸子，腸子不屬於戊己。辰戌丑未四個都是土，腸子是未土，是另外一條路子，腸子不屬於戊己。

向下走。

道家講「中宮」是心窩子以下。男女老幼最好守中宮，這樣至少胃健康，守竅不如守中宮，這個我倒同意。你們守上竅下竅，問題多得很，修道到最後，還是靠這個中宮起作用。修到中宮充滿了的人，可以不吃飯了，就是道家說的「氣滿不思食」。當然不要故意餓，有兩個同學這兩天不吃飯，我警告他，你弄到胃出血開刀我不負責。這不是玩的，要中宮氣充滿才可以不吃。你說我吃不下，這是病，能夠一個人吃得完一桌酒席，或者可以不吃，這個叫不吃。你說我吃下去不舒服，也是胃病，不叫工夫到。所以真正工夫到了，一桌菜飯可以吃完，胃口大沒有問題，不過吃下去打坐會昏沉想睡覺，要花半天幫助消化。不吃的話也可以個把禮拜不吃，這個才是工夫。

訪道青城後山

我講個真實的故事給你們聽。我們當年訪道，比你們時下青年可憐多

了。我從十二歲起，不曉得拜了多少老師，那真叫訪道。有些地方要爬山，還要帶著錢，拜老師要錢，至少要買禮物。當年在四川灌縣青城山有個周神仙，是非常有名的劍仙。我們年輕哪分得出真的假的！加上幻想，假的都當成真的了。我有個四川和尚朋友聖明法師，跟他是方外之交，他是帶著媽媽出家的。我就邀他陪我上青城山，非要把周神仙找到不可。

灌縣離成都有一百二十里路之遠，我們兩個人路上花一天，到了青城山的上清宮，向當家的老道士打聽，得知周神仙住在後山。後山有土匪，有老虎，他勸我們晚上不要去，現在只剩一個多鐘頭天就黑了，山路又險很難走。我跟和尚說，訪道要有誠心，給老虎吃了都應該，我那時候也傻得很。我們在廟子上買了火把，老虎怕火的，走到半路天全黑了，我看這個和尚快要「一佛出世，二佛涅槃」，臉色有點變了。我說不要怕，老虎來了我在前頭，現在我們有進無退，你會念咒子，大悲咒什麼咒都拿來念，我來打火把。這樣走著看到前面山上有一點燈光，我跟和尚就叫，周神仙啊！出來救人啊！徒弟在這裏！

一陣亂叫，結果把神仙的徒弟叫出來了，是個道士提著燈籠，盤旋而下。我對他說，我是下江人，千里訪名師，萬里求道法，三步一拜上山來。我江湖術語全都拿出來了，半真半假。他就招呼我們進去，院子很大，真是別有洞天。先讓我們洗腳，再招待我們吃飯。一問周神仙，他說升天了，自己是他最小的徒弟。那請問周神仙這套有傳人嗎？有！他的姑奶奶。

這位姑奶奶叫周二娘，修道的。我們就要求拜這位姑奶奶為老師。我有好幾位女老師，我當年的宗旨你有道我就求，求來了我自己摸索摸索，不對的丟掉，對的就留下來。周二娘一出來先像法官問案子，把我們審問一番。我告訴她我練過劍，沒有碰到名師。她就要我練一套劍給他們看，我也老實不客氣，拿下壁上掛的劍就比一套。她大為欣賞。我說，那些靠不住，我要學的是白光一道。後來送了她一些禮物。晚上住在那裏，到閣樓一看，供了位菩薩看起來就像媽祖。我心裏想中國到處都一樣，道家儒家搞不清楚，再看這位菩薩，非佛非神。那天晚上我對這菩薩就很不恭敬

了，我先叩個頭，然後摸摸她的臉，說塑得蠻漂亮。和尚就說如果給他們看到，這個是犯忌的。

我就託這個和尚下去給小道士打個交情，你們都是本地人，就說我有心求道，一個目的，真正練劍怎麼練？真正青城山的道法是什麼？我說希望她明天早晨傳我道，她要是不傳，我們吃完早飯就下山。他去交涉了半天，回來說這位女師父講看你那麼誠心，是正人君子，明天早上再說。不過拿來一張黃紙，她把秘訣寫在上面，只准你看。我打開一看，畫了兩個圓圈，在那個中間點了一點，旁邊寫了兩句話，「識得青城有大道」，這是恭維我的話，「明也傳來暗也傳」。黃紙寫了這兩句話，叫做神仙傳口訣。我一看叫做「和尚不吃葷，肚子裏有數」，就對和尚說，你看吧！沒有什麼秘訣，我已經懂了，明天吃過早飯就下山。她所講的就是守中宮，道家經常講這術語，這個方法我早就知道，原來如此，害得我夜裏上山還要怕老虎。唉！我常常為了訪道傻事做得多了，不像你們真有福氣，坐在這裏。我當年穿的是草鞋，腳都走破了。

我懂了，道我也得了，她暗也傳了，我也不想學了，因為我看她四十多歲已經發福了。真正有道有工夫是不會發胖的，這是肯定的。筋骨堅強了，肥肉不會這樣鬆垮垮的，我就曉得她沒有工夫。再一看眼神，兩眼無神，差不多了。「明也傳來暗也傳」，早就傳給我了。

第十九講

方伎之學的長生術

　　我們前面講過，用中國文化「金木水火土」五行的道理，說明人體生命的作用。在道家的術語，有兩個重點，一個是藥物，一個是火候。講到藥物，就要追溯到春秋戰國的諸子百家。所謂百家包括了陰陽家以及方伎之學，「方」就是方術，一種方法；「伎」就是現在專家技術，也包括了醫藥。現在所謂的化學、物理這些科學方面的東西，在我們舊的文化都屬於方伎之學。那時候北方的燕齊魯一帶，出了一幫方伎之士，倡言人的肉體生命可以長存。我常說世界上所有各民族的文化，對於生命的希望都寄託在死後，沒有像我們祖先這樣，想辦法使它永生，永遠活下去。這是很難兌現的一張支票。我們常做一個有趣的比喻，每一個宗教好像只管死去的事，都在招攬生意，說不要怕死，死了就會得救，而且聽我的話，到我

開的那個豪華飯店，叫天堂，招待周到，樣樣俱全，而且免費永遠可以住下去。佛教也開了一家，在西方極樂世界，比天堂還要漂亮。回教也開了一家，在月亮出來太陽落下去的地方，也是非常之好。

前兩天看到一份報紙，有位太空人最近皈依了回教，因為他登陸過月球，在月球上聽到一個聲音「嗡…」，他在世界上到處找不到，最近到了回教的教堂去，看到回教徒在那裏做禮拜，「嗡嗡…」就是這個聲音！找到了，因此他皈依了回教。我說他找對了，回教是以月亮星星為標準。宇宙中有三個基本的聲音，佛教的密宗知道，就是「嗡啊吽」這三個基本音，一切咒語都有這個基本音。至於這個音聲的神秘、力量之大，那是說不完的。尤其是「嗡」跟「吽」兩個音，你們讀《濟公傳》，濟顛和尚一邊吃狗肉，一邊喝酒，一邊唸「嗡嘛呢叭咪吽」，後腦一拍，神光就出來了。既不拍前腦也不拍胸口。懂得修道的人，你們沒有研究他為什麼拍後腦？

譬如佛教用「嗡嘛呢叭咪吽」，你們讀《濟公傳》，濟顛和尚一邊吃狗肉，一邊喝酒，一邊唸「嗡嘛呢叭咪吽」，後腦一拍，神光就出來了。既不拍前腦也不拍胸口。懂得修道的人，就曉得這個寫小說的非常內行。基督教禱告完了說「阿門」，回教法師叫

「阿訇」，都有「嗡」，很多聲音都是「嗡」，乃至阿彌陀佛綜合攏來，也是「嗡」！這是音聲瑜珈。我們人體的內部，也有這三個神秘的聲音。

所以有人睡不著覺躺在枕頭上，或者有時候打坐，就發現耳朵裏有這個怪聲音，不是外來的，是人體的內部有的聲音。

道家的看法，我們這個生命，起碼可以活十二萬億年。但是我們為什麼變成那麼短命呢？喜怒哀樂、七情六欲把它消耗了。我們大笑一下，壽命去了十年，對人家恨一下，去了十年、二十年。七情六欲一動就減壽，這個帳一算下來，活個三十年已經了不起了。另外再簡單地算我們的壽命，假定活六十年，一半在睡覺，去了三十年。剩下三十年當中，前面十二歲不懂事去掉了；後來老了有七八年迷迷糊糊的活著；再扣掉三餐飯大小便和生病，一個人活到六十年，真正過日子，不過幾年而已。

所以道家說我們把生命蹧蹋得很厲害，因此這一幫方士專研究恢復生命的功能，永遠活下去，而且永遠是青春。那要怎麼做才辦得到呢？有一本道家的經典，叫做《高上玉皇胎息經》，實際上是方士們的醫書，中間

有句名言：「上藥三品，神與氣精」，說世界上真正的藥只有三樣，就是「精氣神」。道家修煉長生不老之術，第一要認清楚什麼是「上藥」，這個藥是什麼東西。「精氣神」我們都知道，上次提到伍柳派是絕對禁欲的。雖然印光法師非常呵斥伍柳派，我卻是很讚嘆他們的持戒。但是以道家真正的精神之說，把有形的精血認為是生命的這個精，也是錯誤的。

我們修道要認識什麼是精，有形的精蟲卵臟乃至細胞、紅血球、白血球、荷爾蒙等等總匯起來都是精。而真精的作用是什麼呢？只有釋迦牟尼佛在《楞嚴經》說：「心精徧圓，含裹十方」這句話，透露得最清楚。我們心意識清明、精神充沛、思想健旺，只是有形的精。這一切是哪裏來的？是背後那個東西，那個才是精，包括了全部這些東西。寧靜起來，就是「心精徧圓，含裹十方」，整個的虛空都包含在它之內。

修栽接法的老人

道家所講「精氣神」，拿現在觀念來比喻，就是物理上的「光熱力」。神就是光，精就是熱，氣就是力，力量。古代聖人研究生命，很多地方都是相通的，只是地區不同，像印度、中國或者歐洲，表達就兩樣。生命存在，在佛教的唯識裏頭叫「煖壽識」，同「光熱力」或者「精氣神」沒有兩樣。佛教的這個「識」，有時候中國佛學把兩個字連起來叫「神識」。換一句話，不管你怎麼表達，這個生命是一個東西，各家表達的方法不同。

這個地球的生命，地球的文化，一切靠太陽的光明「神光」所照。地球吸收太陽的光，變成地球的熱能。地熱由地球的中心再上升出來，回轉來能夠生長萬物，所以「神光化氣，氣化精」，凝結起來。我們要把這個生命恢復，使青春常在，就要走相反的路。我們的肉體是有形的東西，先要把有形的精，有形的東西，修煉變成有形無形之間的那個氣。然後再進

一步，把有形無形之間的氣，修煉回到那個形而上的神光。能修到這個地步，壽命是可以長存的。不過，人到了老年，身上的所謂上藥的本錢沒有了，因此道家方士派，又產生一種方法叫做「栽接法」。如果老年人懂了這個方法修煉，也可以返老還童。

不過大家不要聽了就抱很大的希望，所謂有人成了道成了仙，都是聽說的而已，最後訪問結果，都是「事出有因，查無實據」。你們去看古書《抱朴子》，那是道家正統的書，葛洪寫的，神話特別多，所以說，不說神話不叫做道家。但是道家這個理論絕對是正確的，我可以說保證是真的，只是人不容易做到。原因是什麼？修道家有一個條件，「善行為先」，要多行善事功德，只顧自私在那裏打坐修道，不肯為他人做一點事情，那是世界上最自私的人，不會成就的。我常常說修道的人最自私，兩腿一盤，眼睛一閉，說我要修道，不要吵我，什麼事情我都不管，萬緣放下。拿萬緣放下這一句話逃避現實，實際上他什麼都沒有放下，他最大的欲望擺在前面，就是想長壽。道家的老祖宗老子講的：「後其身而身先，

外其身而身存」。你把自己擺下，先為人，不怕你不活著；如果先自私為自己，最後你先走路。

老年人最希求「栽接法」，這是很難的。我向諸位聲明我不懂道，也沒有工夫，據我從書本學術的研究，這個栽接法有沒有呢？有！道家密宗都有一套。栽接法老年修不成，就要修一個法叫做「奪舍」法，是道家的名稱，前面已經說過。在密宗藏文名稱叫「頗哇法」。頗哇是藏文，翻譯成中文就是往生，有時候叫「遷識法」。遷識就是神識遷移。我們這個身體壞了，把這個戶口遷移，修好了這個法，死後靈魂一定有把握往生極樂世界。根據道家理論，栽接修不成，必須修奪舍。不過這個方法在道家不能亂用的，條件很嚴謹，若你自問功德不夠而用它，是犯法的。當然不是犯我們人間什麼法，是犯天條。修道人所謂「罪犯天條」，是天上的憲法，比我們人間憲法還要大。

桂湖寶光寺奇事

前面提到因為不懂藥物，沒有辦法修成功，神識離開，回不到肉體廬舍才要奪舍。再告訴大家一個資料，當年我們學禪宗的時候，離四川成都三四十里，有個縣叫新都。當地有個名勝桂湖，「荷花千朵桂千株」，尤其秋天，我覺得比杭州西湖，另有一番風味。還有個禪宗的叢林寶光寺，禪堂起碼容納五六百人打坐修道。這裏的方丈老和尚告訴我，前好幾年，廟裏來了一個和尚，很有工夫，在禪堂打坐入定，坐了半個多月也沒有下座，只有身體有一點歪了。廟上有個管事的知事，認為這掛褡的和尚不守規矩，應該下來行香，他也沒有下來，摸摸氣也沒有了。那個叢林人很多，有時候幾百和尚從十方八面來的，查到他只有登記終南山下來掛褡的。管事的就說，不行了！遷化吧！就是送涅槃堂火化。

遷化後第二天，他回來了，回來找不到這個佛家叫色殼子，道家叫廬舍的肉體了。這位老兄，拿道家來講，起碼陰神成就得很堅固了，他就在

禪堂裏叫，我呢？我呢？到處找「我」！所以道家講「散而為氣，聚而成形」，他雖然「凝結」還沒有「聚而成形」，還有一部份工夫沒有成功。他找自己這個我，是我見身見解脫不掉！白天叫沒有關係，晚上一叫，大家坐不住了，禪堂裏只剩下兩三個老和尚敢打坐，其他的人都告假走了。後來，陝西一位老和尚來到這裏掛褡，發現稀稀落落沒有人，原來他是那位被火化和尚的同參道友。他就要知客師晚上燒一盆火，旁邊放一缸水，他自己就在堂上打坐。等到我呢我呢……叫起來了，他就叫他的法名，某人，你在火裏頭呀！一盆火燒得很大，沒有聲音了，這個傢伙跑進去找了。等一下，又我呢？我呢？又開始叫了，他說，某人，你在水裏頭，沒有聲音了。過一陣出來又我呢？我呢？老和尚說，師兄呀！你怎麼搞的？現在火裏也去得，水裏也去得，還要那個色殼子幹什麼呀？就這麼幾句話，恍然大悟，哈哈一笑，從此沒有了。

陰神同佛家講「中陰成就」不同，這是講到五行藥物栽接法，中間插了故事給諸位做參考。

第二十講

五金八石的外丹

剛才報告這個故事，是我當年訪道親自經歷的，這些給我的啟發很多。我們要修長生不老之術，第一先要認識「藥物」是什麼，「藥物」認識了，還要知道「火候」。這個火候是道家的專門名辭。為什麼他用火候呢？因為道家學術的淵源從方士煉丹而來，這是世界上物理與化學兩門科學最早的鼻祖。普通講丹有天元丹、地元丹、人元丹三種。人元丹又分外丹、內丹。外丹就是靠化學的草木、五金、八石這些藥物幫助身體；五金（黃金、白銀、赤銅、青鉛、黑鐵）八石（朱砂、雄黃、硫黃、雌黃、雲母、空青、戎鹽、硝石）必須要經鍋爐來煆煉，等於燒柴煮飯一樣。火太大把它燒焦了，火太細溫度不夠不會成功。所以修道的工夫，不管是佛家、道家，最難是火候。自古神仙傳你丹訣，傳你口訣，火候沒有辦法傳

你，因為各人身體生理的稟賦、強弱不同，男女老幼不同，環境思想情緒各有不同，所以火候就很難。等於我們做菜，同樣一個做法，每一個人燒出來的菜口味不一樣，就是火候問題。

一般人以為佛家好像不談這個，其實佛家非常注重火候，在修持的經典上，譬如《禪秘要法》，再三強調做工夫要知時知量，就是「火候」。你某一個方法，某一步工夫修煉到某一個程度，要「易觀」，這是佛學名稱，就是要變更方法。老是一個方法下去，就過份了，就像吃藥一樣，維他命吃多了要出毛病，不夠也要出毛病，所以難處在這裏。外丹的藥是靠這個五金八石，我可以向諸位報告，五金八石我大部份有些常識和經驗，譬如水銀我吃過，硫黃也吃過，吃一點就會死的砒霜，我也吃過一個多月。那真有一點害怕，就發現自己的皮跟肉分開了。要想成仙就要不怕死，要有這個精神。

我小時候，父親在家裏經常有修道的人一起談論，我愛在旁邊偷聽，聽到那些老道士們講：「若要人不死，先要死個人」。這個話莫名奇妙，

要想學到長生不死之法，先要把自己變成死人嗎？我還聽到：「未死先學死，有生即殺生」。實際上是修道方法，就是念頭一起就要把它空掉。

「未死先學死」，所以我每天晚上睡在床上先學死，修道嘛，自己裝死人。死了以後，黑洞洞的，說有個生命的竅在哪裏，我自己在想，「在這……這……」，東摸西摸，什麼上丹田、下丹田，我都試過。你們十二歲時有沒有發現過，早晨睡醒起來，這一帶，由心窩子以下到肚臍以上，哎！有無比的舒服，快感，樂感！我幾十年來問了很多人，只有三個人答覆我有，這三個人都是修過道的。後來我才曉得，這一帶有條腺叫青春腺。這個青春腺真恢復了會得樂，真發快感。「中宮」，當時我就早摸到了，所以後來到青城山訪道，寫來兩句什麼「明也傳來暗也傳」，我看了只好笑就下山了。原來這個樣子是道法，我早曉得了，那還有什麼稀奇。

這是內藥部份。

這個「外藥」部份呢？所以膽子大，「未死先學死」。我們曉得，韓愈反對佛反對道，他吃丹藥，王陽明吃砒霜。這些人表面反對佛家、道

家，背後都偷偷幹的，所以理學家我最看不起。哪像蘇東坡，吃丹藥是公開的，王陽明是吃丹藥砒霜死的，死後身體整個發藍，就是中毒了。

古人為什麼吃五金八石？這些都是最燥烈的藥，他的道理是，我們這個身體是個寄生蟲的世界，道家叫做三尸蟲，而且還取名字姓彭。有個女神仙曹文逸，是宋朝名將曹彬的孫女，修成道家的仙姑，皇帝封她文逸真人。她有部著作《靈源大道歌》，我勸你們學佛修道最好都要背來，真是性命雙修的好東西。像我們都下過工夫背過，中間有兩句話：「三彭走出陰尸宅，萬國來朝赤帝宮」，赤帝代表心，三彭就是人體上的三尸蟲。有人解釋《金剛經》：「所有一切眾生之類，若卵生、若胎生、若濕生、若化生、若有色、若無色、若有想、若無想、若非有想非無想，我皆令入無餘涅槃而滅度之。」他說就是度身上的眾生，道家的解釋，不能說沒有道理。我們身體上，乃至細胞也是生命，它也各有國土。我有一位皈依的師父，是位活羅漢，他比濟顛和尚還要髒，一年到頭只穿同一件衣服，身上都是蝨子，也不剃光頭，留個長頭髮。我們經常看到他身上那個蝨子爬出

來，有個師兄抓住，他就說：「不可以殺生！給我、給我⋯」，把蝨子放回身上，說「這樣牠就不會不服水土」，這也是度身上的眾生。

這個五金八石的藥，都是殺菌殺寄生蟲的，可是古人有兩句話要注意：「服藥求神仙，反被藥食誤」，一般人吃外丹藥吃出毛病的太多了，從秦始皇開始，漢代唐代幾個皇帝，乃至一般名士，明朝更多了，都服食外丹。這些外金丹的藥，有沒有效果呢？我自己大部份試過，效果很大，對人體好。但是有一個條件，一般人做不到的，假定做得到，吃藥一定有效果。什麼條件？要清心寡欲，飲食、男女一定要戒除。這些皇帝，這些文人像王陽明、韓愈、白居易等等，有福報，又聰明，修道家神仙朋友也多，這藥吃下去以後都是壯陽的，陽氣來了以後，男女關係戒不掉，這一崩潰比普通人厲害萬倍，一下就送命了。其次，飲食也大有關係，吃一些外丹的藥要有服氣的本事，可以不吃飯，光喝水、喝茶，但他們做不到，結果就送命了。

未有神仙不讀書

譬如硫黃可以治很多病，它是起死回生的藥，道家的五金八石之一。硫黃有毒，吃下去會死人，那麼要什麼方法令硫黃沒有毒呢？就是豬油，加上豬油製煉了以後，硫黃的毒性沒有了，吃下去陽氣會旺。如果不能戒除飲食，碰到一點動物的血，那個毒性照樣發作。所以他們這些帝王名士們，飲食不肯斷去，男女之欲不肯戒掉，這個外丹藥吃下去只有短命，哪裏能夠長生！這是第一點。第二點，古人說：「未有神仙不讀書」，譬如我們讀書的時候，老師們一定要你看看《洗冤錄》，這一本書就是古代法醫學。《洗冤錄》說，假使驗屍拿出來那個骨頭抓到手上一捏，變成黃粉下來，那是中了硫黃毒死的。硫黃吃多了骨頭鬆了，一捏就成粉。

一看這個書，就懂了一件事，硫黃礦的旁邊那個泥土都是鬆的，像糞土沒有黏性了，因此你就會懂《論語》中一句話，「糞土之牆，不可杇也」。硫黃雖然能夠殺菌，它也有化掉地、水、火、風四大之中地大這個

骨骼的作用，所以能夠清心，但也不能常吃，必須中和。因此丹藥的配製，都有互相中和制衡的作用，所以修道家的人，必須懂得醫藥。

現在我們主要還是講這一段，五行同藥物的關係。《參同契》這裏提到這個五行，只講內丹方面，沒有提到外丹。「坎戊月精，離己日光」，這一段配合天干地支的作用，朱真人下面的註解很清楚，諸位自己可以研究，不要我來向大家報告浪費時間。前面報告過了有形的內部「心肝脾肺腎」，配合顏色，配合五行金木火水土。我上次提到，你們諸位守中宮的還好，尤其現代人不要守上下竅。不止這兩竅，守竅的種類多得很，有一派道家佛家守竅守背上、守腰，這個方法是從白骨觀修法來的。白骨觀裏頭有修腰竅，也有修夾脊這一竅。修夾脊這一竅，同密宗的頗哇往生法，同道家的出陽神、陰神等等的修法都有密切的關係。從學術的觀點來看，說明在東漢末期，魏晉南北朝的階段，佛道兩家修持的方法已經融會起來，彼此在摻和了。

守哪個竅

道家守竅有各種各樣的古怪之處，現在我們講到《參同契》這一段，我貢獻諸位最穩當的方法，我是不主張守竅的，只偶然也可以用。我不說滑頭的話，你們自己去研究。偶然可以用，知時知量，就是「火候」問題，最穩當的是守中宮，不會錯。中宮準確的部位，就是心窩子之下，用八個指頭橫著疊起來，在肚臍以上，差不多四指的地方，不是在肚皮表面，在這個部位的中間。守中宮修久了的人，有一個效果很快會出來的，就是飲食可以減少，甚至可以一天吃一餐都沒有關係。在《孔子家語》中孔子說的：「服氣者壽」，吃氣的人，不靠五穀飲食的會長壽。「不食者神明而不死」，乃至服氣都不需要了。我們這位老師聖人他都知道，可見道家的方法是準確的。雖然一般學者不承認《孔子家語》是真的，我還是提出來給大家參考。所以這一段最後是「皆秉中宮，戊己之功」。

我們大家學中醫修道的，就要瞭解這個道理。真正中醫的治病方法不

是頭痛醫頭，腿痛醫腿。譬如我們中國是黃種人，容易得肝病。照西醫的治法，肝病就醫肝補肝了，但不一定對，雖然也會治好病沒有錯。真懂得中國醫學，懂得《易經》，懂得道家這個方法，就知道肝是木。什麼生木？剋木的又是什麼？我們曉得水生木，金剋木。或者這個人肺呼吸系統有問題，或者感冒太久，支氣管炎，慢慢影響肝臟功能變差，這就要先治療肺。要培養肝功能健康，不是針對肝臟，而是針對腎臟，因為肝腎同源，把腎水的功能培養好，水生木，肝的功能也好了。但是這個不是呆定的啊！要活用，也要懂得算命的道理，就是水多則木漂。水固然生木，水太多，把木漂起來沖到太平洋去，這根木頭就完了。

我現在告訴諸位的是學理上的「五行生剋」之理，你搞清楚了以後，自己對於修道的功能，各部份的調整就容易了，這是講有形的。但是，是不是《參同契》的原意？是不是所謂正統的道法？就不一定了。道家所謂正統道法有一個名稱叫上品丹法，很不容易達到，很不容易求得。據說上品丹法求到了，七天可以成仙。當然，這個是據說，是靠不住的。只講學

理的說法，上品的丹法，是在有形無形之間，不在這個肉體內部，但是也不會離開肉體的。

上品丹法如何煉

根據道家的正統道法，上品丹法的觀念，金木火水土是個代號，不一定指有形的東西。譬如這一段所提到的坎離兩卦，坎離代表水火。在《易經》卦名當中，水火是既濟，既濟是好的；顛倒過來火水就未濟，未濟是不好。那麼，什麼是水火既濟呢？我們看到做飯燒茶，水在上面，火在下面燒，就是好的。火在上面燒，水在下面毫無用處，這個是很簡單的物理，要懂得。所以，諸位修道打坐，上面的頭腦「嗡嗡」地發熱，紅光滿面，心思不定，妄念不斷，就是火在上面；水在下面，這是氣虛。所以老子講：「虛其心，實其腹」，這就是火下降了。因此禪宗祖師利用老子這兩句話罵人，說有些人沒有悟道，自己以為悟道，就是「空腹高心」，剛好與老子這個話相反。上面妄念不能停，就是心火不能下降；精氣神不能

歸元，就是坎水不能歸元；念多就是虛火，心不清淨。佛經經常用清淨圓明，就是代表取坎填離這個道理，要心境凝定，元氣才充盈。

中宮是土，這個土究竟指的是什麼呢？道家有一個名稱，叫「真意」，提到真意這個名稱，我們又有值得研究的地方。佛學講唯識的第六意識我們大家都容易瞭解，第六意識的根是第七識，叫末那識，也叫做「意根」。末那識是梵文，很難翻譯，包括了很多，佛學名稱又叫「俱生我執」，與生命同時來的有個我。這個我不用思想去想它，生命自然有我，是本能的活動。這個末那識有時在別的佛經上，就乾脆用中文真意來代表。如果我們研究學術思想，就看到唐代以後佛道兩家思想上有了交匯，修持的方法也融會了。真意在道家就是真土，這個是戊己土。所謂真意真土是什麼呢？就是有念無念之間，也就是上次我們提到「一陽初動處，萬物未生時」那個一念不生的境界。

禪宗佛家講空，一念不生不是沒有東西，是有個東西，這個東西就是真意。唐宋以後的禪宗靈知之性這一念，有形無形停留在中宮內外，沒有

妄想沒有雜念，這個是內丹基本的一步。所以「皆秉中宮，戊己之功」。

拿佛家來比喻，這個時候等於是無念，無念之念是為正念，永遠定在這個境界。對於身體方面，就停留在中宮這一部位。保留久了而靜極，用老子的話，就是「致虛極，守靜篤」。「致虛極」就是空到極點，靜極空極在這個中宮，五行就歸元，就是集中起作用了。正統道家，在這個時候，真正的精氣神才搞得清楚，它的消息才起來，才能把握得住。但是不要過份，因為無念太過，虛靈太過，要出毛病的，這個就是火候問題。

那麼要如何來調配呢？下一章會提到這個問題。在這個境界久了以後，把藥物調整好才可以談服食，吃這個丹藥。為什麼無念清淨境界要吃丹藥呢？在理論上沒有辦法懂，如果真做工夫，到那個境界就曉得，若有若無之間，並沒有一個有形的東西，但是的確有這麼一個作用。所以老子說：「恍兮惚兮，其中有物」，空空洞洞，若有若無之間是有東西。你說真有嗎？沒有，也就是佛家講「非空非有、即空即有」。

《參同契》上篇前五章是講「御政」，這個第二章，我們講到「戊己

之功」，先認識藥物同服食的基本原理，然後再說如何用這些方法。這些方法就在下面第三章「日月含符」。

第二十一講

《參同契》上卷主題是「御政」，包括了五章。第二章最後的結論是「戊己之功」。

戊己兩個都是土，戊土是脾的功能，己土是胃。普通我們講腸胃不好，脾胃是脾胃，腸子不好是排泄系統不好，不一定是胃的毛病，這個不能混為一談的。西醫的治療同中醫是兩個路線，但一樣有功效，只是基本的學理不同。

所以我經常分類，西醫的哲學建立在唯物，建立在機械上，它也有高明的一面；中醫建立的哲學基礎是精神的，是唯心的，也有它高明的一面，而且治療的方法往往不是頭痛醫頭腳痛醫腳。頭腳為什麼痛？必先找出根本原因才能加以治療。

真土真意與孟子

戊己在道家有形的修法是守中宮，中宮就是真意，也叫做真土，所謂「住意」，意識住在中宮。上次我給大家貢獻的意見，不管男女老幼，如果用有形有為的道家修法，守上丹田或者守下丹田，通通不及守中宮可靠穩當。這些都是有為的修法，不是無上道法，無上的道法是無形的真意。

拿佛家來比較，佛家唯識的八識中，第七末那識就是俱生我執，那是沒有思想意念以前，它天然若有若無的有這個我相的存在，這個是意根的作用。所以唐宋以後的道家講無上道法，所謂真意，它採用的名稱就是佛道兩家的混合。真意真土的境界，在若有若無之間不守任何一處，心境都擺在中和的狀態。

如果用儒家的道理來說明，所謂真意就是《中庸》的原文：「天命之謂性，率性之謂道，修道之謂教」。這個道，所謂「喜怒哀樂之未發謂之中，發而皆中節謂之和，致中和，天地位焉，萬物育焉。」這其中，差不

多十分之六是理論哲學的道理，十分之四是真工夫；莊子也一樣，有許多話是真工夫，很難做別的解釋。我們一般唸《中庸》都讀錯了，我們要注意，孔子、孟子、曾子、子思都是山東人，唸他們的文章最好要懂山東話。《中庸》的「中」要唸成去聲，我們跟山東朋友談話，對了沒有？中中！山西人也有這個話，中了就是對了。開鎗打靶，子彈打中了沒有，這是中了。所以「喜怒哀樂之未發謂之中」，喜怒哀樂都沒有動，等於佛家講「一念未生處」。「發而皆中節」，該用的時候還是要用，並不是只要清淨、虛無。發而能夠中節「之謂和」，一動一靜之間和起來，「致中和，天地位焉，萬物育焉」，這個是儒家修養的境界，也就是《參同契》第二章的所謂「皆秉中宮，戊己之功」的道理。

我們就拿煉氣的工夫和養氣的學問來講，這就是孟子在〈盡心篇〉裏頭所講的，「可欲之謂善，有諸己之謂信，充實之謂美，充實而有光輝之謂大，大而化之之謂聖，聖而不可知之之謂神。」這完全講的是工夫，沒有辦法講理論啦！假使不從真正修養工夫來解釋，孟子就是只講空洞的理

論，那孟子豈不是自欺欺人！真實做工夫才知道所謂亞聖並不是偶然得來的。他講「我善養吾浩然之氣」，什麼是「浩然之氣」？在〈盡心篇〉講得很清楚，「可欲之謂善」，喜歡修道只能講善行開始，不一定要有基礎工夫；到了第二步「有諸己之謂信」，是工夫要到身心上來，自己知道。

拿《參同契》這一章來比就是「戊己之功」到了。

我不曉得你們諸位見過多少真正修道家的人，像我們當年所看到道家的老前輩們，有時候正在跟我們談話，忽然不講了，把眼睛一閉，什麼都不理。我們也懂得就走開了。過了半天再去看他，拿佛家的話說，他慢慢地出定了。不是他去找工夫，是工夫找上門了！像這一種情形，到那個時候身心自然的非進入那個境界不可，就如孟子所講「有諸己之謂信」。

「信」有兩個解釋，一個自己確信不疑了，另一個解釋就是「消息」，工夫來找你，不要你去找工夫。我們大家修道找工夫，找那個境界找不到；等它自然來找你時，自然清淨了，自然要進入那個定境。

真正的戊己土，是真土是真意，不在有形的身體內、外、中間，但是

與身體的中宮之氣有關係。所以到了中宮之氣充實了，就是道家所謂「氣滿不思食」，這個時候自然可以斷除飲食；不是完全斷去，是不吃飯的時間可以拉長。「精滿不思淫，氣滿不思食，神滿不思睡」，到了這三種境界我們也不要把他看成很高，在我看來基本上等於孟子所講的「有諸己」；在道家來講道已經上身體了。我們普通修道不管你氣脈通了也好，別的什麼也好，道還沒有上身呢！只能說「可欲之謂善」，只是喜歡做這件事而已。

日月含符章第三

　　易者象也，懸象著明，莫大乎日月。日含五行精，月受六律紀。

　　五六三十度，度竟復更始。窮神以知化，陽往則陰來。輻輳而輪轉，出入更卷舒。

　　易有三百八十四爻，據爻摘符，符謂六十四卦。晦至朔旦，震來

受符。當斯之際，天地媾其精，日月相撢持。雄陽播元施，雌陰化黃包。混沌相交接，權輿樹根基。經營養鄞鄂，凝神以成軀。眾夫蹈以出，蝡動莫不由。

偉大的日月

我們有了這個瞭解以後，現在是〈日月含符章第三〉，先讀一下朱雲陽真人註解這章的一句話：

「**此章，特著日月之功用，究藥物之所從出也**」，這一章特別顯著的說明天地之間太陽月亮運行關係，瞭解了這個日月的功用，以及這個天體運行法則，然後才可以瞭解身心性命大藥的究竟。道家稱為大藥就是「精、氣、神」，三位是一體的。我們上次也提過宇宙的法則，我給它一個代名辭「光熱力」。神是宇宙太陽的「光」能，化成一股「力」量，就是氣；氣產生而發「熱」，這是精。神變成氣，氣變成精，我們後天的生命是順著來的，由先天變成後天。修道是相反的，要返回先天，所以煉精返回去化

成氣，再煉氣化神。精氣神三種實際上是一種，都是神所化的。所以許多的宗教，處處都講到光，大家修淨土宗，講到西方極樂世界處處光明，基督教也一樣，耶穌教的《聖經》〈約翰〉一章說：「神就是光」。

「易者象也，懸象著明，莫大乎日月。」《易經》講宇宙的現象，天地之間這個現象掛在那裏，「懸象」就是掛。所謂八卦就是掛出來的現象，宇宙最大的現象是天地日月風雷山澤，這八樣東西很明顯掛在那裏，所以「懸象著明」。我們抬頭看得最明白的現象，「莫大乎日月」，所以日月叫「大象」。

現在我們就進入了中國古代文化物理哲學，古代的科學是科學的一種，它同現代的科學是否相同是兩回事。中國上古的物理邏輯講：「日含五行精」。太陽代表火，太陽不是只有火，而具備了五行的精華。太陽是至陽，至陽裏有至陰，所以太陽裏頭有一個黑點。我們兒童時讀的古書神話，太陽裏頭有個鳥，像公雞一樣，叫「金鳥」，就是太陽裏那個黑點。太陽代表了光，一個光就代表了金木火水土五行。

「月受六律紀」，修道的首先注意月亮，最後注意太陽。月亮是小周天，太陽是大周天。月亮上半月由小變到大圓；下半月由大圓變成黑暗。這是小周天的行度。大周天行度是太陽在天體的行度，舊的天文學稱為躔度。太陽在天體中走一度，在這個地球人世間算一天。所以一年三百六十五度有多，這就是大周天。大周天下面還會討論，現在重點在小周天。

我們手邊的十二辟卦代表了一年十二個月，也代表了一天十二個時辰，也說明了一個月。「律」就是「律呂」，這是中國文化的專有名稱，是同音樂有關係的。一提律呂又是麻煩的事，在中國文化裏也是重心之一。我們的老師孔夫子整理中國文化，刪詩書訂禮樂，可惜這一部《樂經》失傳了。現在我們保留的只有五經。五經的《禮記》中有一篇〈樂記〉，勉勉強強還保留這個精神。中國古代講的音樂與西洋的不同，中國音樂的學理是律呂。

律呂兩個字在《二十五史》裏頭都有，現在講中國文化難了，譬如一

部《史記》，大家讀了漢高祖劉邦傳以為看了《史記》，再不然在中學背了《伯夷列傳》，也以為懂了《史記》，其實連影子都沒有！真正中國文化中心在《史記》的「八書」，譬如〈天官書〉就是中國上古天文學，後來每一代的歷史天官都有所沿革，或者叫〈天官志〉或〈天文志〉。《漢書》裏頭還有〈五行志〉，就是中國物理科學。又譬如「八書」裏還有一篇叫〈平準書〉，就是講經濟學、財政學，所以「八書」很重要。當然我們普通人不是專家，專門研究歷史的人只講歷史，不一定懂歷史哲學和中國文化的傳承。後來史書上有〈律曆志〉，是專門研究律曆的，也包括天文象數。我也看過一些現在的文章談中國的律曆，他們連影子都還沒有摸到，那是與曲子調子都沒有關係的。可是要真的懂得做曲子，非得懂律曆不可。我在前面也提到過。

回到「月受六律紀」，我們前面講過五天叫一候，三候叫一氣，所以一氣是中氣。六候，「五六三十度」為一個月，這是講月亮的出沒。講到一年有二十四個氣節，我告訴大家一個秘密，這裏有好幾位西醫的權威，我

們的腦神經有十二對，不多不少，學過解剖的都曉得。學道家就懂，十二對腦神經和二十四個氣節關係密切。你把十二對腦神經真修通了，就跟宇宙連起來了，當然就有了神通。可是你不要去玩！我常說你們玩得不好就玩成第二號神經了，第一號才是神通。信宗教、修道、學佛的，多數都走上這個二號的路子，所以千萬不要亂來。

「度竟復更始」，三十度走完了。每月陰曆初三月亮在西南角上出現。加上五天是初八，從正南出來半個月亮。初八加五是十三，一直到十六完全是東方出來西方下去。這個月亮的出沒以前都講過了，也就是「度竟復更始」。

「窮神以知化」是叫我們修道先要懂學理。到底謂之「窮」，到頭了。「窮神」是把這個「神」的作用，研究透頂。這是我們自己生命的根本，在佛家叫「性」。所以要明心見性，或者是佛學翻譯的「真如」、「菩提」、「涅槃」，這是根據梵文。中文來說這個就是神，神就是光，光就是神。「以知化」，這樣你才知道每時每分每秒都在變化。這個宇宙

的變化不是偶然的，懂了《易經》就曉得宇宙的變化都有法則有規律，一點沒有辦法逃過這個規律。因為我們文化不帶宗教觀念，所以把這個規律叫做造化。在西方文化中就是主宰、神的意思。這個造化的法則是不變動的，等於春夏秋冬一樣，等於早晨晚上一樣。所以修道的次序，工夫的進度，也是呆板的，不是說這個人根器好，一下就跳過去了，不可能的。

知道了這個變化，就懂得「陽往則陰來」，陽的光明去了，黑暗來了；黑暗去了，光明又來了。春去秋來，就是這個樣子。「輻輳而輪轉」，「輻輳」是車輪子的楗子，車輪子就是那麼旋轉。

「出入更卷舒」，月亮從初三開始一直到二十八，一出一入之間，「卷舒」，好像我們卷畫一樣，等於說初三開始，天地間慢慢一點一點拉開，到十五拉滿了，然後十六以後開始卷，到了二十八統統卷好了。要注意的是，卷好雖然沒有亮光，但它的「神」永遠不會喪失，不過一出一入之間有這個「卷舒」的作用。

卦變及人事之變

《參同契》的內容包含了全套的中國文化，每段下面有清代朱雲陽真人的註解。他的學問非常淵博，是真正的正統道家，可惜此人無法考據。

以我的想法，這個人應該是真修成仙了，因為考察不出資料，所以我更相信他成了神仙。他不要名，什麼痕跡都不留，太高了！希望諸位自己研究他的註解，假定有不懂，有機會可以問我，我也許可以幫忙諸位瞭解。你真懂了這些法則，懂了關鍵地方，道書一看就懂，而且曉得哪本道書講得對，哪一本不對。

「易有三百八十四爻」，這個要再說明一下了。《易經》的先天八卦，每一卦都由三爻組合而來，畫卦要從下面一爻一爻畫到上面。換句話說，卦是從內畫到外。後天卦是由兩個先天卦重疊組合而來，所以每卦六爻，一共八八六十四卦，就有三百八十四爻。

這個爻是什麼呢？剛才講天地間宇宙萬物人事都有個規律，是爻變而

來的。爻是交易、交變來的，內外相交，上下相交，互相變化。所以精神跟物理也無不相交變化，生理跟心理也互相交易變化，男女朋友之間感情也是互相變化，一切都是相對。但是變化是漸變！《易經》的道理說，宇宙間沒有突變，都是漸變！我們偶然說這是突變！但如果你追究突變的前因，就會發現仍是漸變來的，是一爻一爻變化來的，也是一陰一陽相對變化來的，這是宇宙間的法則。

「據爻摘符」，「符」合也，就是配合。宇宙間一切變化的法則，都符合一個原理。拿現在的話講，都符合它的邏輯道理。「據爻」是說《易經》每一卦都有卦辭、爻辭、象辭。譬如說「乾為天，天行健」這個卦辭，乾是代表天，天怎麼樣呢？「天行健」，天體永遠在動。

當年有一位大師講中國文化害在一個靜字，因為大家都主靜。後來我講了句難聽話，我說放狗屁！根據什麼說中國文化主張靜？中國文化早就說宇宙間的萬事萬物都在動啊！尤其是《易經》，經典裏頭的經典，哲學裏頭的哲學，提出來「天行健」，這個天體永遠在運動，太陽月亮永遠轉

動。「天行健」卦辭下面：「君子以自強不息」。所以人要效法天體，不斷的前進，只有前進沒有後退。中國文化誰說是靜態呀？所以《大學》上講「苟日新，日日新，又日新」，人效法天地，只有明天，滿足於今天的成功就是退步了。修道也好，做學問也好，人生的境界永遠看明天，只有明天，不斷地前進，生生不已，這就是我們中國文化生生不已的道理。

所以「符謂六十四卦」，每一爻每一步都是對的，都符合天體道理，歸納起來叫做六十四卦。下面有一個《易經》的大發明是道家的秘訣，「晦至朔旦，震來受符」。每月陰曆三十謂之「晦」。「朔」就是初一，「旦」就是天亮早晨。

第二十二講

天地陰陽相交

剛才講「晦至朔旦，震來受符」，震是卦名，先天震卦上面二爻是陰，從坤卦變來的。一陽從下面開始畫的，也可以說是一陽從內向外慢慢成長。《易經》的卦象「震為雷」，雷就是雷電。後天卦非常注重震卦，這也是個秘訣。我們現在老啦，把這個秘訣都要告訴年輕人了，有許多人學看相算命，看陰陽風水，先天後天都搞不清楚。最重要的都是用後天，後天以震卦為主。所謂震又代表帝，皇帝的那個帝。這一句就是每月初三月亮剛剛出來，所以「震來受符」是講月亮的現象。

「當斯之際，天地媾其精，日月相撢持」，在中國古代的看法，天地也有陰陽相交，每月相交。每月二十八以後月亮不見了，凌晨才看到在東北方，天一亮就下去了。二十八起到初二這個五天當中，夜裏真黑得一塌

糊塗，這個時候是純陰的境界，是天地在媾精，陰陽相交的時候。這時太

陽和月亮兩個結合在一起，古人認為這個現象是「日月相撢持」，兩個的

結合是陰氣與陽氣的結合。

「雄陽播元施，雌陰化黃包」，這個時候天地的陽氣、陽精就放射出

來。月亮同地球代表這個「雌陰」吸收。所以雄性的是放射，雌性的是吸

收，一放射一吸收之間互相結晶，等於男女的交媾一樣。「黃包」就是中

土，黃色代表中土，包就是陰陽像一個雞蛋一樣。

「混沌相交接，權輿樹根基」，這時陰陽像混沌交接的境界，是交接

不是混合。混沌這個名稱是莊子提出來的，等一下提到做工夫方面會給大

家說明一下。「權」是權柄中心，講把握，等於天體一樣，星辰轉動都是

北斗星在指揮。孔子在《論語》〈為政篇〉上也講到：「為政以德，譬如

北辰，居其所，而眾星拱之。」好的領導人在中間不動，就像是北斗一

樣。北斗有七個星，是人為劃分的，後面四個前面三個。所謂斗就是舀水

的瓢，古代叫做斗。這個斗柄前面還有兩顆星特別亮叫做「招、搖」，我

們說這個傢伙招搖撞騙，就是這兩個星名。天體是以北斗星為主，正月斗柄正指東方。過去沒有鐘錶沒有日曆，山中無甲子，晚上出來看天象，現在幾月了？一看，哦！三月。天體像個平面，這個「權輿」像個車輪一樣在平面上轉。「樹根基」，打坐修道就在這個時候紮根。

「經營養鄞鄂，凝神以成軀」，懂了這個道理要「經營」，像做生意一樣慢慢一點一點賺起來。「養鄞鄂」，鄞鄂是堤防，自己要做一個堤防，像城牆一樣。我們常講達摩祖師的徒弟二祖神光問，禪宗要怎麼用功？達摩祖師講：「外息諸緣，內心無喘，心如牆壁，可以入道。」其實佛道兩家都一樣，《參同契》成書的時候達摩祖師還沒有到中國來，是二百年之後才來的。達摩祖師所講的這句話，和「經營養鄞鄂，凝神以成軀」是同一道理，表達不同而已。達摩祖師說的「外息諸緣」，我們容易懂，修道人外面什麼都不管了，眼睛閉著打坐，死了人都不管，真正自私自利了。修道學佛是絕對自私的，自私自利到了極點才能大公無私呀，先把自己度好才能度人嘛！像游泳一樣，你不會游泳怎麼跳到海裏去救人

啊！這個「無喘」是心不動念了，到這個時候呼吸已停住了，念頭也跟著清淨了。「心如牆壁」，內外隔絕了，牆外跟牆內隔開了，這樣還不是道哦！達摩祖師說「可以入道」了。所以要注意後面這一句，有些人說「外息諸緣，內心無喘」就是道了，不對！這只是說做工夫要能內外隔絕，才有資格來入道進門，這也就是「經營養鄷鄂」，一陽來復的時候。

「凝神以成軀」，這時在學佛的人來說叫修定，得定；道家是講功用，不跟你講原理。「凝神」最厲害了，好像凍結不動，凝結攏來，「凝神以成軀」，把這個功能凝結攏來，慢慢構成一個身外之身，在生命之內或之外成就新的生命。

「眾夫蹈以出」，一般男女交媾生人，就叫「蹈」。所以人一代一代生下去。「蠕動莫不由」，欲界的生命，這個天地，都是陰陽交媾而來，所以佛學叫做欲界。修道沒有這個東西還不行，就靠這個地方迴轉才行。

我們再把原文這一段做個研究，希望大家還是自己研究朱雲陽的註解。「易有三百八十四爻，據爻摘符，符謂六十四卦」，這句話就是講天

地運行的法則，《易經》把這個原則都講完了。所以你要留意它一步有一步的工夫，一步有一步的象徵，象徵就是「符」。你的工夫到達哪一步，外形就現出來了。「據爻摘符」，一點都沒有差的，符合於那個原則。六爻為一卦，八八六十四，合起來一共是六十四卦。

大周天　小周天

「晦至朔旦」，每一個月來講，六爻第一爻開始動，由上個月尾到這個月初三「震來受符」。震卦是一陽出現，在《易經》六十四卦中，就是地雷復卦。復者恢復了，上個月的黑暗去了，光明又恢復了，所以叫做一陽來復。我們曉得《易經》上復卦的爻辭講「七日來復」，講到數字，東方文化妙得很，同西方、印度都一樣。西方的基督教第七天是安息日，現在叫星期日休息日。

那麼這個七天同五天的關係呢？七天是講太陽的系統大周天，五天是講小周天。現在把這個秘密告訴大家，你們讀書就不會搞錯了，不然你疑

問重重。我現在告訴大家的好像簡單幾句話，可是當年我腦子轉了十幾年，不知道這個問題錯在哪裏，解決不了。問那些修道的老師，會修道的不懂學問；問那些學問高懂《易經》的，他又不會修道。痛苦啊！最後自己總算悟到了，再一翻古書完全貫通了！所以說讀書修道有如此困難。這是我花了幾十年工夫才弄通的，成本很大。

佛家修行上有一句話：「不破本參不入山，不到重關不閉關」，不初步悟道，住山的資格都沒有。你說要到山上修道，你道都沒有悟，到山上修個什麼道啊？「經營養鄞鄂」還不過是破初關，還沒有資格住山呢！

「凝神」以後還要到重關，所謂身外有身這個境界，才可以真正的閉關。現在人反正門一鎖就叫做閉關，在關裏讀書也可以，寫字也可以。那不叫做修道，修道做工夫閉關，連書本都不要的，什麼都沒有，或者只有一個床舖，甚至只有一個蒲團，一天到晚在入定，這才叫閉關，也是「先王以至日閉關」的意思。

精從腳底生

講到「震來受符」，每月到這個時候一陽來復，老實講，「震來受符」就是一陽初動處。上一次跟你們提過邵康節講：「冬至子之半，天心無改移，一陽初動處，萬物未生時。」佛學從心理入手，到達了萬緣放下，一念不生，真正清淨到極點，那不過是「震來受符」的一陽初動。拿生理來說，什麼是震卦境界呢？我們上次講伍柳派認為男性陽舉的時候，女性胸部乳房堅挺，所謂春情發動，認為這是一陽來復。對不對呢？不是不對，但不是完全對。究竟什麼是震卦境界？就是當我們睡眠剛醒的時候。人為什麼睡夠了會醒？睡眠是陰境界，就是在充電，電充夠了，就發亮了清醒起來。就在那個將醒未醒之間，這個生理上是有作用的。

我們大家都有睡覺的經驗，我常常問人兩個問題，修道的朋友怎麼睡著的？怎麼醒來的？睡了一輩子覺，不曉得怎麼樣睡著怎麼樣醒來。這個真懂了，可以修道了。這不是說笑話，因為很難懂的，但是有一個現象我

告訴你們，你們回去體會。人哪裏先睡著呢？你們總以為頭腦先睡，錯了！腳趾頭先睡著，由下面一節一節睡著，蔓延到上面就睡著了。越是睡不著的時候，越是感覺下面腳和腿很重。早上一個人看著好像還沒有醒，但腳趾頭動起來，就知道他已經醒了！一陽來復，從下面動上來。

精從腳底生，所以我常常講，你看老年人，如果兩個腳底心冬天都發燙發暖，走路兩腿非常靈活有力的，一定是長壽之相。老化是從下部先開始老。你看嬰兒愛玩腳，躺在那裏兩個腳蹬來蹬去。大了就愛跑，所以小孩子六歲七歲狗都嫌，他閒不住的，非跑不可，在成長中他精力旺盛。到了二十幾歲，就要坐咖啡館不大動了；到了四十多歲，坐在那裏兩條腿蹺起來；六十歲的時候腳蹺得更高，才叫做舒服，因為兩條腿硬棒子一樣彎不動了。所以打坐也坐不住，當然會腿發麻，下半身早已經報銷到閻羅王那裏去了。兩個腿的氣走通以後，打坐時兩個腿是無比舒服！坐在那裏不肯下座的，那個就叫真正的得樂了。

那什麼是「震來受符」呢？這是身心兩方面的，剛剛「一陽初動處，

「萬物未生時」，平靜的，陽氣發動，可以說從腳趾頭開始發動。所以你看釋迦牟尼佛高明啊！白骨觀叫你由腳趾頭開始修，修白骨觀到中間第十四、十五觀，佛就明顯告訴你這個陽氣都從下面來。一般人看經的看不懂，也不去研究，自己想修道又偷懶，好像閉著眼睛打坐就算是修道了，這就是蠻幹！道是有個道理的，道理不通，怎麼去修？

混沌與昏沉

「當斯之際」，當這個時候，天地在媾精，如果你們做工夫時，自己覺得昏沉，大家打坐都有這個境界，普通人也有的。像中飯吃過後，坐在那裏昏昏沉沉的，自己覺得沒有睡，但你真睡著了。只要這樣一刻鐘，精神就來了，天地媾精就是本身的陰陽二氣在交，換句話說是在充電了。你說心裏是不是清楚？不清楚嗎？好像有人進來也知道，講話也聽到，講些什麼？不知道。你說沒有睡著嗎？睡著了。真睡著了嗎？沒有睡著，這個境界並不一定在昏沉。有許多同學搞不清楚，他說我又昏沉了，

怎麼修呢？老師可以告訴你方法，沒有辦法幫你修呀！這個要用你自己的智慧了。不過我會說書，會講書本上道理給你聽，這個千萬搞清楚。

「天地媾其精」，這個時候是「日月相撢持」，人的日月，在道家講是兩個眼睛，神在這兩個眼睛裏。中國陰陽學家乃至面相講法，左眼為日，右眼為月。所以看相的說左是日谷，右是月谷，要搞清楚。還有男左女右，女人要倒轉來數的，這邊是太陽，那邊又變成太陰了。這裏女同學很多，你們不要學了一半把我的招牌打破了啊！所以你們要搞清楚，這個時候「日月相撢持」，要眼神內斂。

「混沌相交接」，有時候你工夫昏沉不是「混沌」。這裏要先介紹一下佛家名稱，佛學講人的生命一天只在兩個境界中，不是散亂就是昏沉。思想不能停叫做散亂，我們平常清醒時腦筋都在散亂中，借用現在科學的名稱就是放射，放射就是消耗，一天到晚都是在放射消耗掉。有時候我們似睡非睡，並沒有去思想，但是，還是有點知道輕微的思想或者像做夢一樣，這個叫做掉舉，比散亂輕一點點，是輕的散亂。一個人不散亂不亂想

時幹什麼呢？就昏昏沉沉。有時候不是真睡著了，有一點迷迷糊糊，譬如中午吃飽飯疲倦迷糊一下，那是細昏沉。人生的境界不散亂就昏沉，睡醒沒有下床腦子就開始思想，就散亂了。不散亂不想時就睡，所以學佛的人不能得定就是這兩個原因。不散亂也不昏沉叫「定」！這就很難，定是絕對清明的，清明當然沒有昏沉。但是清明過頭就開始思想了，就是散亂。

有時碰到「混沌」的境界也把它當昏沉就錯了！所以通了佛家不通道家又不行。道家所講的「混沌」可不是昏沉哦！但是同昏沉差不多，當身體上陰陽相交接，就是剛才提到孟子所講的「有諸己之謂信」，這個時候信息來了。老輩子修道人講，工夫來找你的時候，一身都發軟。發軟到什麼程度？我告訴各位，有時候連拿一張紙都拿不住，到這個境界一定認為自己是出了毛病，這我當年都經驗過。有時候走在路上覺得頭在下面腿在上面，倒過來了，我根本不理，拿不住就讓它拿不住，我就不拿，充其量這個時候死了！過了這個時間，照樣的鋼條都可以抓！這也是一個經過的階段。

老母雞抱蛋你們看到過沒有？這個老母雞要抱蛋的時候臉都發紅，蹲在那裏迷迷糊糊，也不吃也不睡，晝夜就伏在上面一身發燙，它這個熱力把蛋抱出小雞來。這時候你碰牠都不動的，在「混沌」狀態，眼睛也不睜開。所以禪宗祖師也說「如雞抱卵」，「如貓捕鼠」。修道的工夫到了這個「混沌」境界好像是昏沉，但又不是，昏沉跟「混沌」分別得清楚。「混沌」這個名稱誰提出來的？是莊子。莊子原文不是那麼詳細，我把它編一編，意思完全一樣的。

莊子說「中央之帝為渾沌」，有個中央的皇帝就是「中宮」，名字就叫渾沌。南北二帝在中宮相遇，中帝對他們很好，二人就想要如何來報答中帝的恩惠。想來想去，想到中央之帝什麼都好，就是「渾沌」不通竅。這兩個人講，我們給他開竅。所以一天給他打一個竅，七天七竅開，等於我們兩個眼睛，兩個耳朵，兩個鼻孔，一個嘴巴，可是「七竅開而渾沌死」，他的生命完了！所以後天的聰明一打開，先天生命的真體就完了。

什麼叫真正的「混沌」呢？拿佛家一句話來解釋，「六根大定」就是眼耳

鼻舌身意六根都對內，就是剛才提到達摩祖師的話「外息諸緣，內心無喘，心如牆壁，可以入道」，這就是「混沌」境界。

水源與採補

現在我們站到伍柳派的立場來講一陽來復，認為在男性那是陽舉的時候，在女性是乳房發脹。這是陽氣發動，所以要把陽採回來叫「採補」，但是不准動男女淫欲之念，然後把這個精煉化為氣了。這對不對？也有它一部份道理，不是完全錯，也不是完全對。這裏頭又講水源有清濁，如果陽舉過份，已經配上男女的欲念，就不能採回來了，因為水源已經濁了，採回來也不能用！

據我所知，今天社會上很多人學的都是採補的工夫，忍精不漏，認為是修道。這些人一看就知道，一臉烏黑，一看那個眼神就是邪門鬼道的樣子。我告訴大家要注意哦！這樣下來非得心臟病肝病不可，不是嚇唬你的啊！這樣的人，一天到晚胸口這裏是悶的，一塊板一樣，那不得了的。再

告訴你忍精不洩，有時候把膀胱的尿氣拉回來，尿中毒，或者是大便中毒，到腦神經就不得了。所以有許多人修道，就是這樣修出病來的。伍柳派這個說法，就是認為濁氣就不能採，不能化。那麼水源什麼時候清呢？是陽舉未舉之前，將舉未舉欲念根本沒有，這個時候才叫做清的水源。這是伍柳派的立場哦！講到這裏，我要給伍柳派打兩個圈圈，因為這一點很有道理。

但是要認清水源的清濁，還是著相的，還不是上品丹法。上品丹法的一陽來復，剛才講過，在將醒未醒之間，身心陽氣精從足底生。你們多去體會足底，足底有很多的穴道，年紀大了腳趾甲變成灰趾甲了，左邊或右邊的腳趾頭不動了。腳趾頭不動是腎氣虧損，心臟也不對囉！所以先要把陽氣認清楚了，配上意念平靜，再就是「經營養鄞鄂，凝神以成軀」。這個時候是指六根都收回不向外走了，拿佛家來講就是「一念不生全體現」。這個神是指六根都收回不向外走了，拿佛家來講就是「一念不生全體現」。這個時候「凝神」凝轉來，老母雞抱蛋一樣「凝神以成軀」。為什麼我多年來提倡修白骨觀？白骨觀修煉得好就是「凝神以成軀」，身體一定健康

的，袪病延年健康長壽不成問題。因為白骨觀一觀成，那就是真正的「凝神以成軀」。其實不是真的白骨，是「凝神」凝攏來的。

第二十三講

人老有藥醫

上一次我們大概提到伍柳派的「一陽來復」「水源」「清濁」的說法。有人提出有關《無根樹》的問題。《無根樹》是道家張三丰所作的，他是元朝到明朝的道士，是太極拳的祖師。另有一個是張三豐，也是一個修道家的人，是南宗的，講男女雙修，這兩個人不能混淆。《無根樹》詞裏提到栽接法：

　　梅寄柳　桑接梨　　傳與修真作樣兒
　　自古神仙栽接法　　人老原來有藥醫

他以物理的道理說明，人老可以修到返老還童。梅樹如果不用別的樹來栽接，是不會結成梅子的，所以「梅寄柳」，這是中國古代農業的科

學，我們用了幾千年。梨樹要結成梨子是用桑樹來接，才能夠結果，不然光開花不結果。這個作用傳給我們修道人，當生命衰老快要死亡時，可以使他返老還童，可以使他不死，這個是「栽接法」，所以說「人老原來有藥醫」。

這個返老還童是什麼藥呢？當然主要不是外藥。道家的外藥，什麼長生不老丹藥，什麼小還丹、大還丹等等，好多方子，千萬不要亂服啊！在藥理上醫理上講，絕對有道理，可是有時候吃下去精神特別好，反而把人吃死了。不是藥把你害死了，是因為精神太好，自己以為了不起，做了許多的壞事促成你快死。至於金石之藥，礦物配的外丹，那效果更快。如果自己戒律不清淨，死亡得也更快。修道基本的原則是清心寡欲，乃至於絕欲，這是最高的守則。如不能做到絕欲，甚至基本的清心寡欲也做不到，想返老還童是不可能的。

宋朝筆記小說中寫一位老先生，七十幾歲，等於現在部長之流，功成名就告老還鄉，家裏很有錢，地位也很高，妻妾也很多。他覺得年紀大

了，怕死。聽說有一位修道的人已經八九十歲，看起來只有四十許，所以就把他請來，要向他求道。這位道人說你不要修道了，你官做得很大，又富貴高壽，你應該滿足了，修道是很苦的事，不簡單。如果一定要求道，第一個條件要離開你這些太太們；聲色犬馬，吃喝玩樂的一概都不能要，然後才能跟我修道。這位先生一聽，就送了道人很多禮物把他送走了。

人家說你不是要求長生不老，把這個神仙請來了嗎？為什麼又不學呢？他說人活了一輩子，除了吃喝玩樂之外還有什麼好玩的？叫我這些都放棄去修道，那又何必長壽呢！這也是一種哲學，沒有錯！可是從這一個故事，我們就瞭解，世界上的人樣樣都要，功名富貴要，錢也要，名也要，無所不要，最後還要成仙成佛！哪有這樣便宜的事！我常說有那麼便宜的事，他們出家又幹什麼呢？不是白出家了嗎？有這一點好處就不會有那一點，很公平的！如果飲食男女不能遠離不能絕欲，那丹藥吃下去就會早死。

「人老原來有藥醫」是靠內藥，內藥是煉精氣神。像張三丰的詞，道

家稱這些書為丹經，《參同契》就是道家丹經之鼻祖。修長生不老之道是中國道家開創的，但是密宗的講法又不同。很多人懷疑密宗許多的修法是中國道家傳過去的，也有人懷疑道家的許多修法是印度當年傳過來的，這個考據起來都很困難，反正是東方文化。講密宗這些修法是道家傳過去不無理由，也可以有很多的證明。在歷史上，最重要的是唐太宗將一位宮女，號稱是他的文成公主，下嫁西藏王。這個時候西藏還沒有文化，開始引進了佛教。文成公主下嫁西藏的時候，帶過去有好幾位儒生，就是讀孔孟之學的讀書人，其中也有道士。所以在西藏可以看到太極圖、八卦圖。嚴格研究起來，這是很有趣的一個問題。我們也可以綜合而論，人類文化研究生命永恆存在的，幾乎是同一條路線來的。

真正的栽接法

我們回轉來講，密宗同道家一樣也有栽接法，可是一般人把栽接法誤解了，所謂長生不老之藥，是本身內丹真氣發動，這才是真藥。老子也提

到如嬰兒一樣，真氣發動，毫無欲念，這個清的水源，才可以採回來，這也是伍柳派的運轉河車理論。運轉河車成為九轉還丹，這兩句話包含了工夫方法，每一步有一步的效驗，一步一步有不同的方法配合。我們借用佛家的話，每一步都有助道品（法）幫助他化煉。

究竟真元陽氣這個藥物的開始在哪裏呢？丹經鼻祖的《參同契》另有說法。但是伍柳派的旁門左道很多，譬如說古代的《素女經》《玉女經》《洞房秘訣》等等之流，其實都是醫書，這些醫書可以說是自我治療的方法。可是其中提到了許多男女關係，現在在國外很流行，法文、英文翻譯得一塌糊塗！密宗更不得了，在歐洲、在美國都是公開還加一塌糊塗！這是真的！都變成男女雙修，所謂「採陰補陽，採陽補陰」。假定世界上真有這一種辦法叫做「栽接法」，我是第一個堅決地反對！一個修道人怎麼能損人利己呢？如果損人利己也可以成仙成佛的話，那世界上儘管做惡人好了！

至於說正統的栽接法有沒有？有！譬如西藏密宗所謂頗哇法，就是往

生法，也就是道家的奪舍。這個在前面都講過，要修到一念專精才能往生、佛家講念佛要念到一心不亂。在道家來講，要昇天入地必須修到一念專精而不散，也就是要陰神堅固，才能有把握往生。陰神不堅固沒有用的，這還談不到陽神。所以密宗頗哇法跟彌陀法連在一起修，但是修彌陀法的人，必須同時修長壽法。長壽法的佛是藥師佛，往生法的佛是阿彌陀佛，這兩個是連著的。換句話說，阿彌陀佛也是藥師佛，也是長壽佛！這中間有一個秘密，那就是栽接法的作用。不過在佛教密宗的修法裏，他配合了佛教的形態，配合佛教的學理，是走另一個路線。

至於道家的栽接法，不管咒語，也不管觀想，因為道家不談這些，道家沒有宗教東西。根據佛說，一切音聲皆是陀羅尼（咒語），就是我們現在講話也是在念咒。道家的栽接法同佛家的長壽法非常有關聯，可是我們只能講理論，道家要修煉到什麼境界呢？借用莊子的話，就是「與天地精神相往來」才是最好的栽接法，那是真的！假使有人懂這個方法，可以說一刻之間，等於我們靜坐半個鐘頭以內，就可以把生命轉過來。

有一位同學研究密宗很深的，他修長壽法、不死法，他寫日記寄給我看，要我批。他說不食不死。我說，你說的沒有錯，不過越修越死。人要不死太難！而且你修的這個不死法還不是密法真正的不死法。密法有這個法，太容易也太難！先要把本身的氣脈通了，就是「與天地精神相往來」，到死的時候，自己曉得身上的氣脈快要封閉了，你必須先有這個把握。就像一般人肚子痛，你問他哪裏痛？他有時候指下面，有時候指上面，身體部位差一個指頭就差很多。他連一個肚子痛就搞不清了，何況是氣脈！普通人對內在的氣脈不會瞭解，所以必須要做到「內照形軀」，可以照見自己內部才行。

譬如佛家修白骨觀的，真修到了以後，他對內部經脈的流行，看得很清楚，不用眼睛，只要一體會就很清楚，曉得哪一部份不對，哪個地方有阻礙了。密宗修不死法到那個程度時，把這個氣脈流動認清楚，就要閉氣，停止後天的呼吸一個時辰。我們平常呼吸不能夠停掉，所以一定要有了這個工夫，才能修不死法。要死的時候就在這一個時辰，這個時辰給你

一拖過去就可以不死。不過我還沒有死過，我是說書的，沒有經驗也沒有工夫。這在理論上絕對通，工夫上做起來就難了。這是不死法，同栽接法沒有關係，栽接法是補法，等於吃補藥。我叫了好幾年，你們好好研究白骨觀，這個裏頭就有補法在裏頭。可是叫歸叫，沒有人信，怎奈眾生不上船，你不上船，有什麼辦法！

提到張三丰祖師的《無根樹》，文學很高喔！「梅寄柳」，人是可以用自己的精神採補回來的。再說，我們平常的精神是向外放的，六根都是向外走，怎樣把精神做到內斂，與天地的精神相往來，與虛空結在一起，這就是「栽接法」，並不一定靠外藥，更不是靠男女關係才叫栽接法。我現在所看到的，幾乎是萬修萬錯！這些道法，一般人知道的都是渣子，不會真的知道，太難了。這是答覆同學這個問題。

天符進退章第四

于是，仲尼讚鴻濛，乾坤德洞虛。稽古當元皇，關雎建始初。冠婚炁相紐，元年乃芽滋。

聖人不虛生，上觀顯天符。天符有進退，屈伸以應時。故易統天心，復卦建始萌。長子繼父體，因母立兆基。消息應鍾律，升降據斗樞。

三日出為爽，震庚受西方。八日兌受丁，上弦平如繩。十五乾體就，盛滿甲東方。蟾蜍與兔魄，日月炁雙明。蟾蜍視卦節，兔者吐生光。七八道已訖，屈伸低下降。十六轉受統，巽辛見平明。艮直于丙南，下弦二十三。坤乙三十日，陽路喪其朋，節盡相禪與，繼體復生龍。

壬癸配甲乙，乾坤括始終。七八數十五，九六亦相當。四者合三十，陽炁索滅藏。八卦布列曜，運移不失中。

元精眇難覩，推度效符徵。居則觀其象，準擬其形容。立表以為範，占候定吉凶。發號順節令，勿失爻動時。上觀河圖文，下察地形流。中稽于人心，參合考三才。動則循卦節，靜則因象辭。乾坤用施行，天下然後治。

金丹　火候

現在我們繼續《參同契》的本文，「天符進退章第四」，朱雲陽真人

註解：**「此章，言天符進退，乃金丹火候之所取則也」**。道家說的「金丹」是個代名辭，就是自己生命的根本動力。把生命根本的動力抓住了，那個作用叫做金丹，並不是黃金煉成丹。不過古人有吃黃金做的丹，這個方法我知道，所謂吞金死人，不是黃金把你毒死的，是金子吞下去以後，下墜把胃穿了孔，腸胃就破裂了。

我們這裏有一位同學，有一天夜裏十二點給我打電話說，老師啊不得了！某一個同學把金牙齒吞到肚子裏去，這怎麼辦？我說，快吃韮菜！叫

他切長一點，鍋裏頭拿一點油鹽炒一炒吃！可以化金，第二天金牙齒還能找回來，當然明天自己要在那個地方（馬桶）找一找。結果這位同學很聽話，去買了韭菜，也吃下去，仍然覺得還在肚子這裏。我說叫他明天一早去照Ｘ光，不對就去開刀嘛！到了第二天，照了胃鏡，沒有，下面腸子照相，也沒有牙齒。到了下午，電話來了，老師，某某人牙齒找到了。哪裏找到？當然從那裏出來了，水沖沖洗照樣可以戴上去（眾笑）。

金屬的東西吃下去，有些會中毒的，像金、銀、銅、鐵、錫，都是容易中毒的，在道家可都是煉丹的藥。黃金先要把它化成液體，黃金加現在的化學藥品，化成水不能喝啊！一下去了以後連腸子、胃都要燒爛了。道家的發明，黃金萬一中毒了怎麼辦呢？吃鷓鴣鳥的肉可以解。這個話本來不想講，這一講就要殺鷓鴣鳥了。我在試驗這些丹藥的時候，都要先把解藥找來。我想這些古代神仙，為什麼要喝黃金？有什麼好處呢？我現在沒有結論，我這個藥沒有試，別的藥我試過了。譬如水銀我試過，砒霜硫黃我試過。你們同學們不要隨便去試啊！不是好玩的。當我試吃這些藥的時

候，那就是等於自殺，準備就跟你們諸位不見面了。

我們曉得金丹是個代號，有些人誤解，把這個金丹代號當成打坐。尤其是伍柳派，經常提到「圓陀陀，光爍爍」，金丹呈現。因此現在有些守上丹田，守眉間的，打坐久了，眼睛看到亮光，喔！這是道！在我看起來那是鼻孔漏氣的道。我們這裏同學打坐的都會隨時看到亮光，那有什麼稀奇！那全是第六意識的幻影。道家有一派搞不清楚，打坐看到亮光一點，哎喲！這是金丹現前！要把它停留住。

修密宗的人把這個亮光叫光明定，有相的光明定是最下等的，要修到無相光明定還差不多，可是仍然還不究竟。有些人誤解這個事情，認為是精神鍛鍊成的。也不是的，那是光影。所以禪宗祖師罵人：「落在光影門頭」，自以為是悟道了，那是走了岔路，非常著相。

金丹這個代號，等於佛家講顛撲不破金剛的意思，丹就是袪病延年不死之藥，把這兩個觀念合攏來就是金丹。再說在中國的陰陽五行裏頭，金是代表西方，木是東方，阿彌陀佛是屬於五行裏頭西方金的方法，藥師佛

是東方木的方法。所以東方是生生不已的，西方是不生也不滅的，而「金丹」這個道理，只是一個形容。

「火候」呢？不同了！這個道家名辭我非常佩服，火候只有道家用，用得好極了。任何佛法或道家的修法，可以傳你丹訣，沒有辦法傳你火候，這個火候非常重要，只能由你自己體會。你說佛法修持裏有沒有火候？有啊！譬如修「白骨觀」，佛經常提到要「易觀」，到了某一個程度，你要換方法，這就是道家的火候。某一個方法，修到某一個程度不能繼續修下去，再修下去就因藥而成病了。

這個道理永嘉禪師在《永嘉集》，修止修觀上面講得也很清楚。譬如昏沉是病，惺惺是藥；散亂是病，寂寂是藥。但是你寂靜太過了就變昏沉，惺惺太過，也就是清醒太過了，變散亂，都是因藥而得病。道家修法也是這樣。所以我看許多修道的，萬一說那個工夫太對了，就變成不對了，因為他不知道火候，該止的時候不知道止，該進的時候不知道進。所以孔子在《易經》上說：「知進退存亡而不失其正者，其

天地開始只有陰陽

「于是，仲尼讚鴻濛，乾坤德洞虛」。仲尼就是孔子的號，孔夫子讚鴻濛，讚嘆《周易》。《周易》是由乾坤兩卦開始，鴻濛是形容宇宙的開始，也就是莊子所說的渾沌，「乾坤德洞虛」是讚乾坤兩卦的重要。「稽古當元皇，關雎建始初」，我們的文化是實證的文化，所以講道家的學術，一般人容易誤會是男女雙修的問題，這個地方誤會就來了。「稽古當元皇」，我們上古文化的《詩經》，第一篇由講男女愛情開始，「關關雎鳩在河之洲，窈窕淑女君子好逑」，我們小時候唸到就搖頭了，然後同學你看我做個鬼臉，我看你做個鬼臉。現在把色情叫黃色，我是反對！黃色

唯聖人乎」，這就是火候。作人做事也一樣，買股票有該買的時候，有該賣的時候；做官有該退休的時候，有該辭職的時候。火候雖然那麼難，我們這位丹經鼻祖的作者魏伯陽，這位千古神仙的領袖火龍真人，他告訴我們，火候並不難，而是要懂學理也懂得學問。

是我們中國人好的本色，何必自己打自己的耳光。我們本來把這個東西叫做桃色，多好聽呢！偏要把它弄成黃色，顛倒眾生毫無辦法。《參同契》說「關雎建始初」，天地開始只有陰陽，人倫開始只有男女，動物生物開始有雌雄，都是兩性。其實這個兩性不要想錯了，這是正反兩個力量，一正一反，陰陽兩個是代表的名辭。

「冠婚炁相紐，元年乃芽滋」。中國文化古禮，男子「二十而冠」，不叫童子，準備成年了，頭髮就編起來，戴個帽子叫做「弱冠」。我們中國古禮是「女子二十而嫁，男子三十而娶」，中間年齡距離十年非常正常，現在拿醫學來說，才曉得我們老祖宗大有研究。「冠婚」就是講年輕男女結婚，「炁相紐」是電感的作用。這個「炁」你要注意啊！中國古文是无火之謂「炁」，上面是個「无」，沒有，空的，下面四點代表火。拿現在話講是生命那個「能」。「相紐」是陰陽二氣，互相結合。「元年乃芽滋」，我們這些書上印的「元」都是唐朝以後改的，原來是「玄」。古書的「玄」，我們這些書上印的「元」「元」都混合起來用，因為唐明皇叫唐玄宗，皇帝的年號不可

以亂用，所以唐明皇的後代把那個「玄」字都換成這個「元」了，是避諱來的。

「元年乃芽滋」，他說男女兩情相愛而結合同電感一樣，陽電同陰電一接觸，「乃芽滋」才發芽。我們想想看，物理世界陽電陰電接觸是什麼？轟！打雷了！雷不是壞事，這個時候陽能才發動。修道的人有時候是會打雷的，有些人打坐，自己肚子裏頭砰！爆炸一聲，把自己嚇成神經了。小說上叫做走火入魔，其實火也沒有魔也沒有。有些人腦神經氣脈走通以後，閉眼坐在那裏，聽到天空中一聲炸雷，比夏天雷還要大聲，張開眼睛什麼都沒有。這個都是「元炁」發動最初的現象，最初的作用。

第二十四講

如何對應天符

「聖人不虛生，上觀顯天符」。這句話就像《易經》的作者形容：「仰以觀於天文，俯以察於地理」；又像倉頡造字「見鳥獸蹏迒之跡」，構成將天文、地理、人類、動物、植物，一切生物各種的變化綜合攏來，構成法則。所以聖人仰觀天文，「顯天符」。這個天體的運動，一年十二個月，一月三十天，一天十二個時辰，一個時辰三刻，一刻有多少分有多少秒。整個宇宙的運動和所有生物的生命息息相關，逃不出這個法則。你血液的流行，脈搏的跳動，呼吸的次數都是固定的法則，不能隨便，你沒有辦法改變，此謂「天符」。

「天符有進退」，進退就是一消一息。「屈伸以應時」，「屈」就是內收，內斂；「伸」就是向外伸長，都有一定的時間。所謂一定的時間，

是天體自然的法則。我們的生命也有一定的時間，人身是個小天地，大致上同宇宙的法則配合，可是有時候法則雖一樣，並不一定配合宇宙的時間，這個要活用了。前面說過《易經》所講「周流六虛，變動不居」，就是這個道理。「屈伸以應時」，怎麼「應時」法？這個要注意！普通我們修道家的，有一個問題，現在要討論一下，像修伍柳派講的打坐，要在子午卯酉四個時間打坐，前面已經提到過。

為什麼在這四個時辰打坐呢？因為子午是地面正應對天體的磁場，也就是物理上的磁場正好對應，這個時候打起坐來容易得定，心境容易凝靜。但是半夜子時是「一陽初動處」，正午午時是「一陰初生處」，所以陰陽不同。卯酉是陰陽正平的時候，所以卯酉沐浴，就是《易經》孔子講的：「洗心退藏於密」。拿佛家來講，是把念頭空掉，連空也空，空到徹底，就是沐浴。

前面講過「子午抽添，卯酉沐浴」，「抽添」是用有，不是走空的路。但是這個有，不是故意的有，是妙有。子時是添火，生命功能天然有

陽氣上升，是修道要配合的，但是心理不要幫忙，凡事要寧靜下來，讓它自然發展。一般不懂的人，身上陽氣發動，就要幫幫它，喔！過關了，經過那裏經過這裏，在那裏做鬼相！人還沒有先修好，鬼是先修成了。

所以這個時候是「應時」，應陽能發動時，你不要妨礙它。佛在《心經》上說「不增不減」；孟子講不可揠苗助長。但是許多人修道做工夫都在揠苗助長，所以吃虧了。「冬至一陽生」是指陽生起時，念頭不去做主，只是看著它。《心經》說「照見五蘊皆空」，只是照著，這個是「抽添」的

「抽」，陽長時你心反而寧靜。到了中午時分陰生了，容易昏沉，你倒要「添」，提高警覺了，也就是永嘉大師所講的「惺惺」，不能昏沉。所以「屈伸以應時」的道理是如此，工夫自己去應用就是火候。

「故易統天心，復卦建始萌」，你們懂了這一句，也就懂了《易經》。日月之謂易，「易」包括「天心」，天心就很難解釋。《易經》的乾坤兩卦代表陰陽，陰陽是道的用，不是道的體。陰陽、動靜、善惡、是非，都是道的用，道的相。這都是相對的，有陰就有陽，有是就有非，有

動就有靜，有善就有惡，有光明就有黑暗，這都是相，不是道。道的體，那個能陰能陽者，不在陰陽上面，那個是道，要把這個搞清楚才能修道。那個道，在佛家是「明心見性」，佛說萬法唯心；道家叫做「天心」，永遠居中而不動。「易統天心」是講陰陽法則的用，這就要懂得修道了，你要「天心正運」。換一句話說，你念頭越空，把身體越忘掉，那個生命力發動得越快。

這個時候「復卦建始萌」，地雷復卦上面五爻都是陰，下面一爻是陽，一陽初動處，萬物未生時。這個卦上卦是坤，代表地；下卦是震，代表雷，這個電能從下面發上來。地雷是什麼時候打？春天驚蟄時候打，那個地雷打起來聲音都不同，這就是所謂「驚蟄一聲雷」。依中國的農業科學，這個時候才可以開始耕地種稻插秧了。不到驚蟄你那個稻子插下去都不會成長，所以驚蟄一聲雷開始農忙了。這個雷配八個卦，天雷無妄，水雷是屯，山雷是頤……共有八種雷。現在只講復卦的震，震為雷是雷電，第一個發動，震者震動也。在這個圖表上，震卦在陰曆的十一月是地

雷復卦「冬至一陽生」。我們每天的震卦呢？就是我們這個生命的「活子時」，也就是你休息睡眠到極點，陽能發動的時候。真的陽能發動不止生理方面，所以我常常問諸位同學，人怎麼樣醒的？怎麼樣睡的？為什麼睡夠了會醒？這些現象要先把握住，這就是「復卦建始萌」，剛剛萌芽的意思。

長子和海底

「長子繼父體」，《易經》八個卦，乾坤叫做父母卦，乾卦是陽，代表父親，坤卦是陰，陰就代表母親。震卦是坤卦的第一爻變成陽，所以謂之長子。中國的家庭制度，大兒子代表家長，父母生了一個大兒子，表示繼承「父體」。在修道上，父母給我們這個生命，女性超過十三四歲，只要第一次經期來了就進入後天生命。男性十五六歲後情竇一開，生命就是後天破損的開始。要想恢復到父母所給先天無漏之體的生命，就要把握長子這「一陽初動處」。

「因母立兆基」，坤卦代表母親，代表陰性。陽能怎麼發動呢？就要靜極則陽生。靜極就是坤卦母體，是陰極；動極就是父體。中國過去的家庭制度，男主外，女主內。現在無所謂了，因時代不同了。「因母立兆基」，這個震卦是由坤卦來的，代表了陰極了就陽生。你打坐為什麼要求靜呢？因為靜到了極點，陽能才發動。

「消息應鍾律，升降據斗樞」，陽能發動是一步一步，一點一點動的。譬如我們人身背脊骨的二十四節，代表一年二十四節氣，也等於十二個月。所以當「冬至一陽生」時，尾閭發脹，一路上來，二十四對神經等於一個天梯接起來。這個陽氣發動在身上，一消一息「應鍾律」，意思是對應十二律曆的十二個月，或者十二個時辰。像過氣節一樣，一節有一節的作用。我們身體這個小天地，血脈等於長江黃河溪流樣樣都有。宇宙間所有的一切，身體內部都有，當然也有很多眾生，有細胞也有寄生蟲。

譬如天體有北斗七星，我們身上有沒有北斗七星呢？有！但是你不要著相，真的北斗七星是什麼？就在人的內心、念頭、七情六欲。講有形的

我說 參同契(上) 384

人體北斗七星，你看臉上有七個。而且人體很妙的，都是三角形的，密宗有時候畫壇城是三角形的，現在我把密宗也給你們公開了。密宗所謂生法宮，是生命來源的地方，普通叫做海底。海底在哪裏？男女都一樣，在前陰後陰的中間，就是前面生殖器和後面肛門的中間的三角形地帶，不過這麼一點點大。這個地方是生命來源的根本，瑜珈把這個地方叫做靈蛇的窟穴，像龍蛇潛伏在那裏，死後它就跟四大化掉了。如果經過修道把握得住，生法宮升起的生命能，可以修成不死不漏之果。所謂不漏之果，是絕對無欲念，由欲界天昇華到色界天去了。

我們人體上，外表兩個眼睛到鼻孔，兩個乳房到肚臍，都是三角形，對不對？這是人體的奧密，還有七角形八角形的。懂了人體這個奧密，氣脈的轉動就會很清楚了。所以密宗不告訴你，只畫圖案三角形。那麼密宗這個圖案怎麼來的呢？《易經》和河圖洛書怎麼來的呢？我們歸根結柢，應該說是來自上一個冰河時期的人類。以佛教來說，上一個佛，迦葉佛的末法時代，人類文化已經達到了最高峰，生命的科學也到了最高峰，可是

天地毀壞，留下這些圖案給下一個時代的人，慢慢再去研究恢復。所以在人類文化達到最高峰的時候，這個地球又崩掉了，這也就是成、住、壞、空的法則。所以佛道兩家要我們趕快修，跳出來這個循環。

再說太陽月亮

「升降據斗樞」，這個一升一降就靠北斗中樞做主。真正的中樞是什麼？在人心，我們這個心臟。佛家密宗講「脈解心開」，顯教講「意解心開」，都一樣。這個心臟的外形看起來就像八瓣蓮花一樣，所以禪宗真到開悟，密宗到修成功的時候，心脈輪一定打開了。但這並不是心臟張開了，不要當成有形的開。人的心臟外面有八瓣，裏面有七竅，像是個小漏斗一樣在動，七竅就像是「斗樞」，念在心（廣義的心念之心），因此我可以告訴你們，修觀心法門都在心的（廣義的心）部分，不要在腦子裏幻想。腦子是與第六意識分別有關，不要多用，你還是觀心，先觀有形的心的部份，你慢慢就可以得凝得定了。這個道理也就是「升降據斗樞」，因

為「斗樞」還是在心。

「三日出為爽，震庚受西方」。我常常說古人的詩：「人生幾見月當頭」是真的！一個人活了一輩子，一年有十二次月圓，可是我們一年當中見過幾次月圓啊？很多次月亮升起的時候，你去睡覺睡掉了。我常說，曾在雪山頂上看過明月，那個時候披著一個紅色的斗篷，裏頭是皮的，站在峨嵋山頂上，冬天十二月，月亮一出，萬山冰雪，這個琉璃世界看了真不想睡覺。世界上幾人享受過這個味道？那真好！那才叫做清福！所以我曉得福報享受完了，就該死了，但是現在還沒有死。

我有一個老鄉在南洋大學教書，退休以後研究中國天文，每天夜裏不睡覺，跑到房子頂上去看天文。他說研究《易經》同天文有關係，蠻有道理，可惜缺乏師承，沒有好老師教很痛苦，摸了很久，還是沒有摸到關鍵。所以師承重要但很難。

現在講天文現象講到月亮，「三日」是每月的初三。「出為爽」，爽是「晦爽」，一個文學名辭，指天快要亮時。「震庚受西方」，初三的月

亮，下半夜在西南方看見。震是東方，庚是西方，是《易經》的卦象。震跟庚，就是東跟西配攏來。「震」代表「一陽來復」東方的生氣，代表太陽的光。月亮本身不發光，它同地球一樣，吸收太陽的光反映出來。所以震，太陽的光明照到初三月亮，那時月亮剛剛在西方出來，就是在庚方。「受西方」，在西方接受。

如果拿道家的學理來講佛學，修阿彌陀佛淨土法門，是「生法」，不是「死法」，所以生西方極樂世界是「長生不死」之法。慧遠法師在盧山創白蓮社修淨土法門，因為他原來是修道家的。你把這個學術源流一查清楚，就知道淨土宗了不起了，那是長生之法，不是叫你死後往生，那只是方便之說而已。所以修「彌陀大法」，一定跟「藥師法」「長壽法」配在一起，這樣密法的秘密你就懂了！

五天叫一候，初三再加五天是初八，「八日兌受丁」，後天卦兌卦是在西方，初八的月亮，上半夜大約十二點鐘，看到月亮在正南方，像半截燒餅一樣，文學上叫上弦月。怎麼叫上弦呢？古人拉弓拉平了叫上弦，

「上弦平如繩」。初八的月亮，陽氣就慢慢增加，增加到一半「十五乾體就」，到了十五，完全是乾卦，純陽之體的圓滿月亮從東方出來。

「盛滿甲東方」，我們以前講過：「日出沒，比精神之衰旺。月盈虧，比氣血之盛衰。」有時候同學問我，老師，這兩天睡不著覺啊！這個時候是「盛滿甲東方」。但是你必須知道，睡不著以後會怎麼樣？一下反過來就要想大睡了！好幾天都是想睡覺。所以不懂道理，天天問老師也無用，老師不會幫你成道啊！火候要自己知道。

「蟾蜍與兔魄，日月炁雙明」。中國人比喻，月亮裏頭有個蟾蜍，是有毒的癩蛤蟆，但是它可以治大病的，可以做起死回生的藥。你們看那個畫的神仙叫劉海蟾，他是五代後梁人，是燕王的宰相，後來修道出家了，民間叫他劉海仙。劉海仙用銅錢來釣蟾蜍，你們看到畫的一個神仙站在海邊，釣竿上套了三個古代的錢，釣上來海裏一個三角蟾蜍，這是比喻海底的丹，是道家的修法。那麼你懂了以後，道家的畫也會看了，這三個錢代表了精、氣、神。

第二十五講

圓月　眉月　鉤月

上次《參同契》正說到月亮的出沒與生命是同一個法則，月亮的出沒影響到人的情緒，影響到生理的變化。在美國有很多科學的調查，這裏朱先生有一篇文章就是這個統計調查，現在國外的司法單位也在研究犯罪與這個月亮圓缺的關係。月圓的時候人的情緒較為高漲，月亮暗淡的時候人的情緒低落，乃至地表的潮水水氣候都受到影響。

講到「蟾蜍視卦節，兔者吐生光」這兩句話，我們中國人講月亮裏頭有一個三角的蟾蜍，那是個影像啦。究竟月亮那個圓球裏頭什麼情形，我們不要冒然的下結論。現在人已經登陸月球的表面，月球的內容還搞不清楚呢！當然不會像我們古代那麼講，月裏頭有個仙子啊，有一棵桂樹啊，這是神話。有個蟾蜍，有個兔子，也是神話，代表了古代科學的符號說

明。這裏也借用這些神話，但是這裏講的是科學，就是月亮裏頭的黑點。

「七八道已訖，屈伸低下降」，「七八」是七天加八天，就是每月陰曆的十五，月亮圓滿，陽氣已經到了頂。陽極則陰生，所以月亮開始在變了，就是光芒在減了。

從陰曆十六開始計算，「十六轉受統」，轉了。十五以前是陽氣統受，十六以後是陰氣統受了。「巽辛見平明」，「巽」是巽卦，巽下斷，下面一爻斷為陰，是一陰初生，上面兩爻還是陽。「辛」是天干，代表西方，「見平明」，早晨看得見。

那麼到了「艮直於丙南」，「艮為山」是卦名，艮卦跟震卦相反，艮下面都是陰，上面留一爻還是陽的。「艮直於丙南」，就是說到了陰曆二十三以後就成艮卦的現象，南方看見「下弦二十三」，叫下弦的月亮。

那麼再加五天就是二十八到三十，就是坤卦純陰了，看不見月亮。「坤乙」，甲乙是東方。「三十日」，每月的月尾，「陽路喪其朋」，月亮完全沒有了。這是講艮、震的道理。

「喪其朋」出自《易經》坤卦卦辭：「西南得朋，東北喪朋」。假使要出門，卜到坤卦，向西南方走最好，那是大吉大利，「得朋」是有貴人相助。如果向東北走呢？就不好了，「喪朋」，跟朋友鬧翻了或者打官司，或者有朋友過世了，這是照字面的解釋。

朋友與光明

但是我們研究《易經》的學問，想知道古人何以斷定西南會「得朋」，東北會「喪朋」，所以就要研究古代什麼叫「朋」，為什麼這樣寫。

我們先講「寶貝」，因為上古民族在西北在河南一帶，貝殼很不容易得到，物以稀為貴，所以老祖宗用貝殼代表錢。什麼是「朋」呢？就是兩串的貝殼，掛在身上出門，這是「朋」字的象，就是錢很多，後來朋友就用這個「朋」了。我們研究中國字，想想有道理！交朋友就要錢，沒有錢就沒有朋友，「有酒有肉皆朋友，患難何曾見一人」。這個「朋」字就是

兩串錢掛上去，所以寶貝，是貝亦是朋。

如果卜到坤卦，「西南得朋，東北喪朋」，古人《易經》的註解多得很，西南方，剛才講過是生方；加上卦的方位及干支，再加上種種理由，各家的說法一概不同。我有一個老朋友是有名的學者，原本同意要把《易經》翻成白話，還沒交卷就過世了。當時台灣商務印書館負責人王雲五先生託人來跟我講，無論如何勉為其難，把它完成！我沒有辦法就答應來做。開始覺得無所謂，但是把《易經》翻成白話，一開頭就麻煩啦！譬如碰到「西南得朋，東北喪朋」，平常我們不寫成文字，解釋很容易，告訴你們就好了，變成學術一解釋，完了！我本來想六十四卦，一天一卦就解決了，結果三年也動不了幾卦。後來實在沒有辦法，其他事情也越來越多，只好交給學生幫忙交卷寫好，不算數啦！他成書後我也發現有些錯誤地方，不過那個學生能擔起來實在已經了不起了。

在那一本書上也提到，這個「朋」字可能自古就錯了，應該是光明的「明」。原版《易經》古人是刻在竹板上的，用久了，翻過來調過去，變

了一點點就不同，明字就變朋字了。所以不是「西南得朋，東北喪朋」，是「西南得明，東北喪明」。它道理是什麼？坤卦代表是月亮，每月初三先見於西南方，所以「西南得明」，到每月月尾二十三，天亮在東北方看見眉毛之月，這個時候是「東北喪明」。因為《易經》流傳下來的版本是寫「朋」字，這個「易更三聖」，中國聖人的文字誰敢碰它！朋就朋到底吧。所以後人只好加上許多理由來解釋，而我也不敢講我的說法一定對，你們自己判斷吧。

封禪　禪讓　禪與

「節盡相禪與，繼體復生龍」，一節過完，剛好一個月。「禪與」就是禪位的意思，後來佛法用到禪字，古代這個禪字也代表宗教，就是所謂「禪讓」。中國古代統一天下的帝王，最嚴重一件大事就是「封禪」。秦始皇封禪，漢武帝封禪，但歷史學家認為這些皇帝都不夠格，除了我們老祖宗黃帝，還有堯與舜才有資格去封禪。封禪是幹什麼？封禪是代表全國

的人民，代表全民族，到山東登到泰山絕頂，舉行儀式，燒起大火來，表示這個皇帝成功了，有大功德，可以向上天報告，我做了幾十年，對得起國家，對得起老百姓，所以可以告慰向上天交卷，可以「封禪」。

司馬遷寫《史記》的時候，特別寫了一篇封禪書。這一篇文章，他列舉了我們中國歷代的皇帝有資格封禪的；然後講到秦始皇統一天下，也來到泰山封禪。他到了泰山，一方面封禪一方面求神仙，想求得長生不死之藥。秦始皇的封禪有這一個企圖，所以到了泰山碰到大雨，在五棵松樹下面躲雨，後來就封這五棵松樹做五大夫，松樹都封了官。據說他雖然沒有碰到神仙，也碰到一個人，教了秦始皇鞭地之法，就是縮地法，可以把地縮攏來。如果我們有這個方法的話，到美國去不要買飛機票了，畫一個符，唸一個咒子把地球縮攏來，踏一步就到了。這縮地法也叫鞭地法，拿鞭子打地就可以縮攏來，是神通啊！他描寫這些諷刺秦始皇，也諷刺了他自己當時的皇上漢武帝，封禪也是不夠格的。這幾個皇帝封禪一次，那個文武百官的隊伍，由河南起到山東，一路的部隊連結不斷好幾個月，那個

威風之大，消耗之大！所以司馬遷寫封禪書是諷刺的文章。

外國人講「你們中國人沒有宗教的精神」，其實只要你把封禪書一讀就懂了，在我們文化裏，對於宗教迷信思想，認為是很丟臉的，很沒有面子的。司馬遷就有這樣的看法。但是他並不是反對宗教，他認為真正的上天，真正的道，或者後世講真正的佛菩薩，並不需要你去封禪，去拜祭的。你真作好人，真做好事，那個神菩薩會來找你，這是真正的天人，真正佛菩薩。如果你去拜去求，他才來保佑你，這個菩薩已經變成薩菩了，不夠資格！佛菩薩、神、天人，無所不照應，善人要照應，使你更好，壞人他也在照應，照應你改過。這是天地之心，司馬遷寫的是這麼一個道理，這個書要如此去讀。

講到這個禪字，牽涉了封禪，我們文化上還有一個很重要的「禪讓」，也是這個禪字。堯舜禹三代公天下，皇帝當到功成名就身退，選出來繼承人，禪讓給他，自己自動退位。所以上古的歷史，說到這幾位了不起的皇帝，堯舜禹都成仙了。這個禪字很妙，是「示」旁，是向天道告

示，旁邊是個「單」字。中國姓氏裏頭有「單」姓，不要唸成簡單的單，而是與「禪」的古音同音。這個禪字，它的道理包括了很多，與天道有關，也代表了形象。

《參同契》這裏「節盡相禪與」，這個禪字，是禪位的意思。每月二十八是月尾，月亮的光明沒有了。光明代表陽氣，陽氣沒有是不是斷了呢？這個裏頭有個問題，道家跟佛家的哲學就來啦！我們做工夫修道的也要注意。所以女性「二七天癸至」，這是出於《黃帝內經》，十四歲第一次月信開始，父母生下先天的生命，變成後天了。假使講修道，這個時候已經破了身，所謂破瓜，一個完整西瓜切開了。男性十六歲，拿現在講，性知識開發了，不過現在都市青年都提早了。由先天變成後天，就是「禪與」的意思，表示改變了。

更年之後如何

《法華經》上講龍女八歲成佛，她沒有到達二七十四天癸至，這個叫

做童真入道，不分男女相。女人能不能成佛？絕對能！小乘批評女人不能成佛，大乘沒有這一套了，成佛不分男女老幼。所以女性四十九歲以後開始修道，如果拿伍柳派的看法，那要加兩倍的功，先要做到月經再來，來了以後再把它修斷，這個斷了月經的修法叫「斬赤龍」。這等於男性修到「馬陰藏相」，返回到男性是八歲、女性是七歲前的童體。這種「斬赤龍」的論調，一般修道的很流行講。

這個理論準不準確呢？不一定準確，也可以說很準確。為什麼？拿有形氣血的生命來講，不是沒有理由，有道理。你說陽氣完啦，經期完啦，難道四十九歲的女性都活不下去了嗎？還有活到九十幾一百多的呢！她另外自己那個真的生命功能起來，就是接近《參同契》這裏所說的「繼體復生龍」，她生生不已的那個生命的功能在發動。「龍」不是說女性斬赤龍，而是指乾卦，代表陽氣。乾卦在《易經》上都用龍來做代表，坤卦代表陰體，在動物是以馬來做代表。《易經》的坤卦不是普通的馬，是以母馬來代表。「牝牡之精」還不是公馬。所以研究《易經》要很小心，以動

物代表的說法，是要把物理研究清楚才懂得它的道理。

我們要知道，女性的陽氣，在停經之後繼續的生命，我們可以給它一個名稱「第三重宇宙的生命」，這個名稱是我臨時創造的。我們由入胎到出生，女性到七歲，男性到八歲，這是第一重宇宙的生命。男性十六歲，女性十四歲，這個先天與後天的分界，可以說是第二重宇宙的生命。到經期斷了，男性五十六，女性四十九，先天的陽氣用完了，父母給我們充的電用完了，此時再產生的電能是我們自己充來的，就是「繼體復生龍」。

所以叫它第三重宇宙的生命，並不是說陽氣絕了就不能修道了。

這裏有個東西了，像女性的月經，它這個生滅變化不絕，新陳代謝不已，去了以後又有新的生命生長。但是真的生命功能不在這個新陳代謝。新陳代謝是現在科學名稱，佛學叫「生滅」，道家是「陰陽變化」，陽極陰生，陰極陽生。能生滅、能變化的這個生命功能，並不在生滅上。所以伍柳派認為把後天有形的精收回來煉，是煉精化氣，全錯了。在座很多懂得醫學的，還有大醫生坐在後面，知道人的生命細胞、血液，隨時新陳代

謝，由毛孔等排泄出來。

所以說，不要認為化氣是把有形的精蟲卵臟化成氣，氣再化神，那是伍柳派的看法，至少在科學哲學上站不住腳。中國神仙道家的「煉精化氣」不是指這個精。道家煉精化氣包括了荷爾蒙全體作用，以及氣血一切的生長等等全套的作用謂之「精」，要整個轉化才能脫胎換骨，其中取之不盡，用之不竭。

所以人這個生命，不管男女，最後一口氣未斷之前，得了真正的正法、道法，專心一念之間可以把生命拉回來。可是就是難！真正的道法在哪裏？「繼體復生龍」，這一條生命的陽氣像龍一樣，它還不一定在你身體上，但是當然又離不開身體。所以密宗講什麼中脈呀！講了半天，老實講同伍柳派的道家一樣，都在有形那一面講。所以要瞭解真正正統的道家，對中國文化真正通達，這一本書就要好好研究了。

這本書之難讀，怪不得朱熹朱夫子啃了幾十年，啃不進去。其實他並沒有那麼差，這些都懂，什麼道理啃不進去？就因為他一方面反對佛法，

反對道家，又想做神仙，又不肯拜師，哪個人肯傳給他？所以只好自己研究，又研究不通！

配卦與陰陽

「壬癸配甲乙，乾坤括始終」，壬癸兩個是天干代號，屬水，屬北方黑色；甲乙屬木，屬東方青色；丙丁火是屬南方赤色；庚辛金屬西方白色；中央是戊己土屬黃色。那麼「壬癸配甲乙」怎麼講呢？北方怎麼配起東方呢？水怎麼配木呢？壬癸屬水，這要懂得河圖洛書了，「天一生水，地六成之，地二生火，天七成之」。現在順便講一點河圖洛書，應用就不講了，因為掐指一算那就多了。

先講哲學「天一生水」，這個天不是代表有形的，是指中國文化形而上宇宙原始本體。這個地球，這個世界形成，第一個是水，水就代表液體，同希臘有一派哲學一樣，認為這個世界是水開始的。等於我們冰凍的水果凍攏來，這個地球是冰凍而成的。「天一生水，地六成之」，凍攏

來形成地球，六合就是四方加上下。壬癸代表水，「配甲乙」，所以《易經》叫配卦，就把這個法則引用到這個作用上，配攏來用。甲乙東方木，代表生生不已。這就是說明月亮，一個月當中六次的變化，所以五天叫一候，六候叫一節，六五是三十天。第七天是休息日，星期天，陽氣重生的日子。「乾坤括始終」，是陰陽二氣變化的道理。

第二十六講

繼續講「乾坤括始終」。乾代表天體太陽，陽氣；坤代表月亮，陰氣。這個「括」字也要注意，古文之所以受人尊重，是因為每一個字都不虛用。括字從《易經》坤卦來，說到括囊，像口袋一樣收攏來。我們說囊素，上面開口的袋子是囊；兩頭開口的是素。「括始終」，到了陰曆月底的五天月亮的光沒有了；實際上不是沒有，是另一個陽在培養，含藏在陰之中，陰到極點新的生命陽生了。所以我們打坐、靜坐、修道，有時候不一定是昏沉哦！

有時候感覺提不起來，或者做工夫的，有一段時間只想睡覺。常常有同學問我這個問題，我說你們這些人還修什麼道！那麼沒有氣魄，道法自然，該睡就讓它睡個夠嘛！有些同學不滿意，說老師不肯正經答覆我。其實我講的都是老實話，他聽不懂有什麼辦法！好幾位禪宗祖師一睡就好幾年，動都不動！你能夠真的這樣睡，也是成功的睡法。那當然不是普通的

睡，也不是得了睡病。一般能夠睡並不一定是壞事，那是陰極，下一步就是陽生。

修道裏頭有一派，號稱「華山派」，何以稱「華山派」呢？是因宋代的道家神仙陳摶老祖，高臥華山用睡功而得名。實際上他並不是真睡，打坐是用功的方法，睡覺也是用功的方法。譬如我們中國人畫的阿彌陀佛都是站著的，站立也是用功的方法，歪著也是用功的方法，各人不同。哪一種方法適合哪一個人，也是各個不同。

「七八數十五，九六亦相當」。七加八是十五，九加六也是十五。七是陽，八是陰，陰陽交，產生另一個生命。九是陽數極點是老陽，六是老陰，老陽老陰相配，就表示另一個生命要產生，陰極陽生，陽極陰生。總而言之，拿數運來講，每月「七八數十五」是上半月；「九六亦相當」是下半個月，也是十五天。

袁枚的八索

「四者合三十」，這四個數字合攏來是一個月的三十天。「陽炁索滅藏」，索是一條繩子，什麼樣的繩子？我們畫八卦的一爻，就是這一條繩子。講到這裏，想起清代文人名士袁枚（子才）的趣事。他做了兩任縣長以後，年紀輕輕，就退休辭官不幹。這個學問好又聰明又有錢的人，把位於南京《紅樓夢》小說背景的大觀園買下來，當時叫做「隨園」，他的文集有《小倉山房尺牘》《隨園詩話》。

袁枚的錢不是貪污來的，因為滿清入關後，看到明朝官吏的貪污，所以就公開給官員高薪，自然就不貪污了。「一任清知府，十萬馬蹄銀」，考取功名，清心寡欲的人，一任之後不想再做官了。袁枚在小倉山房，四十多歲退休，一輩子詩文滿天下。他專門收女弟子，所以很多人誣蔑他。他本來沒有兒子，七十幾歲才生一個兒子。一般人講男人八八六十四歲陽氣已經完了，不會生了，他老兄反對道反對佛，七十幾歲還生兒子。

他兒子的名字叫阿遲，太遲了，不過他自己還活到八九十歲呢！我們現在看看小倉山房，在乾隆年代，那個窗子已經用外國進口的彩色玻璃，你看他多會享受！

在他的住處，掛了一副對子在大門口：「此地有叢山峻嶺茂林修竹」，形容他那個小倉山房風景之好，有山有水；下聯是：「是能讀三墳五典八索九丘」。八索九丘這個書難讀喔！八索就是八卦，九丘就是陰陽家所用《書經》洪範篇的九疇。袁子才掛了這一副對子，同時代另一個名人趙翼，是歷史學家，也是大文豪，傳說曾故意來挑他。趙先生有何指教？「今天來沒有別的事，只向你的主人借書！」佣人向袁子才報告他來借「八索九丘」，害得袁子才趕快叫佣人把門口對子拿下不掛。我們插進來這麼一個故事，是講「陽炁索滅藏」的「索」字。這個「索」字就是卦氣，卦氣是不絕的，等於後世的文字「不絕如縷」；一條絲還吊著，一口氣還沒有斷絕以前，好像是沒有氣了，其實生命能還在。

中的道理

「八卦布列曜，運移不失中」，八卦的分佈像一個月亮，一個月五天一候，每五六天的變化不同，配合八個卦的現象，同天體上每個星座有關係。這一種關係運移旋轉，與天體的旋轉一樣，第二個月又是這樣變化。變化是現象，有一個不變的東西，那個是道！「運移不失中」，就是不失中央的戊己土。所以道家、佛家、儒家沒有兩樣的，真理只有一個，表達的方法不同而已。我經常說佛教沒有反對其他任何的宗教，更沒有看不起任何一個教主，《金剛經》上一句話說得最透徹：「一切賢聖皆以無為法而有差別」。這個意思是說，一切賢聖多少都得了道，只不過深入的程度不同而已！佛說的是無為法，中國文化表達就是「運移不失中」，不離中央戊己土的道理。

那麼如何是「中」呢？這是個問題。我們懂了這些道理，不要在生理氣脈的變化上、身體的感受上做工夫，不要認為這就是道。剛剛我們在休

息時，一位朋友來說，老師啊，你不要笑我老是搞氣脈。我說，你又錯了！我平常罵人搞氣脈，因為你們執著氣脈就是道，所以我才罵你們不對。可是有些人根本不懂氣脈，卻罵氣脈不是道，那我就會強調氣脈是道。我這個人講話亂七八糟靠不住的，東說西說，有時候你說不要錢，我就拚命講錢怎麼好。袁子才的話：「不談未必是清流」，天天表示清高，口口聲聲不要錢，不談未必是清高。倒是玩錢玩慣的人，他不要錢是真的，因為他玩慣了，花也花慣了，不在乎。一輩子清苦的人，清不一定高，他沒有看過錢，錢一壓就把他壓死了。

什麼道理都是一樣，氣脈不可以執著，那不是道。氣脈有沒有關係呢？同道有絕對的關係，氣脈的變化就像月亮的運行，只是現象。所以「日出沒比氣血之盛衰」，你的道在哪裏？道看不見，現象看得見；現象固然不是道，沒有元氣，這個現象也出不來。這個要搞清楚！下面一段這個「中」，他又叫「玄精」。這個要把它改過來，不要寫元精，原本是這個「玄」，但是元也可以通啦！

「元（玄）精眇難覩，推度效符徵」。魏伯陽真人也告訴我們，道在身上，但是煉精化氣那個元精，不是有形的精蟲卵臟。譬如說這個元氣不發動，這個精還有沒有呢？有的男性精蟲不足，不會生孩子，就拚命培養精蟲，這絕對是錯的。只要培養元氣根本，火力旺了，無形的精就會變成有形的精，就會有活力了。元精是一個氣，精蟲是現象，不是根本。所以學醫要懂這個道理，否則頭痛醫頭，腳痛醫腳，那只能說是一個技師、醫技，不是懂醫理的醫師。

這元精就難了，它非精神非物質，而精神物質都是它變的。所以他告訴我們「元精眇難覩」，看不見摸不著，無形無相。釋迦牟尼佛在《楞嚴經》中說：「心精徧圓」那就是元精的道理，這個東西就在我們後天生命上；最嚴重的是下面這句「含裹十方」。「含」把它包含了，「裹」把它裹攏來了。那麼你說督脈、任脈，打起坐來這裏氣動，過那個關，對不對呢？答案是，只要不執著就對了。

「推度效符徵」，這同月亮在天體上的出沒一樣，一步有一步的工

夫，一步有一步的效驗，一步有一步的符。符者符合那個現象，徵就是那個徵候。那個現象那個徵候一定出來的。譬如我們看某人工夫修到什麼程度，內行一看這個人的印堂像月亮一樣亮，他到某一步，某個現象就出來了。看女性很簡單，她經期前後，一望而知。學醫要學到這個程度，修道也要修到這個程度。然後你一看這個人年齡大概多少，臉上病氣在哪裏，也一望而知了。本來的元精、元氣、元神，是摸不著，看不見的東西；既有此理，當然很難無此事。但是要像自然科學一樣拿出東西來看，是拿不出來的。你說拿不出來嘛，它表現在生命上，在肉體的表現上，一步有一步的「符徵」，做了工夫就有效，真能祛病延年。

了解進度和易觀

「居則觀其象，準擬其形容」，平常要觀察天體，太陽、月亮、地球，各種的物理現象。所以要懂得《易經》，懂得象數。「準擬其形容」，我們這個身體是個小天地，自己知道準確的徵候，看別人更清楚。

「其形容」，有它的形象，有它的外形可以表達。

「立表以為範，占候定吉凶」，所以陰陽家把它變成一個科學，就是科學「立表」，立了一個度數。表就是一個統計的規格，到那一步就一定出現那樣的境界。修道也是一樣，所以真正修道，先把理論搞通了，做起工夫並不困難。「占候定吉凶」是說火候最難！修道的口訣容易，火候難。真正的工夫，只有一個規範，沒有兩個，所以叫做不二法門。在一個規範之下，一個真證道的人，對於旁門左道的象徵，眼睛一看就知道。

南宋大禪師大慧杲語錄上講，你們在這禪堂裏冒充，騙飯吃啊！你們有沒有道，在我前面走三步路，你的命根已經在我手裏。因為他一望而知你的工夫到什麼程度。為什麼他會吹這樣的大牛？就是這個「立表以為範，占候定吉凶」的道理。這個聽起來容易，但是困難得很呢！不要說大慧杲，就算釋迦牟尼佛、呂純陽、火龍真人親自收我們做徒弟，把丹法傳給我們，我們修不修得成，還是疑問。

最難是「火候」，任何方法都是活的，到什麼時候就不能用，就要

換，到某一步工夫就要變，或者抓緊，或者放鬆，或者提起，或者放下，不一定。釋迦牟尼佛在《禪秘要法》露了一句修道重要的話，他說工夫修到此時，「慎自易觀」，自己謹慎小心，要易觀，就是換方法。重要道理就在這裏，所以要「占候」，五天一候，三候一氣，中氣就來了。

「發號順節令，勿失爻動時」，我們打坐做工夫，這個做主的是什麼？剛才講「運移不失中」，無論道家、佛家，這都是重點，做主的就是這個中。中在哪裏？在一念之間，就是心性這個心。工夫到了這個時候，經驗曉得應該變一種方法。譬如說上丹田，現在一貫道、同善社的，點竅都指這裏，密宗叫眉間輪。中丹田在兩個乳房中間，下丹田在肚臍下一寸三分。我開始就告訴大家不要亂守，尤其年紀大血壓高的人，學那些亂七八糟的都得毛病了。女性更不要守下丹田，會得血崩，很嚴重！至少欲念會加重。

這個要自己曉得調配，萬一氣機到了上庭，到了頭頂怎麼辦？譬如有些人說，哎呀，頭頂像裂開一樣，尤其修密宗的人，修頗哇法的，一天到

晚頭頂發脹，要裂開似的，下一步怎麼辦他就不知道了，因為「占候定吉凶」不知道。你光在上庭守，守久了血壓會高，所以最後都是腦溢血而死。修道、修密的我見得多了，不是死在腦溢血，就是死在心臟病。因為氣脈的變化到了某一步時，問題都出在這個火候。不知道火候，你自然會跟著氣脈的象徵，跟那個感覺跑的。佛法就高明，說色受想行識是五受陰，受陰離不開感受，都是依他起。你的氣脈在那裏動，你的感覺自己都曉得，可是你那一點感覺空不掉，而被受陰牽走，就是依他起。所以要了解受即是空，空即是受，受不異空，空不異受。但是你做不到啊！能空掉才可以，所以這個時候要知道「占候定吉凶」。

當你知道「徵候」已到，陽極上了頭頂，趕快要入陰境；陽極陰生，現在需要陰了，純陽境界，這一陰是多需要啊！所以修道要懂這個道理，這個時候就不要再用功了，你趕快睡覺去吧，趕快想辦法走入陰境。所以說「發號順節令，勿失爻動時」，爻動就是卦變，一個卦一個現象，六爻就有六個步驟，每一個步驟都有變化，卦就變了。譬如乾卦六爻，陽到了

極點，陽極陰生，下面一爻由陽變陰，乾卦變成「天風姤卦」。也就是說你氣機真到頂的時候，一身精氣充沛，頂門都在跳動，你趕快需要進入「天風姤」，就是「一陰來復」，不是「一陽來復」！

第二次再一變，卦又變了。第二次變有兩種變法，第二爻陽變陰，這個叫「天山遯」，這個時候人就昏昏迷迷要睡覺去了。這個「遯」不是睡覺，是進入混沌狀態了，這是一種變法。還有一種變法，第一爻還是陽爻，第二爻變陰，上卦還是乾，下卦「離中虛」變成離卦了，離屬火，六爻卦變成為「天火同人」。假使我們打坐做工夫，上面腦子一念不生乾卦，下面整個身體在佛學叫作「得煖」，道家叫做「陽火」就是離卦，表示工夫到了。

拿得起　放得下

你們看過《七真傳》的都知道，那個劉長生在妓女館做工夫，達摩祖師來看他，他也曉得達摩是來度他的，也不說穿，只像平常一樣，叫了一

個妓女來，茶壺盛冷水放肚子上，一邊跟達摩祖師談話。不久水開了，沖茶給他喝。達摩祖師喝了這個茶說：「好！你可以在這裏修道」。他雖然在這裏「火裏生蓮」，並沒有敗道，沒有漏氣，沒有漏丹，陽氣還是那麼充足，這個是「天火同人」卦，在佛學就是得煖。所以要曉得這樣變，叫做「勿失爻動時」。

八萬四千法門都要懂啊！修道那麼簡單嗎？佛法說菩薩要通五明：內明、醫方明、工巧明、因明、聲明都要通。修神仙丹道也是一樣，要天文、地理、人事、陰陽術數、兵、農什麼都要懂。所以說，未有神仙不讀書。但是一般學佛修道的人，嘿！都是八個字「得少為足，閉屋稱王」，這怎麼行啊！所以「勿失爻動時」，這一句話很重要。

「上觀河圖文，下察地形流，中稽於人心，參合考三才。」你看這個道家的祖師魏伯陽，火龍真人，他這部千古丹經要多少學問才能寫成？

「上觀河圖文」，要懂得《易經》的「河圖洛書」；「下察地形流」，下知於地理，因為修道是科學，同地球物理、天文物理都是一樣；「中稽於

工夫境界到哪一步，你就曉得該用哪一個法門，所以

人心」，中間還要通人事。「參合考三才」，天、地、人謂之三才，一切學問法則都要瞭解。

「動則循卦節，靜則因象辭」，每進一步的變化，拿《易經》來講叫卦氣，卦氣一動，「循」是追查，「卦節」，每一節每一步怎麼走，每個境界來自己知道是什麼現象。所以「動則循卦節」，是一定的步驟，它是個科學。「靜則因象辭」這句話，他說你要看《周易》的〈象辭〉，因為這時佛學還沒有傳入中國。象是野獸的名字，《易經》都用獸來代表，譬如龍、馬、象、羊等。古代說象這個獸，鐵被牠牙一咬，嘣！就斷了。所以孔子註《易經》作〈象辭〉，就是作決斷語的意思，告訴我們這個卦講什麼。但是孔子作的〈象辭〉，並不是光講物理或哲學，中間還有修道的道理在內，所以孔子懂，不是不懂。「靜則因象辭」的「靜」，就是要像象辭一樣有決斷，能斷就斷；念頭說不起就不起，像象一樣切斷。古人翻譯《金剛經》，有的加兩個字《能斷金剛般若波羅蜜經》，像金剛一樣切斷，提得起放得下；能斷也就是「靜則因象辭」。

把握動靜之間

「乾坤用施行，天下然後治」，這是講政治哲學的應用。乾坤兩卦的一陰一陽，就是生滅的現象。懂了以後，你把這個應用的法則把握住才懂得修道；然後治天下大事，則天下太平。儘管你到了八九十歲，懂了這個理，下手修持用功，一樣可以袪病延年，返老還童，長生不老。真的！不過今天我聽到個消息，有個朋友跟我講，醫藥已經研究出來啦，絕對可以抗拒老死，試驗了幾十個老頭子。他說，半年以後再檢查身體，一切都健康了，而且退回到四十歲的狀況，這個方子快要出來了。我說這個是外藥、外丹，也是中國的古方，加上新的科學研究試驗，但是要懂得「乾坤」兩卦的應用。

關於「火候」這一篇，有個重要的道理我們要知道，釋迦牟尼佛告訴我們，一切法是生滅法。佛法的偈語：「諸行無常，是生滅法，生滅滅已，寂滅為樂」，這是小乘所追求的，可以成羅漢。要一念不生全體現，

在心理上講是生滅的念頭切斷；但是在生理上也有生滅法。所以有幾天你念頭清淨，覺得戒律清淨，然後看別人就像著魔似的！你看我多好呀，對境心不動啊。嘿！過不了幾天，你動得比別人還厲害。這是什麼道理呢？是心理生滅法.；身體也有生滅法，這是一陰一陽。能陰能陽者，那個是不生滅的。生滅法並不妨礙呀，你要懂得才行，所以後來在大乘佛法上，佛就不那麼嚴厲批駁生滅法了。道家現在告訴你，一陰一陽之謂道，這個法則是呆定的，生滅與不生滅是不二。這個消息在《維摩詰經》《法華經》《圓覺經》都透露了。

所以要明白修法的道理，修煉氣脈是生滅法，一步有一步的現象，一步有一步的徵候，能把握住那個不生不滅的話，最後修證到不生不滅才成道，這個問題諸位去研究。你們在座的很多深通儒釋道三教，但是掉到儒釋道三教的缸裏爬不出來的還蠻多。怎麼爬出來？這是很重要的題目。

「火候」之道是講生滅法，在生滅法中有現象，要把握住的是一動一靜之間。把握不住的話，在道家講是敗道法門，成功了還是會失敗的；把握得

7/21/13

住才真懂得中國正統的道家，才不冤枉研究《參同契》了。

國家圖書館出版品預行編目資料

我說參同契 / 南懷瑾講述. －－ 臺灣初版. －－
臺北市：老古, 民 98. 03
　　冊；　公分

　ISBN 978-957-2070-88-8（上冊：平裝）

　1. 太玄部

231.65　　　　　　　　　　　　　98003401